PETROC™

LEARNING TECHNOLOGIES & LIBRARY SERVICES

Please return this item on or before the last date shown below

13 JAN 2017

2 6 JAN 2017

WITHDRAWN FROM STOCK

North Devon Campus: 01271 338170
Mid Devon Campus: 01884 235234
Email: library@petroc.ac.uk

This reader is one part of an Open University integrated teaching system and the selection is therefore related to other material available to students. It is designed to evoke the critical undertstanding of students. Opinions expressed in it are not necessarily those of the course team or of the University.

Social Policy
and
Social Welfare

A Reader edited by
Martin Loney, David Boswell and John Clarke
at the Open University

OPEN UNIVERSITY PRESS
Milton Keynes

Open University Press
A division of
Open University Educational Enterprises Limited
12 Cofferidge Close
Stony Stratford
Milton Keynes MK11 1BY, England.

First published 1983
Selection and editorial material
copyright © The Open University 1983

British Library Cataloguing in Publication Data

Social policy and social welfare
1. Social policy
I. Loney, Martin   II. Boswell, David
III. Clarke, John
361.6'1   HN17.5

ISBN 0-335-10408-8

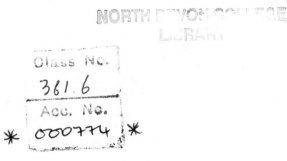
Text design by W.A.P.

Phototypeset by
Gilbert Composing Services, Leighton Buzzard, Beds.
Printed in Great Britain by
M. & A. Thomson Litho Limited,
East Kilbride, Scotland.

Contents

Preface

This Reader has been designed to complement the Open University course **Social Policy and Social Welfare.**

The editors would like to acknowledge the assistance of Gloria Channing and Marie Day in typing parts of the manuscript. We particularly wish to acknowledge the valuable role played by Carol Johns in preparing the manuscript for handover to the publishers.

Acknowledgements

The Editors would like to thank the following for giving permission to include in this volume revised versions of previously published work: *Futures* and Patricia Thomas, whose article first appeared in the February 1982 issue, Vol. 14, No. 1 pp. 2–10; the British Sociological Association and Alan Walker, whose article first appeared in *Sociology* Vol 15, No. 2, May 1981; Jens Alber whose work first appeared in 1982 as *European Institute Working Paper* No. 15; Basil Blackwell Publisher for Alan Maynard's article which first appeared in *Social Policy and Administration* Vol. 15, No. 2, Summer 1981; and Heinemann Educational Books for Adrian Webb's and Gerald Wistow's work which first appeared in Public Expenditure and *Social Policy* edited by Alan Walker.

PART I

The Welfare State in Perspective

Introduction

This collection has been put together at a watershed in the history of welfare in Britain. We are experiencing a period in which the relationship between the state and welfare which has dominated the field of domestic politics in post war Britain is being reassessed from every point on the political compass. The 'commitment to welfare' — even when given grudgingly — formed one of the main elements of cross party political consensus in the thirty years after 1945. That commitment can no longer be taken for granted. Equally importantly for this book, the revival of political conflict over the future of welfare has been paralleled by intellectual disputes in the study of social policy itself. The diverse articles collected in this volume have been selected for their contributions to examining this crisis in welfare, its ramifications through a variety of policy areas, and the problems it has highlighted for those engaged in the study of social policy.

In this introduction, our purpose is to explore these two emergent conflicts — the political and the intellectual — which form the context in which the articles collected here have been written. These conflicts of explanation and direction reflect very powerfully, the emergent crisis of welfare in Britain. The quiet retreat from the commitment to welfare can be dated from Labour policies in the late 1960s, with their reduced spending on social programmes. By the mid-1970s, James Callaghan was announcing the death of Keynesian remedies in the face of a deepening world recession, and Labour settled on substantial cuts in public spending in 1977. In part, the quietness of this retreat might be attributed to the absence of any clear alternatives from which policy might be directed and through which popular support could be rallied to a 'temporary' regime of hard times. However, while this tacit withdrawal was being constructed on one side of the parliamentary battlefield, a significantly louder trumpet was being blown on the other.

A revamped Conservative party, under the new leadership of Margaret Thatcher, equipped itself with a new intellectual armoury and declared war on the sacreds cows of the post-war consensus. One of the foremost political targets of the new Conservativism was the burden of 'unproductive' state spending. They identified state spending as one of the main constraints on individual freedom — both at the point of taxation where enterprise and hard work was discouraged by the disincentive of lost earnings, and at the point of state intervention where individual choice was being crushed by state monopolies. The state's welfare activities were identified as placing a further burden on the spirit of initiative — that of the scrounger who abused the soft regime of welfare.

Since the 1979 election, conducted in the shadow of Conservative promises to cut taxation, roll back the state, 'free' initiative and get tough on the welfare

3

scroungers, the retreat from welfare has continued with more gusto. This period has seen the imposition of 'cash limits' on public spending, the erosion of the decision making powers of local authorities, cuts in the staffing of welfare services and in the level of provision of services. This has been accompanied by a substantial increase in the numbers on the 'payroll' of the welfare state, though not employed by it. But this economic dimension is only one part of the crisis of welfare in the nineteen eighties. The 'new Conservatism' was not just about cuts in state spending pragmatic but based its approach to public spending on a re-opening of the long silent debate on the 'proper role' of the state. The achievement was to go beyond the question of how much the state ought to be spending on welfare to the question of whether the state ought to be in the business at all.

The return of that question to a central position on the political agenda overturned not just the political consensus of 1945 and after, but also the rather longer span of political assumptions about welfare since the turn of the century. The answer which the new Conservatism provided — the need to reassert the power of individual choice and market forces — was no mere electoral flourish. It was grounded in an array of intellectual argument and institutions— variously termed monetarism, the radical right and neo-liberalism. The theories of Friedrich von Hayek were rehabilitated, and his demonstration of the irreconcilability of the collectivist state and market freedoms adopted. The intellectual products of the Institute for Economic Affairs, and subsequently the Centre for Policy Studies, came to occupy a central place in the formulation of the politics and policies of the new Conservatism. A new philosophy of welfare was constructed based not just on a hostility to the collectivist state, but on the propagation of a positive alternative: privatization — the revitalization of 'individual choice' and 'consumer sovereignty' (erected by some as *the* democratic process; Seldon, 1980).

The depth and scope of this argument, together with the visible crisis of welfare itself, gave rise to other political reassessments of the achievements of '1945'. The split in the ranks of the Labour Party leading to the formation of the Social Democratic Party involved an effort to construct a new politics of the centre.

In keeping with the broad outlines of the new party's commitments to decentralization and popular politics, two of its leading members (Williams, 1981; Rodgers, 1982) provided commentaries on welfare which identified the 'failures' of 1945 with the overcentralized and overbureaucratic structures of service delivery. Instead, they argued the need to decentralize and create closer integration with the needs, activities and resources of local communities, stressing the themes of participation and voluntary work. Meanwhile, the Labour Party itself, while taking on the mantle of defending the welfare state, has also been engaged in trying (in some sections of the party, at least) to develop a more positive strategy towards welfare. In part, this has consisted of linking the redistributive possibilities of welfare provision to the development of social and economic programmes (grouped under the rubric of 'The Alternative Economic Strategy') and suggesting that the overbureaucratic and overcentralized structure of welfare requires *political* decentralization to accompany service decentralization.

One further reassessment of welfare needs to be mentioned — for though it may be less visible in the sphere of parliamentary politics, it is no less profound in its potential consequences for the future of welfare. From the Women's Movement have come a number of criticisms of welfare directed at the way welfare provision makes assumptions about the family and women's role within it, which have profound material consequences for the possibilities of women's lives. A number of particular issues, about the conditions under which benefit is provided (the cohabitation rule in supplementary benefit); about crucial gaps in welfare provision (the provision of refuges for battered women); and about the assumptions under-pinning policy initiatives (how 'community care' assumes the availability of women to do the caring) have highlighted a general conflict over both the form and content of welfare provision which challenge old assumptions about the 'benefits' of welfare in a very pointed way.

While the political and economic conditions which upheld the commitment to welfare have been transformed, they have, in the process, posed new difficulties for the study of social policy. Social administration — the applied 'non-discipline' of the social sciences — has had some of its certainties and commitments eroded by twin pressures. The 'external' crisis of welfare — the profound changes in social administration's very subject matter — has forced the consideration of the structural forces of politics and economics into the calculation of policy making and policy effects. The theoretical revival of other disciplines in the social sciences — the surfacing of competing models, paradigms and theoretical diversity — visible from the late 1960s, made its presence felt in social administration from the mid-1970s. An increasing number of articles, books and teaching courses addressed themselves to the need for a more theorised approach to the study of social policy — in a subject which had been characterized by (often, indeed, prided itself on) its a-theoretical and eclectic approach. The first signal of this emergent controversy within the discipline was perhaps the pioneering work of George and Wilding (1976) with their insistence that what the discipline had previously treated as 'values' (the standpoints of individual scholars) in the study of welfare could be better grasped as the deployment of systematic ideologies of welfare. Subsequent writers have developed more elaborated analyses of the conflicting models, paradigms and theories which have been used in the study of explanation of welfare policy. This insistence on a greater level of theoretical self-consciousness and argument has parallelled (though it is not the same as) the disintegration of the political consensus.

Some of the old intellectual certainties which had provided the core of social policy came under powerful criticism. The 'whig' conception of the history of welfare, embodying a belief in the incremental progress towards a better society, was challenged not only by contemporary changes but also by substantial historical reassessments of the social forces and interests involved in the construction of welfare (e.g. Wilson, 1977; Thane, 1978). Similarly, the Fabian tradition of social policy research and its uneasy coexistence with Labourist policy making was attacked for its neglect of wider structural questions of the inequalities of class and gender in Britain.

Although much of this new analysis in social policy reflected the rehabilitation of Marxist theory in British academic life (e.g. Gough, 1978; Ginsburg, 1979; Taylor-Gooby & Dale, 1980) as well as the development of feminism (e.g. Wilson, 1977), such theories were by no means the only contenders. Economic liberalism and its privileging of the market had its intellectual voices, too. The Institute of Economic Affairs — for a long time cast as a voice in the wilderness — became more central with the increasing salience of monetarism, especially in the persona of Milton Friedman. The Institute contributed a number of substantial critiques of public spending and welfare policies (e.g. Seldon, 1980; Parker, 1982). It was joined by the Centre for Policy Studies (founded by Sir Keith Joseph after his conversion to monetarism), and its Social Affairs Unit was also active in promoting the neo-liberal reassessment of welfare provision (e.g. Anderson *et al.*, 1979). In a different way, the social — democratic themes of decentralization and local participation have been reflected in social policy writings about neighbourhood and community based social provision (e.g. Hadley & Hatch, 1981).

These conflicts, and their policy ramifications, form the subject matter of the articles collected in this Reader. The articles in Part One deal with some of the political and ideological conflicts about welfare. Phil Lee and Colin Raban provide a critical review of the uses to which the concept of ideology has been put in the study of social policy since George and Wilding's work. While the identification of different ideologies of welfare has been important, they suggest that the restriction of ideology to the classification of typologies of 'ideal' positions has led to a neglect of other aspects of ideological struggles over welfare. John Saville's article returns to the themes of his famous (and extensively reprinted) article of thirty years ago (1954). He argues that we need to develop an historical understanding of the class forces and conflicts which have profoundly shaped the British Welfare State. Elizabeth Wilson has contributed a powerful reminder about the still-neglected relationship between women and welfare. Her article highlights the development of feminist criticisms of and demands for welfare. Tony Fitzgerald presents an analysis of contemporary neo-liberal ideology of welfare in Britain, and its expression in the Conservative party under Mrs Thatcher's leadership. His articles focusses on how neo-liberalism sees the 'proper' relationship between the state, the market and the family.

Finally Peter Townsend reviews a variety of perspectives on poverty and lays out an alternative 'institutional' approach which, he argues, will provide the basis for a more comprehensive attack which will go beyond traditional social service remedies.

References

Anderson, D. *et al.* (1979) *Breaking the Spell of the Welfare State,* Social Affairs Unit.

George, V. and Wilding, P. (1976) *Ideology and Social Welfare,* Routledge and Kegan Paul.

Ginsburg, N. (1979) *Capital, Class and Social Policy,* Macmillan.

Gough, I. (1978) *The Political Economy of the Welfare State,* Macmillan.

Hadley, R. and Hatch, S. (1982) *Social Welfare and the Failure of the State,* Allen and Unwin.

Parker, H. (1982) *The Moral Hazard of Social Benefits,* I.E.A.

Rodgers, W. (1982) *The Politics of Change,* Secker and Warburg.

Saville, J. (1954) The welfare state: an historical approach, in *The New Reasoner.*

Seldon, A. (1980) *Charge!,* Michael Joseph.

Taylor-Gooby, P. and Dale, J. (1981) *Social Theory and Social Welfare,* Edward Arnold.

Thane, P. (ed.) (1978) *The Origins of British Social Policy,* Croom Helm.

Williams, S. (1981) *Politics is for People,* Penguin.

Wilson, E. (1977) *Women and The Welfare State,* Tavistock.

The Origins of the Welfare State

John Saville

We must start from the fact that all advanced societies in the world today have a wide range of social services we group under the term 'the welfare state'. There are certain important differences between the United States and Japan, on the one hand, and Western Europe on the other, but the tendency for state expenditure on the social services to rise sharply during the second half of the 20th century has been common to all industrial countries, again with the partial exception of Japan. There remain considerable variations in the structure of the social services between all countries, in the principles upon which they are based and in the ways in which they are financed. There are, moreover, divergent approaches to welfare services between different social classes in different countries; and a discussion, therefore, of the origins of the welfare state in Britain offers both generalizations common to all mature industrial societies as well as quite marked distinguishing features peculiar to Britain.

British society from its early industrialization at the end of the 18th century has had a number of economic and social features not found elsewhere until, at least, the most recent decades. Compared, for example, with the United States, Britain was a closed, less expansive economy with vertical mobility for working people severely restricted: emigration being the main escape; while compared with all other industrial societies which emerged out of feudalism, Britain had no peasant class and was overwhelmingly proletarian. It was this fact of a predominantly working-class society — the only example in the 19th century world — that increasingly dominated the political tactics and strategy of the ruling groups in Britain. It was not numbers only but the threat of political cohesiveness that worried the Victorians. The working classes had been kept outside the civic pale for two decades after 1848 — a reflection of the social fears of the years since the French Revolution; but despite the absence of political democracy there had developed a high degree of collective self-help among working people in the shape of trade unions, co-operative societies and friendly societies. Defensive as they were, these organisations encouraged and sustained a sense of class solidarity that was constantly renewed within the social relations of production, and which found expression in radical politics as well as a more

8

elementary perception of 'them' against 'us'. It was an appreciation of these social facts that produced the widespread anxiety concerning 'the leap in the dark' when the vote was first given to sections of the urban workers in 1867. Walter Bagehot, the most subtle of Conservative thinkers in his century, addressed himself to these problems in the preface to the second edition of his famous text *The British Constitution*, published in 1872. He first warned against the two political parties competing for the support of the working man, and then turned to another problem which he almost certainly felt could be potentially more serious. These were his words:

> I can conceive that questions *being* raised which, if continually agitated, would combine the working men as a class together, the higher orders might have to consider whether they would concede the measure that would settle such questions, or whether they would risk the effect of the working men's combination . . .
>
> But in all cases it must be remembered that a political combination of the lower classes, as such and for their own objects, is an evil of the first magnitude; that a permanent combination of them would make them (now that so many of them have the suffrage) supreme in the country; and that their supremacy, in the state they now are, means the supremacy of ignorance over instruction and of numbers over knowledge. So long as they are not taught to act together, there is a chance of this being averted, and it can only be averted by the greatest wisdom and the greatest foresight in the higher classes. They must avoid, not only every evil, but every appearance of evil; while they have still the power they must remove, not only every actual grievance, but, where it is possible, every seeming grievance too; they must willingly concede every claim which they can safely concede, in order that they may not have to concede unwillingly some claim which would impair the safety of the country.

Bagehot recognized how difficult it would be for politicians to follow his advice; how they would be accused of appeasement (although he did not use the word) but he insisted that a prolonged struggle would only reinforce the determination of the working people to build their own organizations and to adopt intransigent attitudes.

As the 19th century went along the ruling groups in Britain proved extraordinarily successful first in containing the upsurge of tensions and discontents and turbulence before 1850 and then in adapting and moulding the working people to the economic and social requirements of industrial society. It was an adaptation that was never complete, but the shrewd and quite ruthless combination of coercion, paternalism and cajolery established an hegemony that confined the working class to a firmly subordinate position in bourgeois society. It is, indeed, striking that in the most working-class of all countries in the 19th century there was no independent working class party of any significance before 1900: one of the major paradoxes of our modern history and a remarkable fact that deserves more emphasis than it is usually accorded.

By the 1870s, in the context of this present discussion, certain leading characteristics of British society can be briefly summarized:

(i) The ideas of socialism, and the existence of socialism as a political movement had virtually disappeared. There were only a handful of Anglo-Saxons who still held to any ideas approximating to 'socialistic'; most of the socialists in Britain were foreigners, and they too were few.

(ii) The politically articulate — a minority — among working men were for the most part attached to the Liberal Party. The social phenomenon of labourism, or lib-labism, was already a leading feature of working-class radicalism: at its most extreme it was solid for trade unionism, anti-landlordism, pro-Fenian and against the Irish coercion, republicanism and neo-malthusianism. Large sections of working people were a-political, conservative and traditionalist: a receptive audience to the religious sectarians in some parts of Britain and easily influenced by the jingoistic ideas which were soon to be of growing importance.

(iii) Bourgeois hegemony, in the area of social policy, expressed itself largely through the acceptance of *laissez faire* as an article of faith and a constantly re-iterated insistence upon the value of individualism, of self-help and the virtues of hard work. The 1834 Poor Law Amendment Act was the most successful piece of social legislation in the 19th century in terms of effectiveness: it played a major part in the processes of labour adaptation; it encouraged the respectable working man to build around himself and his family a barrier against the feckless and improvident of his own class; and above all, it made of pauperism a thing of shame among working people.

In the emergence of the welfare state in Britain the decade of the 1880s is something of a watershed between the heyday of classical Victorianism and the more fluid period — in terms of ideas and social policies — which preceded the First World War. As Sir Montstuart Grant Duff wrote in the spring of 1887 — having returned to England after six years as Governor of Bombay:

> The first change which I may note is one in the climate of opinion. It was well put by a friend who, writing to me early in 1885, said 'You will come back to an England where thoughts are current and things are discussed which were not current or discussed when you went away . . .' The first place where, after landing in Europe, I met anyone connected with my own House of Common's life, was the station at Lentini in Sicily, and the cheering subject of conversation, which he selected, was the spread of Socialism in Scotland (*Nineteenth Century*, July 1887).

Socialism had indeed come back to Britain after an absence of thirty years, and although confined to a quite small minority, it was nevertheless a growing influence. More immediately obvious, by the end of the 1880s, was the increasing numbers of working men who were being elected to administrative bodies which were part of the widening political democracy of the last thirty years of the century: School Boards (1870); Urban Councils (in the 1880s); County Councils (1889); Boards of Guardians (1892–5); Parish Councils (1894). Moreover, the growing weight of a working class electorate was, very slowly but irresistibly, making itself felt in parliamentary elections, and from 1874 manual workers, or former manual workers, began to be elected to the House of Commons. With the third Reform Act of 1884, which enfranchised many workers in rural areas (and thus including a majority of miners) and with the almost equally important re-distribution of seats in the year following, both Liberals and Tories were under pressure to respond to the changing social composition of their constituencies. Such pressures were most obvious within the Liberal Party, in which the radical wing, represented by Bradlaugh, Dilke and Chamberlain, had already begun to work around a radical programme in the 1870s. It was made more precise in the years of the second Gladstone government and Chamberlain formally launched the Radical Programme in the early part of 1885. His first speech provided the occasion for a scandalized torrent of abuse and misrepresentation from the Establishment of the day. 'I ask' Chamberlain had said 'what ransom will property pay for the security it enjoys?'. Now ransom, as Chamberlain's biographer sorrowfully noted, was an 'ugly' word. It went, J. L. Garvin explained, far beyond Chamberlain's real contention which was only that 'private property must pay to be tolerated'. Chamberlain himself immediately recognized his error, and anxious to correct what he appreciated was a serious political mistake, substituted for 'ransom' in all his later speeches, the less explosive 'insurance'. This, wrote Garvin, was what he was henceforth to 'speak and think' (Garvin, 1932).

There are three interrelated strands of change which can be identified as essential parts of the causal sequence of events and policies which culminated in the welfare state of the second half of the 20th century. The first relates to the political calculations of the ruling groups; the second are the economic and social requirements of an increasingly complex industrial society; and the third to the pressures which have come from the mass of the population as the perceptions of economic and social needs have gradually widened and become more explicit.

The politics of the welfare, from the standpoint of the propertied classes, have inevitably been complicated. As with Joseph Chamberlain there had long been the recognition that the divisions between classes was too great for the political health of society, and that the predatory claims of capital upon working people must be mitigated if social stability was to be preserved. There was no question, for Chamberlain, or any who thought like him, that private property would in any way be displaced; but as Cardinal Manning so nicely put the problem to his friend J. E. C. Bodley in 1888: 'If the landlords, Householders and Capitalists will "engineer a slope" we may avert disastrous collisions. If they will not, I am afraid you will see a rough time'. But there were always difficult problems in these matters even for the most far-sighted among the politicians and the men of property. Reforms, whether large or small, have always been opposed by some section or group among the middle or upper classes. The argument *après nous le déluge* has been a powerful delaying influence and has been used continuously to buttress existing traditions and practices. When faced with a challenge at any time to any privileged position, the self-interest of those involved has at all times encouraged and sustained a massive opposition to change. As the engineering employers stated in January 1852 during a lock-out of their workers: 'All we want is to be left alone. With less than that we shall not be satisfied. Until we accomplish that, we shall not re-open our establishments'; and they continued 'we must take leave to say that *we* alone are the competent judges of our own business; that we are respectively the masters of our own establishments; and that it is our firm determination to remain so. To this principle we recognise no exceptions'. It was a statement to which most employers have continued to subscribe; and the point needs making that the men of business, in the past two centuries, have usually been more obdurate and less accommodating than the politicians. There is, further, an additional matter to be taken note of, and one which has proved in our own day, of critical importance. Welfare reforms involve public expenditure, whether financed directly out of taxation or from the insurance principle; and there has to be some degree of income distribution. The 19th century prided itself on the low levels of state and local government expenditures, and the increases in financial provision for new kinds of social services, or for the exten-sion of existing services, have inevitably been opposed by those upon whom some, at least, of the burden would fall. It has invariably been an issue which has united the owners of large scale wealth with the middle and especially the lower middle classes with their reactionary popularist traditions against increases of local rates and national income tax. In general terms, then, there has always had to be a balance struck between the acceptance of demands from below and the political consequences which might flow therefrom. In practice, the policy has been to trim and especially to delay; and the success of the propertied groups in Britain in maintaining their fundamental positions of power and privilege has been a tribute to the political balance of their practice in government.

The second component in the general historical problem of emergence of the welfare state is that which refers to the changing economic, social and technological requirements of an industrialized society: one that has become ever more complex and sophisticated. The central dynamic of capitalism is accumulation; the greater the amount of surplus value produced the larger will be the volume of profits. For the first hundred years of industrialization in Britain the basic problem was the 'adaptation' of the labour force to the requirements of industry: a problem mostly solved by the use of coercive power inside and outside the factory. But capitalism differs from all previous class societies in that the formal relationship between capitalist and labourer is based, not upon status as in feudalism, but on a contract between two parties in the market place. And however much the balance in the early days of industrialization was biased in favour of the owners of property, the contract has increasingly evolved into a free one. Moreover, as a dynamically expanding system, industrial capitalism has been obliged to find ways of encouraging the greatest possible productivity from its workforce. Material inducements and incentives have therefore to be offered, and the system as a whole, if it is to work reasonably smoothly, must encourage the general sentiment that the future will be better than the present or the past. In political terms, this means that capitalist society has to try to win, if not the political confidence of the working people, then at least their political neutrality. At the same time, the economic interests of capitalism and the improvement of the material needs of the working people begin to coincide at various points within the social spectrum. Industrial capitalism requires an increasing range of technical expertise; and that means an improving educational system. A labour force that suffers from a high incidence of disease — the result of dirt, poor housing, inadequate diet — is an inefficient labour force; and therefore the improvement of the physical environment in which working people live, the means for purchasing an adequate food supply, the availability of medical services in sufficient quantity and at a satisfactory level of competence, are all necessary if the industrial machine is to work at full stretch. At the end of the 19th century no group was more aware of these problems than the Fabians. They were also highly conscious of which groups in society were likely to be most interested in the encouragement of efficiency and rationality in economic and social affairs. As Mrs Sidney Webb wrote in her diary on 2 January, 1901 (after complaining of the many obstructions during the previous decade to factory reform):

What we have to do is to detach the *great employer*, whose profits are too large to feel the immediate pressure of regulation and who stands to gain by the increased efficiency of the factors of production, from the ruck of small employers or stupid ones. What seems clear is that we shall get no further instalments of reform unless we gain the consent of an influential minority of the threatened interest.

It is not, however, the abstract calculation of enlightened self-interest on the part of the great employers, or the vigorous consciences of a small minority of middle class humanitarians, that can account for the central direction and movement of social change in Britain. No one denies the unselfish single-mindedness of the liberal pioneers of reform, and no one fails to recognize that certain measures of rational change have come about in all advanced industrial countries precisely because the industrial system could not work without them. In Britain, however, largely because of the much earlier beginnings of industrialization, and the much longer drawn out period of bitter class antagonisms and social tensions, reform, both political and social, has been the product of ideological and class struggle. In the last resort the determining factors in the evolution of the Welfare State have been the degree of organization, and the determination of the working people themselves, to insist upon social change. However reasonable the reform, and whatever the calculation of well-being, and therefore of economic efficiency, the massive weight of tradition, the tyranny of established ideas already well-grounded by the middle of the 19th century, and the general and unrelenting hostility to the mass of the ordinary people on the part of the property owners: all have operated to resist change and to hold back social improvement. Only the development of the working class movement, and the recourse at times to direct action, have been able to shift the mountains of unreason that have built themselves upon the foundations of private property. There have been many occasions when opposition to reform has been calculated and deliberate; there have been many others when the inarticulate major premises of the owners of property have obstructed change. Every generation stumbles and gropes for a comprehension of the emerging problems of its contemporary society; and the enlightened and the stupid, rationality and prejudice, come into continuous conflict and struggle. The pace of social change, with the exception of a few individual years, has always been slow in Britain; and without the pressures from below, it would have been both more protracted and much more uneven in its impact throughout the country as a whole.

It was the Fabians who articulated the philosophy of social change that is summed up in the phrase 'the Welfare State'. From 1889 on, Sidney Webb in particular was constantly emphasising what he later described as 'the inevitability of gradualism' and he was always quoting historical examples to prove his point. Webb argued that the increasing complexity of modern society would itself compel a growing intervention by the State, and that this would be reinforced by the further development of political democracy; by which he meant the progressive awareness by the working people that political power now resided in them as the majority of the nation. Inevitably, Webb went on to argue, the working people, through their representatives in Parliament, would increasingly curtail the powers of property over the lives of ordinary people.

The Fabian theory of historical inevitability, which became the accepted theory and practice of the British labour movement in the 20th century, rested upon one major assumption: that the Government in a political democracy are in full control of the State and State power, and that upon the Government's ability to legislate there are no effective limitations. The central postulate is the political neutrality of the State; any administration that takes office is by that fact in full and complete control of the legislative programme it wishes to implement. This belief in the neutrality of the State — which for the Labour Party has always meant the House of Commons — has been accepted by the Left as well as the Right within the Labour movement; and when things go wrong, as they so often do, with the hopes of the reformers dampened, the central questions of where power in society actually resides are ignored, and some simple conspiracy theory substituted.

It is, of course, true that considerable advances in social welfare have been made in the 20th century, but it is only the parochialism of our fellow countrymen and women which leads them to believe that the rate of social progress has been much greater than elsewhere. There have been three main periods of social change during the past century: the first, the beginnings of welfare services in a minority of urban boroughs before 1914, and the implementation of certain items of national legislation following the large-scale Liberal victory of 1906: school meals for necessitous children; the medical inspection of school children; the first Old Age Pensions Act; the first Act establishing minimum wages in selected industries; and the beginnings of national health and unemployment insurance. The second main period of reform, not as spectacular or as concentrated as that between 1906 and 1911, were the years of the First World War and the two decades between the wars. The pace of change was slower and more uneven, but among the more important reforms were the Maternity and Child Welfare Act (1918); the 1919 Housing and Town Planning Act (which introduced subsidies on a considerable scale and took the Government into the business of housing: although Wheatley's Act of 1924 was the most successful individual item of housing legislation); the 1920 Unemployment Act which brought nearly all workers earning below £250 a year into the scheme; the 1926 Hadow report on education and the slow improvement in educational structure and provision in the years which followed; the 1927 Widows, Orphans and Old Age Contributory Pensions Act; and the 1934 Unemployment Act. The inter-war years, then, although politically dominated by the Conservative Party, were by no means empty of social legislation; but the situation in 1939 was a highly unsatisfactory mixture of uncoordinated social policies, with married women and children being especially disadvantaged, for provision was still being made on the basis of the individual and not the family. The years of the Second World War marked an important change in principle. With the publication of the Beveridge Report a unified and comprehensive programme of social services became a matter of major public debate; and the Labour Government of 1945, brought into office by the political radicalisation of large sections of the population during the war years, proceeded to implement, in quick succession, its promised legislative programme. In 1945 Family Allowances were introduced; in 1946 there was a comprehensive scheme of National Insurance and the introduction of the National Health Service; and in 1948 there was the National Assistance Act. It is a misconception to describe these measures as protecting the individual citizen or family 'from the cradle to the grave', for the deficiencies in provision soon became apparent although for nearly two decades they were masked, or partially masked, by the fact of near-full employment. Nevertheless, had the structures set up in the years immediately following the end of World War Two been added to and strengthened in the next two decades the social services of Britain would not have fallen behind those of Western Europe to the extent that occurred. In part, of course, slower economic growth in Britain inevitably produced a lower rate of investment in the social sectors, but in part also, the political bankruptcy of the leadership of the Labour Party — as the main reforming body — further contributed significantly to the increasing difficulties that have come upon the social services to the point where large parts of the structure, especially those connected with medical provision, are involved in major crisis. But these matters are discussed at length elsewhere.

There are some general points to be made in a concluding section. The first is to emphasise once again the slowness of social change: the length of time it has taken to provide even elementary social provision, long after the need has been identified and fully recognized. Old Age Pensions were an example. The agitation for some statutory provision for Old Age Pensions first developed in the late 1870s. There were three Reports of a Select Committee on the subject in the 1880s; a Royal Commission and a further Select Committee in the 1890s; back-bench private members bills for at least half a dozen years before the 1906 election; the establishment of a pressure group in 1898 with a wide-ranging support; and yet the electoral programme of the Liberal Party did not include pensions among its items in the run-up to the 1906 election, and the first Act did not reach the Statute Book until 1908 when on a sliding scale, a maximum of five shillings a week was given to all those, of either sex, who had reached the age of 70. Those whose annual income was thirty-one pounds and ten shillings, or more, received nothing. As Disraeli said to H.M. Hyndman in 1881: 'It is a very difficult country to move, a very difficult country indeed . . .'

There are other, more spectacular, examples of delay and procrastination but it must not be thought that conservatism comes only from the owners of property, although they are always the main bastion of opposition. But it was many trade unionists in the 1920s who were opposed to children's allowances and much of the delay in developing an educational system for England consonant with the requirements of a technologically-based society has come from within the educational system, especially from the university sector, and most particularly from the universities of Oxford and Cambridge: the latter responsible for so much of the educational deficiencies of the 20th century.

The final point refers to the characterisation of the welfare provision as it has grown, haphazardly, over the past century. Before 1914 there was no problem: the reforms introduced by the Liberal Party were liberal reforms, inserted into the system in order to remedy the worst depredations of a class society with no intention of displacing private enterprise or private property. But with the emergence of the Labour Party as the second main Party in the State, and with the rhetoric of Labour Socialism — that is, Labourism with a socialist rhetoric — the agitation for further social reform often took on a socialist colouring which led many to equate social reform with socialism. And when it came to the legislation of the 1945 government the identification was complete, both from within the Labour Party and from those who were in opposition. By the time the first three years of the Attlee government had passed, the most influential Labour intellectuals were beginning to discern a new kind of society: 'a major historical change' Anthony Crosland called it. In particular nationalization was equated with socialism, with unfortunate consequences for those who continued to argue for a socialist society. Apart from the bemused absurdities of the labour intellectuals, most clearly illustrated by Crosland's contribution to *New Fabian Essays* (Crossman, 1952) it is necessary further to note that the principles accepted by the Labour Party since 1918 were bitterly attacked by many in the Parliamentary Labour Party before the First World War. At that time it was not automatically agreed that social provision should be financed by compulsory contributions but rather should come out of general taxation, especially direct taxation; and as welfare provision has developed in Britain in the past sixty years the contributory principle plus very heavy indirect taxation have together meant that much of the expenditure upon the social services has become a transfer by taxation within the working class itself. As the *Economist* remarked in 1950 of the social services: 'It is still true that nobody — or practically nobody — gets anything for nothing'. Welfare capitalism has made a significant difference to the lives of ordinary people compared with the opening years of this century: it is important to understand and comprehend its limitations, which have evolved over a long period of time, as well as its benefits.

References

R.H.S. Crossman (ed) (1952) *New Fabian Essays*, Turnstile Press, London.
J.L. Garvin (1932) *The Life of Joseph Chamberlain*, Macmillan, London.

The Welfare State: a brief bibliographical note

The more orthodox approach to the history of the welfare state will be found in D. Fraser, *The Evolution of the British Welfare State* (1973) and in a more detailed study by B.B. Gilbert, with an excellent annotated bibliography: *The Evolution of National Insurance* (1966). There is a useful booklet by J.R. Hay, *The Origins of the Liberal Welfare State, 1906 - 1914* (Studies in Economics and Social History, 1975), and this also has a bibliography. The best marxist account is probably I. Gough, *The Political Economy of the Welfare State* (1979); and the most interesting comparative study of the emergence of the welfare state in an industrial society is G. Rimlinger, *Welfare Policy and Industrialization in Europe, America and Russia* (1971). There is a mass of periodical writing which can be traced through the references and bibliographies in Gilbert, Hay and Gough.

Welfare and Ideology

Phil Lee and Colin Raban

The intention of this article is to clarify and contextualize recent discussions about the relevance of the concept of 'ideology' to the study of welfare. Fewer concepts play a larger part in the analysis of historical and political issues, and yet its meaning is often shrouded in vagueness and ambiguity. Whatever else the concept involves, its usage does imply the presence of social determinations and of normative considerations that somehow affect people's understanding of the world. Its intrinsic value for the study of social policy would also appear to be self-evident. As Richard Titmuss once noted:

> We all have our values and prejudices . . . we have a responsibility for making our values clear, and we have a special duty to do so when we are discussing such a subject as social policy which, quite clearly, has no meaning at all if it is considered to be neutral in terms of values [1974, p. 27)].

This is a revealing extract for it serves to remind us — if anyone needed reminding — that to study social welfare is to necessarily engage a battery of 'essentially contested' concepts such as need, right, community, equality and justice. These concepts inevitably involve 'endless disputes about their proper uses' (Gallie, 1955 - 6, p. 169) and they deeply implicate normative argument.

The term 'ideology' has usually been employed in two ways by social administrators. The first of these usages was prevalent during the 1950s and 1960s, and still has an important influence today. During this period most practitioners of the subject were committed to an *institutional* view of social welfare — normative integration through redistributive social policies. The discipline itself was the child of a particular political ideology, social democracy, and social administrators shared the value assumptions of what Donnison (1979) has called 'the Titmuss paradigm'. In other words, value disagreements did take place but within a very narrow, well-defined, space. If one did not share the assumptions of the 'club' you were an 'outsider' — an ideologue — and your views were simply out of touch with 'reality'. The term had no apparent pertinence for social policy analysts during this period, other than to outlaw certain beliefs — 'ideological' ones — from the domain of policy studies.

With the end of the long post-war boom, and with the consequent revival of political critiques of 'democratic-welfare-capitalism' from both the Right and the Left, there has been pressure to expand the intellectual terrain within which it is permissable to practise social administration. In the early 1970s influential figures within the discipline were consequently noting an apparent 'polarization of welfare debate' (Pinker, 1971) and an 'outbreak of ideological warfare' (Marshall, 1972). In such circumstances, and hardly surprisingly, a less judgemental view of ideology was advocated by some of the more 'radical' members of the discipline (George & Wilding, 1972, 1976; Wilding & George, 1975).

This was an important development for the study of social policy but one that, as we hope to demonstrate, was both flawed in its own terms, and restricted by never adequately developing a *theoretical* understanding of the concept.

Social Administration and the End of Ideology

In the same year that T.H. Marshall referred to the incipient 'outbreak of ideological warfare', George and Wilding (1972) remarked on the failure within social administration to give any more than 'ritual mention' to the influence of social values and conflict on the development of social policy. They attributed this to the reformist preoccupations of the discipline, the value it placed on a direct professional liaison with policy makers, and the 'unacknowledged' and 'often unrealized acceptance' of a consensus model of society. The tendency to see 'power and authority as legitimate, and as exercised for the good of all to advance agreed goals', seemed to obviate the need for an analysis of value conflicts in the study of social welfare.

If the failure to consider issues of value conflict was directly connected with the pragmatic empiricism and the implicit theoretical assumptions of social administration, these features were, in turn, products of the discipline's natal environment. The formative period in the development of the subject occurred in the Cold War years and during the honeymoon phase of the post-war settlement. The intellectual and political style of the time was generally based on the presumption that decades of constitutional action, culminating in the establishment of the mixed economy and the Welfare State, had resolved 'the fundamental political problems of the Industrial Revolution' (Lipset, 1960; p. 406). Many Labour politicians, believing that welfare legislation had achieved the historic goals of their movement, revised their traditional 'socialist doctrines' (Crosland, 1956), and vied with one another to present themselves as 'common-sense fellows with no time for theorizing' (Crossman, 1952). Leading academics announced the 'end' of the 'ideological age' (Bell, 1960) and renounced their traditional role as critical and visionary thinkers. The result — a combination of political pragmatism and academic empiricism — was anticipated, some thirty years earlier, by Mannheim's prophetic vision of a world made barren by the absence of utopia. In 1929 Mannheim had written that 'the more . . . an ascendant party gives up its original utopian impulses and with it its broad perspective' the more it is likely to be preoccupied with 'concrete and isolated details'. There is, he suggested, a corresponding change in 'the scientific outlook which conforms to political demands, i.e. what was once merely a formal scheme and abstract, total view, tends to dissolve into the investigation of specific and discrete problems' (Mannheim, 1960; p. 225).

The declared 'End of Ideology' and the practice of 'consensus politics' encouraged the construction of absolute and invidious distinctions between the mainstream activities of value-free scientific enquiry and 'practical politics', and the fringe pursuits of 'ideological' or 'utopian' thinking. The former were defined as progressive and constructive, the latter as destructive anachronisms in the context of the prosperous and democratic welfare states of the West. 'Ideology' came to be defined as a particular *kind* of belief closed, emotive, partial, irrational, false and, above all, un-scientific. Where 'science' was associated with democracy and freedom, 'ideology' was equated with authoritarianism, dogmatism and violence (Abercrombie 1980; pp. 3 - 4). Ideological thinking was, for many contemporary writers, a symptom of the more pathological or malevolent facets of human conduct (Harris, 1968; pp. 5 - 12). The study of ideology was thus trivialized and consigned to the margins of academic enquiry.

With the revivial of Marxist and neo-Liberal perspectives on State welfare activity, more serious consideration was given to ideological issues. One potentially significant contribution was made in 1971 by Pinker's *Social Theory and Social Policy*. Its historical treatment of the intellectual traditions of sociology and social administration appeared to give a new priority to the analysis of the contribution of ideologies and 'normative theories' to the making of social policy. In this respect Pinker's book would seem either to mark the end of an era in the development of social administration or, at least, to provide an exception to George and Wilding's general characterization of the discipline. In fact, the argument he advanced exemplified and perpetuated the neglect of a reflexive treatment of ideological and value issues. Pinker's main concern was to defend his subject, the pragmatic approach and the empirical idiom, against the onslaughts of Marxist theory and critical sociology. He retraced the paternity of social administration to a form of 19th century social enquiry that was 'empirical and sceptical' rather than 'ideological and authoritative'. The former, in Pinker's view, had constituted 'a makeshift rearguard action' against the latter: the historical achievement of the pragmatic and empirical tradition of social administration, and the proof of its intrinsic superiority was, according to Pinker, its success in promoting the advance of 'collectivist forms of welfare provision' with a minimum conflict over welfare aims.

This version of the history of the Welfare State—a form of idealism that echoed the earlier contributions of empirically-minded sociologists—was clearly intended to provide an object-lesson for the present. Pinker argued that, at a time when the academic debate about social policy was becoming 'more imbued with ideological imperatives', the discipline had to be preserved from 'the wilder reaches of ideology'. Although he conceded that the work of the social administrator also springs from 'normative preoccupations', these have 'always been complemented by an equally strong commitment to democratic principles, rational discourse and a respect for evidence'. These qualities sharply distinguish the 'more revolutionary forms of social theory' from the combination of 'pragmatism and moral conviction' found within social administration. In the first case, the ideological abuse of reason and political freedom can only subvert the cause of social justice. Conversely, the empirical tradition, coupled with a willingness to compromise on 'issues of principle', should continue to enrich the subject-matter of social policy and to ensure its future contributions to 'human betterment' and the 'maintenance of democratic values'.

It seems that the purpose of Pinker's contribution to the debate about welfare values was to protect the province of social administration from those forms of discourse that *he* defined as 'ideological'. He thereby excluded from the agenda any reflexive analysis of the ideological properties of the discipline and of 'the sectarian nature of the dominant social values' that it reflects (George & Wilding, 1972; p. 244). We have suggested that Pinker's Canute-like defence of his discipline, and of post-war collectivism, against the rising tide of radical criticism, rested on a definition of ideology and on a set of political and historical assumptions that were more widely shared by an earlier generation of writers who subscribed—explicitly or by default—to the 'End of Ideology' thesis. Criticism of this thesis, and of the political and intellectual styles with which it was associated, was left to the New Left intelligentsia of the 1960s, for whom the 'End of Ideology' was itself an ideology—the ideology of a civil, 'Natopolitan' intelligentsia. (Shils, 1958; Thompson, 1960). Recent criticisms of 'orthodox' social administration have, with one or two exceptions (e.g. Donnison, 1979), come from writers (Mishra, 1977; Taylor-Gooby & Dale, 1981) whose inspiration owes much to New Left analyses of the impact of 'bourgeois ideology' on the development of the humanities and social sciences in Britain (e.g. Stedman-Jones, 1967). It was from these sources that a more comprehensive assessment of the ideological basis of conventional welfare studies and of post-war social policy can and has been constructed. The term 'ideology', has, accordingly, been rescued from its obituarists and brought to bear on the mainstream of political and academic life.

The classification of Welfare Ideologies

Although George and Wilding did not initiate the comparative study of welfare ideologies their review of the various political values and attitudes that have some bearing on state welfare provision formally acknowledges the problematic nature of received assumptions and dominant social values (George & Wilding, 1976). Their contribution to the analysis of the 'battle of ideas' over state welfare was to offer a formal classification in which a potentially bewildering array of beliefs, values and prescriptions are reduced to four logically related 'ideologies'—'Anti' and 'Reluctant Collectivism', 'Fabian Socialism' and 'Marxism'. The interconnecting theme, and thus the basis of their typology, is provided by a range of attitudes to the role the State should play in relation to the capitalist market—whether this be to sustain, supplement or supplant the free play of market forces in achieving an 'equitable' allocation of resources or 'welfares'. As we shall see, part of the value of this contribution lies in the criticisms it has provoked. We shall consider two different, but in some ways related responses to their typology.

In the final chapter of *The Idea of Welfare* (1979) Pinker sets out to 'rehabilitate' the 'middle way of the mixed economy': the first reason for doing so is to counteract the 'continuing influence and popularity of the classical economic and Marxist paradigms of welfare'; and the second is to correct the typological illusion that advocacy of the mixed economy possesses no existence apart from its relation to the polar extremes—'the two paradigms of capitalism and communism'. The novelty in Pinker's argument does not arise from his first reason for rehabilitating 'the middle way', since this leads him merely to reiterate many of the claims advanced in his previous book (Pinker, 1971). Once again he reserves the term 'ideology' for any radical (or 'extreme') doctrine that seeks to transcend the present social order and extant political practices. The two opposed alternatives of classical economic theory and Marxism are portrayed as identical with respect to their political consequences (they tend, for example, to become 'instruments of oppression and diswelfare') and they are unfavourably compared with the pragmatic realism and open-minded eclecticism of the 'prudential philosophy' of the Third Way. This sustained polemic adds nothing to the analysis of welfare ideology that was not already available to the Natopolitan intellectuals of the 1950s.

Pinker does, however, make some important comments on George and Wilding's typology. His specific objection to their categories concerns the equation of collectivism *only* with socialism, and the attribution of 'reluctance' to Keynes and Beveridge who, in Pinker's view, 'were enthusiastic collectivists . . . *because* they were both anti-socialist'. This leads directly to Pinker's more general concern—to retrieve the 'tradition' of 'mercantile' collectivism' from the obscurity thrust upon it by both its detractors and its apologists. Although this tradition antedates both capitalism and socialism its intrinsic coherence and historical complexities have been obscured by the convention of reducing the 'choice' in welfare to a spectrum of alternatives that is defined by the two relatively recent, and 'highly deterministic' theories of capitalism and communism.

In contrast to the general drift of Pinker's argument, which is towards either a *tripartite* (classical economic theory versus Marxism versus mercantile collectivism) or a *dichotomous* (the prudential philosophy of mercantile collectivism versus ideological 'extremism') classification, Peter George (1981) has advocated a two-dimensional typology of welfare ideologies. Like Pinker, George's concern is to correct the distortions arising from the Collectivism/Anti-Collectivism continuum and, for different reasons he, too, is concerned with identifying 'the character of the ideology implicit in and underlying the British Welfare State'.

George starts by observing that, although the terms and the boundaries of their categories may vary, most if not all of the more recent contributors to the analysis of welfare ideologies merely offer variants of George and Wilding's continuum. This point can be diagrammatized as follows:

	Anti Collectivism	Reluctant Collectivism	Fabian Socialism	Marxism[1]
	Market Liberals	Political Liberals	Social Democrats	neo-[2] Marxists
ANTI-STATE	Classical Economic Theory	neo-Mercantilism	Marxisms[3] 'its socialist derivatives'	PRO-STATE
	Residual	Institutional	'Normative' or 'Socialist'[4]	
	Conservatism	Positive State	Social Security State	Social Welfare State — Radicalism[5]

Figure 1
1. George and Wilding, 1976.
2. Room 1979.
3. Pinker, 1979.
4. Mishra, 1977, pp. 35–6 and George and Manning, 1980, after Titmuss, 1974, Ch. 2.
5. Furniss and Tilson, 1977.

As George comments: 'The one-dimensional nature of the continuum used by all these authors could hardly be made clearer. It has economic individualism and the free market at one end and out-and-out collectivists and the command economy at the other, with the Welfare State as the middle way between these extremes supported by a variety of more or less liberal, more or less socialist collectivists'.

George lays the foundation for his two-dimensional classification by criticizing the original continuum for giving such a high priority to those political philosophies that have their roots in Enlightenment rationalism (individualism and collectivism). It consequently neglects the venerable, but nevertheless, living traditions of conservative paternalism and libertarian socialism. Because the former, which is rooted in 'the natural ideology of feudal and . . . land-owning aristocracies', is essentially anti-individualist and advocates active and responsible government, it cannot in any way be subsumed under the rubric of 'anti-collectivism'. The latter, equally, with its roots in 'the peasant commune and the guilds and corporations of the free cities of predominantly agricultural societies', harbours a strong antipathy to the centralized and bureaucratic state, to 'paternalistic collectivism'. George argues that these two traditions embody alternative ideas of 'community' — the one being *hierarchical* with an emphasis on the rights and duties attaching to the various ranks of society, the other emphasising fraternal relations and mutual aid in a *community of equals.*

Thus George offers two dimensions for the classification of welfare ideologies. The first consists of our original continuum and it describes a range of attitudes to the proper relationship between the state and the market; the second describes the various 'concepts of community' advocated by the protagonists in past and current 'welfare' debates. This enables George to identify four distinct ideologies — 'Market Liberalism' and 'Collectivism', 'Conservatism' and 'Communism':

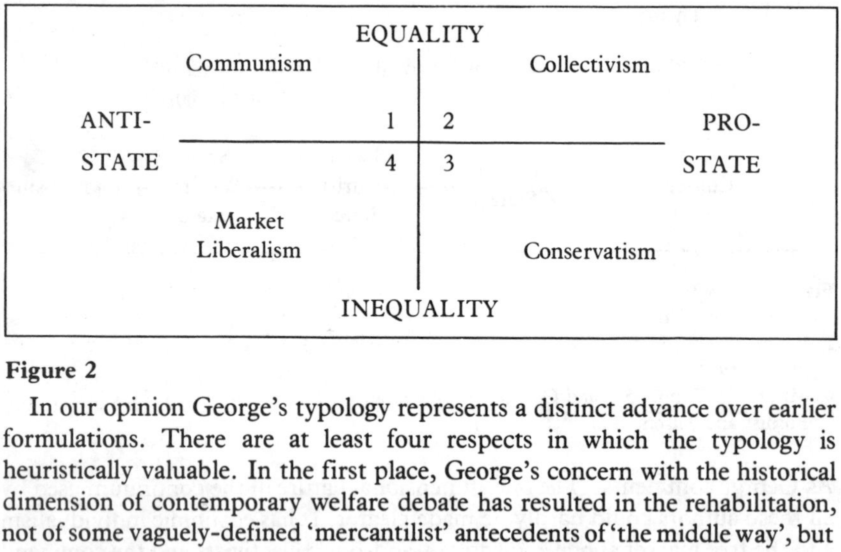

Figure 2

In our opinion George's typology represents a distinct advance over earlier formulations. There are at least four respects in which the typology is heuristically valuable. In the first place, George's concern with the historical dimension of contemporary welfare debate has resulted in the rehabilitation, not of some vaguely-defined 'mercantilist' antecedents of 'the middle way', but of the concrete and mutually antagonistic traditions of Tory paternalism and socialist 'anti-collectivism'. Both traditions have been overshadowed in recent welfare discourse. The former has been eclipsed by the contest between the 'progressive' conservatism of Macmillan and Butler (a conservatism that was presented to the electorate, in the years of the 'Butskellite' consensus, as a qualified form of social democracy) and the 'radical' free-market conservatism of Thatcher and Joseph (one that lays a false but forceful claim to have restored the identity of the Conservative Party). The tradition of libertarian socialism — which includes the Guild Socialism of G.D.H. Cole and the ethical socialism of Richard Tawney — has been obscured by the Webbsean equation of socialism with collectivism. George's framework transcends the preoccupations of recent political debate. It has, for this reason, a particular relevance to the 'welfare' controversies of the 18th and 19th centuries, and it provides the means for re-establishing the linkages between early criticisms of bourgeois society and modern welfare philosophies.

Secondly, the two-dimensional typology makes it possible for George to demonstrate that the ideology of the British welfare state 'is loose, fragmented and often contradictory because it incorporates elements from a number of different traditions in an attempt to promote a consensus in a deeply divided society'. This 'unstable consensus' is, he argues, held together by the notion of 'citizenship' — drawing from Conservatism the ideal of service, from Market Liberalism the idea of the 'minimum', unversalism from Collectivism, and the ideal of 'mutual aid' from the cooperative tradition of British Socialism. Thus the ideology of the British welfare state is not simply the product of a contest between Collectivism and Market Liberalism, but also of an equally important conflict between the 'patrician' and the 'plebian' elements in the national culture. This suggestion is very much more plausible than Pinker's claim that the philosophy of social administration and the welfare state is rooted in a single, though complex and independent tradition of 'mercantile collectivism'.

Third, whilst Pinker draws an invidious contrast between the eclectic plurality (the 'open-ness') of the doctrines of mercantile collectivism, and the ideological coherence and consistency (closure) of both classical political economy and Marxism, George's framework facilitates an analysis of the internal disputes that are endemic to *all* of the traditions. Thus, although the dominant strain within Fabian Socialism might be placed in the second quadrant with a tendency to enter the third, the Fabianism of Tawney and Cole can be squarely located within the first. Modern British conservatism clearly owes much of its vitality to an 'unholy alliance' between the philosophies of the third and fourth quadrants. And the perennial tension within Marxism between its libertarian (quadrant 1) and state-socialist (quadrant 2) forms belies the quality of monolithic homogeneity attributed to it by the ideologues of the 'centre'.

And, finally, the fact that the earlier literature failed to conceptualise the second (vertical) continuum — with its concern for the relations of power between individuals and groups — partially explains the reason why feminism is never granted the status of a welfare ideology. As Wilson (in this text) demonstrates, feminist concern nearly always focuses on the way social policies regulate the 'private' realm of home and community, subsequently reinforcing crucial, and inegalitarian, relations of dependency between men and women, the old and the less old, etc. Feminist critiques of welfare provision are highly sensitive to those questions of unequal resource distribution not reducible to the successful, or otherwise, operations of economic markets. Their work is particularly concerned with 'the monolithic, authoritarian and paternalist form that state welfare provision all too often takes' (Wilson), and with alternatives involving greater consumer participation. It might be suggested that the present attempts by some Labour councils to try to personalise and democratise their welfare services owes much to the impact of feminist criticism.

Beyond Description: Towards Explanation

There are several more general comments that need to be made about the literature that has appeared in the ten years since the publication of George and Wilding's original article. The first concerns the use of the concept of 'ideology' to refer exclusively and in a pejorative manner to the intellectual practices of those who reject the prevailing social order and its received wisdoms. We have suggested that this identification of ideology with 'utopian' thinking (cf. Mannheim, 1960; Ch. 4) has been a prominent and recurrent feature of Pinker's contributions. But the problem is not confined to the work of one author. The usage adopted by Pinker derives from the 'End of Ideology' tradition, and it continues to be implicit in the disdainful attitude of 'orthodox' social administration towards the 'pretensions' of social theorists (see Taylor-Gooby and Dale, 1981; Ch. 1). The term retains its pejorative connotations if and when it is used by radicals to refer only to the beliefs and values of dominant groups and their intellectual agents.

Many of the later contributions to the literature have overcome the pejorative connotations of the concept by extending its range of application, and this has greatly facilitated the interpretive and comparative analysis of welfare ideologies. But, in most cases, the concept is not formally *defined* and 'ideologies' are usually treated, in an uninterpreted way, as either synonymous with or reducible to 'values' ('attitudes', 'normative assumptions', concepts of 'the Good Society'). This precludes any systematic attempt to distinguish the 'ethical' aspects from the belief and practical components of 'ideology', and to examine the ways in which these 'components' are related to one another within the context of self-contained, formally rational worldviews with their own rules of evidence and interpretation. This has two important consequences. First, it means that the resulting typologies remain peculiarly susceptible to the drawing of invidious comparisons between perspectives. The problem arises when the realm of 'fact' is treated as potentially free of ideological 'colouring', and as the source of objective criteria for choosing one rather than another view of welfare issues. The various perspectives represented in a typology can thus be discarded or accepted, either on the basis of an appeal to 'the empirical evidence' (cf. Room, 1979), or by claiming that certain perspectives systematically abuse the canons of science and reason (Pinker, 1971; 1979).

The second problem concerns an apparent failure to produce a coherent analysis of the *programmatic* aspects of welfare discourse. For as long as 'ideology' is equated with 'values', the ideals associated with each of the defined positions will sometimes appear to be contradicted by the political actions contemplated by their adherents. For example, unprecedented powers were conferred on the State at a time when, in the 19th century, Whig and Liberal politicians had at least a notional commitment to the principles of *laissez-faire*. The present Conservative administration has transferred power and responsibilities from local authorities to central government, despite its theoretical commitment to an 'anti-statist' ideology. Marxists, for all their pronouncements about an eventual 'withering away of the state', are described, in the one-dimensional typologies, as full-blooded collectivists in active pursuit of the 'dictatorship of the proletariat', the wholesale nationalization of the means of production, and the establishment of a centrally planned economy (cf. George & Wilding, 1976; pp. 96–9). And the conventional identification of social democracy with gradualist and constitutional strategies would seem to be belied by some of the statements of an earlier generation of Fabian and Revisionist socialists: at some stage in their lifetime, Shaw, Bernstein and the Webbs had each conceded that revolutionary action might be necessary *in certain circumstances*. The last phrase is crucial because it is only when matters of 'belief' — perceptions of current circumstances, issues of 'fact' and 'explanation' — are brought into account that one is able to resolve these apparent contradictions between theory (values) and practice.

If our classifications of welfare ideologies are to be capable of analysing strategic disputes, they must acknowledge the problematic and variable nature of the relationship between 'fact' and 'values'. Although political values may have a relatively timeless and consensual quality, circumstances do change, and it is over the assessment of these circumstances that ideological allies may disagree. The strategic implications of a set of political values will depend on the extent to which there is a perceived discrepancy between the 'ideal' and the 'real': they will depend, in other words, on how certain political goals are thought to relate to current circumstances and future trends. Once these issues are brought within the scope of ideological analysis it becomes possible to understand how and why it is that the same set of values may have radical and revolutionary implications at one stage in their history and yet, at other times and from other viewpoints, they may acquire a conservative and reformist character. Such an analysis might be constructed on the basis of Mannheim's distinction between the 'ideological' and the 'utopian' states of mind (1960; pp. 173–84) and Harris' discussion (1968) of the conditions under which initially radical and oppositional philosophies are translated into conservative defences of the *status quo*. One immediate advantage of this analysis might be that it would reveal the essentially 'ideological' nature of the political empiricism and pragmatic realism of British social democracy (and social administration) in the early post-war period — a period in which the leading politicians and academics of the 'liberal left' regarded the Welfare State as a fair approximation to their collectivist ideals.

If the concept of ideology has at times been used to refer only to particular *kinds* of perspective, or to certain *aspects* of welfare discourse, the empirical analysis and classification of welfare ideologies has generally been confined to the relatively articulate theoretical and philosophical systems advanced by 'key' intellectuals. Peter George (1981) is a possible exception to this, in that his discussion of welfare ideologies does acknowledge the role of the working class and of professional elites as 'carriers' of particular notions of 'community'. Nevertheless, the literature as a whole gives little consideration to the less systematic, and certainly more volatile, *popular* dimensions of welfare ideology. (Whiteley, 1981; Golding & Middleton, 1982). Unless, of course, one were to maintain that policy making is only influenced by the deliberations of a 'free-floating' intelligentsia, the analysis of welfare 'ideologies' will have limited explanatory value for as long as it continues to be divorced from the study of public opinion and political attitudes. Little is really known about such opinions despite the widely held view — optimistic on the Right (Harris & Seldon, 1979) and pessimistic on the Left (Hall, 1979; Corrigan, 1979) — that anti-welfare state sentiments hold sway amongst large sections of the population (cf. Judge *et al.*, 1983). Useful sources for such investigations might be those sociological studies of class images of the social order (Bulmer, 1979) and of working-class culture (Clarke *et al.*, 1979).

Thus far our criticisms of conventional approaches to the classification of welfare ideologies have concentrated on questions originally raised with George and Wilding's frame of reference. Our concern was with suggesting ways in which their *descriptive* and *intellectualist* exercise in taxonomy could be improved in its own terms. In the remainder of this section we want to draw attention to some other, more fundamental, issues raised by the investigation of welfare and ideology.

If the undervaluation, and neglect, of strategic issues and popular values betrays an *implicit* idealism, this tendency is confirmed and made explicit by the failure to satisfactorily address two further questions. These are the critical questions concerning the *determination* of ideologies, and the identification, and understanding, of their *effects*. George and Wilding (1972) do certainly recognise the importance of addressing these more analytical questions in their first agenda-setting article. For they contend that hitherto the study of social policy has contained:

> virtually no analysis of what is meant by social values, of how they are formed, of how and why values change, of how they are transmitted, of the relationship between social values and social structure, of who actually holds the values which are supposed to be important, of the intensity with which social values are held or of the relative importance of different values (p. 236).

Yet because they are entrapped within a descriptive understanding of ideology, equating the concept with value choice, they fail to furnish a satisfactory answer to their own questions. These questions remain not only stubbornly unanswered by the literature spawned by George and Wilding but, as yet, largely unaddressed by the discipline of social administration. It is one thing to *observe* ideas and construct neat classifications, it is quite another to *explain* the operations of ideologies. In fact, it makes no sense to discuss ideology — a concept never actually cited in the index of *Ideology and Social Welfare* — unless one has some analytical understanding of its conditions of existence and appearance (the *determination* of ideologies), and a theoretical grasp of what it is you are seeking to explain when invoking the concept (the *effects* of ideologies). If one occupies an intellectual position that merely equates values with ideologies, the concept can only be employed descriptively to catalogue different value choices, and only certain rather obvious answers can be supplied to such questions. The effects become self-evident; people occupy differing moral and political camps, and the development of social policies simply reflects a process of compromise between them. The origins of these differences, presumably, can only but stem either from personal choice or external manipulation.

George and Wilding's (1972; pp. 240–241) exceptionally brief answer to their own questions is to plump for the notion of manipulation. They specify a number of mechanisms whereby the practices of the dominant capitalist groups guarantee that their 'sectional values and interests come to be seen and accepted as national interests'. These mechanisms include elite control of the mass media, and the fact that the major social institutions are staffed and organised by members of that same elite. Such arguments have a strong pedigree both in instrumentalist variants of Marxism (see Miliband, 1969) and in some of the more progressive themes of the Fabian tradition, notably that of Titmuss (1970). George and Wilding's affinity with the latter political tradition comes over particularly strongly in their argument that certain values (self-help, individualism and competition) requisite 'for the successful operation of a capitalist economy', are 'in clear opposition to the values needed to underpin a successful public welfare system' (1976; p. 118). Change towards such a system will only materialise if, as for Titmuss, changes in values or in *intellect* occur — if altruism can flourish to the exclusion of egoism. Such a change would be largely facilitated by reforming the elite control of the mass media, and so altering the dominant ideologies. Whilst these arguments may make *political* sense the theoretical attention given to our two crucial questions is, nevertheless, grossly inadequate. Determination stems purely from imposition, and the *effects* are to enforce sets of false consciousness. Ideologies are more than mere collections of separate falsehoods, and are better conceived as matrices of thought firmly grounded in the very nature of our social life.

Poulantzas (1973) suggests that we can best appreciate the general function of ideology under capitalism in terms of three effects: (a) masking and displacing (b) fragmentation or separation and (c) the imposition of an imaginary unity or coherence on reality. He argues that Marx's false appearances are better understood as the *re-presentation* of certain relationships — for example, in the sphere of market relations the productive classes appear (or rather are represented) as mere separate economic units and private greed seems bound by 'fair' contracts. Thus representation has the effect, first of *shifting* emphasis and awareness from production to exchange; second, of *fragmenting* classes into individuals; and third, of *binding* individuals into a passive community of consumers. It is in the sphere of exchange that our spontaneous and everyday common-sense perceptions and experiences of the system arise. In essence, the effect of ideology is to re-inforce that which 'passes for common-sense in society — the residue of absolutely basic and commonly-agreed consensual wisdoms' (Hall, 1977; p. 325). Precisely because it 'feels' as if it has always been there, its location is bound to raise complex analytical questions.

We may, for example, be able to agree that certain dominant ideas inform the public understanding of poverty and welfare — '*efficiency* of the labour market, *morality* of the work ethic and *pathology* of individual inadequacy' (Golding & Middleton, 1982; p. 48) — and that the effect of these ideas is to blame the victims of poverty for their predicament. But just *how* these ideas become 'fixed' into the prevailing common-sense requires detailed historical and empirical analysis, and such studies are at present woefully lacking in the discipline. Golding and Middleton (1982) have produced an interesting analysis, containing much useful empirical material, but they fail to resolve the chicken-and-egg question of the causal relationship between media treatments and residual public opinions in the production of ideology. Even within the 'new' critical social policy these questions have been underplayed. Gough (1979) acknowledges as much when he notes that his own political economy approach to welfare 'urgently needs complementing with a study of the ideology of the welfare state' (p. 10). We do not wish to suggest that the answers to such questions are readily available, but there have been interesting developments in those literatures concerned with the emergence of the New Right and its apparent success in capturing the popular imagination (e.g. Hall, 1979, 1981; Corrigan, 1979; Mouffe, 1981; Fitzgerald, in this text), and in recent feminist studies of welfare provision (see Wilson in this text for a useful review of this literature, and Bland, 1979). Rather our argument is, first, that adequate answers to such questions will not be found within idealist discourse. And, second, that even 'radical' social administration texts, such as *Ideology and Social Welfare*, tend to play down these more complex, theoretical questions and celebrate empirical ones.

It has been our contention throughout this paper that contemporary discussions of the pertinence of the concept ideology for explaining welfare issues have been both restricted and restricting. Whilst most of the discussion has concentrated on descriptive and classificatory matters, this has been far from exhaustive. Developments have been further impeded by their atheoretical nature, and by their preference for idealist resolutions of complex problems.

References

Abercrombie, N. (1980) *Class, Structure and Knowledge,* Blackwell.

Bell, D. (1960) *The End of Ideology,* Free Press.

Bland, L. *et al.* (1979) Sexuality and reproduction: three 'Official' instances, in M. Barrett *et al., Ideology and Cultural Production,* Croom Helm.

Bulmer, M. (1975) *Working Class Images of Society,* Routledge and Kegan Paul.

Clarke, J. *et al.* (1979) *Working Class Culture,* Hutchinson.

Corrigan, P. (1979) Popular consciousness and social democracy in *Marxism Today* Vol. 23, No. 12.

Crosland, C.A.R. (1956) *The Future of Socialism,* Jonathan Cape.

Crossman, R.H.S. (1952) *New Fabian Essays,* Turnstile Press.

Donnison, D. (1979) Social policy since Titmuss, in *Journal of Social Policy,* Vol. 8, No. 2.

Furniss, N. and Tilton, T. (1977) *The Case for the Welfare State,* Indiana University Press.

Gallie, W.B. (1955–56) Essentially contested concepts, in *Proceedings of the Aristotelian Society.*

George, P. (1981) *Ideology and the Welfare State,* Unpublished paper delivered to the Annual Conference of the Social Administration Association at Leeds University In July 1981.

George, V. and Manning, N. (198) *Socialism, Social Welfare and the Soviet Union,* Routledge and Kegan Paul.

George, V. and Wilding, P. (1972) Social values, social class and social policy, in *Social and Economic Administration* VI(3).

George, V. and Wilding, P. (1976) *Ideology and Social Welfare,* Routledge and Kegan Paul.

Golding, P. and Middleton, S. (1982) *Images of Welfare: Press and Public Attitudes to Poverty,* Martin Robertson.

Gough, I. (1978) *The Political Economy of the Welfare State,* Macmillan Press.

Hall, S. (1977) Culture, the media and the 'ideological effect' in J. Curran, *et al.* (eds), *Mass Communication and Society,* Edward Arnold/Open University Press.

Hall, S. (1979) The great moving right show, in *Marxism today,* Vol. 23, No. 1.

Hall, S. (1981) The 'little Caesars' of social democracy, in *Marxism Today,* Vol. 25, No. 4.

Harris, N. (1968) *Beliefs in Society,* Watts.

Harris, R. and Seldon, A. (1979) *Over-Ruled on Welfare,* Institute of Economic Affairs.

Judge, K. *et al.* (1983) *New Directions in Social Policy? Public Opinion and the Privatization of Welfare,* Discussion Paper 268, Personal Social Services Research Unit, University of Kent.

Lipset, S.M. (1960) *Political Man,* Heinemann.

Mannheim, K. (1960) *Ideology and Utopia,* Routledge and Kegan Paul.

Marshall, T.H. (1972) Value problems of welfare capitalism, in *Journal of Social Policy* I(1).

Miliband, R. (1969) *The State in Capitalist Society,* Weidenfeld and Nicholson.

Mishra, R. (1977) *Society and Social Policy,* Macmillan.

Mouffe, C. (1981) Democracy and the new right, in *Politics and Power,* No. 4.

Pinker, R. (1971) *Social Theory and Social Policy,* Heinemann.

Pinker, R. (1979) *The Idea of Welfare,* Heinemann.

Poulantzas, N. (1973) *Political Power and Social Classes,* New Left Books.

Room, G. (1979) *The Sociology of Welfare,* Blackwell.

Shils, E. (1958) Ideology and civility in *The Intellectuals and The Powers,* University of Chicago Press.

Stedman-Jones, G. (1967) *The pathology of English history,* in *New Left Review,* 46.

Taylor-Gooby, P. and Dale, J. (1981) *Social Theory and Social Welfare,* Edward Arnold.

Thompson, E.P. (1960) Outside the whale, in *Out of Apathy,* New Left Books.

Titmuss, R. (1970) *The Gift Relationship: From Human Blood to Social Policy,* Allen and Unwin.

Titmuss, R. (1974) *Social Policy,* Allen and Unwin.

Whitely, P. (1981) Public opinion and the demand for social welfare in Britain, in *Journal of Social Policy,* Vol. 10, Part 4.

Wilding, P. and George, V. (1975) *Social values and social policy,* in *Journal of Social Policy,* Vol. 4, No. 4.

Feminism and Social Policy

Elizabeth Wilson

One way of looking at social policy would be to describe it as a set of structures created by men to shape the lives of women. 'Social policy' is a broad term, and is used to define a spectrum of state policies running from economic policy at one end through to the control of crime at the other. Social policy has also been described as 'integrative', that is as policies to produce social integration and harmony (Boulding, 1967). If we concentrate on women and social policy we find ourselves at the mid point of the spectrum, and involved with the core issues that make government *policy social:* education, housing and health; income maintenance and social security; and the care of children and other dependent groups, largely the sick and the old.

These areas of social policy of course provide for both sexes. We find, however, deeply embedded within them, assumptions about women and their role which seem sometimes to operate at the level of the 'taken for granted' and sometimes to be part of deliberate planning for women. Sometimes, that is, it seems as if policy makers simply reproduce unthinkingly traditional, unquestioned views about women's role; sometimes it seems that there is a conscious attempt to create such roles because they *are* believed to enhance 'social integration' anew, to reinforce them and even to punish those who reject them.

The views and assumptions to which I refer operate at two distinct levels. They operate in the way policies are shaped; and they operate in the ways in which those policies are carried out. So, for example, the cohabitation ruling: this states that a woman who is alleged to be cohabiting with a man, that is who is in a relationship with him which is both domestic and sexual, may not claim supplementary benefit, but must be claimed for by her partner, just as if she were married. This is an assumption about women's role at the level of the law and social planning. The behaviour of individual DHSS officers, of special investigators ('sex snoopers'), possibly of social workers and other officials, represents the second level; at which policy is put into practice.

Moreoever, although social policy is directed at both men and women (and children of both sexes) it operates much more in the private than in the public

33

sphere; and is less concerned with the public world of work than with the private world of home and community. Much of social policy therefore becomes policy about the family, or else about individuals for whom the family is missing, especially for those outside the work force who also lack a family — the isolated pensioner, the parentless child.

Here, Boulding's notion of 'integration' comes into play. For throughout the 20th century policy makers have relied heavily on a notion of 'family' as a harmonizing force, as the basis of social peace and stability. In reality, 'family' indicates ever-changing domestic and kinship patterns; yet in our century a fixed and static conception of family has become part of a powerful ideology of what constitutes a healthy society. (Barrett & McIntosh, 1982; Donzelot, 1979). Change — which actually occurs all the time — has as a consequence come to seem very threatening as it relates to the family; and a major feature of 20th century social policy in Britain (and in most other capitalist countries) has been an attempt to preserve the family unchanged. Since women's lives are centrally bound up with family, this has many consequences for them.

What, though, of *feminism* and social policy? Feminism as a movement was attendant upon the rise of capitalism in Britain, western Europe and the United States. During the middle and late 19th century feminists campaigned around many issues: they demanded the right to vote, the right to their own property, the right to work and to education. At the same time new professions or 'semi-professions' were growing — teaching, nursing and social work — and these tended to reproduce in the public sphere the work women had traditionally done on a private basis within the home (Walton, 1975).

More generally, capitalism led to state intervention on an unprecedented scale. State intervention took many forms, and as the 19th century wore on governments found themselves becoming more involved than ever before with the provision of social benefits and necessities. Many of these provisions replaced or at least supplemented the work that women had traditionally performed in the home.

To take one example: once, women had controlled medical processes (Ehrenreich & English, 1979); the care of the sick had been women's sphere and their responsibility. With industrialization came new knowledge, new trainings, new technology — medicine itself became a kind of industry, with the result that women were edged out of their traditional healing role and replaced by men who created a new profession of medicine, relegating women to secondary roles, notably nursing. In the 19th century women of the expanding bourgeois class were excluded from the education and training that would have admitted them to this vigorous new medical profession, and had to fight many battles as individuals (Manton, 1965) in order to gain some sort of foothold there anew. Meanwhile the lore of wise women and midwives, who had tended working class people, was downgraded and despised. The new, expensive forms of medical care were built on the basis of harsh class ideologies as well as embodying ideologies about gender.

Many 19th century feminists fought for a place in the public world from which they were increasingly excluded as the private sphere of the home and family enlarged itself to contain, even to imprison them (Zaretsky, 1975). Yet feminists did not merely seek a place in the public, male world. Nor did they seek the vote simply as a right for themselves. Rather, they saw their participation in public life as making possible the operations of women's values upon a male world (Banks, 1981). They regarded the function of maternity as central to women's identity and moral being. Because of their motherhood role, women, they believed, had a special and a higher moral nature than men. Women's entry into the public sphere of good works, as civic workers, local councillors, teachers and so on, they saw as a moral force that would cleanse the proliferating urban centres from violence, vice and crime (Platt, 1969).

Such feminists — and not all 19th century feminists held these views — shared the ideology of the wider Victorian society. This ideology placed women on a pedestal by virtue of their sacred responsibilities as mothers; but in doing so emphasized their moral purity at the expense not only of their sexuality but also of their intelligence and 'character'. Women were seen as dispensers of love and harmony, as responsive and passive; and *therefore* as unfitted for the hurly-burly of capitalist life outside the home, as unable to reason and as swayed by emotions. Set down thus crudely such an ideology sounds self-contradictory. Nevertheless many feminists themselves accepted it, partly because it did assign a certain superiority to women in terms of their moral nature and sacred role in the family.

Feminists interpreted this ideology to mean that it was their duty to engage in the public sphere in so far as the public sphere was more and more concerning itself with the well-being of the family. Beatrice Webb, a Fabian, although she was not herself a suffragist and would probably not have described herself as a feminist, nevertheless well summed up this view in a letter she wrote to Millicent Garrett Fawcett, the leader of the suffragists, in 1906, to explain why she had decided that, after having previously opposed the demand for the vote, she should now support it (Webb, 1926; pp. 362-3):

> The rearing of children, the advancement of learning and the promotion of the spiritual — which I regard as the particular obligations of women — are, it is clear, more and more becoming the main preoccupations of the community as a whole . . . Whilst I rejoice in much of this new development of politics I think it adequately accounts for the increasing restiveness of women. They are in my opinion rapidly losing their consciousness of consent in the work of Government and are even feeling a positive obligation to take part in directing this new activity. This is in my view not a claim to rights nor an abandonment of women's particular obligations, but a desire more effectively to fulfil their functions by sharing the control of State Action in these directions.

But of course it is not feminists only who have perceived social welfare in the public sphere as peculiarly the concern of women — that has become another 20th century cliché about women's role in public life.

In Britain the struggle for the vote was effectively won by 1918, and the feminist movement went into a period of gradual decline which lasted until the resurgence of feminism in a new form in the late 1960s. A similar trend was seen in the United States. Feminism was by no means dead in the period between the two world wars. It did however subtly change its orientation and its concerns. Some authors have described this as the period of 'welfare feminism' (Banks, 1981). I am not convinced that this label is particularly accurate; yet it reflects a reality — that the most prominent feminists between the wars continued to campaign around issues of relevance to women; and many of these issues necessarily related to welfare. Mary Stocks and others laboured to bring contraceptive knowledge to working class women; women in the teaching professions pursued feminist educational goals; Sylvia Pankhurst campaigned for a better deal for the unmarried mother; the Women's Cooperative Guild campaigned on a range of issues, and as they themselves said later on (HM Government, 1949):

> The development of the social services in this country has come about largely from the prodding and pressure of women who have a very high sense of responsibility, and our own Committee has played a very great part in the development of these services . . . When this Committee was formed in 1916 one of its first campaigns was for the passing of the Maternity and Child Welfare Act, which was passed in 1918. One of the big campaigns that we carried out in the early twenties was for the nursery school, and that came from women who took a very high view of their responsibilities as mothers of families and as housewives in the home.

But probably the best remembered campaign of this period was Eleanor Rathbone's for the 'endowment of motherhood' — which later became in a much reduced form the family allowances of 1945 and the child benefit of the 1980s.

Eleanor Rathbone (McIntosh, 1978a, b) did not see the demand for an allowance for maternity as undermining another and parallel women's struggle of this period: the struggle for equal pay for women. Indeed she supported equal pay. But she saw the demand for the endowment of motherhood as supplementing the struggle for equal pay. She regarded it as unrealistic for women to struggle for equal pay, if equal pay meant that both men and women would receive what had come to be known as a 'family wage'. This was now the traditional male wage, defined by the unions for negotiating purposes as a wage that would support not only a wage earner but also his wife and dependent children.

What Eleanor Rathbone proposed was essentially a redistribution of wages within the working class. Bachelors — and single women — were to subsidize the children of those who were married. The single would be more highly taxed, those with children would receive a benefit. There would no longer be a 'family wage' paid to all men regardless of whether they had family responsibilities or not.

At the same time like many feminists of this and earlier periods, Eleanor Rathbone was less concerned to emphasize the similarities between men and women than to demand that women's special role as mother be given adequate recognition and support. Her emphasis brought her and other feminists into direct conflict with many women active in the trades unions; for these latter at that time opposed family allowances, along with the trades union movement as a whole, on the grounds that family allowances would simply be used as an excuse to cut wages.

This view was changed by the experience of the Second World War. Many more women with children then went out to work, and some of them joined trades unions. For this and other reasons, the demand for family allowances was then taken up by the TUC and a (very meagre) family allowance was legislated for by the wartime Coalition government at the end of the war. (For a good, detailed account of the whole movement for family allowances, see Macnicol, 1980).

The ultimate success of Rathbone's demand was partly due to the support it received from William Beveridge. His was the design for the postwar 'welfare state' (Wilson, 1977). The Beveridge Report, which was the widely discussed 'blue print' for the postwar welfare state, was published in 1942 at the height of the Second World War, and actually became a bestseller. Its proposals were for a proper, organized system of subsistence income on which the individual could depend when work was 'interrupted' through sickness or unemployment, after it had been terminated by old age (pensions) or before work became appropriate (family allowances for children). The Beveridge plan was a response to the demands of the labour movement as represented by the Trades Union Congresss Leadership.

The Unions at this time were bargaining from a position of strength, for the Coalition government needed their cooperation in the war effort; and the Beveridge plan was the price the government was prepared to pay for no strikes and for cooperation in various labour schemes for the duration of hostilities.

What the TUC was asking for was essentially a rationalization and improvement of the existing system, not a new, more 'socialist' system. Nor was it an accident that the wage earner was referred to as 'he'. For the Beveridge plan as it became law after the war institutionalized a dependent status for women.

It was not out of malice that Beveridge turned married women into a special insurance class. On the contrary he firmly believed that his reform would enormously improve both the economic position and the social status of women; and his plan did recognize for the first time the important role played by women in the home in terms of unpaid domestic labour (HM Government, 1942, pp. 49–52):

> In any measure of social policy in which regard is had to facts, the great majority of married women must be regarded as occupied on work which is vital though unpaid, without which their husbands could not do their paid work and without

> which the national could not continue. In accord with facts the Plan for Social
> Security treats married women as a special insurance class of occupied persons
> and treats man and wife as a team . . . The attitude of the housewife to gainful
> employment outside the home is not and should not be the same as that of the
> single woman. She has other duties . . . Taken as a whole the Plan for Social
> Security puts a premium on marriage in place of penalizing it . . . In the next thirty
> years housewives as Mothers have vital work to do in ensuring the adequate
> continuance of the British race and of British ideals in the world.

The Beveridge plan as carried into action did represent a (limited) advance. It
was a more rational social security system, certainly as it dealt with
unemployment. Yet his Plan now reads as deeply conservative in its emphasis
on Imperialism and on familist ideals. Beveridge never questioned the sexual
division of labour in the home, whereby the man becomes a 'breadwinner'
while his wife performs unpaid domestic labour and takes responsibility for
virtually all direct aspects of child rearing and also 'services' her husband — in
return for handing over his wage, the husband expects personal care from his
wife, and in the mid 20th century there was the beginnings of some recognition
that wives were too often reduced virtually to the status of personal servants and
subordinates of their husbands (Wilson, 1980a). And feminists in the postwar
period were concerned, as Eleaner Rathbone had been, with an income for
women within marriage; although as the divorce rate rose questions of
maintenance took the forefront in place of family allowances.

To be fair to Beveridge, no-one expected the great increase in the numbers of
married women going out to work in the period since the Second World War.
But the 'facts' on which Beveridge confidently relied were 'facts' about the
prewar world. Employment patterns for women changed after 1945. Another
'fact' on which Beveridge depended was the stability of marriage. And again, he
was betrayed by history, for the divorce rate has risen fairly steadily since the
Second World War, and consequently disastrous gaps in the Beveridge Plan
have been revealed; for although its architect tried to grapple with the problem
of the deserted wife, his scheme could not accommodate her, and deserted
women with children, whether married or not, have been left to languish on
supplementary benefit.

Yet at the time the Beveridge Plan received rapturous acclaim, not least from
the left, the Labour Party and progressive opinion generally, and it was widely
viewed as being, if not actually socialist, then at least a step in the direction of
socialism. A few feminists alone stood out against it. Elizabeth Abbott and
Katherine Bompass (1943) wrote:

> The status given to the married woman in the Report is not new, it is the reflection
> of her present status in law and insurance, that of a dependant without any right of
> her own person, by way of one penny of cash, though she doubtless can in both
> cases claim a legal right to subsistence . . . It is with the denial of any personal
> status to the woman because she is married, the denial of her independent
> personality within marriage, that everything goes wrong.

But feminist attempts to petition the government to change the scheme were unsympathetically received, and Sir William Jowitt, Minister without Portfolio and later the first Minister of National Insurance, who received a deputation from the National Council of Women of Great Britain, described their demands as 'unreasonable'. It was even suggested that a separation benefit might encourage marriage break up.

Many feminists in the postwar period got caught up in the mild reformism of the labour government elected in 1945 (Wilson, 1980a). They devoted their energies for the most part to the general task of postwar reconstruction, and feminism was even more quiescent in the 1940s and 1950s than it had been between the two world wars.

Built up in the ethos first of postwar 'austerity' and rationing, and then of the 'affluent society' of the 1950s was a very strong ideal of family. Women were openly encouraged to stay at home, to make a 'career' out of homemaking, and to find both sexual and personal fulfilment in the traditional roles of marriage and motherhood. Such an ideal was always talked about as being 'modern' and as involving a 'choice' whether to work or not, yet it was an even more traditional ideal than the 'new woman' of the years between the wars, or an earlier period, the 1890s. Yet it is not true — as the contemporary feminist myth would have it — that women were driven back into the home after the war. A much more contradictory situation arose, because there was an acute labour shortage and married women were drawn increasingly into work (although this was often part-time, badly paid work). It could be argued then that the prevailing ideology of support for the family, which was perpetuated and reinforced within the social policy legislation of the time, and particularly in the many policies for child care, which positively burgeoned in the 1950s and 1960s, ran counter to the needs of the economy.

We could say that there was a contradiction between those state policies needed for the reproduction of the working class, and state economic policies regulating the labour supply in the short term. Or we could put it more simply, and say that there was a conflict between short term and long term needs. And we could also say that there was a split between economic policies, and the management along Keynesian lines of the economy, and social policies, which aimed to preserve family stability and (for a time at least, and quite unsuccessfully) to raise the birth rate. Alternatively, some feminist — and some socialist — commentators have seen the creation of a strong familist ideology in postwar Britain and in the United States as a response to the need of the economy to sell more and more light consumer goods (Friedan, 1963).

In the late 1960s, however, the boom began to falter. The British economy had long been uncompetitive and stagnant by comparison with its rivals. Social change at the same time brought new political ferment, and part of this was the resurgence of feminism in the shape of the women's liberation movement.

The women's liberation movement began with outrage at the inequalities between men and women which still so clearly existed. Women trades unionists were still battling not only *for* equal pay but *against* the indifference, often the outright hostility and prejudice of their male fellow workers. Women who had benefitted by the expansion of the education system found that they did not begin to compete on equal terms with their male peers in the job market, for they were still defined by their reproductive intentions — their role (potential or actual) as mothers was used against them when it came to the question of a 'career'. Meanwhile the 'permissive society' spawned images, advertising, films and a general culture that in emphasizing a new sexual freedom also revealed its extraordinarily sexist nature — women were everywhere portrayed as sexual objects *for men*.

In its early years the women's liberation movement laid great emphasis on the political nature of personal life — and for women that meant life in the home, relationships with husbands and lovers and the battle against the isolation of child care in an essentially unsupportive environment. The early emphasis of the women's liberation movement was on individual change, or change at the immediate, local level: (Segal, 1983) that meant changing your relationships; its also meant campaigns for alternative schools, community nurseries, later for women's refuges. But of course these campaigns immediately brought women up against the state.

In the same period the 'wages for housework' campaign questioned the nature of domestic work. The women's movement rejected the demand since it seemed to most feminists merely to institutionalize the isolated work of women in the home; but it did announce a recognition that 'home-making' really was work.

In the long run early debates on this issue together with the burgeoning campaigns for what turned out to be in most cases extensions of state welfare provision caused many feminists to become much more aware of the welfare state, of social policy and its traditionalist bias. Contemporary feminists, therefore, have traced a line of continuity between their own campaigns for welfare provision and the campaigns of the earlier feminists. At the same time they have radically differentiated themselves from those earlier feminists by virtue of their far more critical attitude to the family and to women's traditional role.

Feminists, however, have never taken up the simplistic slogan 'smash the family'. But because they have often been concerned with short-term goals (such as getting a refuge for battered women off the ground) they have not developed a coherent strategy of demands of the State. In practice there has been an implicit contradiction between feminist demands for independence and equality, and feminist demands for sharing and interdependence. Sometimes women have demanded that men should take more responsibility in caring for others (which is what the welfare state and social policy is all about); sometimes they have argued that men should have fewer rights. Sometimes too the emphasis on individual rights has made it possible for the women's liberation movement to be portrayed as a greedy 'me-too' movement, when really it has been talking about a better quality of life for women, children and men.

Moreoever, in a sense the contemporary women's movement represents a response to the changes in family life that have actually occurred. The high divorce rate has already been mentioned. More women and men are today choosing to have children than ever before; but they choose to have fewer. This means that child bearing and rearing takes up a far smaller time span in any individual woman's life (Titmuss, 1963). More and more women continue to work or return to work after they become mothers. There are many different kinds of *household* in our society — the traditional nuclear family is a minority form, and fifteen per cent or less of us are living in it at any given moment.

Yet — and this applies particularly to welfare provision — in all sorts of ways society just grinds on as though all women were still housewives and mothers; and *nothing else*. The family may be 'breaking down' — it is certainly changing, as it always has — but the ideology of the traditional family is as strong as ever; and nowhere is it more crudely expressed than in the many and various provisions of the welfare state.

In attacking this traditionalist ideology women are sometimes mis-understood as attacking the very idea of love, of sustaining relationships and of consistent nurturance and care for children. But this is not so. Feminists are concerned because social policies and welfare provision *fail* to sustain emotionally satisfying relationships either inside or outside the family; they *fail* to provide nurturance and care, but rely on a largely non-existent notion of an extended family network for the care of dependants. Politicians talk glibly of the 'family' and the 'community' but in practice women's unpaid labour in the home is unjustifiably exploited and extended to fill the glaring gaps in social provision. Some feminists (Barrett & McIntosh, 1982) have argued that we should revise our negative views of institutions; that hostels, homes and special accommodation will always be needed and that the important thing is to banish their authoritarian and patriarchal aspects and make of them places where we would actually like to live, or at least to stay. As things are women are prepared to shoulder what can be or become a nightmarish burden because they *do* love their stroke-stricken husbands, confused parents or severely mentally handicapped children; and because the alternatives for the sick and permanently dependent are often so grim. But what feminists are saying is that these sometimes enormous and shattering responsibilities which can result in mental anguish and physical exhaustion, should not have to be shouldered by women alone, virtually unsupported either by cash benefits (which do exist in some cases but are very restricted) or by alternative and *acceptable* social provision, or by men. Men appear to be virtually exempt even from normal housework, let alone from the task of caring for children, the sick and the old. This is only partly due to their advantaged position in the labour market, their capacity in most cases to earn more than their wives; because even when wives too are in full time work, such scanty surveys as exist suggest that men perform astonishingly little of the day to day domestic work.

Perhaps most dramatically of all, feminists have shown that society in relying on women to be the carers, does not care for the carers themselves. Nowhere has this been more painfully and shockingly illustrated than by the growing recognition in the early and mid-1970s of the nature and extent of violence by men towards women in marriage (Pizzey, 1974; Wilson, 1983; Dobash & Dobash, 1979).

Child abuse had been acknowledged since the late sixties — although as has often occurred in the social work and medical fields mothers were made the scapegoats and the problem was seen as simply due to 'inadequate' mothering, a 'failure to bond' and so on. But what enraged many feminist campaigners was that when it came to violence towards women the welfare authorities simply did not take it seriously. To this day there are few legislative sanctions against it (and they are certainly not enforced by the police); rape remains legal within marriage; and such refuges as now exist for battered women are in almost every case there only because women campaigned and struggled for them.

The women's aid movement to help battered women highlighted another assumption about the family that has become the target for feminist attack: that the family is treated in social policy as a single and indivisible unit, when in fact there are conflicting and competing interests *within* families. It is here that contemporary feminists find themselves returning to what was a major preoccupation of earlier feminists — the division of income within the family.

The Beveridge Plan rested on the comfortable assumption that married couples never argue about money, but that the breadwinner's wage is harmoniously and equitably redistributed within the family. Such few studies (for example, Wilson, 1980a) as exist suggest that this is not the case. Therefore in recent years feminists have begun to push for more flexible fiscal and social security policies, both to suit the many actually existing variations in households, and to give all women regardless of marital status the right to an individual income.

Such demands centre round two important feminist goals. The first is the need to separate the economic functions of marriage and marriage type parternships from the nurturant and emotional functions — to end once for all the similarities, which the 19th century feminists saw, between marriage and prostitution (the exchange of sexual and personal services for money or one's keep). The second is a recognition that the family is not adequate, or even suitable, as an institution to have loaded onto it an increasing range of welfare responsibilities as the welfare state itself is cut back.

At the theoretical level, feminist work on welfare has implied a critique of the existing left as well as mainstream approaches. It is interesting that even those male writers who address problems of welfare from a radical or Marxist perspective appear to remain rather blind to the way in which a nurturant role restricted to women has been enshrined within the welfare state. Ian Gough (Gough, 1979) emphasized the economic contradictions of the British welfare state, caught in the pincers of an economy that combined declining productivity with expanding state expenditure; Paul Corrigan (Corrigan, 1977) reiterated the importance of understanding the welfare state as contradictory in a political sense; that is, welfare is not just a conspiracy to buy off political protest, nor implicitly (though he never mentions this) a conspiracy to keep women in their place; on the contrary the working class has consistently fought and campaigned for many welfare reforms and we must therefore understand welfare as at least partly progressive.

But feminists are aware that Ian Gough's analysis cannot account for the form in which welfare comes and its ideological emphasis on the family; Paul Corrigan in seeking to foreground the success of working class struggles in the creation of the welfare state chooses to ignore the divisiveness of aspects of that welfare state in its treatment of women as only and always nurturers and dependants — in other words, in some respects the welfare state has sharpened the sexual division of labour and the public private divide.

The feminist analysis carries theoretical and political implications possibly unwelcome and unfashionable 'on the left' or amongst progressives at the present time. One of the main criticisms levelled at it has been that it is 'left functionalist'; that is that feminists have understood welfare as a system that meets the 'needs' of capitalism and is therefore *functional* to it (hence the term functionalism); this so-called left functionalism is compared unfavourably with the approach that has emphasized class struggle and the contradictory nature of welfare. But, on the one hand, the feminist analysis *has* always emphasized the contradictions, while on the other hand it does entail a recognition that the capitalist state *does* have plans for women (although these plans are often internally inconsistent) and that we cannot rush to the opposite theoretical extreme and refuse to see the state as ideological planner at all.

This feminist analysis therefore lays more emphasis on the repressive element in state provision; most feminists are particularly critical of the authoritarianism of the centralized state and have argued for more local community involvement and for more involvement on the part of consumers; a democratization of provision (London Edinburgh Weekend Return Group, 1981; but see also Davis, 1981). But some have rightly reminded us that the anarcho-libertarian solution of local, grassroots community provision, now taking on a new lease of life in some Labour controlled boroughs as 'decentralization', cannot be a total solution, for as Mary McIntosh has argued (McIntosh, 1981):

> Feminists in this country have never been for very long attracted to purely anti-statist solutions. Such utopian individualism (or even small-scale collectivism) is a possible dream for men who can envisage a world of self-supporting able-bodied people. But women are usually concerned with how the other three-quarters live. They have argued for new forms of interdependence based in the community and not the family, and these necessarily involve the state at one level or another . . . There was a clear recognition . . . that women need state provision. Faced with a choice between a chancy dependence on a man on the one hand and dependence

on the state or exploitation in waged work on the other, feminists opt for the state and the wage.

This perspective is now beginning to come under attack, not simply from the right, but from feminists influenced by the ecology movement and its call for the 'abolition' of work. It is therefore all the more important to assert anew the importance both of paid work and of state welfare to women.

The voice of feminism in relation to social policy is the voice of reason and sanity, not of extremism or selfishness. The feminist message to the policy makers is that diverse and varied forms of household — which do actually exist —require diverse and flexible forms of provision of all kinds. It reminds them that the care of all dependants should be the responsibility of society as a whole, not simply of individual fragile households. It is a call for preventative medicine, for local provision, for flexible working hours and genuinely shared care.

Many social policy makers and politicians have found the feminist critique of social policy hard to swallow. This is because most of them are men whose family lives are not only organized by their wives but are massively supplemented by the private market, in the leisure as well as the welfare sphere.

But the goal of feminism is for a society in which a decent quality of life is not rationed by wealth nor built on the domestic drudgery of women. It is for a society that caters adequately for all and does not penalize and punish those many individuals who find themselves outside a family. The goal of feminist social policy would, in fact, be a genuine welfare society.

References

Abbott, E. and Bompass, K. (1943) *The Woman Citizen and Social Security: A Criticism of the Proposals in the Beveridge Report as they Affect Women*, Women's Freedom League Pamphlet, London.

Banks, O. (1981) *Faces of Feminism*, Martin Robertson, Oxford.

Barrett, and McIntosh, M. (1982) *The Anti-Social Family*, Verso, London.

Boulding, K. (1967) The boundaries of social policy, in *Social Work*, Vol. 12, No. 1.

Bridges, G. and Brunt, R. (1981) *Silver Linings*, Lawrence and Wishart, London.

Corrigan, P. (1977) The welfare state as an arena of class struggle, in *Marxism Today*, March, pp. 87–93.

Davis, P. (1981) Review of the political economy of the welfare state, by Ian Gough, in *Critical Social Policy*, No. 1.

Dobash, R. E. and Dobash, R. (1979) *Violence Against Wives: A Case Against the Patriarchy*, The Free Press, New York.

Donzelot, J. (1979) *The Policing of Families*, Hutchinson, London.

Ehrenreich, B. and English, D. (1979) *For Her Own Good: 150 years of the Experts' Advice to Women*, Pluto, London.

Friedan, B. (1963) *The Feminine Mystique*, Gollancz, London.

Gough, I. (1979) *The Political Economy of the Welfare State*, Macmillan, London.

H.M. Government (1942) *Report on the Social Insurance and Allied Services (The Beveridge Report)* Cmnd 6404 HMSO, London.

H.M. Government (1949) *The Royal Commission on Population,* Cmnd 7695 HMSO, London.

Kuhn, A. and Wolpe, A. (1978) *Feminism and Materialism,* Routledge and Kegan Paul, London.

London Edinburgh Weekend Return Group (1981) *In and Against the State,* Pluto, London.

McIntosh, M. (1978a) The state and the oppression of women, in Kuhn and Wolpe (eds.)

McIntosh, M. (1978b) The welfare state and the needs of the dependent family, in Burman, S. *Fit Work for Women,* Croom Helm, London.

McIntosh, M. (1981) Feminism and social policy in *Critical Social Policy,* No. 1.

Macnicol, J. (1980) *The Movement for Family Allowances 1918–1945,* Heinemann, London.

Manton, J. (1965) *Elizabeth Garrett Anderson,* Methuen, London.

Pizzey, E. (1974) *Scream Quietly or the Neighbours will Hear,* Penguin, Harmondsworth.

Platt, A. (1969) *The Child Savers: The Invention of Delinquency,* University of Chicago Press, Chicago.

Segal, I. (ed.) (1983) *What is to be Done about the Family?* Penguin, Harmondsworth.

Titmuss, R.M. (1963) *Essays on the Welfare State,* Allen and Unwin, London.

Walton, R. (1975) *Women and Social Work,* Routledge and Kegan Paul, London.

Webb, B. (1926) *Our Partnership,* Longman, London.

Wilson, E. (1977) *Women and the Welfare State,* Tavistock, London.

Wilson, E. (1980a) *Only Halfway to Paradise: Women in Postwar Britain 1945–1968,* Tavistock, London.

Wilson, E. (1980b) Marxists, the 'Welfare State' and the crisis: A review of *The Political Economy of the Welfare State* by I. Gough, in *New Left Review,* No. 122.

Wilson, E. (1983) *What is to be Done about Violence towards Women?* Penguin, Harmondsworth.

Zaretsky, E. (1975) *Capitalism the Family and Personal Life,* Pluto Press, London.

The New Right and the Family

Tony Fitzgerald

When the Thatcher government took office in 1979 it did so with a pledge to the electorate to radically alter the course on which Britain had been set by previous post-War British governments. For this Conservative government, unlike its post-War predecessors — whether Labour or Conservative — was not committed to social democratic Keynesian forms of economic and social management. The Thatcher government presented the British electorate with its own neo-liberal/monetarist programme which it claimed would solve Britain's economic and social crisis. For Thatcherism did not perceive the problem of Britain's economic crisis (as so many 'Establishment' commentators and politicians did at that time) as being one in which Keynsianism, though once the correct set of principles with which to manage the economy, had now outlived its usefulness. On the contrary Thatcherism perceived Keynsianism as the *primary cause* of that economic and social crisis.

Thatcherism's overall strategy to resolve the crisis had as its grand design: to dismantle the economic and social edifice which it claims has been erected as a consequence of trends set in motion by the (morally) corrupt Keynesian revolution; and to set about restructuring society according to what is seen as its 'true design' — i.e. the design of neo-liberalism.

This ideal society identified by the neo-liberals is a society whose essence is the free market, a free market which is allowed to operate via its mechanisms of supply and demand without interference from the state or other monopoly interests. Social Democracy's conception of society is one in which the necessity for a strong interventionist state is posited because of the thesis that the free market is inherently unstable and unjust. The strong state is necessary so as to be able to ameliorate the injustices produced by the market and its relations. Neo-liberals reject this charge that the market is unjust and on the contrary claim that the free market is the *only* just system. For the free market is said to be an 'objective knowledge process' which through its mechanisms of supply and demand imparts this scientific knowledge (truth) to individuals who use the market in their roles of buyers and sellers. Counterposed to this is what neo-liberals see as the highly subjective 'plans' of the interventionist state. However well intentioned these plans may be they are nevertheless the product

46

of particular interests of particular policy makers — this political nature of su...
plans means that they are not objective and thus have no truth value. Howeve...
while neo-liberalism regrets the need for an interventionist state, they do see
the need for a minimum state, alongside a strong family to act as a support
mechanism for the free market:

> The Ideal Society rests upon the tripod of a strong family, a voluntary church, and
> a liberal minimum state. The family is the most important leg of this tripod
> (Johnson, 1982).

What becomes clear is that Thatcherism's strategy must include not only the
transformation of the economic field from being that of a 'mixed economy' to
that of a free market order, but the transformation of the socio-political — a
transformation which shifts the key role in this field from the state to the family.
In this article we want to concentrate our analysis on this latter set of
transformations — this shift from an interventionist state to a minimum state:
this shift which gives the determining role to the family. For it is by grasping
these shifts that we can fully contextualize and thus comprehend Thatcherism's
social policy objectives.

We can, for the present, state the objectives of this transformation of the
social in general terms: to redirect the state away from its social democratic task
of guarantor of the health needs of the nation, in order that the state can devote
all its energies to what neo-liberals see as its only relevant function — to act as
guarantor of 'law and order'. In neo-liberal terms, this is to provide for the
defence of the nation from both internal and external enemies; and to provide
the 'general rules of conduct' (i.e. to frame laws) which are necessary to the
functioning of the free market order.

This shift also involves re-constructing the role of the family. For the
strategy to dismantle the welfare function of the state is predicated in the neo-
liberal thesis that those goods and services would be better provided by private
enterprise and more efficiently utilized by a 'family' which could, through
market relations, determine its own welfare needs. Thus the 'family' is no
longer to have the status, as neo-liberals argue it has under social democracy of
being a passive *client;* it is now to enjoy the 'freedoms' of the market and become
the *consumer* of welfare. The state is no longer to be the agent which calculates
the social needs of the nation ('from the cradle to the grave'), this is now the
function of 'the family' — the family must actively take on the role of policing
its members and the community.

> ... the more society can be policed by the family ... and less by the state, the more
> likely it is that such a society will be both orderly and liberal (Johnson, 1982).

However, such 'freedoms' to police are to be constrained. For the neo-liberal
state still has as its function that of laying down the 'general rules of conduct'.
In this sense, as we shall see, the neo-liberal strategy is just as interventionist as
the social democratic strategy; it is the form of that intervention which changes.

The first point to note in the neo-liberal conception of the family (the 'general rules of conduct' the family shall adhere to) is the thesis of the necessary relation between stable family life and the institution of marriage. A report written by a group of conservative lawyers makes this point clearly:

> . . . the family is formed by the institution of marriage which is a union for life and is the vital link which binds together the family (Conservative Political Centre, 1981; 28).

Marriage, then, is the origin of the stable family life; it acts as the 'moral cement' which binds together the members of the family into harmonious accord. Throughout the report is the strong implication that if life-long marriage was the foundation of every household, then problems of delinquency, truancy, family violence, etc. would largely disappear. The social democratic state is criticized for its interventions into family life which, under the guise of what Keith Joseph once termed 'trendy philosophies' (Joseph, 1974) are said to have led to the conditions under which 'problem families' have been generated. The report concludes by suggesting the Thatcher government should develop not a strategy of interventionism so much as a strategy of preservation — that the government should seek to preserve the institution of marriage, and thus halt what is seen as the trend towards deviant family forms, i.e. the growth in single parent families.

This strategy of 'preservation' would constitute a reversal of a trend which has been taking place in Britain since the 1960s under social democratic administrations, for as Brophy and Smart suggest, the law under such governments

> . . . gradually recognized that the family and marriage were no longer the same thing, and the state began to relax the strategy of regulating family members through strict controls over marriage and divorce (Brophy & Smart, 1982; 12).

This change in the attitude of the state was in part a recognition of the changing reality of familial relationships. Illegitimate births rose from being 6% of the total number of live births in 1961 to representing, in 1980, more than 12%. Amongst those who do marry, many do not now perceive marriage as a life-long union: in 1961 there were some 32,000 divorces granted; by 1980 this figure had leapt to 172,000 (all figures from Social Trends, 1982). In 1971 there were some 570,000 single parent families in Britain; by 1980 the figure had grown to 950,000.

Neo-liberalism regards such trends not as expressions of changes in life-style, but as deviant-pathological forms, generated by the 'permissiveness' of social democracy. The single parent family is the object of a particularly vigorous attack, because of its potentially subversive effects on the ideal form of family. This is due to neo-liberalism's belief in a biological essentialism which asserts that sex roles are biologically given and innate. 'Nature' is said to be the origin of the 'difference' between the sexes; a 'difference' which, it is claimed, must be (re-) asserted in society. 'The two sexes are said to be complementary to each other ('opposites attract'); however, this complementary relation is not one based on equality — it is the product of definite power relations:

> Quite frankly, I don't think mothers have the same right to work as fathers do. If the Good Lord had intended us to have equal rights to go out to work, he wouldn't have created men and women. These are biological facts (Patrick Jenkin, 1977).

The complementary relation is predicated on the so-called natural dominance of the male. The male is perceived as being more rational, as possessing more strength of will, and is thus that sex which provides for and protects the female. He is said to complement the *weakness* of the female. The female sex-role is said to revolve around the privilege of gestation; thus women are in the first place definable by the reproductive function. If the female is the biological mother, it follows that she is the natural social mother; thus her 'place of honour' (Jenkin, *ibid.*) is inside the household. Women are said to be less rational and more emotional; their role is to want to be protected by men and to reward men by gratification of the latter both sexually and emotionally.

> You know, it makes me angry if any woman is made to feel guilty because she chooses to concentrate on providing that warmth and welcome for the family instead of having a career (Thatcher, 1980).

There is no question here of the male parent choosing to carry out the function of giving warmth and welcome to others in the family, for the *natural* parent for this task is the woman-wife. Women-wives are said to have a natural comparative advantage in accomplishing the tasks of housework and the 'rearing of children' (Papps, 1980; p. 28), whilst men-husbands are said to have such advantages in market-orientated work outside the household; thus concludes Papps:

> Men will expect to specialize in market work and women will expect to specialize in household work (Papps, 1980; 29).

The possibility of a reversal of such roles is said to be 'uneconomic'. In a discussion of the Sex Discrimination Act and Equal Opportunities Act — Acts which were intended to assist women gain equality of status in the workplace — Papps warns us:

> . . . that such Acts artificially alter the relative prices of both men's and women's time spent in the household relative to that spent in market work. This will cause women to specialize less and men to specialize more in household production. Such a result is inefficient for society as a whole because time is being used inefficiently in an activity in which it is less productive (Papps, 1980; 52).

The notion of the female as sole breadwinner is anathema to this 'economic theory of the family' (Becker, 1973; Papps, 1980). No attempt is made to offer very vigorous proof of the theory, Papps merely tells us in a footnote: 'For

simplicity I will assume that most mothers assume primary responsibility for
child care . . . it accords with the evidence.'

This appeal to the 'evidence' acts as a closure to discussion, for it allows
Papps to presuppose what it is she is supposed to explain. We witness this form
of circular argument when Papps tells us all women have a conscious or
unconscious 'recognition of the importance of household production' which we
are told helps to 'explain choice of jobs by women' (Papps, 1980). Because of
this recognition: 'Women tend to be concentrated in occupations such as
catering, nursing, teaching of small children and so on, all related to work in the
household.' (Papps, 1980; 29). Such an explanation is disingenuous: women do
women's work because they are women! A more rigorous account would seek to
look at the effects of such variables as education (e.g. see Shaw, 1976) and the
social and economic constraints on women which direct them to do certain
types of work (e.g. see Ruberg & Tarling, 1982).

We see, then, an attempt to construct an economic explanation in support of
the biological essentialism implicit in neo-liberalism. It becomes clear as to why
single parent family forms (and communal forms of household) came to be seen
as deviant — for these forms can subvert the thesis of the complementary
heterosexual relation as the basis for the household's division of labour.

Thatcherism is concerned to construct an alliance of a specific nature with
women-wives — an alliance which, if successful, would create for it a powerful
consensus on which to carry out its overall strategy. This alliance is concerned
to construct its ideological strategy 'as if' it were common sense.

Thatcherism utilizes to the full the fact that Mrs Thatcher is a mother. She
has, since assuming office, utilized this fact by giving numerous interviews to
those journals who are said to cater for the 'traditional women's interest' (e.g.
Woman, Woman's Own).

It is a safe assumption that most of the readers of these journals are mothers.
Mrs Thatcher usually begins such interviews with the disclaimer, 'this is not a
political interview', and attempts to talk as 'one mother to another'. Thatcher is
attempting to construct a personal rapport, in which she is a mother with the
same concerns as every mother has. She is also a 'mother' who sees the
housewife/mother role as creative — for running a home:

> . . . is a managerial job. You're making your own decisions all the time. You're
> budgetting. You're deciding what to do . . . You therefore have an outlet for
> energies which many men don't have in their daily work (Thatcher, 1981).

Women-wives have something of a privileged position, then, which allows
them to develop their energies in a creative direction:

> We (women) have a more practical approach and in the end it's the women who
> are left to cope with all the practical problems (Thatcher, 1981).

The potential for identification with 'ordinary' housewives is evident: *in the
end;* who soothes the upset child, who gets the supper? In most cases it is, of

course, the woman-wife. However, this quote also betrays the true nature of Thatcherism's strategy of alliance, for we see a construction of women as the practical sex. Women are invested with the so-called practical skills to deal with practical problems. The problem with such an 'investment' is that an emphasis is placed on intuitive knowledges, and intellectual knowledges are denigrated so that Thatcher can then claim:

> You don't learn from books . . . you learn from other people (Thatcher, 1982).

Women are said to be more emotional and less rational, thus they have a set of knowledge adequate to this 'mentality': knowledges of an intuitive and spontaneous nature. Women are also said to be passive — their status in the complementary relationship is to gratify and to care for 'others': the agenda as to how to gratify is set by those others; women's role is merely one of personal response to others' needs. They require a set of knowledges which do not contest the basis of this agenda *(status quo)*, but which allow them to give a spontaneous personal response in any particular situation: it is the same in politics:

> It is easy enough to march in protests, but democracy consists of a *personal response*. Am I prepared to work harder? Am I prepared to help that person? (Thatcher, 1980).

The point of democratic politics is not to contest its basis or to create new demands. Women's role in politics must be predicated on their role in the household — individualistic and passive. Women have no need to develop new political strategies such as feminist movements or anti-nuclear movements (e.g. Greenham Common, 1982); politics for women is essentially a local response to particular and local problems.

Thatcher herself, on the basis of her choice to be just one mother among many, sets up the illusion of being just such a 'pragmatic mother'. For Thatcher, her job as Prime Minister is an extension of her role as mother. 'Let us remember we are a nation, and a nation is an extended family.' (address to Conservative Party Conference, 1979). Thatcher presents herself as the nation's mother who is presiding over the economic well being. That economy was allowed to fall ill during the post-war consensus due, in large part, to 'trendy philosophies' of social democrats: social democrats who didn't understand that what was needed was a practical approach to the problems of the economy and society. Neo-liberals accuse social democrats of retreating from such problems, of taking a soft line in problematic areas, of 'giving in' when they should have taken a disciplinarian approach:

> The people who give everything to their children because they don't like to exercise family discipline don't get it right. And it's the same in politics. You've got to do the things you believe to be right and explain them. Some of them will hurt. But you just can't retreat (Thatcher, 1981).

The pragmatic mother is concerned with results ('the proof of the pudding is in the eating') and is not to concern herself with methods. Thatcherism is concerned to deny that it is engaged in a politico-ideological war with social democracy, that is rather a practical expression of the common sense and true values of the British people. It is social democracy with its trendy philosophies which is said to have attempted, after the Keynesian revolution to corrupt the British people from their true values and beliefs.

Whilst Thatcherism makes this claim, it is in fact, a strategy for the containment of women in their 'place of honour'. Women are said to be at their happiest in the home, only a few need to escape this role.

> All right there are some women like me who can take on extra responsibility and would be frustrated without it. For us its right to do it, but just because its right for us, it isn't right to impose it on others (Thatcher, 1981).

The majority of women are said to be content to remain in the home: an alternative is said to be an imposition against their freely chosen will to do the job. Only a small elite ('some women') need to go outside the tasks of the household. The ominous point here is that any other work undertaken by this small elite is seen as an extension of the fundamental tasks of motherhood — it is extra responsibility. Thatcher sees women as essentially definable by their reproductive function, a function which necessitates the household as their 'natural' work place. A work place in which the terms of reference are defined by the male head of that household: Thatcher, the nation's mother, whatever her power, sees herself definable in the last instance in terms of her family:

> You agonize within. Your job is to keep up morale and the moment you go out the door or see other people your job is to keep up morale in spite of tragedy. There is no-one else to look to except your own few who are intimately connected with you. You need your family desperately (Thatcher, 1982).

Women can agonize within — within themselves, within the confines of the home; but on the exterior must be the 'brave face' for as morale-booster women must act as the comforters in times of tragedy. The resolution of tragedies lies within the family for there is no-one else to look to. Women's limits are inside the household and not in the public space of the 'social'. The family is perceived to be a 'refuge' against the harsh realities of that public space—women's task is to make this refuge as warm and welcoming as possible. When problems arise in the family those problems should be dealt with inside the household — to enter the public space of the 'trendy philosophies' of social work agencies is an error, for these agencies of the state operate under a fundamental misconception:

> You can never quite know what goes on behind someone else's front door and thus you can't set out to judge . . . (Thatcher, 1982).

For the family occupies a qualitatively distinct space from that of the 'social' space of the state:

The family is an area of private custom as opposed to public law. It is an alternative to the state as a focus of loyalty and thus a humanising force in society. (Johnson, 1982).

The problem child, the alcoholic husband are not suitable subjects for the interventions of the professional social worker, or the strategies of the psychiatrist; the agent with the *natural* skills and faculties is the biological mother:

> We hear a lot today about social work — perhaps the most important social work is motherhood (Jenkin, 1977).

We have seen that Thatcher, quite correctly, acclaims the status of the worth of the housewife/mother, but she does so only to suggest that this is the sole role for women, and that this role is sufficient for the social and psychological development of women. Thus Thatcher constructs an ideal *Woman* (rather than talk of *women*, with differing needs and desires), a heterosexual woman who knows her 'place of honour' is within the household; a woman who does not question, but responds to the needs of others — her children, her husband. We note that scant mention is made of the needs of women themselves — for the Thatcherite woman has no needs (except to serve others) and if she should develop any, then she must 'agonize within'; for this Thatcherite woman has no public 'voice'. She is definable purely in terms of the space of the family. She complements the dominant role of her husband, by offering warmth and welcome to him and her children. Because she is more emotional and caring, the Thatcherite woman is said to be the perfect social worker; this complements the so-called rationality of the male head of the household.

Thatcherism perceives this 'balanced' family as the alternative to the welfare state, in the calculation of welfare needs. The economic role of this ideal family is that of the consumer of welfare goods and services provided by private enterprise in a free market of real goods. This corresponds to the longer term project of Thatcherism: to dismantle the welfare state.

Thatcherism's critique of the welfare state is derived from its more general critique of all forms of interventionist state. The Ideal Society in neo-liberal philosophy is one where there exists a minimal liberal state — Hayek uses an analogy to describe its main function:

> . . . it is somewhat like that of a maintenance squad of a factory, its object being not to produce goods or services to be consumed by the citizens, but rather to see that the mechanism which regulates the production of these goods and services is kept in working order . . . (Hayek, 1973L; 47).

The liberal state should restrict itself to formulating the 'general rules of conduct' (the law) which allow individuals to act freely in the market place. The interventionist state is said to repress the free market, which is the regulatory mechanism to which Hayek refers.

One of the methods by which the market produces knowledge is in the form of its price mechanism. In a free market individuals use prices as signals; signals as to whether to buy or sell or use another part of the market. The free market is progressive because it induces the healthy competition, risk taking, and social movement (trade) on which civilization is said to be based.

Thus firms must be competitive to hold their markets; they must cheapen their products by developing new technologies which cheapen the production process; firms must take risks by opening up new markets where there is a demand. The attraction of neo-liberalism is the construction of the consumer as sovereign and its thesis that market accountability, as distinct from political accountability is the most democratic form of participation. The critique of the welfare state involves the assertion that it is not accountable to the market — instead it monopolises and represses the market in welfare goods and services. This lack of market accountability creates selfishness and lack of efficiency.

In the first place, because many of its goods and services have no (market) price, and hence its clients are not constrained by the prices of the market as signals, infinite demand will be generated, which will seriously strain the efficiency of the Welfare State. The 'logic' of this thesis is derived from the neo-liberal contention that individuals are by nature selfish and always act in self interest, thus they will always look for something for nothing. It is from this thesis that neo-liberals develop their notion of the Welfare State as necessarily generating laziness, scroungers and delinquents. The Welfare State deforms individual character because it represses the risk-taking competitive spirit that is necessary to society — society as the free market order.

Secondly this lack of market accountability is said to generate bigger and bigger bureaucracy. For those who work for the Welfare State have no interest in competitive marketing and thus in the demands of their consumers, instead they, because working in self interest, will 'feather their own nests' being more concerned to safeguard their monopoly, than to produce quality products for their clients.

Both sets of social groups, the clients/consumers and the bureaucrats, are potential scroungers — scroungers who have been allowed to gain 'immoral' earnings from their deity — Master State. Thatcherism argues for a radical change.

> ... it is time to change the approach to what governments can do for people and to what people can do for themselves: time to shake off the self-doubt induced by decades of dependence on the State as master not as servant ... (Thatcher, 1979).

This change involves opening up once again this market which the Welfare State has repressed — to open up the market to allow spaces for individuals to 'exit' from state provision.

> ... the very efficiency of the social services in so far as they must be provided by government would be strengthened by the maintenance of a market in education and medical care, by enabling if not positively helping people from the state services through exits to private services ... (Brittan, 1979).

Thatcherism's strategy is to sell off parts of the Welfare State, so that these exits may exist for individuals, until the whole edifice is dismantled. This is the policy of privatization. In late 1982 the details of two government Think Tank reports were leaked to the media. The first proclaimed the desire of the government to transform council tenants rent payments into mortgage payments, thus automatically making them home buyers. The second report though betrays the real underlying 'logic' of the privatization strategy. It argued that the Government could save £4,000m by dismantling the whole welfare state — this would include replacing the NHS with a private health insurance scheme, and the abolition of all state funding of higher education.

This substitution of 'private' welfare provision for state services has a 'logical' basis in Thatcherism's concept of the economy. In general terms this concept divides capitalist economies into two parts; a private sector based on the market and a public sector. The former is said to be productive and wealth creating, whilst the latter is said to 'live-off' the former's wealth.

The productive sector is said to be made up of two constituents — the household and the firm. However there is no doubt that the former is seen as the most privileged constituent, and that the firm is largely a derivative of the household.

> ... the family must be the centre of our thinking ... a large part of our production and services comes from the *family firms* which are the backbone of economic and community life . . . (they are) . . . the indispensable basis not just of economic vitality but also of political liberties . . . (Joseph, 1975).

Firms which are small and take the family form are second only to the family itself — these firms are the very essence of democracy.

Thatcherism uses the 'family' as a model by which to assess the productiveness or otherwise of other sectors of the economy. We have already noted Thatcher's attempt to be *the* disciplinarian mother of the nation, we can now note her attempt to be *the* prudent housewife for the nation's budget. For this ideal family Thatcher is constructing a relation of identity which not only subscribes to the 'family discipline' but subscribes to values of prudence and virtuousness in matters financial:

> Paying your taxes on time, paying your bills on time, *living within your income*, having some savings, being prudent and conscientious (Thatcher, 1982).

These are Mrs Thatcher's standards, but they are acclaimed to be those of all responsible, self-disciplined people as well. The disciplinarian family is also the financially prudent family who live on income from work done. That is the family *earns* its income.

However the public sector does not receive its income from work done, it receives its income from the creation of government debt, and by the levying of taxes (fiscal policy) from the productive sector. That is the public sector receives its income *before* the production of its goods and services. Mrs

Thatcher has found a (super) scrounger within the nation-family; a scrounger in the shape of the public sector which does not work for its money so much as coerce the other productive sectors of this family into giving it money, it is something of a mugger, a veritable 'enemy within'. It gets something for nothing. Indeed when it gets this money it does not act prudently or with thrift, like a child in a sweetshop it 'spends-spends-spends' on itself for it reproduces itself becoming ever larger as it does so. It sets a bad example to others, by allowing others to rely on it and themselves to develop in its own image — as scroungers. There is only on way to deal with such a delinquent 'child'.

> You've got to teach children to exercise responsibility. Any mother will tell you that . . . (Thatcher, 1982).

The 'responsibility' in question is the discipline of prudence:

> . . . your first priority must be spending on digs, the second must be to save money . . . and only then do you think about spending (Thatcher, 1980).

This articulation of the economic strategy with the family seeks to 'ground' the former so that it appears 'as if' it were bereft of ideology, and merely an extension of the 'obviousness' of common sense. The central agent in the prudent family is the mother/housekeeper who plans her expenditure within the constraints of the income the family receives for work done. The deviant family is that which (like the caricatured Keynesian policy maker) spends beyond these limits of income, or worse still that family which gets its income without having 'earned' it, (i.e. those who receive state benefits).

As the prudent mother of the nation (designated as an extended family) Mrs Thatcher claims that she must do as the 'ordinary' housewife does, she must cut public expenditure in order to balance her budget, for there is no alternative (T.I.N.A.) to this obvious common sense. In her speeches on economic policy Mrs Thatcher frequently constructs this ideal, prudent housekeeper as proof of the validity of her monetarist policies: 'As every housewife knows . . . we need to balance our budget.' 'Any mother will tell you . . . you need to save'.

However Thatcherism's economic strategy is part of a political and ideological attack on social democracy. This can be seen if we examine the specific nature of the 'cuts' the Thatcher government has implemented since taking office in 1979.

These cuts have not been felt by all the agencies within the public sector, as we might expect they should be if Thatcherism was that extension of common sense — balancing one's budget — which it claims to be.

What has in fact occurred is a change in the direction of government spending, in which money is 'saved' on areas of social policy, and these savings appear to be given to those agencies which are concerned with social control. Thus Education, Housing, Transport, and the personal social services have experienced real cuts; whilst Defence and Law and Order have received real increases since 1979 (indeed the item Social Security has increased as well, though this is an unintended consequences of Thatcher's monetarist policies elsewhere, e.g. weeding out the so-called uncompetitive firms with the resulting high unemployment rate).

Thatcher's thesis of 'balancing one's budget' is in fact a veil — a veil which marks the true nature of her strategy. Beneath this veil lies the 'logic' of neo-liberalism's concept of the minimal state. A state which has as its functions, the defence of the nation, both from within and without its borders; and the codification of 'general rule of conduct' to protect the free market order. Thus monies are found for militaristic and police purposes; monies are found for private education. Whilst 'savings' are found in state education as well as the general welfare function of the state.

The necessity for the existence of the disciplinarian/prudent family in Thatcherism's strategy becomes evident: it constitutes an alternative caring/control agent to that of the state — it constitutes a 'saving' of public monies; this family also becomes the 'consumer' necessary for the operation of the free market in welfare goods and services.

References

Becker, G.S. (1973) a theory of marriage, in *Journal of Political Economy*, July/August.

Brittan, S. (1979) *Participation Without Politics*, I.E.A., London.

Brophy, J. and Smart, C. (1981) From disregard to disrepute: the position of women in family law, in *Feminist Review*, No. 9, October.

Conservative Political Centre (1981) *The Future of Marriage*, London.

Donzelot, J. (1980) *The Policing of Families*, Hutchinson, London.

Hayek, F. (1973) *Law, Legislation and Liberty, Vol. 1*, Routledge and Kegan Paul, London.

Jenkin, P. (1977) Speech to Conservative Party Conference.

Johnson, P. (1982) Family Reunion, in *The Observer*, 10 October.

Joseph, K. (1975) My kind of Tory party, in *The Daily Telegraph*, 31 January.

Meuret, D. (1981–82) Political economy and the legitimation of the state, in *Ideology and Consciousness*, No. 9.

Papps, I. (1980) *For Love or Money*, Hobart Paper, No. 86, I.E.A., London.

Ruberg, J. and Tarling, R. (1982) Women in the recession, in *Socialist Economic Review*, Merlin Press, London.

Shaw, J. (1976) Finalising school: some implications of sex segregated education, in *Sexual Divisions and Society: Process and Change*, Barker, D. and Allen S. (eds.), Tavistock, London.

Office of Population and Censuses (1982) *Social Trends*, H.M.S.O., London.

Thatcher, M. (1979) Speech to Conservative Party Conference.

Thatcher, M. (1980) Interview in *Womans Realm*, 6 December.

Thatcher, M. (1981) Interview in *Womans Own*, 17 October.

Thatcher, M. (1982) Interview in *Woman*, 11 September.

A Theory of Poverty and the Role of Social Policy

Peter Townsend

During the last 20 years public and academic interest in the phenomenon of poverty has increased dramatically. In public discussion and academic work the term was rarely mentioned in the years immediately after the Second World War. Partly this was because economic and social management of the rich countries was dominated by neo-Keynesian assumptions about the Welfare State. Full employment, high taxation and State sponsorship of social legislation were believed to have largely eliminated poverty. And partly this was because many of the poorer countries were caught up in the process of de-colonization and little attention was being directed towards their internal living standards. The empires of European nations were quickly disintegrating and former colonies were becoming independent. Exaggerated hopes were placed in the capacity of new nation states to transform established structures and the hungry conditions of their people.

Today all that has changed. Poverty was said to have been 'rediscovered' in the United States and the United Kingdom in the 1960s (Harrington, 1962; Bull, 1970). An official 'war on poverty' was launched in the mid-1960s in the United States, and one European state after another has come to recognize poverty, sometimes slowly and grudgingly, as an important internal social and political problem. (See for national examples, France, 1981; FRG, 1981). Political and academic interest have both, in fact, accelerated. In the late 1970s and early 1980s several reports of both an individual and organisational kind on poverty in Europe were published (Sawyer & Wasserman, 1976; OECD, 1976; CEC, 1977; ECSWTR, 1979; Roberti, 1979; George & Lawson, 1980; Espoir, 1980; Ferge, 1980; Walker, Lawson & Townsend, 1983). At the end of 1981 in particular bulky reports from all the member countries of the European Commission on pilot schemes and studies to combat poverty were published. (See especially the final report, CEC, 1981 and Brown, 1981, who summarized the reports). When piled on a table single copies of all these 'pilot' reports amount in depth to more than four feet. This interest in Europe has been matched in Australia, (see, for example, the Henderson Report, 1975), South Africa (e.g. Maarsdorf & Humphreys, 1975) and Canada (Caskie, 1979;

Senate of Canada, 1970) as well as the United States (Miller & Roby, 1970; Plotnick & Skidmore, 1975).

Interest has also been concentrated on poverty in the so-called 'Third World'. Attempts have been made to measure the extent of poverty in African and Asian Countries (e.g. India, 1978; Malaysia, 1976). The World Bank, perhaps paradoxically, and the Brandt Report (1981) have done much to popularize the enormity of the problem.

But it must not be supposed that this mounting interest in poverty signifies either agreement about the nature and causes of the problem or greater willingness to do something about it. On the contrary, mounting interest may signify growing conflict between opposing political and theoretical views of a problem. In beginning a study of poverty people should be advised not to expect simplicity or agreement. There are self-interested groups who are eager to influence not merely the policies to alleviate poverty but the causal theories seeking to explain poverty and even the very meaning of the term itself.

This must not be misunderstood. The definition of poverty has implications for the numbers measured to be in poverty according to that definition as well as the policies required to combat poverty. There are those who take the view that poverty is virtually non-existent and others who believe it is widespread in rich industrial societies. Then there are those who are inclined to suggest that poverty is inevitable — because of innate individual shortcomings or tenacious sub-cultural traditions or even as part of the structural price of competitive economic progress — and others who believe it is unnecessary and can be eliminated through redistribution. Yet again, there are those who do not accept much connection between poverty and inequality, and who argue that economic development or growth — in which all classes share — can eliminate poverty in both the First and the Third World, whereas others consider that this is shortsighted because it permits ruling interests to go unchallenged and existing inequalities to be maintained, permitting poverty to be reproduced.

In terms of understanding the relationship between poverty and social policy five steps seem to be important. These are:

(i) to briefly identify the principal alternative theoretical approaches to knowledge of the relationship between social policy and social development.

This sets the theoretical scene:

(ii) to explain how perceptions of poverty take root socially so that we can understand differences attached to the meaning of poverty and difficulties in its measurement;

(iii) to explain why certain theoretical approaches to poverty have to be set aside;

(iv) to outline a 'structural' or 'institutional' approach to the explanation of poverty and

(v) to examine the implications of that approach for policy. I will draw heavily on the approach set out in *Poverty in the United Kingdom* (1979) but I will also draw on a large number of further contributions to the subject, including the more analytic reviews of that approach in different countries, which have raised issues which deserve to be accepted and criticisms which deserve to be answered. (Bryson & Eastop, 1980; Bryson, 1981; Cass, 1982; Colasanto, 1981; Desai, 1981, 1983; Donnison, 1979, 1980, 1981; George 1982; Golding, 1980; Gough, 1981; Gubbay, 1981; Henderson, 1980; Klanberg, 1982; Klein, 1980; Lambert, 1981; Leibfried, 1981; Madge, 1981; Marshall, 1981; Miller & Tomaskovic-Devey, 1981; Piachaud, 1981a; Saunders, 1980; Sen, 1982; Shorrocks, 1980; SWRC, Australia, 1980; Social Welfare Policy Secretariat, 1981; Tulloch, 1980; Wedderburn, 1981; Whiteford, 1981).

The Need to Identify Different Theoretical Approaches To Social Conditions and Policy

In considering current controversies about the meaning and extent of and solutions to poverty it is necessary to appreciate the different theoretical traditions and not just political perspectives within which ideas and arguments about poverty have been based. In the 1970s and early 1980s a number of general introductions to social policy theory have been published. (See, for example, Mishra, 1977 and 1981; Gough, 1979; Ginsburg, 1979; Room, 1979; Taylor-Gooby & Dale, 1981; Pinker, 1979; George & Wilding, 1976.) These should be consulted as background to the account given here.

There may be said to be at least three separate approaches to the explanation of the relationship between social policy and social developments, or the rise of the Welfare State. The first may be called *The Liberal-Pluralist* approach, which has ingredients supplied by orthodox economists, some sociologists and some political scientists. Social policy is conceived as subordinate to economic policy, and to be restricted in scope principally to the five public social services, which have been supposed to provide basic benefits and services for the poor but also for the population generally, representing significant social progress, and yet progress which is treated as being dependent on economic growth. Social problems like poverty tend to be seen as temporary problems of economic development, or as inevitable problems of adversities like individual illness or poor inheritance of intelligence and skill. They are not seen as large-scale or endemic problems. Liberal-Pluralist theories are predominantly concerned with the explanation of the development of social services as *residual* institutions in the evolution of the market, or as functionally necessary to the smooth operation of the economy, or as the conditional support for people unable to earn a living or make private provision for their own support. Conflicts of interest are believed to have been resolved by a process of compromise and representation. Just as poverty is often seen as relatively marginal to a market society so the social services are also seen as relatively marginal to the organization of the State.

The sources of this approach are varied, and will not be traced here. In the 19th century classical economic theory concentrated more on the aggregate income share of land, capital and labour than income distribution among persons. Neo-classical as well as monetarist theory in the late 20th century neglects the low income of those outside the market and of dependants, and 'explains' poverty predominantly in terms of personal characteristics rather than structural features of industry or the State. Functionalist theory within sociology and social anthropology has many points of correspondence with such economic theories and also puts stress on personal characteristics, although with more recognition of acquired skills. It shares with economic theories an acceptance of institutionalized inequalities as an inevitable consequence of advanced industrialization. The ruling ideology of the State has undoubtedly influenced these traditions of the social sciences, as I shall argue later.

— The second is the Marxian approach, which has generally concentrated on social policy under capitalism, and has sought to explain the development of social services as an instrument of the ruling class, acting through the machinery of the state. Poverty is seen as endemic to capitalism and the social services as a means of regulating the relationship between poverty and profit. Major themes are the interpretation of the evolution of the social services as means of social control, incorporating labour into the Capitalist State, reproducing labour, and maintaining the non-working poor at cheapest cost. But the approach is sometimes ambivalent, and interprets welfare as also a success of working class struggle. In certain respects this can be regarded as unradical. New legislation may be taken at face value, and the actual implementation in detail of laws and statutory provisions ignored. Again, the Welfare State may be represented as a big advance on previous conditions experienced by the working class. But advocates of this approach are sometimes inclined to overlook the patient accumulation of evidence of contemporary deprivation, that is, the 'relativity' of deprivation to present conditions. Thus, in acknowledging improvements in certain benefits and forms of treatment, relative to the conditions of the past, the question whether they simultaneously represent deterioration or greater inequality, relative to the conditions and resources of the economy of today, must be confronted. With social development new instruments of poverty and inequality may have been fashioned. For example, it would be impossible today to neglect the major distributive effects of fiscal and employer welfare, the institutions by which wider or more comprehensive social policies operate to reinforce inequalities. The class structure has also become more hierarchical, with consequences for the poorest ranks which have also been insufficiently identified. Thus, there are significant differentials among the employed manual classes and the problems of vast numbers of non-employed poor are insufficiently emphasised. Again, the problems of poverty and low income in State socialist societies, while often smaller, are real enough and deserve more attention, not least because even when there is no longer private ownership of the means of production there can be a tyrannical State bureaucracy.

The third may be called the 'radical' social administrative approach. In some respects this could be said to be more radical and more relevant than some Marxist analyses — especially when the strongest elements of the Marxian tradition are accepted into it. It could be said to go beyond Fabian gradualism because the analysis implies the need for dramatic change or transformation of social structure and of corresponding social and economic institutions, though not necessarily implying revolution in the sense of political seizure and abandonment of the democratic process (Examples can be found in the work of Richard Titmuss — on the health service and particularly on the tax system and insurance companies. See also Holman, 1978; Walker, 1981; Sinfield, 1978; and Townsend, 1975). Strands of this approach go far back in the history of the social sciences and of the labour movement — identifying large scale poverty and calling for large-scale redistributive policies. Moreover, this approach cannot be said to be synonymous with the history of social administration in our universities and colleges. Much social administration has been, and is, conformist with the Liberal–Pluralist tradition. Some has been myopically and uncritically preoccupied with the management of structures whose opinions and benevolent administration go unquestioned. But there are nonetheless features of the approach which have extremely radical implications both for social criticism and for social transformation. These include

> (i) welfare as the attempt to meet need (which involves extensive empirical knowledge and therefore communication); (ii) welfare as the assertion of social or collective over individual interests; (iii) welfare as compensation for the social costs or "diswelfares" of economic, technological and social change; (iv) welfare as the pursuit of social equality and (v) welfare as the reorganisation of private relationships.

The defect of this approach is its lack of theoretical coherence — but then this is a problem for the other two approaches as well. Its strength rests mainly in an informed knowledge of the operation of modern legal and social institutions and the morality of social equality.

Perceptions of Poverty

With these warnings it is possible to make more progress in understanding different perceptions of poverty. There are variations of usage within the population of each country and variations between societies. Thus, in Britain, individuals in a sample survey were asked to describe poverty. A small percentage answered in terms of the idea of starvation or malnutrition; a larger percentage spoke about groups like pensioners, disabled people and unemployed or low-paid groups; a third of the sample spoke of 'basic' or 'subsistence' needs, that families needed enough money for food, shelter and clothing; and another small percentage thought of it as a condition relative to the living standards of people among whom they lived. (Townsend, 1979; Ch. 6). For convenience these might be labelled the

(i) starvation, (ii) minority group, (iii) subsistence and (iv) relative approaches to the meaning of poverty.

In the survey there were certain residual meanings and overlappings, which will be ignored for the purposes of this chapter.

Such a preliminary classification of meanings of poverty is very helpful. It shows that any meaning which is preferred has direct implications for any explanation or theory, because our attention is directed to a restricted or preferred range of causal possibilities. The classification also has implications for policy — in two senses. First, meaning is related to number. If a 'starvation' rather than 'relative' approach is applied to the population of the United Kingdom, for example, then the number found to be in poverty will be very small in the former case and much larger in the second. This has implications for policy. Second, meaning is related also to aspect of life. A 'starvation' approach implies an anti-poverty programme limited to ensuring an adequate diet. A 'subsistence' approach implies an anti-poverty programme limited to a minimum level of food, shelter and clothing. Whereas a 'relative' approach to the meaning of poverty implies action to restrain the resources and standards of living of the rich and the more prosperous majority of a society for the benefit of the 'poor'.

But are these different perceptions true also of other societies? They appear not to be quite the same. The meanings held by some sections of the British population appear to be more severe, or less relevant to the actual conditions experienced in present national life than in other, neighbouring countries.

In the late 1970s a survey carried out for the Commission of the European Communities into perceptions of poverty revealed some big differences between the populations of different nation states. Compared with Italy, Germany and France, markedly fewer people in the sample interviewed in Britain recognised the existence of poverty, and more blamed individuals (e.g. laziness, drink, lack of willpower) than the Government for such poverty. (CEC, 1977; pp. 66–72). More people in Britain than in any of the other eight countries believed that the authorities were doing too much for people in poverty (*ibid.*, p.77). Correspondingly, fewer in Britain than elsewhere were agreeable to money being spent to combat poverty (*ibid.*, p. 78). Britain was identified as having the highest proportion of so-called cynics, that is, those who were liable to say 'Poverty — what's that?' and to have 'a set of beliefs whereby the poor are primarily responsible for their social disgrace'. There were 27% in this category whereas the next highest percentage was 17%. These were in the United Kingdom, in the words of the report, 'the hard core of social egoism and conservatism of the most reactionary type' (*ibid.*, p. 83). Two national studies largely confirm this depressing feature among the population. Both studies found minorities who did not perceive any or much poverty. Both demonstrate high representation of people ready to blame individuals for poverty where it exists (Townsend, 1979; Golding & Middleton, 1982). One study also found that four people in every five thought that too many in Britain depend on welfare, and seven out of ten agreed that welfare had made people lazy. 'On the one hand it is widely believed that little or no poverty persists, other than an unavoidable degree of hardship in old age. On the other hand, where poverty is recognised, it is explained in terms of the individual culpability of its victims . . . Blaming the victim is a deeply entrenched philosophy'. (Golding & Middleton 1982; pp. 168, 199–200).

While no one would claim that the evidence of perceptions of poverty in the United Kingdom is conclusive it suggests both that the distribution of perceptions is very different from some other, even capitalist, societies and that the perceptions of (*substantial*) sections of the population are altogether out of tune with reality. How then do we explain how such ideas about the meaning of poverty take root?

So far I have tended to discuss statistical evidence collected about the perception of *individuals* about poverty. The fact that there are differences of perception among a population places the onus upon the social scientist to explain the origins of these differences. After all, he or she must attempt to resolve such differences and find whose approach is to be preferred or why all the approaches have to be rejected in favour of some alternative, more objective, approach.

Variation of individual perception or, alternatively, different stock reactions on the part of individuals belonging to certain social groups or classes, can only be explained in relation to the development of *social* perceptions. The perceptions of individuals are filtered through the perspectives adopted by their families, work groups, neighbourhoods, schools and training courses. This social schooling of perception ranges from the earliest absorption of parental attitudes and teaching, through the influence of the media to the edicts of professional economists, sociologists, architects and others in universities and research centres. This is one interpretation of what sociologists understand by the process of 'socialization'. We have to adopt a healthy, sceptical attitude to opinion formation. It would be over-generous to suppose that the definitions recommended in a school or a university are *necessarily* more authoritative or acceptable than those picked up and developed by working people as a result of their experience of life. It is essential to make this point because it must be made if we are ever to be in the position of comprehensively rejecting, as reject we must, some objectionable social theories, especially some of the more objectionable theories, for example about race and genetic selection, which have in the past and also contemporaneously attracted support from social scientists holding positions of great influence but whose beliefs have little or no validity. (For example, see Philip Green's discussion of the work of Jensen, Herrnstein, Goldber, Friedman, Nozick, Cohen, Bell, Glazer and others, 1981).

There are, of course, perceptions of poverty which are rooted in culture and class. Social attitudes are passed on through generations, and then absorbed and reflected, in turn, by the youngest generation. The harsh attitudes reflected by some ruling groups in the United Kingdom can be traced through the 1834 poor law and the administration of public assistance, and not just the administration of the law and the police. Because millions of working people depend upon these ruling groups for work and status the attitudes of the latter exert disproportionate influence and command disproportionate attention. It is not surprising that they are reflected in widely held public attitudes. What is interesting is that these attitudes are not so much confronted as redirected politically by opposition parties. They are also reinforced in some academic quarters rather than modified. I mean that the source of the values of assumptions on which the conventional social science theories are based is rarely investigated and on the whole academic social scientists are deeply influenced by orthodox opinion. But they, in turn, can often provide a means of adapting orthodox responses to gathering criticism and contrary evidence. While this is not the place for a full discussion, public, political and academic opinion are interconnected, and each set of opinion formers respond to each other and, while maintaining a powerful cohesion, transmit new messages.

The social sciences are greatly influenced by the state and by ruling groups, for example indirectly through laws and regulations governing the operation of universities and professions, and directly by provision of studentships and research grants. Often they offer legitimation for conventional ideas and practice and thereby serve the state, for example, accreditation of status and honorary degrees. More importantly, they provide the means of reproducing the status quo by bringing ruling principles and ideas up to date and infusing political and social administration with renewed authority. While the social sciences can also serve other functions, it is as well to remember the important ways in which they connect with, and reinforce, the authority of the state.

Social scientists' conceptions of 'malnutrition', 'subsistence' the 'national minimum' and 'basic needs' could be said to be examples of this process. At various times such conceptions have been taken over by governments and popularized, conditioning administrators and administered to attach a rather minimal value to human need — or so I believe it is possible to argue.

Government and Scientific Conceptions

There are three alternative 'official' or professionally sponsored conceptions of poverty which are currently discussed. First there is the *subsistence* concept. In 1899 families in Britain were said to be in poverty if their 'total earnings are insufficient to obtain the minimum necessaries for the maintenance of merely physical efficiency'. (Rowntree, 1901; p. 86). At that early date for a family of father and mother and three children the poverty line was operationalized at 17s 8d, that is, 12s 9d for food, 2s 3d for clothing, 1s 10d for fuel and 10d for household sundries. Rent was treated as an unavoidable addition to this sum, and was counted in full. A family was treated as being in poverty if income minus rent fell short of the poverty line.

Today this 'subsistence' concept is upheld and applied in rich and poor countries alike (though without any attempt to suggest that it is comparable in the two contexts). Since the mid-1960s it has provided the rationale for the U.S. administration's measurement of poverty; because the standard was defined in terms of an absolute purchasing value for a particular year poverty in the U.S. *(was believed thereby to have fallen)* to 11.6% by 1974 (U.S. Department of Health Education and Welfare, 1976, Expert Committee on Family Budget Revisions, 1980). In India the Government's Planning Commission has defined a poverty line on the basis of recommended nutritional requirements of 2,400 calories per day per person for rural areas and 2,100 for urban areas. These are lower standards, it should be noted, than those generally adopted in rich countries, like the United States and Britain. The poverty line is then established by taking the 'mid point of the expenditure class in which the calorie needs are satisfied'. (India, 1978, p. 50). On this basis poverty was estimated at 46% in 1977–78 *(ibid.,* p. 50). On the same basis the World Bank estimates that 48% of those in low income countries live in poverty (World Bank, 1981; p. 18).

Second, there is the concept of *basic needs.* Two elements were identified within the idea of 'basic needs', for example by the International Labour Office in the mid-1970s. 'First they include certain minimum requirements of a family for private consumption: adequate food, shelter and clothing, as well as certain household equipment and furniture. Second, they include essential services provided by and for the community at large, such as safe drinking water, sanitation, public transport and health, educational and cultural facilities . . . In no circumstances should it be taken to mean merely the minimum necessary for subsistence; it should be placed within a context of national independence, the dignity of individuals and peoples and their freedom to chart their density without hindrance'. (ILO, 1976; pp. 24–25; See also Ghai *et al.,* 1977).

Different international agencies, and in particular the ILO and World Bank, have illustrated this formulation. Thus, a profile has been given of basic needs in Kenya, showing large proportions of the population lacking facilities for water, medicine and nursing and education as well as lacking a sufficient income to ensure minimum nutrition (Ghai *et al.,* 1979). Planning agencies of poor countries (e.g. India, 1978) have developed the argument. The statistical description that is given is rather fragmented, however, and rarely is any attempt made to represent severity of need or even experience of multiple types of basic need.

Third, there is the concept of *relative deprivation*. 'Individuals, families and groups in the population can be said to be in poverty when they lack the resources to obtain the types of diet, participate in the activities and have the living conditions and amenities which are customary, or are at least widely encouraged or approved, in the societies to which they belong. Their resources are so seriously below those commanded by the average individual or family that they are, in effect, excluded from ordinary living patterns, customs and activities'. (Townsend, 1979, p. 1. See also the European Commission's definition of poverty, CEC, 1981, p. 8, which was agreed in principle although not operationalized).

According to this approach it is the intersection between resources and style of living — or the threshold of income (defined in its widest sense) below which deprivation tends to increase disproportionately to falling income — which is critical. The dual feature of this conceptualization has been frequently misunderstood or misrepresented in commentaries by government agencies and neo-Keynesian as well as monetarist economists. Government agencies seem to have difficulty in accepting that testable criteria of need for income should be provided — perhaps because they realize that that would oblige them to defend publicly the criteria according to which existing social security benefits are paid (a particularly interesting example is a report prepared by the Department of Social Security and the Bureau of Statistics in Australia, Social Welfare Policy Secretariat, 1981). In such commentaries a 'relative deprivation' standard for income is misread as an arbitrary cut off of a proportion of units ranked by income. Other commentators are able to distinguish between the attempt to define relative deprivation and to measure low income and, while recognising the operational problems, see the scientific (and political) importance of establishing better criteria of need and adequacy (see for examples of the controversy in Australia, Whiteford, 1981 and Tulloch, 1980). There is a different kind of argument among economists. Even those who recognise the value of strong public intervention in the 'free' market and who have undertaken significant work on poverty (for example, Sen, 1981; Piachaud, 1981a, b) seem unable to accept the idea of the relativity of need and its social determination. They seem to find difficulty in accepting that expenditure, and other behaviour which reflects human needs may be socially conditioned and determined and not be a simple matter of individual taste (Townsend, 1981b). This has been recognised by some radical economists. To escape 'the neo-classical trap (of assuming the atomistic isolation of the agent and impersonality of market forces) it seems essential to frame the problem of poverty not in the individual optimising framework but as a social relation'. (Desai, 1983, p. 5).

There is *prima facie* evidence that the idea of 'relative deprivation' can be a operationalized for the rich countries of the world (Townsend, 1979) and for poor countries. Thus, the construction of a deprivation index on the basis of the concept which could be applied to a representative sample of the population of Hong Kong also led to the finding of a 'threshold' on the income scale below which deprivation became disproportionately marked (Chow, 1981).

Problems of the Three Alternative Conceptualizations

The main problem about the first alternative is that human needs are interpreted as physical — for food, shelter and clothing — rather than as social, and yet the crucial fact about human beings is that they are social beings rather than physical beings. It is their social relationship and their social roles — as parents, partners, neighbours, friends and citizens — which govern and define their needs. They are also actors and producers and not only consumers. Moreoever, this criticism cannot be regarded as implying mere amendments of the subsistence approach to definition — as some commentators have supposed (see Piachaud, 1981; and the rejoinder, Townsend 1981b). It implies that a different approach in principle has to be adopted.

—The main problem about the second alternative is that it is only a slightly extended version of the first alternative. While there is some recognition of the need for an environmental infra-structure of physical services for local communities it stops short of full recognition of social need and of both international and national determinants of such need.

— The third concept, of 'relative deprivation', meets the objections at least in principle. If membership of society is the governing idea in our approach to the needs of human beings, then deprivation can take many forms, because people may fail to match the health, diet, housing, work conditions, educational opportunities and access to roles and relationships which are commonly experienced or customary. Deprivation cannot be engraved on stones like an historical benchmark. Deprivation is relative to the society of which people find themselves members. They are excluded from commonly accessible material and social conditions, and the effects upon them can be studied and measured. They are living in the society of the 1980s, not the society of the 19th century. By this criterion the conditions of some in Britain in the early 1980s, for example, are as bad, or worse, than the conditions deplored by Dickens more than 100 years ago.

In understanding deprivation, however, its obverse must be understood at the same time. If deprivation is linked inevitably to current conditions then the styles of life and social customs and relationships, as well as goods and services, which are constantly evolving in every society must be identified, observed and explained. A picture of national development and prosperity has to be given. Initiatives are taken to make laws, promulgate codes of practice and desirable patterns of activity, as well as take advantage of new forms of technology and manufacture products on a mass scale. Customs subtly change. New standards of behaviour, like the code of practice at public demonstrations or the wearing of seat-belts, or parental activities on behalf of the education of their children, are gradually being established. It is this positive process which has to be described, related and explained.

Therefore, to discern and measure forms and degrees of deprivation a full account has to be given of the roles which people are expected to play, the obligations which they are expected to fulfil, and the customs, amenities and activities which they are expected to share and enjoy as citizens. By registering and maintaining a concern with these matters it is possible to remain in touch with the changing nature and extent of deprivation and poverty.

Deprivation is not poverty, however, and poverty is not inequality. Prosperous people may experience forms of deprivation and very poor people can sometimes perform heroic feats to minimize or displace deprivation. Thus, there are parents, for example, who maintain household amenities and meet some of the needs of their children by withdrawing from relations with friends, neighbours and workmates. They 'save' on obligations or courtesies expected of them in these relationships. Although income (broadly defined) is correlated with deprivation, the two are not uniform in their relationship.

Poverty is more than 'low-lying' inequality by virtue of its effect on individuals and families. As income diminishes, people tend first to reduce the satisfaction of roles, responsibilities, customs and shared activities and then pull out of them altogether. The relationship between falling income and increasing deprivation does not seem to be proportional. There appears to be a threshold of income for each type of family below which the risk of deprivation multiplies disproportionately to falling income. This threshold is difficult to define, and a lot more work will be required to substantiate it.

Examples can be given. If income falls people will tend to take cheaper holidays, but below a certain income will not go on holiday at all. Unemployed people or pensionsers may go less frequently, and then not at all, to see their friends in a pub. Again, rather than scrimp and save to keep up appearances on behalf of their children attending school, some parents may encourage or condone absenteeism on days when the children are expected to have money for an outing, or clothing for sport.

The regularities of poverty are not easy to describe, for reasons which should be given. Deprivation can take different forms, and its observations and measurement tend to be greatly restricted by administrative authorities. A lot of the indicators which are used are not satisfactory. And because of strong social values in favour of 'privacy' and the opportunity to lead a 'private life' a lot of deprivation is not enquired into and is privately experienced. Again, the distribution of income is poorly documented, and the collection of information about the augmentation of cash income through wealth employer benefits in kind and other resources is almost non-existent.

The Extent of Poverty

In fact, none of the alternative approaches to the meaning of poverty as listed above, are fully worked through and put into operation and used by Governments to measure the extent of poverty. (The British Government's measures of low income invoke the Supplementary Benefit rates currently paid rather than any reformulation of the subsistence, or any other 'standard'.) Substitute 'indicators' are used — rather like the rough estimates made by the CEC, OECD, ILO and World Bank, quoted above. The international poverty line which has been used in studies undertaken for the OECD, ILO and Commission of European Communities has been defined in terms of having less than half or two-thirds average disposable income per head. (OECD, 1976; CEC, 1981; Beckerman, 1979a, b).

The European Commission found that for different years in the 1970s there were the following number in poverty (by the criterion of 50% of net income per adult equivalent unit per year): Ireland 23%; Italy 22%; France 15%; Federal Republic of Germany 6½%; United Kingdom 6%; Netherlands 5%; (CEC, 1981, p. 84). These results must be treated as provisional. There are difficulties in interpreting the different collections of data on income distribution. In particular the findings for those countries with substantial agricultural populations are not amended to take sufficient account of income in kind from the land. And indicators of income inequality rather than poverty were applied.

For Britain official estimates have been published of low income. The latest are for 1979 and depend upon comparing the incomes of a random sample of household and income units and their presumed entitlement to supplementary benefit. The rates payable under the supplementary benefit scheme have a distant relationship to the 'subsistence' standard of benefit recommended by Beveridge in 1941. The scale rates originally introduced after the war nearly matched his recommendations and have since tended, with a number of important qualifications, to have kept in line with average earnings. Just over two millions had incomes lower than these rates; about four millions were actually receiving supplementary benefit and another five millions had incomes only marginally above (from 0 to 40 per cent) these rates. In relation to actual population of 54 millions the corresponding percentages are 4, 8 and 10.

A Theory of Poverty

The development of a theory of poverty is, of course, intimately connected with perceptions and measurement of the phenomenon. Theory must be grounded in history — of the social sciences as well as social and economic structure. The theories which were influential in the early years of the industrial revolution were themselves influenced by the intellectual and social climate of the times, as

I have argued above. The virtues of thrift, subservience to one's social superiors, moral propriety, diligence, sobriety and individual self-reliance were reflected in the theories adopted by the classical economists. It was up to the individual to avoid or escape poverty. Poverty was said to be caused by idleness, by improvidence and insobriety, which were defects which could be overcome by discipline and new attitudes. There were of course inescapable problems of sickness, old age and death of bread-winner, but the causes of these tended also to be ascribed to the individual. The various individual characteristics were believed to represent states of poverty which could only be 'relieved'. The new poor law of 1834 was based on these theories of poverty. The idea of 'less eligibility' was central to the system that was developed, and showed the widespread acceptance of individual causation of poverty. This doctrine underpinned Victorian social policy and was expressed in the following quotation:

> The first and most essential of all conditions is that the situation of the individual relieved should not be made really or apparently so eligible as the situation of the independent labourer of the lowest class.

As one economic historian expressed it, there was a tendency to:

> oversimplify the causes of poverty and to ascribe to weakness of character destitution which was the result of an ill-organized labour market or an ill-drained slum (Rose, 1972; p. 20).

Poverty had to be prevented by national strategies designed to discourage individual malpractice.

The work of Booth and Rowntree helped to shift attention to the 'deserving' poor, and to the problems of illness, unemployment or irregular employment and low wages, but they made little or no attempt to explain these phenomena in their turn. However, their work did contribute to the development of more lenient social policies designed to improve the conditions of the casualties of the economy, without intruding too much into the institutions and processes of that economy.

One theme in the entire history of the development of theories of poverty could therefore be said to be that of 'character deficiency' or personal fault. Empirical studies of the population in general and of the poor in particular throughout the last hundred years (including the work of Bowley, Pemberton Reeves, Llewellyn Smith, Ford, Harriett Wilson and others, as well as Booth and Rowntree) have exposed this as wholly mis-placed or, at the most, as a very small factor in the multiple causation of poverty. But the theme has reappeared and gained new momentum in different societies during different periods of the 20th century. Thus, the theory of the sub-culture of poverty put forward by Oscar Lewis was influential in the United States in the 1960s and was used to concentrate attention on the allegedly insidious influence of parental up-bringing and the local community upon children and young people. This theory gained credence because poor people tended to be concentrated disproportionately in certain, especially urban, areas and because it suggested elements of subversion to the rich and prosperous and appealed to their prejudices while confirming them in their belief in their own rights to their good fortune. A variant of this theory was brought to prominence in the early 1970s in Britain when Sir Keith Joseph, Secretary of State for Health and Social Security, put forward a view about a 'cycle of deprivation'. Deprivation and poverty were assumed to be transmitted from one generation to another. Again, the spotlight was turned upon family mores and conventions rather than other social institutions. The theory implied that the policies which required strengthening were those related to probation, family therapy, social work and education. These theories have been critically assessed elsewhere (Townsend, 1979; Chapter 2; Holman, 1978; Brown & Madge, 1982).

The second theme in the history of theories of poverty has been the analysis of the personal characteristics of the casualties of the economic and social system. Those who advocate a free market argue that if the market is left to operate without interference prosperous conditions can be assured the majority of the population. People must be free to invest and apply their skills. Quite how they acquire the wealth to invest and the skills to apply is not a subject for close scrutiny. Inequality of structure is believed to be the necessary counterpart of a system of incentives for individuals. It is assumed that there have to be jobs of markedly different levels of skill, which have to be filled and related to different levels of earnings in order to attract people of the right ability and qualifications. It is recognised that the functioning of a modern 'free' market can produce difficulties, because of the introduction of technological changes or because of the rise and fall of particular forms of manufacturing industry and service employment. It is on this kind of basis that conventional theory is developed to explain how the economic and social system fits in with the view that the cause of poverty is to be found within the individual.

The latter-day theories of neo-classical economists depend on assumptions that poverty is of small extent; that much of it is temporary or 'frictional'; and that the remainder reflects states of dependency which cannot attract high levels of income support, because that would conflict with the priority in values accorded the productive members of society and the system of minority incentives and inequality underpinning the free market.

In the last 20 years those working within the traditions of neo-Keynesian economic thought and social administration and representatives of pressure groups for various social minorities, have been changing the nature of the analysis. For example, those seeking to explain low pay and the unequal pay of men and women have shifted attention from the individual characteristics of the low paid towards the structure of the labour market and the subtle ramifications of the roles which men and women are expected to play in society generally. Studies of the homeless have called attention to the failings of the local and national housing market as well as the scope and procedures of the housing departments of local authorities. Studies of the non-employed poor have concentrated attention on the arbitrariness of income maintenance and the short-comings of the redistributive mechanisms of society. And, inevitably, the recent reappearance of mass unemployment in many of the richest countries has made the reiteration of individualistic explanations of poverty unpersuasive. It has become increasingly obvious that the institutions of world trade and management of the international economy, as well as the particular policies of the managers of national economies, and of the more influential employers within those national economies, must be elements in explaining the changing as well as variable rates of unemployment, and hence rates of poverty. (In recent theoretical discussion of poverty this is reflected in the work, for example, of Hallam 1975; Leifried, 1979; Frobel *et al.*, 1981; and Gough, 1981.)

An Alternative 'Institutional' Approach

An alternative approach must therefore be global, institutional and class-based. I mean that if we have to explain the variations in poverty between different countries we have to explain not merely the unequal distribution of income in its most comprehensive sense but the continuing development of an inter-related set of national cultures or styles of life. The international context has to be analysed. A full account has also to be given of the national as well as international institutions which (i) produce, disseminate and control resources and (ii) establish the norms of social association and activity. And the two-way relationship between these institutions and different layers or classes of international and national populations has to be spelt out.

The functioning of international institutions is a necessary part of the explanation not just of the poverty of what is called the Third World but of poverty within both rich and poor nation states. I can do no more here than sketch some of the elements. (Fuller exposition will be found in Townsend, 1970; 1979, especially Chapters 2, 9 and 27; 1981a and 1983). First, the interdependence of the world's monetary system must be recognised.

At the end of the Second World War the United States was one of the two dominant world powers. This is symbolized by the establishment of the headquarters of the United Nations in New York. The western powers met at Bretton Woods in New Hampshire in 1944 and set up two instruments for international financial and monetary control; the International Bank for Reconstruction and Development, now known as the World Bank, to provide loans to assist the reconstruction of Europe and Japan, and for the Third World, and the International Monetary Fund to be the regulator of currencies, promoting stable exchange rates and providing liquidity for the free flow of trade. Both of these were established in Washington. The Marshall Plan and what later became known as The Organisation for Economic Co-operation and Development helped to fulfil the plans for the reconstruction of Europe. A parallel organisation, the Council for Mutual Economic Assistance — also known as Comecon — which consisted of the eastern powers, was established at Moscow.

The analysis of the financial arrangements between nation states and the rules by which trade can be continued, has to begin with the description of the structure and control of the net-work of such international organizations. The United Nations and related agencies were developed to deal with different aspects of international poverty — the World Health Organization, the International Labour Organization, the UN Development Programme, the Food and Agriculture Organization, the United Nations Educational, Scientific and Culture Organization and so on. Money talks, and the origins and staffing and financing of these organisations helped to explain not only how the pattern of world trade is supervised and disciplined but how world resources are distributed, and wealth produced at the expense of the poor. In the broadest terms, the various alliances between nation states, in conjunction with their respective military power, underwrite and institutionalize these inequalities in the distribution of resources.

Many of the accounts of Third World poverty give insufficient attention to this international power structure (exceptions are Hoogvelt, 1982; and Hayter, 1981). The first report of the Brandt Committee provides an example. It assumes that nation states are predominantly autonomous. Thus

> . . . the governments and people of the South have the primary responsibility for solving many of their own problems; they will have to continue to generate most of their resources by their own efforts, and to plan and manage their own economies. Only they can ensure that the fruits of development are fairly distributed inside their countries, and that greater justice and equity in the world are matched by the appropriate reforms at home (Brandt Report, 1980; pp. 41–2).

Analytically, this assumption picks up and reinforces the individualistic theories of poverty within nation states. The victim is blamed. The causal responsibility of the rich is neglected.

The Brandt Committee recognize that there is a crisis of confidence in the world and that new measures are required to prevent the gap between rich and poor countries widening. But their recommendations, namely of more aid, a more powerful voice for the poor countries in trade and the fixing of commodity prices and the establishment of new monetary institutions designed to diminish dependence, can be said to be unrealistic when compared with the existing distribution of military and financial resources in the world. In some ways the policies recommended are no more than the reformulation of policies which have been tried in the past and have failed. The analysis might be said to avoid principal issues of the origins of world poverty and to lead to recommendations for change which will not make much difference to the *status quo*. That is not to say that the proposals should not be supported if there is no other analysis or policy which has any prospect of attracting political favour and support. Too often policy-making is the choice of the lesser of different evils.

The second important element in an 'institutional' theory of poverty is the internationalisation of industry. Trans-national corporations have become a major force on the world scene and some of the biggest are establishing a kind of independence of control from any single nation state. Half the hundred wealthiest powers in the world are trans-national corporations and not nation states. Exxon and Standard Oil, for example, have larger budgets than does Switzerland or Saudi Arabia. A third of all trade can now be traced as being between the different subsidiaries or divisions of the trans-national companies rather than between nations. Their power is exercised in the relocation of manufacturing industry in countries of the Third World — like Brazil and South Korea. Labour is cheap and new forms of technology make it possible to restrict the range of skills which have to be taught to, and practised by, partly skilled workers. The manufacture of some products can be divided between countries, so ensuring freedom from national take-overs. Improvement in communications and the development of international professional management makes possible the complex juggling of these huge companies. By switching production from the rich countries to overseas subsidiaries they have weakened the local bargaining power of trade unions.

The emergence of the EEC is not unconnected with the growth in fortune of such companies. The European Community has paved the way for the abandonment of tarrifs, the liberalization of trade, the free movement of capital and the relative decline of special subsidies for poor regions. Thus, the European Commission discouraged member states from pursuing certain internal regional policies and has sought to restrict the size of financial inducements offered (Armstrong, 1978). Regional groupings like the EEC have been taking over certain powers from national governments to control national economies — without the same mechanisms of union and democratic accountability, and with proportionately fewer resources committed to ameliorative social policies.

The influence of international organizations and trans-national corporations upon national economies and upon the distribution of national resouces also requires a larger share in any theory of poverty than it has attracted hitherto. For example, a considerable part of the rise in unemployment in Britain is attributable to the relocation of industrial production overseas and the redirection of financial investment to Europe and elsewhere.

Nationally, it is important in explaining the scale and severity of poverty to examine factors controlling not merely production but the social distribution of employment, and the institutions which govern the allocation of wealth and income. The key factors include the development and application of economic and social policy at the national level; the institutions which govern the inheritance and accumulation of wealth including its scale and distribution; and the institutions which shape and change the wage-system, as well as those which govern the scope and rates of the social security system. This helps to explain the distribution of resources.

A second strand of analysis is required to explain how human needs are socially created, (which resources are required to satisfy). The state enacts laws, produces regulations and encourages conformist behaviour, which defines 'citizenship' and therefore defines the needs of people in their capacity as citizens. The obligations and expectations naturally carry an implication of cost in order that they be fulfilled. Similarly, the employer fixes the terms and conditions of employment, with some overview from the state, so that the obligations and expectations attached to the 'work role' and therefore the needs of workers may be defined. But people do not only play the roles of citizen and worker. The same line of analysis can be pursued with the roles they play in the community, the family, among friends, as consumers, homemakers and so on. The terms and conditions which define peoples' membership of groups, and the customs and conventions which they observe naturally as a consequence, also define their needs. At all levels of human association there are powerful forces seeking to influence the specification of what it means to be a member of society and observe social customs and advantages. The state takes an active interest in levels of education, training and skill. Commercial organizations influence patterns of consumption and the performance of family and neighbourly roles. The professions also have high expectations of their clients and set exacting standards of compliance for those who consult them.

It is in following this line of analysis tht the full implications of existing class structure can be seen. Thus, the rich are not only the favoured recipients of the allocative mechanisms of society. They play a positive function in at least two respects. They reinforce their own financial power by securing their interests in the financial institutions which reproduce the unequal distribution of wealth and income. Secondly, through the initiatives of the market and also the professions and senior administration they influence and to a large extent construct the national style of living which is to prevail. So the elaborate system of classes is maintained not just by means of the institutionalised differentials of the wage system and social security but by the differentiated expression of nationally approved styles of living which class positions denote. People *act* by virtue of class position and not only reflect *status*.

The Implications for Social Policy

Theory invariably has direct implications for policy. At the present time there is growing interest for example, in the causes of unemployment as a principal element in the growing extent of poverty. In Britain the government's emphasis on monetarist values in the management of the economy and therefore its affiliation to a monetarist ideology within the Liberal-Pluralist approach to economic and social development has resulted in a higher rate of unemployment than in some neighbouring countries. This appears to have been accompanied by relative reductions in pay at the lower end of the wage system as well as in the substitute incomes of those not in employment. The government has taken the view that 'real' unemployment, like 'real' poverty, is smaller than even official figures seem to suggest—in accordance with the restricted perceptions discussed earlier. Secondly, belief in the virtues of the free market has weakened dispositions to intervene to maintain employment. The only policies which are acceptable are those which moderate the flow of redundancies or prepare individuals temporarily for subsequent work of an ill-defined kind. A careful watch has been kept on the wages paid to those in the employment programmes and also social security benefits in order to deter claims for higher wages and to increase individual incentives to get back into work, on the mistaken assumption that a lot of unemployment is individually self-imposed.

Alternative theories would of course have different implications for policy. A neo-Keynesian approach would be to take action to reflate the economy to create more jobs, to put more stress on training and less on work experience, and to spend public money to secure better employment for disabled and ethnic minority workers, for example, and finally, to initiate and subsidise new forms of industry (though not to a very substantial extent). A radical social administrative or Marxian approach would envisage more public ownership, and greater state control of employment and not just of the economy. A radical social administrative approach would envisage more experiments in work cooperatives, industrial democracy, and decentralization of planning as well as probably more recognition of the employment rights of women, the elderly and people with disabilities.

The link between theory and policy is more frequently recognized in the discussion of taxation, social security and wages as well as employment. (See for an example applied to Britain, Berthoud *et al.*, 1981; and for examples applied to different European countries ECSWTR, 1979; and Walker, Lawson & Townsend, 1983). The approach outlined above, however, suggests more thoroughgoing policy.

A structural or institutional theory of poverty would imply radical programmes not just of international aid to Third World countries but the re-structuring of the terms and conditions of world trade and the opportunities to develop new forms of manufacturing industry and agricultural production. International action would be required to regulate, and change the pattern of ownership, of trans-national corporations. Nationally, a more positive approach would have to be taken towards social planning, and especially the coordination of economic and social policies. Instead of the redistributive mechanisms of the social services, emphasis would be placed on the allocative mechanisms of the economy — a fairer distribution of wealth, the withdrawal of the right to inherit vast wealth; the introduction of a less unequal wage system, including a maximum as well as a minimum wage; the introduction of a closer correspondence between work and non-work incomes; and enlargement of the rights of citizens to participate in the establishment of the institutions and services of the local community.

This kind of strategy has been outlined elsewhere (Cripps *et al.*, 1981, especially Chs. 13 and 14; Townsend, 1981c), it differs from the history since the war of the welfare state in two important ways: first, it envisages a growing need for collaborative international action to reduce global poverty and inequality; and secondly, it envisages a preventive or creative role for social policy rather than a casualty treatment role.

References

Armstrong, H.W. (1978) Community regional policy: a survey and a critique, in *Regional Studies*, Vol. 12.

Beckerman, E. *et al.* (1979a) *Poverty And The Impact of Income Maintenance Programmes*, (International Labour Office, Geneva.)

Beckerman, W. (1979b) The impact of income maintenance payments on poverty 1975, in *The Economic Journal*, 86.

Berthoud, R., Brown, J.C. and Cooper, S. (1980) *Poverty and the Development of Anti-Poverty Policy: The United Kingdom*, Policy Studies Institute, London.

Brandt, W. (Chairman) (1980) *North–South: A Programme for Survival*, Pan Books, London.

Brown, J. (1981) Policies to combat poverty, in *Annex VII to Chapter IV of the Commissions's Final Report to the Council on the First Programme of Pilot Schemes and Studies to combat Poverty*, Commission of the European Communitities.

Brown, M. and Madge, N. (1982), *Despite the Welfare State*, Heinemann Educational Books, London.

Bryson, L. and Eastop, L. (1980) Poverty, welfare and hegemony, 1973 and 1978, in *The Australian and New Zealand Journal of Sociology*, 16(3).

Bryson, L. (1981), Poverty and poverty research in Australia, in Hiller, P. (ed.) *Class and Inequality in Australia*, Harcourt, Brace Janovich, Sydney.

Bull, D. (ed.) (1971) *Family Poverty*, Duckworth, London

Caskie, D.M. (1979) *Canadian Fact Book on Poverty*, Canadian Council on Social Development, Ottawa.

Cass, B. (1982) *The Social Construction of Poverty: The Outcome of Class and Gender Inequalities*, Social Welfare Research Centre, University of New South Wales.

CEC, (1977) *The Perception of Poverty in Europe*, Commission of the European Communities, Brussels.

Chow, N.W.S. (1981) *Poverty in an Affluent City: A Report on a Survey on Low Income Families in Hong Kong*, Department of Social Work, The Chinese University of Hong Kong.

Clark, S., Hemming, R. and Ulph, D. (1981) On indices for the measurement of poverty, in *The Economic Journal*, 91.

Coates, K. and Silburn, R. (1981, new edition) *Poverty: The Forgotten Englishmen*, Penguin Books, Harmondsworth.

Colasanto, D. (1981), Review of poverty in the United Kingdom, in *Public Welfare*, 39(2).

Commission of the European Communities (1981) *Final Report from the First Programme of Pilot Schemes and Studies to Combat Poverty*, Brussels.

Cripps, F. *et al.* (1981) *Manifesto*, Pan Books, London.

Dennett, J., James, E., Room, G. and Watson, P. (1982) *Europe Against Poverty: The European Poverty Programme 1975–80*, Bedford Square Press, London.

Desai, M. (1981), "Is Poverty a Matter of Taste? An Econometric Comment on the Piachaud-Townsend Debate", London School of Economics.

Desai, M. (1983) *On Defining and Measuring Poverty*, London School of Economics (publication forthcoming).

Donnison, D. (1979) Poverty and Politics: a review of Peter Townsend's 'Poverty in the United Kingdom', in *Poverty*, CPAG, No. 44.

Donnison, D. (1980) The meaning of poverty, in *New Society*, 24 July.

Donnison, D. (1981) *The Politics of Poverty*, Martin Robertson, Oxford.

Drewnowski, J. and Scott, W. (1966) *The Level of Living Index*, United Nations, Research Institute for Social Development, Report No. 4, Geneva, September.

ECSWTR (European Centre for Social Welfare Training and Research) (1979) *Anti-Poverty Measures in European Counties*, Eurosocial Report No. 14, Vienna.

Espoir (1980) *Europe against poverty, evaluation report of the European programme of pilot schemes and studies to combat poverty*, Espoir, Canterbury.

Expert Committee on Family Budget Revisions (1980) *New American Family Budget Standards*, University of Wisconsin-Madison and Columbia University.

Fendler, C. and Orshansky, M. (1979) Improving the poverty definition, in *America Statistical Association*, Social Statistics Section: Proceedings.

Ferge, Z. (1980), *Dynamics of Deprivation: The Social and Individual Reproduction of Poverty. Framework and Guidelines for an International Study*, European Centre for Social Welfare Training and Research, Vienna.

Fieghan, G.C., Lansley, P.S. and Smith, A.D. (1977) *Poverty and Progress in Britain, 1953–1973*, National Institute of Economic and Social Research, London.

Fields, G.S. (1980) *Poverty, Inequality and Development*, Cambridge University Press, Cambridge.

France (1981) *Contre la Précarité et la Pauvreté*, report to the President of an inter-department working party, Paris.

F.R.G. (1981) *Poverty study for the European Commission*, interim report, E.E.C.

Frobel, F., Heinrichs, J. and Kreye, O. (1979) *The New International Division of Labour*, Cambridge University Press, Cambridge.

George, P. (1982) Review article: poverty in the U.K., in *The Sociological Review*.

George, V. and Wilding, P. (1976) *Ideology and Social Welfare*, Routledge and Kegan Paul, London.

George, V. and Lawson, R. (1980) *Poverty and Inequality in Common Market Countries*, Routledge and Kegan Paul, London.

Ghai, D.P. *et al.* (1977) *The basic needs approach to development: some issues regarding concepts and methodology*, ILO, Geneva.

Ghai, D. Godfrey, M. and Lisk, F. (1979) *Planning for Basic Needs in Kenya*, ILO, Geneva.

Ginsburg, N. (1979) *Class, Capital and Social Policy*, Macmillan, London.

Golding, P. (1980) From Charles Booth to Peter Townsend: poverty research in the

U.K., in *Social Policy and Administration*, 14(2).

Golding, P. and Middleton, S. (1982) *Images of Welfare*, Basil Blackwell and Martin Robertson, Oxford.

Gough, I. (1979) *The Political Economy of the Welfare State*, Macmillan, London.

Gough, I. (1981) Poverty in the United Kingdom, in *International Journal of Health Services*, 11(2).

Green, P. (1981) *The Pursuit of Inequality*, Martin Robertson, Oxford.

Gubbay, J. (1981) Capital and the State — Part 1: welfare and non-capital investment, in *Sociology Discussion Paper No 1*, University of East Anglia.

Hallam, R. (1975) The production of poverty, in *Economy and Society*.

Harrington, M. (1962) *The Other America*, Penguin Books, Harmondsworth.

Hayter, T. (1981) *Creation of World Poverty*, Pluto Press, London.

Heinze, R.G., Hinrichs, K., Willy Hohn, H. and Olk, T. (1981) Armut und Arbeitsmarkt: Zum Zusammenhang von Klassenlagen und Verarmungsrisiken im Sozialstaat, in *Zeitschrift fur Soziologie*, 10, 3.

Henderson Report (1975) *Poverty in Australia*, report of the Commission of Inquiry into Poverty, AGPS, Canberra, Australia.

Henderson, R.F. (1980) review article: poverty in Britain and Australia: reflections on poverty in the U.K., in *The Australian Quarterly*, 52(2).

Holman, R. (1978) *Poverty: Explanations of Social Deprivation*, Martin Robertson, Oxford.

Hoogvelt, A.M.M. (1982) *The Third World in Global Development*, Macmillan, London.

ILO (1976) *Employment Growth and Basic Needs: a One-World Problem*, report of the Director General of the ILO, International Labour Office, Geneva.

ILO (1977) *Meeting Basic Needs:* strategies for eradicating mass poverty and unemployment, conclusions of the World Employment Conference 1976, International Labour Office, Geneva.

India (1978) *Five Year Plan 1978–83:* Planning Commission, Government of India, Delhi.

Klanberg, F. (1982) Anmerkungen zur Gestaltung Kollectiver Mindesticherungssysteme, in *Nachrichtendienst des Deutschen Vereins fur offentliche and private Fursorge*.

Klein, R. (1980) Inequality and politics, in *Political Quarterly*, 51(3).

Lambert, T. (1981), La pauvrete en Grande Bretagne, handicaps et inadapations, in *Les Cahiers due CTNERNI*, Paris.

Layard, R. *et al* (1978) *The Causes of Poverty*, Royal Commission on the Distribution of Income and Wealth, Background Paper No. 5, HMSO, London.

Leibfreid, S. (1979) The United States and West German welfare systems: a comparative analysis, in *Cornell International Law Journal*, Vol. 12.

Leibfreid, S. (1981) Zur Sozialpolitik der Verteilungsformen in der sozialhilfe. Einige Anmerkunge zur Regelsatz diskussion, in *Nachrichtendienst des Deutschen Vereins*.

Maasdorp, G. and Humphreys, A.S.V. (eds.) (1975) *From Shanty Town to Township: an economic study of African poverty and rehousing in a South African City*, Juta, Cape Town.

Madge, C. (1980), Poverty in the U.K., in Brown M. and Baldwin, S. (eds.) *Yearbook of Social Policy in Britain*, Routledge and Kegan Paul, London.

Malaysia (1976) *Third Malaysia Plan 1976–80*, Govt. Press, Kuala Lumpur.

Marshall, T.H. (1981) Review Article: poverty or deprivation?, in *Journal of Social Policy*, 10(1).

Marx, K. (1946) *Selected Works*, Vol. I, Lawrence and Wishart, London.

MacGregor, S. (1981) *The Politics of Poverty*, Longmans, London.

Miller, S.M. and Roby, P. (1970) *The Future of Inequality*, Basic Books, London.

Miller, S.M. and Tomaskovic-Devey, D. (1981) review symposium, in *British Journal of Sociology*, XXXII(2).

Mishra, R. (1977 and 2nd edn. 1981) *Society and Social Policy*, Macmillan, London.

OECD (1976) *Public Expenditure on Income Maintenance and Programmes* studies in Resources Allocation No. 3, OECD, Paris.

Payer, C. (1974) *The Debt Trap: The IMF and The Third World*, Pelican, Harmondsworth.

Piachaud, D. (1981a) Peter Townsend and the Holy Grail, in *New Society*, 10 September.

Piachaud, D. (1981b) *Children and Poverty*, Poverty Research Series 9, Child Poverty Action Group, London.

Pillay, P.N. (1973) *A Poverty Datum Line Study Among Africans in Durban*, Occ. paper No. 3, Department of Economics, University of Nepal.

Pinker, R. (1979) *The Idea of Welfare*, Heinemann, London.

Plotnick, R.D. and Skidmore, F. (1975) *Progress Against Poverty: a Review of the 1964-1974 Decade*, Institute for Research on Poverty, University of Wisconsin-Madison, New York Academic Press.

Roberti, P. (1979) counting the poor: a review of the situation existing in six industrialized nations, in DHSS Social Security Research, *The Definition and Measurement of Poverty*, HMSO, London.

Room, G. (1979) *The Sociology of Welfare*, Basil Blackwell and Martin Robertson, Oxford.

Rose, M.E. (1972) *The Relief of Poverty 1834-1914*, Macmillan, London.

Rowntree, B.S. (1901) *Poverty: A Study of Town Life*, Macmillan, London.

Rowntree, B.S. (1918, new ed. 1937) *The Human Needs of Labour*, Longmans, London.

Royal Commission on the Distribution of Income and Wealth (1978) *Lower Incomes*, Report No. 6, Cmnd. 7175, HMSO, London.

Saunders, P. (ed) (1980) *The Poverty Line: Methodology and Measurement*, Social Welfare Research Centre, Report No. 2.

Sawyer, M. and Wasserman, M. (1976) *Income Distribution in OECD Countries*, Paris.

Schlesinger, B. (1966) *Poverty in Canada and the United States*, University of Toronto Press.

Sen, A. (1979) Issues in the measurement of poverty, in *Scandinavian Journal of Economics*.

Sen, A. (1981) *Poverty and Families*, Oxford University Press.

Sen, A. (1982) Poor, relatively speaking, in the 15th Geary Lecture *Oxford Economic Papers*, publication forthcoming.

Senate of Canada (1970) *Proceedings of the Special Senate Committee on Poverty, 24 and 26 February 1970*, Ottowa, 1970.

Sheeham, M. (1974) *The Meaning of Poverty*, The Council for Social Welfare, Dublin.

Shorrocks, A. (1980) Poverty in the United Kingdom, in *The Economic Journal*.

Sinfield, A. (1978) Analyses in the social divison of welfare, in *Journal of Social Policy*, Vol. 7, No. 2.

Social Welfare Policy Secretariat (1981) *Report on Poverty Measurement*, Canberra, Australia.

SWRC (1980) *The Poverty Line: Methodology and Measurement*, Kensington, Social Welfare Research Centre, University of New South Wales.

Taylor-Gooby, P. and Dale, J. (1981) *Social Theory and Social Welfare*, Edward Arnold, London.

Townsend, P. (ed) (1970) *The Concept of Poverty*, Heinemann, London.

Townsend, P. (1975) *Sociology and Social Policy*, Allen Lane and Penguin Books, Harmondsworth.

Townsend, P. (1979) *Poverty in the United Kingdom*, Allen Lane and Penguin Books, Harmondsworth.

Townsend, P. (1981a) *An Alternative Concept of Poverty*, Division for the Study of Development, UNESCO, Paris.

Townsend, P. (1981b) Poverty in the Eighties, in *New Socialist*, Vol. 1, No. 1.

Townsend, P. (1981b) Rejoinder to Piachaud, in *New Society*.

Townsend, P. (1983) Understanding poverty and inequality in Europe, in Walker, R., Lawson, R. and Townsend, P. (eds), *Responses to Poverty in Europe*, Heinemann, London.

Tulloch, P. (1980) The poverty line: problems of theory and application, in Saunders, P. (ed), *The Poverty Line: Methodology and Measurement*, Social Welfare Research Centre, Paper No. 2, University of New South Wales.

US Department of Health, Education and Welfare (1976) *The Measure of Poverty*. A report to Congress as mandated by the Education Amendments of 1974.

UNESCO (1978) *Study in depth on the concept of basic human needs in relation to various ways of life and its possible implications for the action of the organisations*, UNESCO, Paris.

Wachtel, H.M. (1974) Looking at poverty from radical, conservative and liberal perspectives, in Roby, P. (ed), *The Poverty Establishment*, Prentice Hall, Englewood Cliffs, N.J.

Walker, A. (1981) Social policy, social administration and the social construction of welfare, in *Sociology*, Vol. 15, No. 2.

Walker, R., Lawson, R. and Townsend, P. (1983) *Responses to Poverty in Europe*, Heinemann, London.

Wedderburn, D. (1981) Review symposium, in *British Journal of Sociology*, XXXII(2).

Whiteford, P. (1981) The concept of poverty, in *Social Security Journal*, Australian Department of Social Security.

World Bank (1981) *World Development Report*, Oxford University Press, London.

PART II

Social Science and Social Policy

Introduction

The discipline of social administration, as it developed in the United Kingdom, was inextricably concerned with questions of social justice and equity. Drawing on a variety of established subjects it took as its focus the development of state welfare and, as its raison d'etre the expansion of that same welfare.

An explicit Fabianism frequently seemed to inform the discipline, a commitment to gradual improvement based on the presentation of cogent arguments backed by strong evidence. It is a tradition characterized by John Rex as 'the book-keeping of social reform' (Rex, 1978, p. 295). The strength of the tradition, for Rex, lay in its ability to document injustice, its weakness lay in its inadequate political grasp. 'One could only make sense of what they were saying on the Fabian assumption that there was a government which would be moved to act on behalf of the people by the presentation of facts' (Rex, 1978, p. 295).

The tradition was explicit in that Titmuss, the founder of Social Administration at the London School of Economics, was an active member of the Fabian Society whilst others played key roles. Brian Abel-Smith and Peter Townsend, for example, both chaired the Society at different times.

It is easy to be wise in retrospect and it is important to remember that social administration developed in a period when the welfare state was growing, when there was optimism about its potential achievements and the high degree of consensus about the fundamentals of state education, the National Health Service and public housing. There was also at least a rhetorical commitment to the government intervention to secure greater equality, of opportunity, if not condition. It is worth noting that the declining official consensus over state welfare, precipitated perhaps by a realization of the depth of the British economic recession paralleled the outbreak of greater theoretical controversy within the discipline of social administration.

Social administration had never shied away from controversy and indeed, unlike its American relation, social policy, it had largely avoided a narrow fascination with techniques of evaluation and programme implementation. A fascination which, in that country, sometimes threatened to turn social policy into little more than the handmaiden for whoever controlled the public Treasury. What critics argued was that social administration lacked theoretical vigour or even sometimes any theoretically informed concern at all. It had no adequate notion of class or state, no sense of the welfare state as an outcome of intense ideological and political struggle and finally, even, an inadequate grasp of the real extent of the appropriate subject matter. Accepting the conventional definition of social welfare, as those goods provided in the public sector in the traditionally defined social services, it ignored other important distributive and redistributive mechanisms, including the important use of private welfare. In fact while the theoretical sophistication of the discipline has clearly developed, there is perhaps a tendency to overstate the naivety of earlier writers. Certainly there were many, including Townsend and Titmuss, who recognized the importance of wider issues. In the final article in this section Alan Walker argues for a far more comprehensive area for the discipline and in doing so draws on the earlier work of Titmuss on the social division of welfare.

In the new enthusiasm for a theoretically sophisticated, politically aware and comprehensively directed approach it is worth recalling some of the strengths of the old tradition. Amongst these must be the designation of the social services as an important area of academic study, the input into the training of social service workers, the willingness to take insights from older academic disciplines and apply them to the study of welfare, and the careful documentation of need and the monitoring of the impact of social programmes. Muriel Brown provides a useful summary of this background and the growth of new directions which, she argues, have changed but not transformed the field.

The wider political controversies over welfare have sharpened an awareness of the old tradition. Amongst these must be the designation of the social services politicians frequently appeal to principles of freedom or equality in seeking to galvanize support for contemporary measures. In practice such appeals may appear to offer straightforward links between value and policy or even posit clear choices but a closer inspection shows that political convenience is at the expense of logical rigour. Indeed the terms themselves invite a variety of interpretations. Weale, in his contribution, argues against the notion that the welfare state is necessarily antithetical to freedom. Social philosophers may elucidate the debate but, as Weale notes, ultimate answers must depend on the political process.

The growing political controversy not only prompted greater attention to conflicting interpretations of the growth of welfare, and its shape and intent, whilst reminding us of the competing values at stake, it also necessarily cast doubts about the role of research in policy formation. The old book keeping of social reform could hardly make sense in the face of governments whose hostility to the social sciences was a matter of public record.

If, as Daniel Bell apparently thought, ideology was dead, if all that was required was the marriage of the research skills of social scientists to the commitment of government to overcome social problems, then there was no need to question the virtues and role of research, only the sophistication of technique and the thoroughness of application.

Daniel Moynihan, exemplified this ultimate denial of the politics of social reform:

> the anti-poverty programme . . . is far the best incidence of the professionalization of reform yet to appear. In its genesis, its development, and now in its operation, it is a prototype of the social technique of action that will amost certainly become more common in the future. . . . It is also a technique that offers a profound promise of social sanity and stability in time to come (Moynihan, 1965, p. 8).

The potential progeny of this marriage of government and the social sciences were considerable. The abolition of poverty certainly seemed to be at hand:

> The prospect that the more primitive social issues of American politics are at last to be resolved need only mean that we may now turn to issues more demanding of human ingenuity than that of how to put an end to poverty in the richest nation in the world (Moynihan, 1965, p. 16).

This is a far cry from those Conservative politicians of today who condemn social science research precisely because it might call attention to social problems and implicitly or explicitly back demands for government action.

Digby Anderson, a critic of state welfare provision, has raised further argument against government intervention based on the inadequacy both now and in the forseeable future of social science knowledge:

> Those who would further increase the role of the state in social intervention must presumably regard this knowledge as adequate for the task or capable of being made so fairly rapidly. Those who object to the increased intervention of the state in social matters may use, as *one* of their grounds, the suggestion that this knowledge is inadequate to justify the scale of current intervention and likely to remain so (Anderson, 1980).

From a somewhat different perspective Patricia Thomas cautions against expectations that social science research can resolve political controversy or provide straightforward solutions to social problems. Thomas does assert the continuing importance of social science research in illuminating the nature of those problems and challenging assumptions based on inadequate investigation or prejudice. Such research may not solve social problems but nonetheless can play an important role in clarifying the choices open.

Clearly, irrespective of the overt hostility directed at the social sciences by the New Right, the discipline of social administration is continuing to develop. Its persistent attention to the questions of social welfare and equity, is surely one of paramount importance in any democracy.

References

Anderson, D.C. (1980) *The Ignorance of Social Intervention*, Croom Helm, London.
Moynihan, D.P. (1965) The professionalization of reform, in *Public Interest*, No. 1.
Rex, J. (1978) British sociology's wars of religion, in *New Society*, 11 May.

The Development of
Social Administration

Muriel Brown

The academic study of welfare, or, more specifically, of the Welfare State in Britain, forms the subject known as Social Administration. Unfortunately the term is neither self-explanatory nor so familiar that the user can dispense with definition. Social administration is undoubtedly a clumsy term suggesting a subject matter of a rather mundane practicality, akin perhaps to bookkeeping. But it is widely used in the academic world to describe a variety of courses offered within social science faculties leading to degrees or diplomas or forming an essential component of social work training, so it deserves some clarification.

Social administration as an area of study has existed since before the First World War but it has expanded dramatically in the post Second World War period. The academic subject is linked to the growth and development of welfare services themselves, which likewise have existed since the turn of the century but which were expanded and consolidated in the late 1940s. We shall see in considering the development of social administration that the state of the welfare services in terms of their role in society has continued to interact powerfully with the state of the subject.

When social administration was just established as a subject of study at the London School of Economics in 1912 it was designed 'for those who wish to prepare themselves to engage in the many forms of social and charitable effort'.[1] This meant it was designed for intending social workers and the course offered a combination of theoretical study and practical work. The social science certificate course was not a professional social work training — professional courses were established later at LSE and elsewhere — but it was a practical and intellectual preparation for work within the social services. This vocational orientation characterized most social administration courses in the early years of the subject. Field work became an integral part of certificate, degree and diploma courses and indeed remains so at many universities.

People who wanted, ultimately, to work in the expanding statutory or voluntary social services wanted information about them. There was, accordingly, considerable emphasis on learning about the structure and functions of social services although this was never the exclusive concern of social administration. As services changed and expanded, and legislation increased, the need to keep pace with service development intensified. The Charity Organization Society produced 'A handy reference book for almoners, almsgivers and others' to provide information about the public services in 1882. The National Council of Social Service compiled a handbook on the Public Social Services in 1917 and another on the Voluntary Social Services in 1928. These handbooks were widely used by practitioners and students of social administration. Revised versions continue to provide basic information about services even today.[2]

Social administration emerged, therefore, essentially as an institutionally based subject. It was, at first glance, the study of the social services. Such concern for definition as there was tended to concentrate on the identification of social services and the need to distinguish them from public utilities such as transport or street lighting.

'The generally accepted hall-mark of a social service is that of direct concern with the personal well-being of the individual' wrote Penelope Hall in her important and durable textbook *The Social Services of Modern England* (Hall, 1952). Although the major social services such as income maintenance and health or education were always seen as vital areas of study so too were a host of smaller services, voluntary and statutory, for disabled people, for children or for youth — including wayward youth. This followed logically from a definition that stressed individual well-being as the hall-mark of social service and it suited the vocational interests of intending welfare workers and probation officers.

As the scope of service provision, particularly statutory provision, widened out, so too the textbooks for social administration students expanded. The spate of legislation after the Second World War was widely regarded as marking a new era of welfare. Piecemeal social provision was superceded by the Welfare State. Social services existed to tackle all the 'giants on the road to progress' identified by Beveridge (Beveridge, 1942). Social services had not only expanded they had become much more clearly the responsibility of the State, either directly administered by Central Government or indirectly through the increasingly subsidized and centrally directed local government machinery. Income maintenance was, by 1948, the year the Poor Law ceased to have effect, an impressive array of National Insurance schemes, plus Family Allowances, backed by the safety net of National Assistance. The National Health Service was created to provide comprehensive health care to all citizens through a complex tripartite administrative structure. State education was expanded, new local Children's and Welfare departments were set up, local government headed the post-war housing drive and the wartime employment services for the disabled were put on a permanent footing.

In terms of its institutional focus social administration had plenty to do keeping pace with these new developments simply describing the legislation and outlining the new organizations. But the subject, perhaps inevitably, caught some of the general rhetoric of the immediate post-war years. A Welfare State was established and it deserved to be celebrated and social administration turned to history to document the transformation of society. The evolution and development of the social services were described in numerous lectures and books which followed the general historical theme of: 'from Poor Law to Welfare State'. Maurice Bruce's *The Coming of the Welfare State* is a good example of this genre — a highly readable, general narrative tracing the development of social security provision, health services, education and so forth, from the dark days of the nineteenth century through liberal enlightenment and interwar depression into the splendours of the post war reconstruction (Bruce, 1961).

In a more specialized category the marvellously detailed studies by Jean Heywood on the history of child care services (Heywood, 1959) and Kathleen Jones on the development of mental health policy (Jones, 1954; 1960) are classics of their kind.

The emphasis on an historical perspective during the 1950s and early 1960s provided social administration with a vast quarry of information about institutional development but relatively little theory to explain it. The general development of a collective response was strikingly evident but often too simply explained by references to a vaguely defined social conscience or a rational, problem-solving process.

Eclecticism and Empiricism

It is important to understand, however, that while social administration as a subject was undoubtedly service oriented in origin its students were rarely confined to learning simply about the structure, background and development of the social services. One major reason for this was that social administration developed on social science or social work courses as only one subject among several. Most students learnt something of government and public administration, many studied political science and philosophy. Some acquaintance with economics was usually considered necessary for a degree or diploma course in social administration and, particularly by the 1960s, sociology was widely taught. Moreover most of the teachers of social administration itself had come to the subject from other, related fields. So the study of services was never uniform nor confined to organisational detail. Different angles were exposed by economists or political scientists, for example, to counterbalance the more descriptive and historical approaches. This eclecticism was strongly defended by David Donnison who argued that:

> Social Administration should be taught in close and carefully planned conjunction with other subjects. Since it demands — indeed, virtually, consists of — a capacity to relate and apply other disciplines it must be preceded by those disciplines, taught and studied for their own sake (Donnison, 1962).

Donnison argued for a clearer understanding of the social services in their total social, economic and political context. Increasingly social administration was concerned with social needs and problems on the one hand, and with the response to the problems, with social policy, on the other hand. Both areas of concern needed to draw on other disciplines to make sense: neither social problems nor social policies can be studied in a vacuum. As it developed as a subject social administration drew on philosophy, to clarify definitions, statistics and methods of social investigation to establish incidence and trends, sociology to examine role and develop theory, psychology to understand personal impact, economics to consider costs. In looking at social policy it drew on history and political science to expand and explain development, on government to understand the political and administrative processes, on philosophy to elucidate objectives and identify values, on economics to identify constraints.

More importantly even than this eclecticism there was always some evidence of another tradition alongside the vocationally oriented, practical, information-giving aspects of the early social administration courses: the empirical tradition of social investigation. The first department of Social Science and Administration, at LSE, was the outcome of a somewhat uneasy amalgamation between the Charity Organization Society's training programme for social workers and the Ratan Tata Fund's research into the prevention and relief of poverty. Teaching and research were to proceed alongside one another in social administration as in other academic fields and this partnership of interests has generally remained true of the subject, especially as it has developed within universities.

The research tradition, it is probably true to say, has tended to be more concerned with social needs and problems than with the social services themselves. There has been much valuable research into the institutional framework of service provision[3] but the bulk of investigation has been concerned with the underlying problems to which the services respond. Research into such topics as poverty and ill health, child neglect or the housing problem has consistently leavened the service oriented approach.

The teaching of social administration has always concerned itself not only with social investigation but with the relationship between social surveys and social action. The pioneering surveys of Charles Booth and Seebohm Rowntree, at the turn of the century, were considered to have influenced the development of income maintenance, for example. It seemed clear to many enthusiasts that if needs were known and understood then services would be developed to meet them. Information about the homeless, the disabled, the deprived or the deviant was widely regarded as the first step towards the development of an appropriate caring response. So students of social administration were expected to be familiar with the methods and the findings of social investigation. Research reports, official enquiries and social surveys were included on reading lists and students were encouraged to participate in academic research into social needs.[4]

Field work, except where it consisted of research type projects, probably reinforced the service orientation of social administration, because it took place largely within services often, though not necessarily, within the more obvious social work services.[5] But field work also undoubtedly leavened the subject and stimulated interest in a wide range of enquiries, particularly about the effectiveness of social services. Field work tended to remind students that the subject had a fundamentally practical orientation, a basic concern for action in the real world. As Richard Titmuss remarked:

> Social Administration is not alone in having difficulties in its external relationships. Sociology has to bear the cross of being associated both with socialism and social work (Titmuss, 1968).

But for many students of social administration the political aspect of the subject was shouldered with as much enthusiasm as the vocational. More than a hint of a crusading mentality has affected teachers and students alike in their eagerness to hasten the creation of a better world, rather than refine the academic understanding of the existing one.

The Growth of Criticism

Social administration then, developed into an essentially eclectic study of the social services with a marked historical and developmental emphasis and an equally strong concern for empirical social investigation. During the 1950s and 1960s the subject became firmly established in the Universities and Polytechnics and it was widely taught on a variety of extra mural courses. In 1952 Richard Titmuss was appointed to the first chair of Social Administration at the London School of Economics. Chairs were established at other Universities and social administration departments grew in size and in the range of courses they offered. In 1967 the Social Administration Association was founded to bring together teachers of social administration from the various institutions at regular meetings.

This expansion and consolidation of the subject coincided with a period of growth within the welfare state. Although there were arguments about the precise scope and purpose of the statutory social services their existence was basically accepted and both the scale and cost of their activities grew steadily. Criticisms of the failure of the Welfare State were countered by vigorous action to extend the social security system, reorganize the National Health Service and the personal social services, improve the delivery system and find new initiatives for positive discrimination in housing and education. Social administration itself expanded because higher education expanded and social work services grew and proliferated to absorb people from the various courses.

In this expansionist phase the subject of social administration developed rapidly. Alongside the growth in numbers of courses and teachers and students there was a veritable information explosion, an unprecedented upsurge of survey material, textbooks, social facts and social theories. The number of questions asked about the social services increased so fast that the first modest questions, about the origins and purposes and structure and organization of the services, almost got lost. Interest shifted towards a more critical and evaluative approach and simple 'nuts and bolts' descriptions of the purposes and processes of social services were regarded by some teachers with near contempt. A new generation of social administrators looked at the services and asked: how far had they succeeded — and how far had they failed? who had benefitted from them? whose interests did they serve? what influenced their operation and determined their outcomes?

Social administration became a more lively and critical subject though not a more tightly defined one. As more and more penetrating questions were asked about the social services the institutional framework of the subject was increasingly seen as an arbitrary constraint. Even in terms of social problems the service orientation operated to restrain the range of enquiry. As I have argued elsewhere, 'the scope of social action itself in part determines what we mean by social problems' (Brown, 1969) when it comes to social policy the formal social services were clearly seen to be no more than a part of the total response to need. In his immensely thought-provoking lecture on *The Social Division of Welfare: Some Reflections on the Search for Equity*, Richard Titmuss, as early as 1956, suggested that we must consider three systems of social services — 'Social Welfare', the familiar public services that comprise the Welfare State but also 'fiscal welfare', allowances and reliefs from taxation, and 'Occupational welfare', the benefits received by employees through their employment (Titmuss, 1956).

Martin Rein went much further claiming that:

it is not the social services alone but the social purposes and consequences of agricultural, economic, manpower, fiscal, physical development and social welfare policies that form the subject matter of social policy (Rein, 1970).

Arguably, Rein's approach, though logical, would lead to an unmanageable subject. A somewhat more limited but pretty demanding agenda was suggested by Titmuss when he addressed the first meeting of the Social Administration Association. He put forward eight areas for study by students of social administration:

1. The analysis and description of policy formation and its consequences, intended and unintended.
2. The study of structure, function, organization, planning and administrative processes of institutions and agencies, historical and comparative.
3. The study of social needs and of problems of access to, utilisation, and patterns of outcome of services, transactions and transfers.

4. The analysis of the nature, attributes and distribution of social costs and diswelfares.
5. The analysis of distributive and allocative patterns in command-over-resources-through-time, and the particular impact of the social services.
6. The study of the roles and functions of selected representatives, professional workers, administrators and interest groups in the operation of social welfare institutions.
7. The study of the social rights of the citizen as contributor, participant and user of the social services.
8. The study of the role of government (local and central) as an allocator of values and of rights to social property as expressed through social and administrative law and other rule-making channels (Titmuss, 1968).

Titmuss, as Brian Abel-Smith pointed out in an obituary note 'was more responsible than any other individual for the form which the study of social policy and administration has taken in Britain' (Abel-Smith, 1973). He was a charismatic teacher and an inspired writer and he influenced more than one generation of academic social administrators. Titmuss was supremely and elegantly eclectic in his approach but he was perhaps more influential in his insistence on the importance of values in social policy. He did not introduce values in any remote academic sense but in terms of an over-riding interest in the actual impact of social policies on individuals. All his work, his research and teaching and administration, had a distinctly, unashamedly moral character — indeed his whole life appears to have had that quality. Titmuss lent authority and credibility to moral involvement in social administration.

The value commitment of social administration, combined with the durable tradition of historical analysis and vocational concern, effectively prevented social administration from falling into a more abstract 'sociology of welfare' mode of thinking. Sociology also expanded rapidly in the 1960s and, to many of those who were disillusioned with the institutional social service constraints of traditional social administration, it appeared to offer an attractive alternative approach, at once more scientific and more theoretical (Warham, 1973). But although social administration has borrowed much of the methodology and theoretical construction of sociology it has done so in its usual eclectic way, taking only what has suited its distinctive angle on social affairs. And this distinction is above all the essentially moral and practical purpose of the subject which marked its inception years ago and which was indelibly stamped upon it in the years of Titmuss' intellectual dominance.

By the 1970s, therefore, it was clear that social administration was concerned with much more than descriptions of the social services. Questions about the scope and purposes of the traditional social services remained — and given the pace of actual social policy development in social security, health, personal social services and so forth, the answers were not only lengthy ones but they required constant revision year by year. But important questions were also raised about inputs and outputs: the distributional impact of the Welfare State was increasingly regarded as a critical aspect of its operation.

The question: 'Whose welfare state?' was raised back in 1958 and it has continued to trouble social administrators ever since (Abel-Smith, 1958). It was linked to the Social Division of Welfare argument put forward by Titmuss in 1956, as we noted earlier, and elaborated in his Fabian pamphlet *The Irresponsible Society* (Titmuss, 1960) which has also remained an active issue.[6]

Basically, it had been widely claimed that the social services were financed by the rich to help the poor and that, as a result of this redistribution, there had been a dramatic reduction in inequality in post-war Britain. These assumptions were sustained within social administration by the emphasis, in definition and explanation, on the role of social conscience. Social services were considered, in Donnison's happy phrase:

> Like a good deed in a naughty world — a charitable, non-productive burden borne on the back of the 'normal' productive institutions of the economy (Donnison, 1962).

These notions were steadily challenged, particularly by Titmuss and his colleagues, as it became clear from empirical work that the burden of taxation was not as progressive as it first appeared and that the social services, particularly health and education, disproportionately benefitted the middle classes (Abel-Smith, 1958; Douglas, 1958; Titmuss, 1962; Townsend, 1962; Robbins, 1963; Milner Holland, 1965).

Increased concern with the impact of social services and social policies — including the impact of fiscal and occupational aspects of welfare as well as of the primary statutory services — has intensified the traditional interest in values. The objectives of social policy have become a matter of profound interest. This no doubt partly reflects an intensification of argument about policy objectives in the real world of social action.

Early in the 1960s it appeared to some observers that there was broad agreement about social ends and that social means were increasingly practical matters, subject to rational decision making processes. 'There is little difference of opinion as to the services that must be provided, and it is generally agreed that, whoever provides them, the overall responsibility for the welfare of the citizens must remain with the State' Marshall optimistically concluded in *Social Policy* (Marshall, 1965).

By the late 1960s that consensus, if it had ever truly existed, had clearly broken down. Political conflict about welfare accelerated and arguments about values were rehearsed once more by academic social scientists, often in the guise of political pamphleteers. Fierce debate took place about the relative merits of universal or selective provision of social services. Selectivists argued for a residual role for statutory social services. State help should only be available to the minority who could not provide services such as health or education or personal care for themselves. The majority should utilize the marketplace to buy the welfare they needed (Friedman, 1962; Grey & Seldon,

1969). Universalists argued that services should be available for all people, as a right of citizenship, without test of need. Universal provision reflected the institutional model of welfare in which the State naturally extended its collective responsibilities for all its citizens (Townsend, 1968; Titmuss, 1968; Reddin, 1970).

Arguments about the different models of welfare led to a search for a more systematic appraisal of the values inherent in welfare. George and Wilding's useful textbook *Ideology and Welfare* began with the statement that 'it is impossible adequately to understand the views of those who write about social welfare policy without taking account also of their social values and their social and political ideas' (George & Wilding, 1976). To the study of classical philosophers and grand social theorists were added the works of contemporary scholars such as John Rawls. Equity versus equality became a major topic for social administration students struggling to make sense of notions of social justice and apply them to the practical dilemmas of the Welfare State (Rawls, 1979).

The broadening of debate about the ends and means of social policy shifted the focus of concern away from the narrow statutory sector of welfare. Interest in distributional issues and allocative patterns could not be constrained by a narrow service framework. Questions of social justice and the search for equality crossed the boundaries of accepted welfare provision. A whole range of social institutions came increasingly to be examined and seen as relevant to social policy in the light of questions about needs, distribution and welfare purposes. Interest was revived in the family and in kinship networks, in neighbourhoods and social groups, in occupational welfare voluntary organizations, fiscal devices and commercial services in terms of their contribution to welfare alongside the traditional social services.

This exploration of alternative patterns of welfare was undoubtedly related to the growing interest, from the late 1960s, in comparative social administration. It became obvious from the comparative studies that the statutory social service orientation of the subject was a peculiarly British tradition. Comparative studies, as Barbara Rodgers wrote in her pioneering *Comparative Social Administration* 'permit the cross-fertilization of ideas and encourage creative thinking about new solutions to old problems . . . (and) will often lead (the student) to new interpretations and fresh evaluations of social institutions with which he has long been familiar' (Rodgers, 1968).

Put bluntly, comparative studies taught social administrators that there were other ways than the British one of achieving welfare objectives. The study of social administration had been a peculiarly British affair for a long time. The discovery that other societies had welfare states stimulated a more critical outlook but it was itself the outcome of increased concern for evaluation in social policy and increased dissatisfaction with the institutional framework and atheoretical stance of traditional policy studies (Higgins, 1981; Mishra, 1977).

Comparative studies of different service areas in different countries are now quite widely taught on many social administration courses. Even where specialist courses are not available a comparative perspective is generally regarded as a valuable aid to policy analysis. In practical terms this approach has gained impetus from Britain's membership of the European Economic Community. At the practical level European social policy must now be understood and certain dimensions of it must be conformed to — it can no longer be regarded merely as a quaint alternative to the British model. This has stimulated academic interest in what other countries achieve in different areas of social policy.

The comparative approach is one important aspect of the recent development of social administration that has weakened the service orientation of teaching. Another is the growing interest in different client groups. There has always been some client group teaching within social administration but in the past it has tended to be focussed on social work client groups. Thus the disabled and the aged have attracted teaching and research that has cut across service boundaries. But in the main the strong functionalist tradition of social services has asserted its influence on patterns of teaching so that most specialization has been by service area rather than by group.

Interest in minority rights, particularly the rights of disadvantaged ethnic minorities has stimulated much more inter-service analysis, and indeed inter-departmental teaching. Disadvantaged blacks have clear social needs and race relations are a tricky social problem but there is little by way of direct service provision to study. Similarly the growing interest in gender as a determinant of life chances has provoked concern for sex and social policy studies but the position of women cannot possibly be understood in service terms alone. A shift of emphasis towards social groups tends to put the social services rather clearly in context as fairly marginal to the basic distribution of resources and opportunities in our society.

The Search for Theory

Social administration has widened the scope and direction of its enquiries. Stimulated by comparative studies and by social and political changes such as immigration but, most importantly, by scepticism about the outcome of social policies, it has become a vastly more critical subject. It has moved on from descriptive and historical approaches to the social services to adopt an analytical stance concerned to measure patterns of distribution and allocation and outcome. It has queried the values within social services and explored the implicit and explicit objectives of social action. Most fundamentally it has rejected the constraints of the original institutional framework of study and redefined the scope and nature of social policy.

As the subject has developed a growing concern for theory has become apparent. In part this reflects a certain maturity of academic status about the subject: it is no longer so tied to vocationally oriented courses for social workers and personnel managers. In the 1960s and 1970s a growing number of undergraduate and higher degree courses were established which had less and less connection with direct practical or professional outcomes. Unlike sociology which had expanded at roughly the same time, social administration had failed to develop a distinctive theoretical tradition.

Several writers have noted the apparent lack of interest in theory among social administrators (Pinker, 1971; Carrier & Kendall, 1973; Townsend, 1975). According to Warham 'Ignoring from its early days the theories of Marx, Durkheim and Weber, concerned though these were with the nature of social order and of social change and with the problems connected with these phenomena, social administration chose instead to ally itself with the empirical approach to social problems exemplified by Charles Booth, Seebohm Rowntree and the Webbs' (Warham, 1973). This concern for social facts rather than social theories suited the early, vocationally minded students of social administration. Moreover 'while sociology pursued the elusive goal of value-freedom, social administration was unashamedly, and some might say naively, committed to a practical view of social reform as a means of ameliorating bad social conditions'. Thus the political and moral commitment of many social administrators can be regarded as as great a barrier as the empirical tradition to the development of an independent theoretical position.

Warham argues that social administration is likely to increase its dependence on sociological theory and it is certainly true that not only are most students now taught about the theories of Marx, Durkheim and Weber, but more and more books about social administration are being written from different theoretical standpoints (Mishra, 1977; Gough, 1975; Pinker, 1979).

But arguably the essentially eclectic nature of social administration will ensure that no one theoretical position will ever be adopted wholesale. The eclecticism derives from the ultimately practical nature of the subject. It is concerned with actual social needs and real social action and it cannot afford to get too lost in abstract theorising. Considerable refinement of the conceptual tools of social administration has taken place and theory — political and economic as well as social theory — now plays a larger part in education for social administration. But the theory of social administration itself remains tentative — albeit growing.

Social administration is nowadays more clearly focussed on social policy — broadly defined — rather than on social needs or social services. The emphasis on the policy process has developed rapidly in recent years, by use of case studies. The ways in which policies are formulated, implemented and changed have been identified and theories of policy making are now emerging (Donnison & Chapman, 1965; Hall *et al.*, 1975; Banting, 1979).

Donnison and Chapman were primarily concerned to examine the role of the administrative process in social policy. At the simplest level their work demonstrated that policy must not be equated with Acts or statements of intention — for example they pointed out that 'Formally approved changes in policy announced by the governing body may simply recognize and codify a process worked out over several years by people at humbler levels of the providing group'.

➤ In *Change, Choice and Conflict in Social Policy* Hall *et al.* considered why social policies were introduced or modified at the national level and they paid particular attention to the political context of change. They were highly critical of the simplistic accounts of policy developments that had prevailed in social administrations which relied on social conscience explanations for change. Many policy studies, they suggested, offered confused and conflicting accounts of change because they proceeded in a conceptually muddled way and tended to fall back on a consensus view of development in default of a more systematic analysis. They argued for a combination of painstaking case studies and explicit conceptual framework with which to analyse social policy, and put forward some propositions about the nature of policy change.

These studies have helped to encourage a much greater awareness amongst social administration students and teachers of the intricacy of both administrative and policy processes. They have encouraged a new emphasis on policy analysis which has shifted the traditional 'needs and problems' orientation of much research and sharpened the conceptual awareness of many students of the subject.

Conclusions

The academic study of social administration has clearly developed markedly over the years. Has it changed out of all recognition from the mix of learning about poverty and the social services that was first provided for intending social workers?

Clearly the vocational connection remains — social administration is still an important element on professional training courses for social workers. But the range and variety of non-vocational courses of social administration has expanded dramatically and with it the scope and complexity of the subject.

The essential eclecticism of the subject remains. It continues to be taught alongside other social sciences, to recruit people from other academic disciplines and to borrow facts, ideas, methodologies and theories from other studies. The tradition of social investigation is also still an active part of modern social administration. Methods of social research have been refined and developed but the concern for a sound empirical base has remained constant.

Interest in social reform and the moral traditions of commitment to welfare is a major aspect of the subject that has endured. The nature and meaning of 'social reform' has altered over the years, and of course it has always meant different things to different people. But a general sense of social criticism, and an eagerness for reforming social action continue to characterize a wide range of academics who research and teach within the broad ambit of social administration. Diverse views there may be about what is wrong with society and how best to tackle its ills, but detachment is not a common attribute of academic social administrators. Academics in this field have continued to boast a high degree of involvement in political and social action seeking to influence the direction and outcomes of actual policies.

It is apparent that many of the traditions associated with the subject have remained active over the many decades it has developed. But the range of topics studied within the subject and the focus of interest have changed quite markedly.

The statutory and voluntary social services, particularly the 'big five' of the Welfare State, are still an important topic for students of social administration. Many textbooks are written and courses organized around them. But the focus of interest in the social services has altered from a predominantly descriptive and historical one to a predominantly analytical one. There is a major interest in the distributional and allocative impact of social services and a concern to measure performance and evaluate provision. There is reserved interest in the policy making process and the detail of administration.

Most importantly perhaps, there is now a sustained attempt to clarify the values involved in social services and develop more theories about approaches to welfare.

So the traditional social service topic is still part of social administration although its dominance is strongly challenged. The concern for values and the search for theory, together with the growing influence of comparative studies, have led to criticism and even to outright rejection of the institutional framework of study. It is argued that students should be concerned with the whole range of policies and structures that must ultimately affect the well being of individuals and societies and not just those that are apparently developed with explicit welfare aims. It is further argued that starting with the social services fundamentally inhibits the development of an unprejudiced approach both to explanations of social problems and to alternative strategies for welfare.

The trouble with the more radical criticisms, which often, it could be said, derive from equally constraining theoretical positions, is that by abandoning the distinctive focus of social administration they could end up with a hopelessly vague and unmanageable subject area. Social administration emerged and has developed as an essentially eclectic subject but eclecticism must have something to focus on, preferably something more tangible than a sense of moral purpose. The social services are clearly limited in practice and possibly constraining in theoretical terms, but they are an enormously useful starting point. Against the analysis of social services the student can sharpen his perceptions of the complexity of processes and purposes involved in welfare. Some of the structured criticism that is developed on the social services can be applied to other social institutions and more of the ideas of politics and sociology and such like can be borrowed to sharpen it. But the basic concern with welfare and the way it has been perceived and developed in our society through statutory and voluntary action is intrinsic to the subject.

In my opinion, therefore, and it is only one opinion in an increasingly large and intellectually active field of study, the subject of social administration has rightly retained not only its historical, practical, empirical and moral traditions, but also its primary focus on the formal welfare state. This has allowed it to extend and develop in many directions, as I have sought to demonstrate, but not quite out of the recognition of its founders.

It is important to acknowledge that, as the subject has developed as an academic area of study, it is now taught at a variety of levels from the short introductory course of extra mural lectures to specialized masters' degrees. It seems appropriate, therefore, for it to be taught with a diversity of approaches and standards which reflect the different interests, backgrounds and purposes of different students. It would also be appropriate at the more academic levels for social administration to be taught from different theoretical orientations, which can increasingly be recognized, and with different emphasis and interests which can be clearly sought out by intending students.

In practice, I suspect, the subject will retain enough coherence to permit its continued existence not least because of its tradition of involvement with the real world. One major development on most courses of social administration in recent years is the growth of teaching about public expenditure. The relevance of economics to social policy and administration is abundantly, practically relevant from the impact of the cuts in state spending which have affected all the social services. The cuts imposed by the present Government have been accompanied by attacks on the role of the social services which amount to blatant opposition to traditional welfare values. Simplistic 'limits to welfare' arguments have blamed the welfare state for economic decline. This assumption has been powerfully challenged but the fundamental inter-dependence of social policy with the economy has been widely acknowledged (Glennerster, 1980). Social administration has rallied to the defence of the traditional welfare state, despite its shortcomings (Brown & Madge, 1982). This is not just because the social services are under threat but rather because the values of social justice and citizenship themselves are being challenged. State welfare may only very imperfectly embody these values but at least it formally acknowledges them. The present defence of social services within social administration reflects the most desirable element of its long tradition — the basic commitment to welfare.

Notes

1. See *Changing Course: a Follow-Up Study of Students Taking the Certificate and Diploma in Social Administration at the London School of Economics, 1949-1973* by Kit Russell, Sheila Benson, Christine Farrell, Howard

Glennerster, David Piachaud and Garth Plowman (London School of Economics, 1981) for details of the early years of the Department of Social Science and Administration.

2. The Charity Organization Society's Guide, originally the Introduction to the first edition of the *Charities Register and Digest,* is now the Family Welfare Association's *Guide to the Social Services.* The latest edition in 1982 is the 100th edition of this handbook. The National Council for Voluntary Organisations, still publishes *Voluntary Organisations: A NCVO Directory,* latest edition 1982–3.

3. For example, the studies on Health Service administration carried out by the Nuffield Provincial Hospitals Trust or the work of the Brunel Institute of Organization and Social Studies.

4. See Kathleen Jones, *Opening the Door: a Study of New Policies for the Mentally Handicapped* (Routledge and Kegan Paul, 1975) for an example of published staff/student team work on a research project.

5. See the handbook *Field Work in Social Administration Courses* edited by Eric Sainsbury (National Council of Social Service, 1966) for details.

6. See, for example, *The Strategy of Equality,* Julian le Grand (Allen and Unwin, 1982) for a recent discussion.

References

Abel-Smith, B. (1958) Whose welfare state?, in N. Mackenzie (ed.), *Conviction,* MacGibbon and Kee, London.

Abel-Smith, B. (1973) Richard Morris Titmuss: Obituary, in *Journal of Social Policy,* 2 March.

Abel-Smith, B. & Townsend, P. (1965) *The Poor and the Poorest,* Bell, London.

Banting, K. (1979) *Poverty, Politics and Policy,* Macmillan, London.

Beveridge, W. (1942) *Social Insurance and Allied Services,* Cmnd. 6404, HMSO, London.

Brown, M. (1969) *Introduction to Social Administration in Britain,* Hutchinson, London.

Brown, M. & Madge, N. (1982) *Despite the Welfare State,* Heinemann, London.

Bruce, M. (1961) *The Coming of the Welfare State,* Batsford, London.

Carrier, J & Kendall, I. (1977) The development of welfare states: the production of plausible accounts, in *Journal of Social Policy,* 6 March.

Donnison, D.V. (1962) *The Development of Social Administration,* LSE, London.

Donnison, D.V. & Chapman, V. (1965) *Social Policy and Administration,* Allen and Unwin, London.

Douglas, J.W.B. (1965) *The Home and The School,* MacGibbon and Kee, London.

Friedmann, M. (1962) *Capitalism and Freedom,* University of Chicago Press, Chicago.

George, V. & Wilding, P (1976) *Ideology and Welfare,* Routledge and Kegan Paul, London.

Glennerster, H. (1980) Public spending and the social services: the end of an era?, in M. Brown and S. Baldwin (eds.), *Year Book of Social Policy in Britain 1979,* Routledge and Kegan Paul, London.

Grey, H. & Seldon, A. (1969) *Universal and Selective Social Benefits*, Institute of Economic Affairs, London.

Gough, I. (1979) *The Political Economy of the Welfare State*, Macmillan, London.

Hall, P. (1952) *The Social Services of Modern England*, Routledge and Kegan Paul, London.

Hall, P., Land, H., Parker, R. & Webb, A. (1975) *Change, Choice and Conflict in Social Policy* Heinemann, London.

Heywood, J. (1959) *Children in Care*, Routledge and Kegan Paul, London.

Higgins, J. (1981) *States of Welfare*, Basil Blackwell and Martin Robertson, Oxford.

Jones, K. (1954) *Lunacy, Law and Conscience*, Routledge and Kegan Paul, London.

Jones, K. (1960) *Mental Health and Social Policy*, Routledge and Kegan Paul, London.

Jones, K. *et al.* (1975) *Opening the Door*, Routledge and Kegan Paul, London.

Marshall, T. H. (1965) *Social Policy*, Hutchinson, London.

Milner Holland (1965) *Report of Committee on Housing in Greater London*, Cmnd. 2605, HMSO, London.

Mishra, R. (1981) *Society and Social Policy*, Macmillan, London.

Pinker, R. (1971) *Social Theory and Social Policy*, Heinemann, London.

Pinker, R. (1979) *The Idea of Welfare*, Heinemann, London.

Rawls, J. (1971) *A Theory of Justice*, Oxford University Press, London.

Reddin, M. (1970) *Universality and selectivity*, in W. Robson and B. Crick (eds.), *The Future of the Social Services*, Penguin, Harmondsworth.

Rein, M. (1970) *Social Policy: Issues of Choice and Change*, Random House, London.

Robbins, (1963) *Report of the Committee on Higher Education* Cmnd. 2154, HMSO.

Rodgers, B.N. *et al.* (1968) *Comparative Social Administration*, Allen and Unwin, London.

Townsend, P. (ed.) (1968) *Social Services for All?* Fabian Society, London.

Townsend, P. (ed.) (1975) *Sociology and Social Policy*, Allen Lane, London.

Titmuss, R.M. (1962) *Income Distribution and Social Change*, Allen and Unwin, London.

Titmuss, R.M. (1960) *The Irresponsible Society*, Fabian Society, London.

Titmuss, R.M. (1956) *Essays on the Welfare State*, Allen and Unwin, London.

Titmuss, R.M. (1958) *Commitment to Welfare*, Allen and Unwin, London.

Warham, J. (1973) Social administration and sociology, in *Journal of Social Policy*, Vol. 3.

Issues of Value and Principle in Social Policy

Albert Weale

Introduction

Consider the following examples. A local authority decides to experiment with educational vouchers. A hospital is closed in London in order to provide more resources for previously underfinanced areas like Sheffield. A researcher proposes that the scale rate of Supplementary Benefit be increased because at present the amounts allowed to claimants do not cover items of essential expenditure for the typical poor family. A government committee of inquiry suggests that the management of schools can be made more democratic by involving more business, trade union and parent representatives. Or a policy evolves of securing access to jobs for previously disadvantaged groups by enforcing the practice of quota hiring on large employers.

Each one of these examples will typically occasion political argument about the rights and wrongs of the proposal that it contains. Some of the people involved in the argument will be partisan. Their jobs or their local service will be at risk, or they will have to pay higher taxes towards financing the cost of the proposals. But not everyone who is concerned, and therefore involved in the argument, will be partisan in this sense. The effects of the policy may not touch some people, or, when they do, they may be broadly neutral in financial terms. Even those who are partisan will need to frame their arguments in terms that are generally appealing, if they are to get a public hearing. The partisan will not speak solely of their own interests, but they will use a political vocabulary that draws its stock from the prevalent political culture. They will speak of disappointed expectations, or of infringements of freedom, or of miscalculations of judgement. Like those who are more detached, the partisan will have to base their arguments on values and principles if their voice is to have more than a cynical hearing.

When we are concerned with issues of value and principle in social policy, we are concerned with understanding the logic of political arguments about just these sorts of policy decisions. We are especially concerned with understanding one particular aspect of this logic, involving not the prediction of expected consequences of policy decisions but an evaluation of the state of affairs at which the policy is aiming. An example will make this distinction clearer. Le

Grand (1982) has argued that many policies in the welfare state are ineffective in reducing material inequality, especially as measured by class access to and use of certain services. The medical care system, the educational system and the system of housing subsidies appear to do little to reduce the difference in the standard of living enjoyed by the professional classes on the one hand and unskilled manual workers on the other. In some cases, as with the public subsidy to higher education, social policy may actually have the effect of increasing these inequalities. Now one can argue a great deal about the validity of Le Grand's analysis — he does not include in his analysis for example the effects of the social security system, which Stephenson (1980) among others shows to be the most redistributive aspect of the welfare state. One can also argue a great deal about the likely effects of policies aimed at reducing these inequalities. Yet, amid these arguments, someone, sooner or later, will question whether the sole purpose of social policy is to reduce material inequalities as measured in class terms, and will propose alternative goals, such as the redistribution of resources from the well to the sick, or ensuring the professional competence of those working in the human services, or the fostering of home ownership. As soon as these sorts of questions are raised we are concerned about the value of equality as a goal of policy compared to other values that social policy might promote. At this level we are concerned not simply with determining the consequences of a particular set of policies but with the use of political principles in appraising the value of those consequences.

A political principle in these contexts is a general statement of the basis on which government policy ought to be made. 'Governments should promote a high rate of economic growth', 'Governments should not infringe the privacy of individuals' or 'Governments should promote home ownership' are principles in this sense. These principles do not specify how governments are to achieve what the principle demands; they specify instead the goals towards which government policy should aim, or the constraints to which government policy should be subject. A person may value such a principle either as an end in itself, in which case it has intrinsic value for that person, or because its implementation will contribute towards some other end which that person values. In this latter case the principle has instrumental value for that person. A person's 'values', in the colloquial sense, comprise those principles which have intrinsic value for that person.

To be concerned with issues of political principle in this sense is to be concerned with issues of political choice. Many of the relevant choices will occur at the margin of existing programmes. As Klein (1974, 1975), Wildavsky (1964), Glennester (1975) and others have pointed out, the vast bulk of public expenditure is committed from one year to the next and to that extent it is out of political control. Since most social policy depends in one way or another upon public expenditure, this means that the scope for changes, and hence for changes in the political principles being pursued, is limited at any one time.

However, experience shows that in the medium term little can be taken for granted in the world of social policy. To choose some examples more or less at random: in the last sixteen years of British social policy there have been two far-reaching changes in the Supplementary Benefits system, three sets of pensions' proposals, the introduction of Family Income Supplement, the creation of mass comprehensive education, and a serious investigation into the financial basis of the National Health Service looking at its possible replacement by compulsory insurance. Political argument about social policy cannot be confined simply to problems concerned with marginal adjustments to existing policies. It will also concern the existence and nature of these policies and the institutions within which they are pursued. Indeed, at their most basic level, it will concern the justification and appraisal of the welfare state itself.

In the remainder of this chapter we shall look at the ways in which two political values, equality and freedom, enter into discussions about social policy. Our task will be to see whether a connection can be established between these values and the functioning of social policy programmes within the welfare state.

Equality and Social Policy

Let us begin our investigation by looking at the principle of equality. There are three reasons for beginning with this principle. Firstly, the principle of equality is central to an understanding of contemporary political debate. Indeed Brittan (1968, p. 11) has seen the principle of equality as being the sole value which divides left and right, and it is an observation at least as old as Aristotle (1962 edn., p.192) to note that division over the principle of equality lies at the root of conflict in politics. Secondly, the welfare state may be characterized as a system of redistribution. Although it does little to redistribute income and life-chances between social classes, it does redistribute resources in other ways, for example from small to large families within income classes. Within the welfare state there is both vertical and horizontal redistribution (Culyer, 1980, pp.64–69). In order to understand the extent to which such redistribution is justified, and which form should be given priority, we need to understand the principle of equality, namely the principle that Tobin (1970) has termed 'specific egalitarianism', the belief that certain specific scarce commodities should be distributed less unequally than the ability to pay for them. The commodities Tobin had in mind were such goods as health care, education and access to legal services. These commodities are available to the general public at zero or subsidised prices in all economically developed states, and in many underdeveloped ones as well. The existence of such widespread practices and policies calls for some discussion and evaluation. We need to appreciate not the general political arguments about equality, but the arguments about the particular form that egalitarianism takes in the welfare state.

To appreciate these arguments we should look first at the meaning of the concept of equality itself. In order to understand any statement of equality, it is useful to think of it as being broken down into three components (cf. Rae, 1981). These three components will specify:

(1) the subjects among whom the equality is to be promoted;
(2) the goods or benefits that are to be distributed;
(3) the degree of equality which is aimed at.

For example, under (1) the subjects may be individuals, families, households, social classes or other sorts of groups. Under (2) the benefits can include income, wealth, educational attainments, health status, skills, opportunities or rights. Under (3) the degree of equality aimed at can be either complete or a reduction in some existing inequality. The reason for making these distinctions is to stress the point that there can be no simple commitment to equality as such. An equal distribution in one of these respects will mean an unequal distribution in another. For example, if the incomes of all individuals are completely equalized, then household incomes will be unequal because households vary in size so that those with more members will have larger incomes than those with fewer members. Hence we cannot talk about more equality or less without qualification. We must instead talk about defined types of equality in relation to particular goods and particular sets of persons.

What sort of equalities can be promoted by the instruments of social policy? In summary terms we can say that the welfare state can promote greater equality in household access to a specific range of goods and cash benefits than would be the case with no public provision but with the prevailing distribution of original income. Note how restricted the relevant equalities are. In social policy we are not talking about redistribution of private wealth, nor about altering the pattern of rewards in labour markets. Instead we are talking about the household consumption of those specific commodities to which Tobin drew attention, including the receipt of benefits consequent upon unemployment, sickness or old age.

In specifying the types of equality that are characteristic of the welfare state, we are implicitly posing problems of value and justification in social policy. From one point of view less is involved in seeking to justify specific egalitarianism than is involved in justifying equality in more global terms. Less claim is made upon available resources by specific egalitarianism of the sort to which Tobin draws attention than would be involved, say, in a general redistribution of income. From another point of view, however, it might be harder to justify specific egalitarianism because we have to explain why there should be an equalisation in respect of just those services and benefits and not other commodities. As a way of considering these problems of justification, let us look at some arguments that have been advanced in favour of specific egalitarianism.

1. The argument from common needs

Consider a benefit like income support in old age or a service like health care. It can be argued that these are common needs which all persons have. No one can survive in a modern economy without some form of income, and those who are ill will require medical treatment if they are going to resume normal physical and social functioning. Moreover, these needs are common in the sense that they are shared by all persons in our society. Each of us is vulnerable to the poverty that comes with lack of income, or to the malfunctioning that is consequent upon illness. So in a community in which needs are to be satisfied, the meeting of common needs, it would seem, is best done by supplying certain common services.

Although possessing some appeal, this argument will not establish the desired conclusion. For a number of reasons we cannot infer from the existence of common needs the ideal of state provided services available to all on equal terms. Firstly, there are some forms of service currently provided under social policy programmes where it cannot be said that fundamental human needs are at issue, for example cosmetic dental surgery. So in these cases the common needs argument would fail to justify the particular form of provision that is available in the welfare state. Secondly, the public authorities can discharge such obligations as they have for meeting common human needs without creating a service or a benefit generally available to all. Having enough to eat and drink is presumably a common human need, and yet the political authorities for the most part can ensure adequate provision in these matters by regulating private markets to control the quality of the product that is supplied. Similarly the political authorities could ensure that people had sufficient income to avoid poverty in periods of unemployment or ill health by requiring of persons that they took out compulsory private insurance. Some special reasons have to be advanced therefore, over and above a concern with equality, as to why some commodities are properly supplied as public services. Finally, the argument from common needs would establish only that some minimally adequate level of service be available to all persons; it would not establish that the best available form of service be available to all, which is the ideal incorporated in the National Health Service for example. Some other argument then, other than an appeal to common human needs, is required to justify the specific egalitarianism of the welfare state.

2. The argument from common citizenship

This argument can take a variety of forms. For example, according to Tawney (1952, pp. 119–157) access to certain common services overcomes class divisions and helps create a bond of common human feeling among members of the same political community. In Marshall's (1950) parallel formulation the development of social rights, involving equal access to certain public services and benefits, is necessary to complement the civil and political rights that hitherto were considered the hallmarks of citizenship.

Like the previous argument this position treats equality as an instrumental value, the basic value in this case being that of humane social relations or a sense of common citizenship. To be successful as an argument therefore it would have to show that equality of access to certain services and benefits really did contribute towards a sense of common citizenship. This contribution is difficult to show, however. We have already noted that inequalities in service use still persist in the welfare state, despite more than thirty years of there having been common services. Moreover, when it is possible for people to substitute private provision for public provision, the public supply may well become a second class alternative, as has happened with much council housing. Where there is supplementation of public supply, as with pensions for example, then the existence of the public supply may make little difference to the perceived inequalities. Finally, even if there were a connection between social policy provision and a sense of common citizenship, it is difficult to establish the direction of causality. Perhaps it is the sense of common citizenship that is necessary to provide the state services rather than vice versa.

3. The argument from democracy

An important argument in defence of specific egalitarianism depends upon a certain conception of altruism within a democratic political system. According to this argument the form of redistribution within a political community will depend upon the preferences of voters and what they are prepared to support. If voters are concerned about the health care consumption of the poor, but not for example about their consumption of newspapers or entertainment, then it will be quite sensible to transfer resources in kind for specific purposes rather than promote general egalitarian measures. The pattern of services we observe, it is argued, is just what we should expect if we posit caring preferences on the part of the electorate for specific items of individual well-being. (Culyer, 1976, pp. 81–95; 1980, pp. 179–203).

How valid is this argument? Perhaps its most serious weakness is that we do not observe a pattern of services that alone would be consistent with the posited caring preferences. It may be argued that preferences of this sort are most consistent with charitable services rather than those supplied as of right to the public at large (cf. Sugden, 1980). What is more, it is difficult to obtain evidence on voter preferences independently of the existing pattern of services, so the justification for those services in terms of voter preferences threatens to become circular. Finally, there are forms of social policy, most notably those involving the regulation of otherwise private contracts, as with old peoples' homes in the private market, which it is difficult to justify in terms of an altruistic desire on the part of voters to supply to those too poor to support themselves a specific range of services.

The above three arguments all give the equality typical of the welfare state an instrumental value. Equality is to be promoted because it in turn promotes other states of affairs having intrinsic value, for example a greater sense of citizenship or the satisfaction of voter preferences. In each case we saw that there were reasons for doubting the *general* validity of these arguments, although they might apply in specific cases. Not all existing social policy, and perhaps some of that which is characteristic of the welfare state, can be justified by appeal to the above arguments. So the question arises whether the specific egalitarianism of the welfare state can be justified by an argument that gives the principle of equality intrinsic value.

Two sorts of arguments might be used here. It might be urged that no society showed concern and respect for its members unless it treated them as equals in certain fundamental respects (Dworkin, 1978, pp. 150–183). Equal treatment expresses the idea of looking on persons as ends in themselves, and not mere means to some further ends. To secure equal treatment in some important aspects of human life, for example medical care and education, is to show this concern and respect. Alternatively, though not necessarily in contradiction, it can be argued that equality of provision expresses a principle of justice, since no one is entitled to claim that they deserve more than anyone else (Ackerman, 1980; Weale, 1978, pp. 33–40). Securing equality in certain limited, but importantly, respects may be the best practical means of giving expression to this more general commitment to equality. The strategy of specific egalitarianism represents an attempt to equalise the most important aspects of persons' welfare.

Both these arguments turn on the idea that equality is constitutive of some basic principles of right or justice that should govern the design of the structure of social and political organisation. However, there is another idea which is frequently invoked as constituting this basic principle of right, and that is the idea of freedom. Yet many people hold that freedom conflicts with equality. So in order to see whether equality can be given intrinsic value and used to justify the pattern of services in the welfare state we must examine the concept of freedom and its relation to social policy.

Freedom and Social Policy

Like equality the concept of freedom can be variously defined, depending on those persons and activities in relation to which it is being considered. Following MacCullum (1967) we may say that freedom consists of a relation between persons, actions and constraints. Depending on how we identify these persons, actions and constraints we shall arrive at differing conceptions of freedom.

To illustrate this point let us consider a specific example. Suppose someone wants a commodity which they cannot afford to buy. Should we say that they are unfree to buy that commodity? An answer to this question will depend on what constraints are thought to constitute a limit on freedom. For example, there are some writers who think that the only things that should be identified as constraints are the intentional actions of other persons, forcibly preventing an agent from obtaining what he or she wants (Hayek, 1960; Rowley & Peacock, 1975). Others by contrast hold that constraints on freedom may well comprise budget constraints. To lack the money to buy something on this second, more extensive, definition is to be legally unfree to buy that thing (cf. Jones, 1982). Whereas on the first definition one may be unable to do something which one is otherwise free to do, on the second definition to be unable to do something is thereby to be unfree to do that thing.

The relevance of this definitional dispute in the present context concerns the way in which we describe redistribution in the welfare state. According to the first definition redistribution involves a loss of freedom, although it represents a gain in equality of material circumstances. The loss of freedom arises because taxpayers give up some portion of their income under threat of legal penalty for not doing so, whereas no such threat is lifted from beneficiaries. On the second definition, redistribution involves no net loss of freedom. The loss of freedom for taxpayers is compensated by the gain in freedom for beneficiaries who are able to consume what previously they could not afford. By this definition, freedom to act and equality of material circumstances are complementary rather than antagonistic.

The moral to be drawn from these definitional points is not that we must choose one 'right' definition of freedom (for by what principles could such a definition be established?); it is that we must specify in detail what freedom we are talking about for which persons. Specific libertarianism then becomes the counterpart of specific egalitarianism. What we have to compare are the specific gains and losses under the headings of equality and freedom as these arise in social policy programmes. Two particular types of freedom are often invoked in libertarian criticisms of the welfare state. These are, on the one hand, the freedom of persons to choose the means by which they achieve the satisfaction of their economic wants and, on the other hand, the civil and constitutional freedoms that are essential to the workings of a liberal democratic community. Let us consider some of the criticisms of social policy programmes that have been motivated by a concern with one or other of these two types of freedom.

1. The argument from the freedom to choose

The first argument for the specific egalitarianism of the welfare state was that it met common needs. As we saw this argument failed to carry conviction. Its failure may be put to use by libertarians, who can argue along the following lines. Given the difficulty of finding a pattern of services that meet needs, we should aim instead at the satisfaction of diverse individual preferences. But state funded and supplied health and education services, the libertarian will argue, restrict the freedom of choice that is necessary for the expression of individual preferences. To see why the libertarian thinks in this way consider the following example. Suppose someone wants a progressive, non-authoritarian education for their children, or suppose they want medical treatment by means of acupuncture. Both these services are unavailable under state schemes, and yet individuals are compelled to contribute towards those schemes by means of taxation. Not only do the state schemes provide a limited range of choice, but their existence compels persons to forego income which they want to put to other uses. On these grounds the libertarian will argue that redistributive welfare state programmes restrict freedom of choice (cf. Friedman, 1962).

There are, however, two related difficulties with this argument. Firstly, it focusses exclusively on those who are net contributors to the cost of welfare services (compared to an arrangement that would obtain if there were merely private markets in these services); and secondly it relies on a one-sided definition of freedom of the sort that earlier we noted was contentious. For consider the position of the person too poor to buy the services that he or she wants in a private market, and who is therefore a net beneficiary from the state scheme. Certainly, if we do not count budget constraints as restrictions on freedom then this person has not received a net gain in freedom by the establishing of the state service, merely an increase in economic welfare. On the other hand, if we do count budget constraints as restrictions on freedom, then this person will experience a gain in the freedom to choose their consumption of commodities. Since the logical point about the appropriate definition of freedom is, to say the least, in dispute, it would be unwise to hang any great weight of political decision on its being resolved one way or the other.

2. The argument from self-reliance

It is difficult to hang any great weight on the notion of freedom of choice considered as an end in itself, because the scope of what is covered by the term is so ill-defined. However, freedom of choice may be considered as a means towards self-reliance. Libertarian criticisms of the welfare state often focus on its supposed tendency to undermine self-reliance. In a way this may be thought a counterpart to the egalitarian argument that social policy measures create the basis for a sense of common citizenship. Libertarians may argue that persons cannot act as responsible citizens unless they develop habits of self-reliance. How can self-reliance be developed, the libertarian will argue (cf. Acton, 1971, pp. 48–49), when major items of expenditure, like health care and education, are taken out of the control of household budgets, leaving private citizens with control over merely inessential items of consumption?

How cogent is this argument? Self-reliance is a difficult notion to define in such a way that the psychological processes it involves could be observed and their direction of change noted in response to changes in public policy. No one has conducted the relevant empirical research to test whether the conjecture is true that social policy provision does undermine self-reliance. Perhaps it is an impossible research project to conduct. So we are thrown back on plausible conjecture rather than hard evidence. This being so, it is at least as plausible to conjecture that it is a combination of welfare programmes and lack of employment opportunities that creates a 'claiming class', rather than this effect simply arising from the existence of benefits and services. Architects of the welfare state, including Beveridge (1942, 1944) always thought that a full employment policy was a necessary condition for the success of social policy, and perhaps all the present criticism amounts to is a reminder of how important it is to combine these two sets of policies.

3. The argument from the tyranny of democracy

The argument from the nature of altruism in a democracy failed to establish the case for specific egalitarianism. The majoritarian aspect of the welfare state may be looked at in another way, however. From its inception critics of the welfare state alleged that the imposition of a single, uniform conception of welfare held by a majority of the community would lead to political totalitarianism (Hayek, 1944). In other words the search for material equality would lead to an undermining of those civil and constitutional freedoms that are at the heart of liberal democratic states. The logic of the argument is quite simple: effective social policy requires central planning and control, and this in turn will destroy the pluralistic sources of opposition that a democracy needs to survive.

Although trenchantly put this argument has never received the empirical support that would be necessary to sustain its strong implications. Those countries, like the Netherlands and Scandinavia, that spend a high proportion of their national income on social welfare measures do not have an obviously bad record in terms of civil and political liberties, to put the point at its weakest. In the United States much social welfare is controlled at state level, and those states which have low welfare spending, most notably the southern states of the old confederacy, are also those states in which there has been the most vigorous resistance to civil rights programmes. Indeed it is striking that there is no advanced welfare state whose political system has gone totalitarian, and those countries which have emerged from dictatorships, like Spain and Greece, also develop social programmes which imitate those in existing liberal democracies. At best then this particular argument must rest as not proven (cf. Wilensky, 1975, p.115).

Equality, Freedom and Social Policy Reassessed

The previous section has attempted to show that there is no general argument against the welfare state deriving from the principle of freedom. We may choose to describe certain forms of redistribution as involving a loss of freedom, but even so we shall still have to weigh up the value of this loss of freedom with the value of the gain in equality. Is it possible to go further than this, however, and to see the values of equality and freedom as mutually reinforcing rather than antagonistic? In conclusion let us consider one of the possible ways in which they might be seen as complementary.

Suppose we wish to live in a community in which basic political and civil freedoms were protected. By our previous argument we can see that these freedoms would not be imperilled by increased public spending on social policy measures. To that extent there is no barrier to our pursuing the goal of greater equality on the grounds that the freedom of the individual would be in danger. Now, if we were asked why we wanted those freedoms protected, we might reply in terms of the right of persons to have their interests weighed and consulted in the making of public policy and in terms of protecting the capacity of individuals to plan their lives in ways that suited them best. More particularly, we might say that we ourselves would not want to live in a political community in which our rights in this regard were ignored, and we have no reason to deny a similar entitlement to others. So our commitment to freedom would already have some commitment to equality built into it. The principle of equal treatment and respect which we note earlier constituted a principle of justice for social organization, applies when we are considering how to secure liberty for persons.

Would the equal weighing of interests and the capacity to plan be protected adequately within a community that merely paid regard to political and civil freedoms? Arguably not. Economic insecurity can threaten peoples' interests and their capacity to plan their lives. The same motive we have for protecting their political freedoms, therefore, would also lead us to want to protect the economic security of persons. This might be done, indeed in a heavily populated world would almost have to be done, by securing minimally adequate levels of income, education and basic amenities for all. Exact institutional arrangements would have to be judged by how well they contributed to these ends. But it is at least plausible to conjecture that a scheme of comprehensive income maintenance, guaranteeing an income sufficient to avoid poverty, and equality of educational opportunity are necessary conditions for protecting economic security (Weale, 1983, pp. 59–79).

Once these minimally adequate standards had been achieved, it would be up to the democratic vote of citizens to decide which particular freedoms and equalities to trade off against one another. Within those political systems that are called welfare states there is an enormous diversity of institutional provision in particular services. It would be difficult to argue, for example, that the Canadian system of compulsory health insurance was obviously superior or inferior to the National Health Service as judged by the tests of freedom and equality. At this level of provision democratic majorities may decide for one system rather than the other in terms which from their own particular viewpoint seem sensible. That some form of welfare state is necessary to protect both freedom and equality is perhaps not in doubt; the exact form of welfare state that is adequate to the task is more open to question. At some point then the political argument has to stop and the voting begin.

References

Ackerman, A. (1980) *Social Justice in the Liberal State,* Yale University Press, New Haven and London.

Acton, H.B. (1971) *The Morals of Markets,* Longman, London.

Aristotle (1962 edn.) *The Politics,* trans. T.A. Sinclair, Penguin, Harmondsworth.

Beveridge, W.H. (1942) *Social Insurance and Allied Services,* HMSO, Cmd. 6404, London.

Beveridge, W.H. (1944) *Full Employment in a Free Society,* Allen and Unwin, London.

Brittan, S. (1968) *Left or Right? The Bogus Dilemma,* Secker and Warburg, London.

Culyer, A.J. (1976) *Need and the National Health Service,* Martin Robertson, Oxford.

Culyer, A.J. (1980) *The Political Economy of Social Policy,* Martin Robertson, Oxford.

Dworkin, Ronald (1978) *Taking Rights Seriously,* Duckworth, London.

Friedman, M. (1962) *Capitalism and Freedom,* University of Chicago Press, Chicago.

Glennester, H. (1975) *Social Service Budgets and Social Policy,* Allen and Unwin, London.

Hayek, F.A. (1944) *The Road to Serfdom,* Routledge and Kegan Paul, London.

Hayek, F.A. (1960) *The Constitution of Liberty,* Routledge and Kegan Paul, London.

Jones, P. (1982) Freedom and the redistribution of resources, in *Journal of Social Policy* Vol. 11, No. 2, pp. 217-238.

Klein, R. *et al.* (1974) *Social Policy and Public Expenditure* Centre for Studies in Social Policy, London.

Klein, R. *et al.* (1975) *Priorities and Inflation,* Centre for Studies in Social Policy, London.

Le Grand, Julian (1982) *The Strategy of Equality,* Allen and Unwin, London.

MacCullum Jnr., Gerald C. (1967) Negative and positive freedom, in *The Philosophical Review* 76, pp. 312-334. Reprinted in Peter Laslett, W.G. Runciman & Quentin Skinner (eds.), *Philosophy, Politics and Society, Fourth Series,* Blackwell, Oxford (1972).

Marshall, T.H. (1950) *Citizenship and Social Class,* Cambridge University Press, Cambridge.

Rae, Douglas (1981) *Equalities* Harvard University Press, Cambridge Mass.

Rowley, Charles K. and Peacock, Alan T. (1975) *Welfare Economics: A Liberal Restatement,* Martin Robertson, Oxford.

Stephenson, G. (1980) Taxes, benefits and the redistribution of income, in C. Sandford, C. Pond and R. Walker (eds.), *Taxation and Social Policy,* Heinemann, London.

Sugden, R. (1980) Altruism, duty and the welfare state, in N. Timms (ed.), *Social Welfare: Why and How?* Routledge and Kegan Paul, London, pp. 165-177.

Tawney, R.H. (1952) *Equality,* with an introduction by R.M. Titmuss, Allen and Unwin, London (fourth edn., 1964).

Tobin, J. (1970) On limiting the domain of inequality, in *Journal of Law and Economics* Vol. 13, No. 2, pp. 263-277. Reprinted in E.S. Phelps (ed.), *Economic Justice,* Penguin, Harmondsworth (1973).

Weale, A. (1978) *Equality and Social Policy*, Routledge and Kegan Paul, London.
Weale, A. (1983) *Political Theory and Social Policy*, Macmillan, London.
Wildavsky, A. (1964) *The Politics of the Budgetary Process*, Little Brown, Boston.
Wilensky, H.L. (1975) *The Welfare State and Equality*, University of California Press, Berkeley, CA.

Social Research and Government Policy

Heyworth, Rothschild and after[*]

Patricia Thomas

Many years before the social sciences came to be generally accepted as a group of academic disciplines, Edwin Chadwick and Henry Mayhew, Charles Booth and Seebohm Rowntree had shown that a systematic collection of information on social problems could influence society's view of itself, although their impact on policy was sometimes slow and the consequences often unintended. In this paper I argue that despite the expenditure of some £50 m a year on social research, in the 1980s the relationship between social research and government policy is exceedingly tenuous.

It is one thing to analyse society's problems, quite another to suggest remedies which should be embodied in legislation. To organize research as a problem-solving instrument — even within government departments — is, in my view, to court disappointment. As a corollary, I would add that for social scientists to try to solve the problems which worry the government of the day is usually wasteful of time and money, even though they, like other members of the community, can occasionally bring about social change by going beyond the research process and pressing their research findings on the appropriate Departments or their Ministers.

Heyworth and its effects

Social science teaching and research in U.K. universities began to grow after World War Two. The number of social science graduates increased fivefold between 1938 and 1962. In 1965 the publication of the Report of the Committee on Social Studies, chaired by Lord Heyworth, led to the setting up in the same year of the Social Science Research Council (SSRC). The Committee was in no doubt about the potential of such a body for promoting the country's social well-being:

> It is our conviction that the additional expenditure by Government that we recommend will in the course of time be more than repaid by improvement in the

[*]This is a revised and extended version of an article which appeared in *Futures*, February, 1982.

efficiency of the national economy and in the quality of our national life (Heyworth, 1965, para. 170).

The term 'policy research' was not in vogue when Heyworth wrote his Report and no significance can be attached to the fact that he did not use it. The Report does, however, make quite clear the intentions of the Committee in this respect:

> The general aim in research is the advance of knowledge over the whole field of the social sciences and to increase our knowledge of how our society works. Advance will come in two ways; first as a result of the free enquiries of researchers, individually or in groups in the universities or colleges pursuing topics in which their own interest and ability promise original achievement; second, through research in response to problems which clearly demand examination (Heyworth, 1965, para. 88).

The Heyworth Report mentioned free enquiries first; problem-oriented research second. More important, it saw the function of social research as examining rather than solving problems. It did not claim that social research was capable of producing the answers to the social problems of the time.

Before the SSRC was set up, the Foundations had played a major role in supporting research in the social sciences. In 1962–63 Foundations spent over £400,000 on social and economic research, more than government or any other sponsor. With the advent of the SSRC the three major Foundations then in operation (the Leverhulme Trust, the Nuffield Foundation, and the Joseph Rowntree Memorial Trust) needed to adapt their activities to meet a changed situation in which their part in funding social research was to diminish.

Rowntree had made the change in 1959 when it relinquished its role as benefactor of the employees of the cocoa works at New Earswick and instead began to support work in the fields of social policy and social innovation. Leverhulme's concern had been, and remained, scholarship and education, but the coming of the SSRC led the Trust to consider other modes of support than the conventional research project. Nuffield, hitherto the main funder of social research, reaffirmed in its 20th Report its Trustees' preference for research of practical relevance (not necessarily to government); (Nuffield, 1965) but in practice continued to support projects which satisfied academic criteria as well as those expected to be useful.

In general the reaction of the three Trusts to the birth of the SSRC was to change tack to some degree (although in the case of Rowntree the change had taken place earlier) and to assign to the SSRC the role of supporting the straightforwardly academic project. The reaction of the Trusts is important because it illustrates the interrelationship of funding bodies and how a change in the grant-giving practices of one institution can affect those of the others.

Whether or not the Foundations supposed that the SSRC should be supporting straightforward academic research, opinion within the SSRC itself has always been divided: some considered academic excellence a sufficient criterion for making a grant, while others looked first for potential usefulness.

The distinction applied not only to the selection of research projects for support, but also to other areas for which the SSRC had a responsibility. To what extent, for instance, should it consider manpower needs when allocating postgraduate studentships to the various disciplines? Should it establish its own units for the study of long-term problems? (It did in 1969.) Should it set up a Committee — the Committee for the Next Thirty Years — which would 'consult with the potential users of research in industry, Government and the social services about the kinds of problem and new developments which might arise in the next thirty years, and on which research might usefully be taken in time to inform necessary major decisions on policy'. (SSRC, 1968). (It did in 1967 but decided against taking the next step suggested by that Committee and setting up an Institute of Forecasting Studies). These developments showed that the SSRC as a whole did not see itself as a passive reactor to research grant proposals (although there were always some members who did) but as having the facility to initiate as well as to react. It was setting up structures which enabled it to interact with government Departments, albeit imperfectly. During the 1960s its place as the major supporter of traditional academic social science remained, however, unchallenged.

The 1970 review of government expenditure led to the first cut in the SSRC's rate of growth, and decisions about priorities in research projects and postgraduate awards became more difficult. For the first time in the SSRC's life there was a Conservative administration and it was a government with mixed, and not especially friendly, relations with the SSRC. The expansion in the SSRC's support for social science was halted, but already in the financial year 1970-71 the Council had committed £2 m to research. (By contrast the Nuffield Foundation spent less than £200,000 on social research in 1971).

While the Foundations were beginning to lose their share of the social research market, government Departments were increasing theirs, so that by the year 1972-73 central government was spending £7.7 m on social research, compared with the SSRC's £2.6 m and the Foundations' £1 m (Rothschild, 1971).

The Rothschild Report on the Organization and Management of Government R and D

In the 1970s there were two developments which changed the nature of the arguments about the kinds of support which the government and the SSRC should give to research. The first of these is embodied in a document which included a memorandum by the government, a Report by Lord Rothschild, then Head of the Central Policy Review Staff, and a Report of a Working Group of the government's Council for Scientific Policy. The best known report is that of Lord Rothschild which concerned itself with the organization and management of government research and development. To avoid confusion this will be referred to as the First Rothschild Report.

Lord Rothschild held the clear view that applied research (which he considered to be the almost exclusive preserve of government Departments) should be undertaken according to the 'customer/contractor principle':

> . . . the customer says what he wants; the contractor does it (if he can); and the customer pays (Rothschild, 1971, para. 6).

The customer might be an individual or division within a Department needing the answer to a question amenable to research, and the contractor an individual or team carrying out research inside or outside the Department. He excluded the SSRC from his review on the grounds that it was still 'in its infancy'. Despite this exclusion, the customer/contractor principle soon came to be applied within Departments to social science research. Application of the principle brought about a new sophistication in the machinery for ensuring contact between contractor and customer.

Rothschild saw applied science as an instrument for solving the problems that worried government. If the problem is the need for a new tank or antibiotic, then applied science is capable of solving it. In applying the principle to social research, government moved on to less firm ground, for social problems involve conflicts of interest between groups, which are usually resolved by political decisions. Whereas Heyworth considered research to be useful in *illuminating* social problems, the application of the principle to social research suggested that it could be useful in solving them.

No British Brookings

The other relevant development of the 1970s was unrelated to the First Rothschild Report, although both grew out of a desire to harness science for the benefit of the nation. In the second half of the 1970s there was much discussion of the need for a new institute of policy studies, modelled on the Brookings Institution in the USA. The proposed institute took on different guises as funding bodies and academics discussed the form it should take, but those who favoured the idea agreed that a need existed for a new independent centre capable of undertaking research relevant to government policy. The criticisms centred on the adequacy of the provision for policy studies in existing institutes and, as it turned out, no such centre came into being — the new Technical Change Centre has a more limited remit. The term 'policy research' took a firm hold on the language of social enquiry and has played a part, I maintain, in distorting the pattern of research funding.

Obstacles to the government's use of research

If research is to be used it must first get a hearing. The output of government-funded research will, it is fair to assume, be read by someone within the appropriate Department, although it may go no further than the research division. The interest with which it will be greeted depends on a number of factors and the chances of all circumstances being favourable seem, on a common sense view, to be small.

If the research output is read, it is arguable that adversary politics offers little opportunity for decisions to be made on the basis of rationality alone, even if it can be assumed that social science research will always produce rational answers. Large social issues are usually resolved on the basis of party politics, although public preference if known, may in some cases affect the nature of solution to some extent. On less important issues policies may evolve slowly, and may be informed by research among other influences. On very small 'housekeeping' issues of efficiency, social or operational research may play a more important part. 'Housekeeping' research is, for obvious reasons, likely to be carried out on the customer/contractor principle inside government or by government contract to a university or research institute. In general, research which bears out the predilections of administrators or their Ministers is far more likely to be used than research which runs counter to them.

The new structures which followed the First Rothschild Report facilitated contact between customer and contractor: in particular officials in policy divisions had regular meetings with colleagues in research divisions or units and in this way were given the opportunity of understanding each other's problems and language. Militating against this advantage were — and remain — the problems of time and presentation. A research project usually takes at least three years to complete and by the time the research is finished and written up it is unlikely that senior administrators who were in the policy divisions at the time the research was commissioned will have remained in the same posts. An official new to the post may not yet have acquired sufficient knowledge of the problem in question to be able to comprehend all the implications of the research findings, even if the topic has remained a live issue and has kept its place near the top of departmental priorities. It is difficult to sustain the momentum of a sense of urgency over a period of three years or more.

The presentation of social research often gives the administrator difficulties. The problem is not merely that the report may be written in a language unfamiliar to administrators but also that in order to present a full and scholarly account of his research the researcher may have written more words than the administrator can absorb.

Faced with this double jeopardy, the researcher is indeed lucky if his research is used in a direct sense. It may, occasionally, have an impact many years later, having influenced public opinion in the meantime, but that is not what Lord

Rothschild appears to have had in mind when he formulated the customer/contractor principle.

Externally funded research is less likely to get a hearing within government, not only because the structures for informing administrators are geared to work in which the customer has expressed an interest, but also because the existence of commissioned and internally conducted work provides an effective barrier against externally funded studies. The competing claims of the Departments' own research make outside research fall very low on an official's list of priorities. All this makes it unlikely for it to be common practice among government officials to look to SSRC research when they are seeking evidence for their policy recommendations to Ministers.

The assertions made above are based on limited observations of the relationship between research and policy. Empirical studies of the attitudes of officials towards research are sparse, but they confirm the view I have put forward. Nathan Caplan, working with colleagues at the Institute of Social Research at the University of Michigan asked 204 senior civil servants whether they made use of social research and, if so, in what ways (Caplan, 1976). He found his respondents well disposed towards social research and most could cite at least two instances in which they had found research useful. A little under half, however, could remember ignoring the conclusions of social research. Caplan observed that these civil servants were more likely to use social science findings to improve their own bureaucratic efficiency. They were able to ensure, too, that only certain types of information came their way. The civil servant:

> . . . does not filter through and selectively utilise the information fed to him by staff aides. He plays a very active role in utilisation by prescribing the information he wants and will ultimately use in reaching decisions on policy relevant matters (Caplan, 1976, p. 194).

Officials' selectivity in allowing only certain information to get through to them extends to the sponsorship of the research used:

> . . . 94% of all research activities represented in the instances of use was either funded by the government, conducted by the government or both; and 86% was funded or conducted by the using agency (Caplan, 1976, p. 189).

Caplan does not tell us how many of his respondents were social scientists (although he knew that some of the sample were social scientists and that others had a legal or medical training). But the high proportion of social scientists in government posts in the USA suggests that in general their receptivity to social research is greater than in the UK. L.J. Sharpe, in his comparison between the relationship of the social scientist and policy making in the UK and America, sees the British civil service as more self-confident and thus less inclined to draw upon social science knowledge in reaching decisions than its US counterpart (Sharpe, 1978). In a study, similar to Caplan's but carried out in the UK, Louis Moss in 1977 undertood a small-scale pilot exercise in the Department of Health and Social Security (DHSS) (Moss, 1977). He asked administrators and professionals who worked with the Research Liaison Groups (RLGs) — part of the departmental machinery for commissioning research — for their views on the usefulness of research. When the respondents were asked whether they could think of any research that they had come across in any departmental activity with which they had been connected, and then whether they could identify examples which they felt had been useful, nearly 40% could identify none or only a few pieces of research which turned out to be useful. It is only fair to add that the study was conducted in the early days of the RLGs, when little of the research of which the officials had had experience had been commissioned through the Groups. Kogan, Korman and Henkel in a study of the DHSS undertaken in the late 1970s noted that professional and administrative 'customers' found the RLGs useful, and that the act of considering potential research had helped them clarify some of their policy needs (Kogan *et al.*, 1980).

When Moss asked his respondents about the sponsorship of 'useful' research which they had experienced in any departmental position, over two-thirds of the sample — and over 80% of professionals — mentioned research sponsored by the Department, a little less than Caplan's result.

In my own research enquiry I found that four out of 12 SSRC- or Foundation-supported projects had brushed shoulders with the policy-making process. The apparently high 'success rate' makes a gloomier reality. In one case, the research findings fitted in conveniently with the views of a new government and were used in framing legislation, but in fact, the recommendations were never put into effect because of a shortage of money. In another case a recommendation, on an important 'housekeeping' issue, was embodied in legislation but the conclusion reached by the researcher simply echoed what the Department had itself decided would be a desirable course. In the third case the successful outcome was that the researcher, because of his externally funded research, was given a government contract to carry out related work which resulted in action. In the fourth case the research was said to be useful, along with other projects carried out within the Department, as an aid to greater methodological sophistication.

None of these case studies showed research to have a direct impact on policy, even though the findings were read in the relevant Departments. (It is worth noting that all the projects came to the attention of the Departments in or before 1972, before the Rothschild reorganization had taken effect. Although government resources for research were growing, the machinery for linking the customer with the contractor was minimal in most Departments and government-funded research had not yet eliminated interest in externally funded work.) In all four partly successful projects the researchers were personally known to senior government officials or their Ministers. These personal contacts had the same beneficial effects as the structures within

Departments which were to link the customer with the contractor.

The use made of these research reports bears out the conclusion of a second observer of the US scene, Carol Weiss. In her book *Using Social Research in Public Policy Making*, she first considers and then dismisses two models of research use; the first, the 'decision-driven model' implies that a social problem is first defined, the missing knowledge needed to solve it is identified and social science techniques are then employed to supply and interpret the knowledge required, the whole process culminating in policy choice; the second, which she calls the 'knowledge-driven model' of research use (more applicable to the physical than the social sciences), suggests that basic research leads to applied research which in time, leads to development and, finally, application. Social science research, according to Carol Weiss, is seldom used in either of those ways but it has a variety of other uses:

> as political ammunition;
> to delay action;
> to avoid taking responsibility for a decision;
> to win kudos for a successful programme;
> to gain recognition and support;
> to discredit an opponent for a disliked policy;
> to maintain the prestige of a government agency through supporting prestigious researchers;
> to keep universities and their social science departments solvent;
> to serve as a training ground for apprentice social researchers;
> to generate further research on topics of social importance.

(Weiss, 1978, p. 15).

On both sides of the Atlantic, then, the relationship between social research and policy is tenuous, although the sustaining myth still prevails that a mutually advantageous relationship exists between administrative officials in government Departments who need to advise their Ministers on policy matters and research workers, housed within government research divisions or in universities and research institutes, supported by government funds or by the SSRC or Foundations. It is closer to the truth to say that research is seldom used but if it is used it is likely to be government funded, and either concerned with 'housekeeping' matters, or able to offer government one or more of the benefits cited by Carol Weiss.

The Second Rothschild Report and its aftermath

Whereas the Heyworth Report expressed the hope that social scientists could illuminate society's problems, the Rothschild principle applied to social research suggested that research could supply the answers. In 1981 the SSRC announced plans for reorganizing its Committee structure with the declared intention of making itself more relevant to the problems of government. The move was in my view misconceived and ill advised but it is only fair to say that it was a response to the critical glances levelled at it by the Conservative Government. In December 1981 Sir Keith Joseph, Secretary of State for Education and Science, asked Lord Rothschild to undertake an enquiry into the work of the SSRC. Social scientists were dismayed at the idea of finding the social sciences once again under the microscope but began to relax as rumours spread that Lord Rothschild seemed to be taking a robust but sympathetic view of the social science community and its work. When this Report was published in May 1982 it came as a relief to the SSRC and its constituents.

The essence of Lord Rothschild's report was that the SSRC was not doing too badly, that its budget should not be cut and that it should be left alone for at least three years without further scrutiny. He did not dwell on the question of relevance and problem-solving, but did remark that:

> . . . directly relevant social science has no outstanding achievement to record comparable with the discovery of the relation between cigarette smoking and lung cancer (Rothschild, 1982, para. 4, 19).

He addressed some well aimed sniping at economics, implicitly regarded by the SSRC as the paradigm of relevance.

> There are conservative economists, socialist economists, liberal economists, SDP economists and, no doubt, Alliance economists; and the fact that economics can be classified in these terms suggests that economics has not the objectivity which is the principal norm of a science (Rothschild, 1982, para. 4, 11).

(Rothschild's stricture can be applied to social research which is intended to help policy-makers solve problems. There are conservative solutions, socialist solutions, SDP solutions and, no doubt, Alliance solutions.) In Rothschild's view the proper role of research was to dispel myths and act as a check on commonsense belief. Both Heyworth and Rothschild expected the social sciences to be useful, but neither saw usefulness as being related to problem-solving.

Any euphoria brought about by the Report was short-lived. Towards the end of 1982 Sir Keith Joseph grudgingly announced that the SSRC was to continue but he imposed an eight per cent cut in its budget.

The present situation is unsatisfactory from every point of view. The Council is still under threat and continues to make itself vulnerable. The government wants research which is useful to itself but, like any other government, will listen only to what it wants to hear. The SSRC is striving to offer it what it wants while attempting to remain unbiased and value-free. The tension between supporting dispassionate research and giving the government the answers it feels it can expect could in time destroy the most robust machine, let alone one brought to a delicate state through an excess of tinkering.

The Council is in danger of losing its role as the main financial backer of research of longer term significance and of theoretical and methodological research and shows no sign of finding a new one.

Alas for Heyworth; The Committee's reasoned arguments for the support of social research as illumination were thoroughly undermined by the application of the Rothschild principle to social research — an application which Rothschild himself has consistently repudiated. For the SSRC to forsake the notion of research as illumination and pursue the myth of research as a solution to problems is to tread a dangerous path towards an ever-retreating goal.

References

Caplan, N. (1976) Social research and national policy: what gets used, by whom, for what purpose and with what effects?, in *International Social Science Journal*, 28.

Heyworth, Lord (1965) *Report of the Committee on Social Studies*, Cmnd. 2660, HMSO, London.

Kogan, M., Korman, N. and Henkel, M. (1980) *Government's Commissioning of Research: A Case Study*, Brunel University, Uxbridge.

Moss, L. (1977) *Some Attitudes towards Research* (unpublished).

Nuffield Foundation (1965) *Annual Report of the Nuffield Foundation, 1964–1965*, Nuffield Foundation, London.

Rothschild, Lord (1971) The organization and management of government R & D, in *A Framework for Government Research and Development*, Cmnd. 4814, HMSO, London.

Rothschild, Lord (1982) *An Enquiry into the Social Science Research Council*, Cmnd. 8554, HMSO, London.

Sharpe, L. J. (1978) The social scientist and policy-making in Britain and America: a comparison, in M. Bulmer (ed.), *Social Policy Research*, Macmillan, London.

SSRC (1968) *Annual Report of the Social Science Research Council 1967/68*, HMSO, London.

Weiss, C. H. (1978) *Using Social Research for Public Policy-Making*, Teakfield, Farnborough.

Social Policy, Social Administration and the Social Construction of Welfare

Alan Walker

Introduction

Whether or not the welfare state is in or on the brink of a crisis, the fact that more than thirty years of institutionalized social services provision has not produced a major change in the unequal structure of British society is now, surely, firmly established. The evolution of this realization has been accompanied by periodic expressions of dissatisfaction about the limitations of the definition of 'social policy', both as an activity or practice and as an academic subject: social administration. Recent analyses of the political economy of welfare have, like their famous predecessors, exposed some short-comings in the current conceptions of social policy, and have succeeded in sowing the seeds of alternative and more sociological approaches. (Crouch, 1975; Westergaard, 1978; CDP, 1977; Gough, 1979). However these critiques have usually remained implicit, and the need for a reassessment of the scope of social policy teaching and research has not been openly and consistently recognized. There are signs that, as a result, the boundaries of the subject are becoming increasingly blurred, with a split emerging between what some social policy analysts do and what is traditionally defined as being the concern of social administration. This is not only confusing for students and others but more importantly, this division may be exploited by those whose interests would be harmed by alternative conceptions of social policy. Furthermore, there are signs that important social developments which affect welfare fundamentally, are not receiving critical attention from social administrators because they fall outside of the compass of the subject as it has developed since the Second World War.

Social administration, as the amalgam of disciplines within which social policy is studied is anachronistically called, is a relatively young and developing subject and it is not surprising, therefore, if its scope is questioned from time to time. However, despite the pioneering work of Titmuss in outlining the three divisions of welfare and Townsend in formulating the basis of a sociological

127

approach to social policy, traditional conceptions of the subject have proved to be remarkably resilient. (Titmuss, 1963; Townsend, 1976). Whilst the coverage of welfare provisions in the private sector, such as health insurance and employers' fringe benefits, has increased in recent years, social administration has continued to concentrate its attention on government action through the five social services: health, education, social security, housing and personal social services. As a result, social administration has not yet succeeded in providing a systematic framework for the analysis of the perpetuation and growth of inequalities in 'welfare state' societies; choosing instead, for the most part, to remain passive, at best describing them and at worst ignoring them. For example, the impact of inflation and income policies on stratification are rarely considered by social administrators, and far from being incorporated into a theory of social policy, they are too often seen as being the province of economists alone. This, of course, partly reflects the fact that economists and sociologists, by and large, have also failed to provide the necessary framework within which to study social development. This deficiency has been exposed starkly by the combination of recession and economic liberalism in Britain in the 1980s, when social development has been so blatantly and relatively uncritically subordinated to economic management.

Despite some well-known exceptions, the study of social administration has focussed its attention almost exclusively on the public welfare activities of government. One important reason for this is the successful social structure construction of 'welfare' as 'the welfare state' or government intervention in welfare. Social administration has, in turn, reinforced this stereotype through research and teaching. But while they continue to concentrate on government and its legislation, social administrators are in danger of ignoring the distributional outcomes of decisions made by other powerful social institutions and groups, including other sectors of the state as well as financial and business concerns. If social administration is to adequately encompass the analysis of welfare or dis-welfare, as the result of the distributional outcomes of various institutionalized social policies, it must at some stage critically re-examine its definition and scope.

This suggested process of re-examination assumes, of course, that it is possible and desirable to arrive at a single definition of social policy or social administration. Titmuss referred to this as the 'unsoluble problem'. (Titmuss, 1968, p.20). However, the problem is not so much a lack of alternative and untainted terms, as an absence of clear agreement amongst analysts on the meaning of concepts that are generally held to be central to the subject. Existing consensus appears to be confined to the study of certain parts of the public policy system. When this lack of agreement, therefore, is translated into a reluctance to investigate some integral parts of the institutionalized policy process, then some discussion of the nature of the subject is clearly called for. This need is further emphasised by the implications for the study of social policy of the failure of the welfare state to significantly reduce inequalities in either the prevailing distribution of resources and power in society or the social differentiation of welfare, and in some circumstances to actually increase them (Le Grand, 1982).

Social Administration and Social Policy

The literature on social administration abounds with definitions of social policy, but most of them are based on the *public* administration of welfare and so would seem to be closer to the study of public administration than *social* administration or social policy (Slack, 1966, p. 14; Marsh, 1965, p. 13; Brown, 1969). What are the main components of existing conceptions of social policy?

There is some consensus amongst authorities that social policy is concerned with collective interventions to promote individual welfare. Marshall defines social policies according to their welfare objectives — security, health, welfare — and contrasts such policies with economic policies which are not concerned with individual welfare and need. Thus:

> Social policy uses political power to supersede, supplement or modify operations of the economic system in order to achieve results which the economic system would not achieve on its own, and that in doing so it is guided by values other than those determined by open market forces (Marshall, 1975, p. 15).

Although Marshall distinguishes three aims of social policies: the elimination of poverty, the pursuit of equality and the maximization of welfare, the 'avowed objective' of social policy is welfare. Furthermore, whilst social policies are concerned with individual welfare, *economic* policies are concerned with the 'common weal'. (Marshall, 1975, p. 12 and p. 15). Pinker has noted the 'general reluctance' of authorities to move far away from a focus on individual welfare despite the illogicality of the distinction often made between individual and collective benefit. (Pinker, 1971, pp. 147–148). For instance, child benefit may be regarded as an individual benefit for a family to spend as they see fit, as a collective benefit for all families with children to bring family income closer to family need and as a national investment by families and others in the future.

Both Donnison and more recently, Mishra, have usefully extended the scope of social policy by stressing *social* welfare rather than individual welfare as the purpose of collective intervention (Donnison, 1962, p. 21; Mishra, 1977). Mishra defines social policy as 'those social arrangements, patterns and mechanisms that are typically concerned with the distribution of resources in accordance with some criterion of need'. (Mishra, 1977). According to Mishra social administration is concerned with intervention and praxis, with 'the advancement of welfare rather than the accumulation and refinement of a body of tested knowledge' (Mishra, 1977, p. 5). In a similar vein, Rein suggests that 'The study of social policy is basically concerned with the range of human needs and the social institutions created to meet them,' and that social policy is 'above all, concerned with choice among competing values,' the primary subject matter of which is egalitarianism (Rein, 1975, p. 20).

In addition to collective provision to meet individual need, several authorities stress the integrative functions of social policy. Writing in 1957, Macbeath said that:

> Social policies are concerned with the right ordering of the network of relationships between men and women who live together in societies, or with the principles which should govern the activities of individuals and groups so far as they affect the lives and interests of other people (Macbeath, 1957).

Titmuss defined social administration as being concerned with 'different types of moral transactions, which have developed in modern societies in institutional forms to bring about and maintain social and community relations.' Thus social administrators', 'primary areas of unifying interest are centred in the social institutions that foster integration and discourage alienation' (Titmuss, 1968, pp. 20–22). In *The Gift Relationship* Titmuss forcefully contrasted the integrative function of 'social' policies, the moral and political nature of the former and the individualistic and hedonistic nature of the latter (Titmuss, 1970, pp. 11–13). Later, in *Social Policy*, he defined the term more clearly as the principles that govern collective actions which concern the non-economic aspects in human relations (Titmuss, 1974, pp. 23–24). Heisler, in a similar vein to Titmuss, sees *integration* as the central focus of social administration. He defines social administration as 'the body of intelligence which contributes to the making of policies and the distribution of sanctions to eradicate social disorganization' (Heisler, 1977, p. 21). In contrast to Donnison and Mishra, Heisler appears to be suggesting a more refined academic (and political) status for social administration.

If this process of listing the definitions of key terms — social administration, social policy and more rarely in the literature, social welfare — continued it would only serve to further emphasize the fact that there are nearly as many definitions as writers on the subject. Common ground has been established on the meaning of social policy, as collective intervention to promote the welfare of the individual or the individual and society. But although a wide measure of agreement appears to exist at this point there is no sign of a broader consensus. There appears to be little point of contact between for example Marshall's and Brown's definitions of the scope of social policy, focussed on government intervention, and Rein and Mishra's apparently broader conception of 'social' institutions and 'social' arrangements. How can such differences be reconciled? Is such a reconciliation necessary?

Social Administration and the Welfare State

The analysis of social policy which follows from what may be termed 'traditional' definitions of social policy as social administration is, not surprisingly, usually circumscribed by formal administrative boundaries, government welfare departments, or government concern in social services. Social policy is thereby equated with collective action through government, or effectively, with that part of government activity known as 'the welfare state'.

Different definitions of the welfare state are more or less specific and may stress helping the poor or attacking poverty, meeting need or increasing well-being, the use of political power to modify the operation of the market system and collective intervention. For example Briggs' definition of the welfare state is similar to Marshall's definition of social policy given earlier:

> A 'welfare state' is a state in which organised power is deliberately used (through politics and administration) in an effort to modify the play of market forces in at least three directions — first, by guaranteeing individuals and families a minimum income irrespective of the market value of their work or their property; second, by narrowing the extent of insecurity by enabling individuals and families to meet certain 'social contingencies' . . . and third, by ensuring that all citizens without distinction of status or class are offered the best standards available in relation to a certain agreed range of social services (Briggs, 1961, p. 22).

But while some models of social policy closely approximate the institutional framework of the British welfare state there is no necessary relationship between the two concepts. The former consists of an institutionalized principle or intention and the latter the activities of the government in relation to welfare. Even in societies dominated by a state bureaucracy there are likely to be 'social' policies outside of the state's institutional network. Herein then, lies a major drawback to traditional approaches to social policy: the tendency to equate social policy with the welfare state. Social administration may be the study of the public services which comprise the welfare state, but 'social policy' implies something more than just these services.

The state in any society obviously will not institutionalize principles of distribution which conflict fundamentally and consistently with those of the dominant economic system; and insofar as such policies are employed, they will be tempered considerably to fit the dominant ideology. Two examples of policies based on principles so modified are the distribution of social security benefits and employment policies for disabled people. (Ginsburg, 1979, pp. 46–107; Walker and Townsend, 1981, pp. 52–72). It is at least questionable, therefore, whether the principles of social justice and egalitarianism will spring from the public sector in a captialist society such as Britain. In fact the capitalist state would appear to be just as unlikely as other captialist employers to aspire to social justice. It follows that if a socially just society is achieved, where 'equality is the accepted principle for the distribution of resources' there will presumably be no role for distributive mechanisms outside of the public sector, since such a policy may have to be institutionalised through state domination. (George & Wilding, 1976, p. 137).

In the absence of a dominant state, non-state agencies retain an important role in distribution and may therefore frustrate or further the principles enshrined in legislation. Furthermore, in the absence of a government which consistently adheres to the principles of social justice the *underlying* as well as professed rationales of public policies must be examined closely. Similarly the administration of policies must be weighed against their expressed intentions, because policies in practice may operate quite differently from their apparent aims, which are usually sketched out very roughly in legislation. State as well as non-state agencies may appear to frustrate the explicit intentions of social policies. For example the commitment enshrined in the Supplementary Benefits Acts to pay benefit to those in need appears to be at variance with the experience of many claimants in trying to secure supplementary benefit and with some of those parts of the officially secret codes which guide the administration of benefits, and that have been made public.

Social Policy and the State

The equation of social policy with the institutionalized welfare state contains some inherent disadvantages which have tended to restrict the policy analysts' investigations of welfare. In the first place, it reinforces the parochialism of British social administration, which as Mishra argues, is partly borne out of its over-riding concern with intervention and praxis. (Mishra, 1977, p. 39). There is a danger, therefore, that British solutions to social problems will be accepted as the only solutions and the best policies available to suit British culture and political institutions. Secondly it may be assumed, implicitly or explicitly, that collective, social or institutionalized policies may only stem from government. This may, thirdly, support the myth that such policies are necessarily beneficial in furthering the aims of 'welfare'. The influence of what Baker has called the 'social conscience' approach to social policy remains very influential today, especially in elementary textbooks on the subject (Baker, 1979). But it cannot be assumed that the aims of public policies or the institution of government are necessarily more moral than those of other agencies. The social construction of altruistic public policies battling against egoistic economic policies, of David against Goliath, falls-down if David, not all he is cracked-up to be, is in the pay of Goliath and the whole confrontation is staged to bolster the morale of the troops. Too cynical and deterministic no doubt, but the important underlying point must stand: the social construction of 'social policies' is one part of the process of legitimation carried out by the state in furthering the interests of the dominant forces in society (this is *not* to suggest a conspiracy but rather an inherent process). At the same time that agencies of the welfare state enable some social minorities to keep their heads above water, if not to make relative gains, these same agencies may also play an important part in the processes of social control and capital accumulation.

The dominant ideology of advanced capitalism portrays the public sector as depending on but quite separate from the private sector. The latter is concerned with the serious business of generating wealth, some of which will be diverted to the ever greedy former sector. The public sector intervenes in the private like Robin Hood, to 'modify the play of market forces' and redistribute income through taxes, transfers and services. (Marshall, 1975, p. 15). This picture is a false one. It ignores the role of state intervention through, for example, budgetary measures to alter supply and demand, wage and price controls and company taxation. All of which, of course, indirectly affect the distribution of income and wealth. But in addition to budgetary intervention, the state plays a major role in the market, at both national and international level, for example, as consumers of the products of 'private' industry, both directly and indirectly through capital grants and subsidies. Also through its nationalization of energy production, it has created differential monopoly markets which favour large industrial consumers. In short, the state in Britain is intimately related at various levels with industry and financial institutions. One example of the importance of this intervention is the relationship between the state and the Vickers Engineering Company:

> The rationalization and diversification carried out by Vickers since the mid-sixties has been done on the basis of profits made from past and present government contracts and the compensation from the rationalization of its steel interests in 1967 (CDP, 1977, p. 78).

Unfortunately because this relationship entails no long term commitment or democratic control, the state's direct or indirect investment, does not imply a guarantee of work for those employed in the industry. The state's intervention to 'help' ailing private capital may merely facilitate rationalisation and the inevitable loss of jobs. It is the workers and their families, therefore, at the different stages of industrial decline and restructuring, who have to bear the heaviest costs.

The definition and pursuit of social policy as the 'welfare state' also fulfils an important political function. One instance of the articulation of this function is the now widely held view that growth is the fundamental prerequisite for 'further' redistribution and increased public expenditure on the social services. Thus it is believed that private enterprise produces surpluses for distribution to the poor and deprived, on the basis of alternative principles such as need. In turn, debates about the welfare state and social services become circumscribed by concern about the economy and growth. In part this reflects the development of social administration in a subordinate relationship to economics and of social policy in subordination to economic policy. But the fact that this philosophy is based on the enduring values of individualism and the privatisation of consumption is rarely exposed to critical comment. Traditional approaches assumed that social policy could operate outside the economy — hence 'social' administration rather than 'economic' or 'political' administration. Yet there is an increasing realisation that these 'social' institutions form an integral part of the apparatus of the capitalist system and do not exist in a moral vacuum.

There is, of course, an inherent contradiction in definitions of the role and function of social policy in capitalist societies such as Britain, as using wholly alternative principles of distribution to those of the market. Social policy can operate, without contradiction or conflict, within the confines of capitalism to meet some of the social costs of industrial production and to assist the market in matters such as training, rehabilitation and health care. But if social policies have genuine 'social' aims and are to be treated as serious attempts at allocating resources according to 'need' or other non-market principles, then clearly these aims are ultimately frustrated by the market itself. As post-war experience in Britain shows, if concern with 'social' aspects is restricted to the public sector this may ameliorate some social problems but will not have much impact on the overall distribution of resources. Systems of distribution are polarized in the minds of some commentators and this may have contributed to the pervasiveness of this distortion of reality in wider society. With the result that social policy is seen as a sort of 'poor person's economic policy'. But as Miller and Rein have argued:

> Effective redistributuve policies must seek directly to alter original income differentials and asset accumulations as well as attempt to offset them (Miller & Rein, 1975).

The perpetuation of this false separation is also a function of the ideology and economic relations embodied in capitalism and the role of the capitalist state in protecting certain interests. The state provides, to a greater or lesser extent, benefits and services for social minorities, without endangering the prevailing distribution of power nor the market system. But as an embodiment of the interests of a dominant class, the state will never intentionally allow alternative principles to become the primary determinant of reward. The professional groups involved in social policy are dependent on the state for support and the institutionalisation of their interests; interests which coincide broadly with those of the social class they belong to. In their reification of market forces, economists and some social policy analysts are apt to ignore these *social* relations which underlie economic life, treating them as autonomous and immutable. For example, in a report from the now defunct Prices and Incomes Board it was stated that 'It can be concluded from the evidence that pay differentials have a great capacity to *reassert themselves*' (Hyman, 1974, p. 183). Such conclusions present, and help to maintain, the image of the market as a natural process working subject to strong laws outside the structure of society. It goes without saying therefore, in such analyses, that social policy does not attempt to meddle with the market. The ways in which such 'a natural process' reflects and embodies the distribution of power in society remain totally neglected in these examinations.

The empirical tradition of social administration has contributed to some extent to the myth that is sometimes promoted that the subject is 'apolitical' and theoretically neutral. As Rose points out, the close relationship between social policy research and government finance is another contributory factor (Rose, 1978). The state institutions are the primary source of funds for research. This is, perhaps, one reason why the analysis of the role of the state is so under-developed in the study of social policy. The growth of research organizations which depend to a great extent on official sources of finance cannot be disassociated totally from the conservatism of many of these bodies. The anodyne nature of some of their research findings masquerades in a cloak of empiricism and political neutrality. Thereby 'The scientized construction of the social work . . . depoliticizes it' (Rose, 1978, p.2).

In addition to this empirical tradition and dependence on government funded research, the close association between social administration and social work (which is persistent) also contributes to the conservatism of much of its legacy. Starting out as a practical guide to the social services 'mainly for the benefit of intending social workers' it has grown along with social work and the public social services over the post-war period (Brown, 1976, p.18). The still close attachment of social administration teaching to social work training probably accounts in large measure for the focus of many definitions on individual and personal welfare and for the 'reluctance amongst authorities to move very far away from this position' (Pinker, 1971, p.148). Thirdly, social policy analysts are also confined by the path that the subject has taken in the post-war period, the particular subject matter and expertise that have gained legitimacy and approval *within* social administration. Of course, the same is true for social science disciplines in general, including sociology. The problem here is that some of the demarcation disputes between different disciplines have led to a failure to apply some of the insights of economics and politics but particularly sociology, consistently to the study of social policy and social administration.

Limitations of Social Administration

Most conventional perspectives on social policy, therefore, would appear to have five main limitations (Townsend, 1975, pp. 2-3). There is first, the danger that the restriction to administrative definitions of social policy and welfare will overlook important sources of social inequalities. For example, measures to meet the needs of low paid workers may be based on state tax or incomes or minimum wage policies, as well as through the social security system or wages councils. In addition, the problem may be tackled at source by employers in different industrial sectors, perhaps as a response to trade union pressure. On the other hand, attempts to redistribute resources through social policies in the public sector may be frustrated by opposing trends in other sectors of distribution, such as employer fringe benefits. In addition to meeting the needs of the low paid, state social security policies may also reinforce and perhaps encourage low pay through the creation of the poverty trap and the subsidy that is effectively given to low paying employers.

Some of the causes of low pay are closely related to industrial structure, the type and scale of production, which particularly influences the cohesiveness of the work-force. Low pay is also created in declining areas as the structure of industry changes, with the breaking-down of the skilled work-force and introduction of new production, often calling for part-time unskilled workers. But the industrial structure of an area does not simply change according to some law of nature. The state itself has a major role in determining the pattern of industry, through its investment and purchasing policies and through its industrial location policies. As some of the CDP projects have demonstrated forcefully, the living standards of individuals in local communities are intimately related to the complexion of local industry (which is in turn, of course, determined by national and international systems of distribution) (CDP PEC, 1979). Thus, *over time* industrial investment and production policies are more important than social security policies in determining living standards. It is crucial therefore, for social policy analysis to widen its focus to include not only the more explicit intentions of state re-location or regional development policies, but also the social consequences of all forms of investment. The study of the social *creation* and distribution of needs and dependencies is sadly under developed in social policy compared with the study of the institutional *responses* to those needs.

There is, secondly, a closely-related danger that the 'second face' of power, the importance of implicit as opposed to explicit decision making, will be ignored (Bachrach & Baratz, 1970 pp. 3–16). Those alternatives which are excluded from policy proposals are as much a part of social policy as the published record. Approaches which concentrate on the latter condone implicitly the prevailing distribution of power, as expressed in the political agenda. In the study of poverty the crucial interconnection between poverty and inequality may be forgotten in the overwhelming desire to make acceptable ameliorative proposals. Thus the structure of inequality may be accepted in the false belief that within it, the problem of poverty can be solved. As part of the social construction of the welfare state as necessarily beneficial, social problem solving may be carried on in isolation from a critique of the social structure. Services come to be seen as ends in themselves. It may then be argued that a service is inadequate, but never irrelevant. The social context is forgotten in the belief that the existing framework of service provision is the best starting point. Furthermore the role of individualized services in maintaining social divisions and the values which underpin them are rarely questioned within the traditional framework. Under a cloak of confidentiality social workers may serve as political atomizers. (They are of course politically atomized themselves, by service administrators.) Moreover, this cloak may be spuriously used to prevent alternative methods of action in direct conjunction with clients, while condoning, if not approving, the open discussion of clients' personal problems within the agency.

Thirdly, policies without explicit 'social' objectives may be ignored by policy analysts. Thus, for example, the transport policies of government, local authorities and private bus companies can have a significant impact on the well-being of citizens. Fourthly, it is clearly absurd to refer to state provision when defining *social* policy. Institutionalized social policies cover not only the welfare policies of the central and local state, but also those of industry and commerce and voluntary bodies as well. The statist tendency in traditional social administration is based on the dominance of the empirical description and evaluation of service provision; concentration that is on the explicit rationales of policies. That this stance inhibits the full analysis of the functioning of social policies is obvious from the growing body of literatures on the aspects of social control embodied in much public welfare provision, the 'dual role' of welfare (Piven & Cloward, 1972; Mencher, 1969).

Fifthly, in attempting to make comparisons among countries, the consideration of government intervention only, although apparently conceptually neat, tidy and manageable, may tell us very little about the welfare of citizens and the range of social institutions which have a bearing on welfare within those countries. To compare social policies in health care between Britain and the United States we must look at both public and private sectors including the medical policies of industry and the state, concentration on one alone will reveal only part of the real world of health care. But we must also study the even wider range of interests and institutions that are involved in the social creation of health and ill-health.

Paradoxically, therefore, the professed aim of social policy to maximize welfare is inhibited by its limited scope. It may ignore sources of inequality and diswelfares which fall outside of the realm of public policies. It does not provide an adequate framework in which to analyse those 'social' institutions which do not 'foster integration and discourage alienation' or which have dual functions (Titmuss, 1968, p. 22). It tends to be parochial, paying insufficient attention to systems of distribution in other countries. In the policy process this adds weight to the reaction against change and supports, and in turn is supported by 'ideological vested interests' (Mishra, 1977, p.8). This facilitates the rejection of solutions to similar problems in other countries. It also provides a distorted picture of the British welfare state as the 'best' solution (with some minor adjustments). The problem is, if the welfare state fails as it patently does in some respects, our social construction of it has become so entrenched that the only alternative appears to be the private market.

Towards a Definition of Social Policy and Social Welfare

Recent developments — such as the social consequences of economic liberalism in Britain and the US — have made it increasingly clear that it is fruitless to abstract for study 'social policies' as traditionally defined in terms of government activity. Even if a broader definition of 'social services' is employed, in line with Titmuss' social division of welfare thesis, it is likely that analysis will still be concerned, at best, with only one part (although usually a significant part) of a many-faceted problem. Social reality cannot be divided neatly into 'social' and 'non-social' institutions. Alternative criteria are needed to ensure that the analysis of welfare is more comprehensive than that possible within the prevailing framework of social administration. To be useful alternative conceptions of social policy must facilitate the analysis of the implicit as well as explicit intentions of state and non-state policies; they must encompass the institutions and processes which create, maintain and attempt to change the distribution of resources, and also provide a framework within which the impact of state policies may be assessed.

The Social Division of Welfare

The basis for an alternative approach to social policy is to be found in the seminal work of Titmuss. Subsequent development of the concept of social policy by Townsend and Donnison, both of whom have considered the *functions* and *outcomes* of government activities, built on Titmuss' historic work (Titmuss, 1963, pp. 34–55). There were two main features of this analysis. First, a consideration of the activities of government in terms of similarities of aims or effects rather than administrative convention. Thus, according to Titmuss:

> The definition . . . of what is a 'social service' should take its stand on aims; not on the administrative methods and institutional devices employed to achieve them (Titmuss, 1963, p.42).

Secondly, he included the policies and functions of other institutions, distinguishing social welfare, fiscal welfare and occupational welfare.

While these divisions remain important in the social construction of the welfare state as operating solely for the benefit of the poor, which I will return to later, there are some albeit slight and inconsistent signs that in the administration of the welfare state, the division between 'social' and 'fiscal' welfare is becoming blurred. For example, since 1978 the annual White Paper on the government's public expenditure plans has contained information on the tax relief and option mortgage subsidy to owner occupiers as well as subsidies to public sector tenants in local authority and new town housing and support through rent rebates and allowances (HMSO, 1979, p.100). The fact that this represents an apparent change of approach by the Treasury and an acceptance of the social division of welfare thesis (though only in part and that heavily qualified) was emphasised in the 1979 expenditure accounts:

> Public expenditure however presents only part of the picture. For an improved

understanding of the role of fiscal policy it is necessary to look also at certain of the reliefs embodied in the taxation system. Such reliefs can have broadly the same effect on the Government's borrowing requirement as public expenditure . . . there is a cse for saying that, where a tax relief benefits a particular group of tax-payers or a particular sector of the economy (HMSO, 1979, p. 17).

The White Paper went on to list, for the first time, the estimated cost of some direct tax allowances and reliefs. But while there are signs of change of policy at the Treasury concerning tax expenditures, the line dividing 'occupational' welfare from fiscal and social welfare continues to be fairly tightly drawn. The recently introduced 'motability' scheme, which provides adapted cars for disabled drivers on a leasing arrangement, would be counted as a social policy by most social administrators in the same what that the provision of purpose-built trikes was. But the exclusion of company cars from the analysis of social policies would follow from most definitions of the scope of social administration.

Although the force of the social division of welfare thesis is enduringly strong, particularly in explaining the social construction of welfare, Titmuss tended to limit his more detailed discussions to looking at social policies that are influenced directly or indirectly by government. When noting the great expansion in occupational welfare benefits in cash and in kind he reasoned that 'Their ultimate cost falls in large measure on the Exchequer' (Titmuss, 1963, p.50). While he classified occupational fringe benefits as 'social services', 'duplicating the overlapping social and fiscal welfare benefits' this classification appears to rest on the fact that they are subsidized by the state (Titmuss, 1963, p.51). 'Such provisions are legally approved by Government and, as in the case of fiscal welfare, they may be seen as alternative to extensions in social welfare. Their cost falls in large measure on the whole population' (Titmuss, 1968, p.192). In *The Gift Relationship* Titmuss' pioneering analysis encompassed altruism and the freedom of choice to give or not to give; but as Mishra argues, he inconsistently related this prescription to the need for the institution-alization of altruism and the structural barriers against such change (Mishra, 1977, pp. 14–15).

One major criticism that has been levelled at Titmuss' own analysis of the social division of welfare, is that while recognising the often self-interested exercise of professional power, he failed to sustain this analysis to include class conflict as a basis of social policy (Wedderburn, 1965, p.138; Sinfield, 1977, p.196). This lack of a framework in which to relate social development to the structure of social relations and the distribution of power, represents a major barier to the operationalization of this concept in the analysis of current developments in the production of inequality, such as the social exploitation of inflation through, for example, state policies on public sector wages and the uprating of social security benefits. (Lewis *et al.* 1975). The social production and reproduction of social problems and the attempts of the state at 'redistribution' must be examined in terms of the dominant interests at various levels in the policy system. The social division of welfare itself reflects the dominance of certain values in social organization and the social creation of various needs and their subsequent legitimation and socialization by the state; and reflects the social relationship between the state and the dominant class interests in society which, in turn, under-pin the development of the division of labour.

Social Policy and Social Distribution

What is it then that distinguishes *social* policies from other forms of policy? Social policies cannot be distinguished on the basis of their expressed rationales alone, on the explicit functions enshrined in official legislation and other rules, since institutions may serve dual functions. Pinker has isolated two major value orientations, the work ethic and welfare ethic, as the two extreme versions of the social contract. But he also points out that they are 'totally inoperable in their pure form' (Pinker, 1974, pp. 3–5). So, as social policy analysts we are concerned with the extent to which they conflict or overlap, often within the framework of a single social service, and therefore cannot define the scope of social policy on the basis of this linear continuum. It is not possible to divide policies neatly into market and non-market, egoistic and altruistic policies, with the implication that one set is 'bad' and the other 'good' or that they will always and everywhere be distinguishable.

The scope of social policy cannot rest on the identification of need or 'states of dependency' similar to those covered by the state, although they are an important part of the subject matter of social policy. If these criteria were employed we might include pensions provided by private companies, but not for example, company cars and clothing allowances. (Titmuss, 1968, p.193). It is at least questionable how far many of the fringe benefits offered by companies have been introduced in order to recognize states of dependency rather than to enhance status and avoid incomes policies. Although Titmuss argued that a substantial part of occupational welfare provision should be interpreted as the recognition of dependencies, he did note that they may also result from a 'drive to "buy" good human relations in industry.' (Titmuss, 1963, p.53). In a 'surprisingly candid' memorandum to the Chancellor after the 1976 Budget, the Engineering Employers Federation insisted:

> It must be recognized that the proliferation of fringe benefits of recent years has been entirely due to the excessive and unreasonable rates of British personal taxation, unparalleled in similar countries (Sinfield, 1976, p.31).

Since fringe benefits are being used in substitution for salary increases the obvious question arises: how should they be distinguished from wages in the analysis of social policies? Furthermore if fringe benefits are included as a now legitimate part of the study of social policy, why is it that the analysis of wage policy and wage structure is so under-developed? Thus the concern of social policy analysis should be as much with the processes by which needs are defined and created as with the social services institutionalized to meet some of them.

The concept of social policy being formulated implicitly here rests on the *distributional* implications or outcomes of the decisions and activities of a wide range of social institutions and groups. This is not to imply that social policy should be concerned only with the distribution of income and wealth, but rather with the production *and* distribution of a wide range of *social resources,* including income assets, property, health, education, environment, status and power. (Townsend, 1974, pp. 15–42). It is assumed that the extent to which these resources are distributed equally or unequally relative to need will determine the pattern of *welfare* in any society. Thus the essence of social policy is the social production and distribution of inequality and welfare. The normative concept of *social welfare* implied here hypothesises a state of individual health and well-being and of social solidarity and co-operation which is in large measure dependent on a socially just distribution of resources. Although significant advances are possible within the existing framework of social distribution a more equal distribution of these resources is dependent on the introduction of radically different forms of social organization (Mishra, 1975, pp. 288–289).

'Social policy' might be defined therefore, as the rationale underlying the development and use of social institutions and groups which affect the distribution of resources, status and power between different individuals and groups in society. Thus, social policy is concerned both with the values and principles which govern distribution as well as their outcome. The task of the social policy analyst is to evaluate the distributional impact of existing policies on social welfare, their implicit and explicit rationales, their impact on social relations and the implications of policy proposals. And his or her concern will be less with the problems of individuals or clients, than with the often multi-faced behaviour of organizations, professions and classes; and less with the consequences of an unequally shared welfare as with the social production of inequality. Once it is grasped that welfare depends on a wide range of social policies both within a society and outside of it, the concept of social policy becomes both exciting and daunting. Some of the problems associated with this conception are discussed in the next section.

The Development of a Radical Approach to Social Policy

In recent years various authorities have begun to set out the basis for a broader approach to social policy. The political economy of social policy discussed here, encompassing all policies which affect the social production and distribution of welfare, is derived chiefly from Townsend's work. He has defined and conceptualized social policy as 'the underlying as well as the professed rationale by which social institutions and groups are developed or created to ensure social preservation or development' (Townsend, 1976, p.6). Social policy is therefore conceived of as a blueprint for the management of society towards social ends. But in the definition of social policy outlined in this paper the concept of social distribution, including the production as well as consumption of welfares, is related centrally to the notion of social policy; and the blueprint, or more accurately, sets of policies which are rarely expressed formally, embody social development in as far as they are concerned with the development of welfare. Clearly social policies may represent social retraction or retrenchment as much as social development.

The sort of development in the scope of social policy suggested in this paper has three main advantages which, in turn, may begin to liberate the study of social policy — as traditionally pursued in social administration, sociology, economics, politics and other social sciences — from its overriding concern with government action in public welfare. In the first place, social policies have hidden intentions, unintended effects, underlying values as well as explicit aims. Indeed part of the challenge of social policy analysis is that few social policies 'are expressed openly' and even those that are, may become adapted, modifed and diverted. Policies such as sexual divisions in social security provision and employment are rarely expressed openly. Secondly, social policies are not only the concern of government, but *all* social institutions and groups which determine the distribution of resources and life chances. Thirdly, this conceptualization of social policy focusses attention on differences of status, power and rewards between individuals and groups in society; broadly, on inequalities of condition and their sources, and thereby provides a framework for the study of welfare within and between societies. The main dimension for such comparisons would be social class, but other important sources of division in society, such as sex and race, would also provide bases for comparative analyses of social inequality. It is *these* social divisions that are so significant to individual and social welfare, rather than the institutional divisions of government intervention which post Titmuss social administration has tended to concentrate on.

The adoption of this approach to social policy also questions other assumptions underlying some conventional approaches which were discussed earlier. For example, it cannot be assumed that all social policies have beneficial effects even to a majority still less to all. It cannot be assumed that all of the outcomes from social policies are planned and that the growth of social welfare and social policies are necessarily tied to economic growth. Nor that growth creates equality. This approach to social policy therefore, not only asks two fundamental questions: who benefits from social policies? And who pays, in terms of freedom, control and command over resources? But also goes on to link the social production and distribution of inequality with the social class and reward structure.

Implications for the Analysis of Social Policies

One of the practical implications of this approach is that institutions hitherto ignored by social policy analysts, such as trade unions, banks and insurance companies must become part of their considerations. For example, trade unions not only pursue improvements in the pay and working conditions of their members but provide advice services and representation of a similar kind to those provided by law centres and welfare rights workers. Simultaneously, in other words, they may, like their members embody motives of self-interest and altruism. This conflict is demonstrated clearly by the different roles adopted by trade unions in relation to incomes policies (Crouch, 1978). How far do they operate to protect and widen differentials in income and occupational benefits as ends in themselves? Or pursue broader social goals, for example by helping the low paid by reducing differentials eroded by some incomes policies, and also by arguing for increased public expenditure.

Institutions and services hitherto considered to be central to the study of social policy might also be considered in a fresh light. For example, an analysis of residential care for the elderly might look beyond the institutional setting and its organisation and the health status or 'dependency' of residents and non-residents. It could begin from an examination of the role of elderly people in society, with an analysis of differentially applied social status as well as with individual need. It would be concerned with the distribution of a range of resources, including income and security, between elderly people and the rest of society, and amongst the elderly according to lifelong social status. It would include an analysis of the conflict between control and care, between institutionalization and dignity. It would encompass an examination of the interests of professional and other groups involved in caring for the elderly, combined with an examination of the exercise of the caring function. Lastly it would be interested in the 'benefit' to society of the increasing use of institutional care for the elderly and the social costs borne by that group.

A further example is provided by an examination of the problem of poverty. The policy analyst may be concerned, for example, with the overall distribution of income and income producing assets; with the social creation of poverty and dependent status, with labour market policies, with the employment and wage policies of enterprises in the public and private sector, with access to employment and various other socially esteemed income producing statuses, with differential rights of access to other resources which buttress income, with discrimination against various social groups, with taxation policy and the role of the state in such areas as industrial investment and job creation as well as social security, and more controversially, with the pricing policies of industry.

The Social Construction of Welfare

The influence of the state in social policy and social welfare is obviously very signficant, but why has the very limited conception of social policy and social administration as public policy and the administration of public welfare dominated thinking in the post-war period, while at the same time the social forces underpinning state activity have remained relatively unexplored? An adequate explanation would include: analysis of assumptions underlying the social construction of the welfare state; analysis of the assumptions concerning consensus over the goals and achievements of social policy and the welfare state; analysis of the assumptions underlying the conception of a steady progress towards welfare; and analysis of the role of the state under advanced capitalism. There is space here only to touch briefly on the former.

The hold that benign functionalism maintains on academic, official and popular conceptions of social policy is perhaps best expressed in the end of ideology thesis. Writing in the late 1950s and early 1960s social scientists such as Bell and Aron were arguing that the major ideological battles were over and that the welfare provisions of all countries would converge (Bell, 1965). Despite the rise of ideological conflict in the late 1960s and the albeit slight prospect of open conflict in the political arena, in the early 1980s, inspired by the Thatcher/Joseph 'social market' approach to social welfare; this thesis still exerts a powerful influence on how many people perceive the welfare state and social policy.

The end of ideology thesis is perhaps, most pervasive amongst those administering the welfare state, as the following quotation from the first annual report of the Supplementary Benefits Commission (itself abolished by the Conservative government in 1980) demonstrates:

> Whatever the starting points of their social security systems, all governments endeavour gradually to correct their weaknesses, and thus to produce patterns of service which tend to converge. It is no accident that the main debates about social security in Britain have for a decade or more focussed on pensions, on family support, and more recently on the needs of the severely disabled. Contentious though they originally were, these debates have at last created a large measure of consensus among the political parties . . . (HMSO, 1976, p.11).

The attractiveness of this thesis to civil servants priding themselves on neutrality and impartiality is obvious.

Stemming from the influence of consensus theory is the idea that the welfare state has been achieved and that in an international context, the British solution is the best, the 'envy of the world'. The battle was won during the war and in the immediate post-war period, all that is needed now as the above quotation illustrates, are various technical adjustments to ensure smooth running, the 'finetuning of heaven' (Rose, 1978, p.3).

Rather than a dynamic concept, over which some groups may have views at variance with those of others and which may itself create inequalities, or be an instrument through which the effects of social changes are managed, the welfare state is seen as a once-and-for-all achievement, that by definition, *creates* welfare. Marshall notes that 'The British Welfare State was the culmination of a long movement of social reform that began in the last quarter of the nineteenth century' (Marshall, 1975, p.99). Other writers have mapped out 'milestones' along the road to the achievement of the welfare state. In this social construction the welfare state is portrayed as being synonymous with social policy and social welfare and represents only government intervention; and furthermore, it is assumed that this intervention is intended only to maximize welfare. Thus as Titmuss noted, the welfare state depends on a 'stereotype of social welfare which represents only the more visible parts of the real world of welfare' (Titmuss, 1963, p.53). Herein lies the enduring force of the social division of welfare thesis (if not the exact structure outlined by Titmuss). We, and the recipients of public welfare in particular, are confronted with only public expenditure on the welfare state, not public expenditure on, for example, tax reliefs and on subsidising fringe benefits nor private expenditure on welfare provision. If they are debated openly then the latter are legitimated by dominant assumptions and ideology of capitalism, and the former stigmatized as a burden on the productive sector. As Sinfield argues the more successful this social construction of welfare is in disguising who really benefits, the less likely we are to accept the need for changes. (Sinfield, 1976, p.148). Growth of 'private' welfare provision for professional and other non-manual groups is seldom debated, though it is as surely paid for out of public contributions, through prices, as is the public sector of welfare, which is the subject of constant debate, paid for through taxation. But one is a legitimate form of social transfer, legitimated that is primarily by the exercise of individual choice, and the other is not.

The successful social construction of the welfare state in Britain creates reactions against both taxation and the able-bodied or undeserving poor. Blame is concentrated on the victims rather than the social structure. As well as the myth that the 'welfare state' has been achieved, or even that we are far advanced on this road, it is widely believed that 'true' poverty or deprivation no longer exists, or that only a small minority still need help. It is also believed that redistribution has been in one direction only, from rich to poor, and despite the large body of evidence to the contrary, that this has gone too far.

Social Planning and Social Priorities

Many of the limitations of the dominant social construction of welfare, as well as some of the contentious ideological questions concerning the welfare state, could remain partially hidden or repressed so long as economic growth was providing, in effect, increasing resources for *both* the public and private sectors. With an ever expanding cake welfare state services provided no real challenge to prevailing capitalist goals and values. (It may be argued in fact that functionalist theories like convergence and the end of ideology, with their timeless assumption that things are getting better depend on economic growth for their credibility.) As soon as growth collapsed questions were bound to be raised about expenditure on public, high profile welfare benefits and services, This is precisely what happened, of course, in the latter half of the 1970s and early 1980s. This is not to support, however, the notion that economic growth is a necessary prerequisite for social expenditure (expenditure that is on the social services). The point I am making is crucial. It is the social construction of social policy under capitalism and especially the subordinate position it has been assigned in relation to economic policy, which has determined its reliance on economic growth rather than any scientific or natural law. Adherence to this view of social policy has been common to a wide range of people on the left, right and centre of the political spectrum in post-war Britain. The collapse of growth then, and the related 'fiscal crisis' of the state, were important reasons underlying the reduction in the growth of resources for the social services first by the Labour government and subsequently by the Conservative government elected in 1979 (O'Connor, 1973). Not only were cuts made in individual spending programmes but changes were made in the public expenditure process to increase the central control of resources.

The implications of the dominant social construction of social policy and social welfare and particularly the relationship between economic and social policy for the future of the welfare state are very serious. It cannot be assumed that growth will increase dramatically in the near future and without it there is no prospect for a substantial injection of resources into the social services, quite apart from the strictures imposed by the current government's antithesis to the welfare state. In a period of nil or negative growth the case for social priority planning is even stronger than usual. This would entail the comparison of expenditure with social indicators such as need, and the distribution of welfare expenditure to meet the most pressing needs first. But changes in the control of public expenditure, including the introduction of cash limits in 1976 and the abandonment of programme analysis and reviews in 1979 (one of the few mechanisms for evaluating policies) have made this task even more difficult. (Glennerster, 1981, pp. 31–52). In view of the importance of assessing priorities to social policy and social planning it is surprising that the analysis of priorities has not been pursued further. Again, the relatively sturdy growth in social spending over the post-war period disguised, to some extent, the need for priority planning. Social priorities have rarely been spelt out as a basis for the allocation of resources. An assessment of social progress and social development has not been attempted consistently in Britain and this means both that cuts in social spending programmes are even easier to carry out and that they are potentially more damaging to those affected.

The prospect is that social expenditure will be further cut back. The predominant economic ideology in the early 1980s is based on the assumption that the market is a superior system of distribution and the most efficient mechanism for allocating goods and services. This effectively places the market mechanism above alternative 'non-market' systems of distribution and ignores the point that both may operate tyrannically. This ideology has fostered attempts at reasserting the influence of the market in welfare, including the move towards 'privatization'. At best such developments cannot answer and may positively hinder, the need for the planned allocation of social expenditure and the achievement of social priorities; at worst they seriously threaten the welfare of the social service clients and potential clients.

The decline of growth and appearance of policies hostile to public expenditure has exposed the absence of long-term strategic planning in relation to explicit social objectives in the distribution of resources for welfare. As the House of Commons Social Services Select Committee recently pointed out, this goal of social planning is far from being achieved:

> This seems to be a clear indication that rather than deciding upon an overall strategy and then adjusting the various elements of the strategy accordingly, policy is made by taking decisions about specific terms (according to whatever criteria may be in use) and then having a retrospective look to see what their combined effect turned our to be (HMSO, 1980, p.xviii).

Indeed according to the select committee the DHSS has no comprehensive information system which would permit the public to assess the effects of changes in expenditure levels and patterns on the quality and scope of services provided. This is a major indictment of the efficacy of the planning record of the main social spending department. Attention has been concentrated on reducing public expenditure as a proportion of national income rather than establishing nationally agreed priorities according to which expenditure may be reduced or expanded. As a consequence not only has social expenditure begun to be reduced, but also the links between social changes, such as increased unemployment, and the demand for expenditure in other sectors, such as health care have not been explored in detail (HMSO, 1980, p.vii).

One important reason for the absence of strategic social planning in this country is the fact that the main form of social planning is carried on in the expenditure planning machinery which itself operates against the achievement of more developed social planning. The Public Expenditure Survey Committee (PESC) system is dominated by the Treasury and the outcome dependent to a large extent on departmental tactics and bargaining skill rather than the detail of programmes. (Bosanquet & Townsend, 1980, p.3). Moreover because it is easier to shift the burden of expenditure onto future generations the PECS system tends to encourage shortsightedness, hence the disproportionate cuts in recent years in capital expenditure. Therefore the expenditure planning process which has evolved over the last 20 years, together with the relatively new tools of expenditure control, are counter-productive to the planned assessment of priorities.

In order to counteract some of the social consequences of economic management and to establish a basis for the planned achievement of social priorities, there is a need for a new social planning machinery. This would provide information on the social conditions of British society, critically assess the operation of public expenditure programmes and the priorities implied by spending, and present regular social accounts of the distributional consequences on changes in expenditure. The establishment of this innovative machinery requires, first, a recognition of the importance of social development as well as economic growth, and therefore the reconstitution of national priorities. Secondly, a recognition of the fact that increases in public expenditure are not *necessarily* beneficial to welfare. The employment of more and better paid professional groups in education, health and personal social services has not been matched by universal increases in the welfare of citizens. Thirdly the introduction of this machinery requires a change in attitudes towards public expenditure, the recognition of much expenditure as an achievement rather than as a burden, and therefore a revision of puhblic expenditure accounting.

There is a need then, for social indicators of the condition of society to enable the assessment of social well-being and progress and secondly, measures of the effectiveness of social spending, in order to assess the performance of society in meeting social need. The process of conducting regular analyses of social well-being would also have the important effect of exposing the extent of social deprivation to the public. If such deprivations are to be tackled and public support given to the raising of revenue to achieve this, they must be publicly perceived as important. The next and most crucial stage is to translate the outcome of this process into social policies. The collapse of growth has emphasised the urgency of this task. It is not simply a matter of deciding *how much* of our national resources can be devoted to a particular social programme but of enquiring first what the aims of individual programmes are and how these can best be achieved.

Conclusion

This paper arose out of a growing personal dissatisfaction with prevailing definitions of the scope of social policy, which appeared to be thrown into greater question by recent developments in British society — developments such as the social exploitation of inflation and economic management, the social creation and management of different forms of dependency.

Social administrators, in concentrating their minds on the public welfare bureaucracy, have tended to overlook other important aspects of state policies. The study of social policy is not simply a description, perhaps accompanied by a critique of administrative institutions and processes, but an analysis of the structures and processes of wider society which create a given distribution of resources and in turn, regulate the institutions through which this distribution is managed. It is not suggested that social policy analysts should study every aspect of policy but that overall a broader range of analyses are desirable. Without a change of focus social administrators will continue to be concerned with only one part — and currently a shrinking part — of the real world of social welfare.

References

Bachrach, P. and Baratz, M.S. (1970) *Power and Poverty*, Oxford University Press, London.

Baker J. (1979) Social conscience and social policy, in *Journal of Social Policy*, Vol. 8, No. 2.

Bell, D. (1965) *The End of Ideology*, The Free Press, New York.

Bosanquet, N and Townsend, P. (eds.) (1980) *Labour and Equality*, Heinemann, London.

Briggs, A. (1961) The welfare state in historical perspective, in *European Journal of Sociology*, Vol. 2, No. 2.

Brown, M. (1969) *Introduction to Social Administration in Britain*, Hutchinson, London.

Brown, M. (1976) *Introduction to Social Administration in Britain* (3rd edn) Hutchinson, London.

Community Development Project (1977) *The Costs of Industrial Change*, London.

CDP Political Economic Collective (1979) *The State and the Local Economy*, Nottingham.

Crouch, C. (1975) The drive for equality? Experience of incomes policy in Britain, in L. N. Lindberg *et al.* (eds.), *Stress and Contradiction in Modern Capitalism*, D. C. Heath, Lexington.

Crouch, C. (1978) *Notes on Incomes Policy and Social Policy*, Social Administration Association Annual Conference, July.

Donnison, D. V. (1977) *The Development of Social Administration*, Bell, London.

George, V. and Wilding, P. (1976) *Ideology and Social Welfare*, Routledge and Kegan Paul, London.

Ginsburg, N. (1979) *Class, Capital and Social Policy*, Macmillan, London.

Glennerster, H. (1981) From containment to conflict? Social planning in the seventies, in *Journal of Social Policy*, Vol. 10, No. 1.

Gough, I. (1979) *The Political Economy of the Welfare State*, Macmillan, London.

Heisler, H. (ed.) (1977) *Foundations of Social Administration*, Macmillan, London.

HMSO (1976) *Supplementary Benefits Commission, Annual Report*, 1975, London.

HMSO (1979) *The Government's Expenditure Plans 1979–80 to 1982–83*, Cmnd 7439, London.

HMSO (1980) Social Services Committee, *The Government's White Papers on Public Expenditure: The Social Services*, Vol. 1, HC702-1, London.

Hyman, R. (1974) Inequality, ideology and industrial relations, in *British Journal of Industrial Relations*, Vol. 12.

Le Grand, J. (1982) *The Strategy of Equality*, Allen and Unwin, London.

Lewis, P. *et al.* (1975) *Inflation and Low Incomes*, Fabian Society, London.

Marsh, D. C. (1965) *An Introduction to the Study of Social Administration*, Routledge and Kegan Paul, London.

Marshall, T. H. (1975) *Social Policy*, (4th edn.) Hutchinson, London.

McBeath, G. (1957) *Can Social Policies be Rationally Tested?*, Hobhouse Memorial Lecture.

Mencher, S. (1969) *From poor law to poverty programme*, University of Pittsburgh Press, Pittsburgh.

Miller, S. M. (1975) Planning: Can it make a difference in capitalist America?, in *Social Policy*, September/October.

Miller, S. M. and Rein, M. (1975) Can income Redistribution work, in *Social Policy*, May/June.

Mishra, R. (1975) Marx and welfare, in *Sociological Review*, Vol. 23, No. 2.

Mishra, R. (1977) *Society and Social Policy*, Macmillan, London.

O'Connor, J. (1973) *The Fiscal Crisis of the State*, St. James' Press, London.

Pinker, R. A. (1971) *Social Theory and Social Policy*, Heinemann, London.

Pinker, R. A. (1974) Social policy and social justice, in *Journal of Social Policy*, January.

Piven, F. and Cloward, R. A. (1972) *Regulating the Poor*, Tavistock, London.

Rein, M. (1976) *Social Science and Public Policy*, Penguin, Harmondsworth.

Rose, H. (1978) *Towards a Political Economy of Welfare*, paper presented to the Research Committee on Poverty, Welfare and Social Policy, World Congress of Sociology.

Sinfield, A. (1976) *Transmitted Deprivation and the Social Division of Welfare*, Report to DHSS/SSRC Working Party on Transmitted Deprivation, November.

Slack, K. M. (1966) *Social Administration and the Citizen*, Michael Joseph, London.

Titmuss, R. M. (1963) The social division of welfare, in *Essays on 'The Welfare State'*. Allen and Unwin, London.

Titmuss, R. M. (1968) *Commitment to Welfare*, Allen and Unwin, London.

Titmuss, R. M. (1970) *The Gift Relationship*, Allen and Unwin, London.

Titmuss, R. M. (1974) *Social Policy*, Allen and Unwin, London.

Townsend, P. (1974) Poverty as relative deprivation: resources and style of living, in Wedderburn, D. (ed.) *Poverty Inequality and Class Structure*, CUP, London.

Townsend, P. (1976) *Sociology and Social Policy*, Penguin, Harmondsworth.

Walker, A. and Townsend, P. (eds.) (1981) *Disability in Britain*, Martin Robertson, Oxford.

Wedderburn, D. (1965) Facts and theories of the welfare state, in Miliband, R. and Saville, J. (eds.), *The Socialist Register 1965*, Merlin Press, London.

Westergaard, J. (1979) Social policy and class inequality, in Miliband, R. and Saville, J. (eds.), *The Socialist Register 1978*, Merlin Press, London.

PART III

Planning and Resource Distribution

Introduction

Contrary to a widespread British assumption, within Western Europe the United Kingdom is one of the lowest spenders on health and social security as a percentage of its gross domestic product. In fact Alber shows that, in contrast to the Scandinavian states, Britain's position has fallen over the last thirty years. Social security systems and social welfare expenditure consist of a variety of universal flat-rate, earnings-related, and selective public assistance measures which are based on quite different sorts of contributory and taxation-based funding and effect correspondingly different levels of income redistribution.

There is no necessary relationship between the amount spent on health and social security and the mode of its distribution within a society. So a more sophisticated type of investigation is required to answer questions about the relationship between levels of economic growth and social expenditure and the use of the latter to effect egalitarian social policies. O'Higgins distinguishes the distributive patterns characterized by social service expenditure on social security, housing, health and education. He questions the crude conclusions conveyed by the radical critique of the welfare state as a means of charging all for what is most beneficial to the better-off — a critique of great value in the armoury of the radical right in its subsequent attack on the welfare state in favour of the market mechanism tempered by selective poor laws. Although social expenditure is most redistributive in the allocation of resources through social security and least through education, O'Higgins indicates that increasing redistribution from rich to poor may simply reflect increasing unemployment, when high employment is a preferable goal, or the fact that the lowest incomes tend to be received by elderly people who do not, in any case, have children still at school and therefore cannot be recipients of redistributed resources through education. In any case the labour market remains the primary means through which incomes are distributed and the primary question concerning equality in social service provisions, for example in health, is that of access not redistribution through the value of services. Taken as a whole social expenditure is mildly redistributive from rich to poor whereas the opposite would be the result of market-generated income for such social services.

Now, ironically, the greatest element of redistribution, although not necessarily the greatest amount which depends on the benefit levels, is represented by non-contributory poor relief, public assistance which in Britain has been redesignated as supplementary benefit. Bosanquet describes not only the rediscovery of poverty after the initial euphoria of welfare policies for, and experience of, improved living standards. What characterized the post-war period of economic management and growth was the marginalization of poor people in various deprived categories without political significance or influence. Contrary to Beveridge's proposals the national insurance scheme did not guarantee a basic income and a variety of means-tested allowances has remained a central feature of the British system of income maintenance. Current government policies during the most intense economic depression since the war have accentuated the general significance of the latter measures because of the extended periods of unemployment which effectively eject large numbers of ex-wage earners as well as their families from the unemployment benefit schemes at the same time as measures have been adopted to discourage the take-up of these benefits.

Alber indicates that irrespective of changing economic conditions, it is left of centre governments that have been most frequently associated with increased rates of social security expenditure since the war and particularly in those countries for which there is evidence of greatest familial instability. An exception to the latter is the United Kingdom. This is further evidence in support of Bosanquet's thesis concerning crises of commitment and retrenchment for it suggests that greater insecurity and dependency have not been matched by greater expenditure to meet such needs. Contrary to assertions that rising social expenditure is a particularly capitalist phenomenon, Alber shows that until the late 1960s, expenditure patterns in western and eastern Europe matched each other. It remains to be seen how effective divergent strategies may be in responding to the shared economic crises of more recent years. In any case rising levels of expenditure need not contradict Bosanquet's thesis because, when adjusted for inflation, they may actually represent falling real purchasing rates.

The differences in scale between social security expenditures in western Europe are reflected in expenditure on health care. Maynard shows that these national differences are reinforced by internal differences in the regional allocation of resources so that a general system of territorial injustice prevails. But the situation is more complicated than that. Resources spent on health care represent only one factor, the other two being the sorts of staff or agency that are provided and the actual outcome of that 'treatment' measured by improved health and needs met. Given the environmental, class and age-related patterns of morbidity and mortality and the apparently unrelated health service patterns of distribution, the scope for various dimensions of inequality is very considerable. In times of cost-constraint, those who command the service, in many cases the doctors through their crucial role in clinical decision making, became its rationing agents. In such a situation the evaluation of services becomes critically important because there is no clearly positive relationship between various forms of expensive treatment and the numbers of employed doctors and the recovery of patients or levels of mortality.

What is true of health services must also be largely true of personal social services in Britain. Webb and Wistow focus on the critically related processes of planning and resource allocation in the major attempt to effect change and development in both services through instituting the drive towards 'community care'. Depending on the point of emphasis on health or social services, and on the degree of government commitment to statutory service participation, so has emphasis been placed on the provision of alternative residential homes to relieve hospital beds for medical and nursing care, or the development of domiciliary services to support those in their own homes, or the compression of demand by resource restrictions without corresponding support for the 'informal carers' who are simply assumed to be a normal domestic resource.

Often concealed within the general discussion of community care policies are the very same people to whom Bosanquet refers, or parallel categories at the deprived end of the resource allocation system for which Maynard provides evidence. Most of the so-called 'priority' groups for whom community care under the aegis of local authority social services are sought, for example elderly infirm, mentally ill, mentally handicapped and physically handicapped, are just those categories for whom the national health services provides least. Although, since 1976, some measures have been introduced to reallocate resources between N.H.S. regions and districts and between health and social services, these date from a new planning era dominated by cost-constraints. Small allocations from national growth funds or earmarked grants can make a considerable difference to certain clients in particular places, but, as Webb and Wistow argue, there is little scope for the major realization of domiciliary support services and well-informed planning decisions without the resources for service assessment and the transformation of social and health service working and service delivery patterns. Community care as a means of compressing the market will simply impose more on those women who can be made to bear these domestic burdens and either abandon those who lack both financial and supportive human capital or continue to project them towards the long-stay sections of the health service whose inadequacy gave rise to the original community care policy thirty years ago.

Some Causes of Social Security Expenditure Developments in Western Europe 1949-1977[*]

Jens Alber

Common trends and national paths of welfare state development

The welfare state has recently become the subject of much scholarly and political debate. In all these debates there is little doubt that the social security schemes whose origins may be traced to the late 19th century still constitute the institutional backbone of present social policies. According to the definition of the I.L.O. social expenditures consist of the outlays for the following six programmes: social insurance (i.e. the schemes which try to protect the population against the standard risk of economic insecurity: old age or death of the family breadwinner, invalidity, sickness, occupational injuries, and unemployment); public health, public assistance; family allowances; benefits for civil servants; and benefits for war victims.

As Table 1 shows expenditure for these purposes averaged some 9% of GDP in Western Europe in 1949.[1] Only Austria, Belgium, France, and Germany had already surpassed the threshold of 10%, while the United Kingdom was close to it. All other nations had social expenditure ratios clearly below 10%, with a minimum value in Norway of 5.5%. In the 1950s all countries increased their shares of social spending in GDP, but the growth of the ratio remained modest. On average the social expenditure ratio rose by 2.1 percentage points, pushing the mean Western European ratio above 11% by 1960. In the 1960s the speed of growth doubled, with a marked acceleration in the second half of the decade. On average the social expenditure ratio rose by 4.4 percentage points in the 1960s. By 1970 social outlays averaged 15.8% of GDP. The maximum value —

[*]This research is based on a data collection which the author compiled for the forthcoming data handbook of the HIWED-project (Historical Indicators of the Western European Democracies). The project was directed by Peter Flora and financed by the Stiftund Volkswagenwerk. The data handbook will be published this year by Campus in Frankfurt under the title: 'State, Economy, and Society in Western Europe, 1815-1975'. The author gratefully acknowledges the many stimulating theoretical discussions with the project director, and the kind comments offered by his colleagues at the European University Institute, Maurizio Ferrera and Peter Mair.

Table 1   Social security expenditure ratios in Western Europe, 1949–1977

Year	AU	BE	DE	FI	FR	GE	IR	IT	NE	NO	SW	SZ	UK	Av.	S.D.
1977	21.1	25.5	24.0	19.3	25.6	23.4	18.3	22.8	27.6	19.6	30.5	16.1	17.3	22.4	4.1
1976	21.0	24.4	24.2	18.0	24.7	23.4	19.1	22.8	27.0	18.9	27.4	15.9	17.4	21.9	3.6
1975	20.2	23.6	22.4	16.1	24.1	23.5	19.7	23.1	26.8	18.5	26.2	15.1	16.2	21.2	3.7
1974	*18.2*	20.9	21.0	*15.4*	*21.6*	*20.3*	*15.8*	*21.4*	*24.8*	*17.8*	24.4	*13.9*	*14.6*	19.2	3.4
1973	18.0	20.0	20.9	15.0	20.8	18.9	13.5	19.0	22.8	18.0	21.5	12.5	14.6	18.1	3.1
1972	18.2	19.4	20.5	15.1	20.3	18.5	*13.6*	20.1	22.3	17.5	20.7	10.4	*14.1*	17.7	3.3
1971	19.0	18.5	18.7	14.3	15.5	17.4	12.6	18.5	21.1	16.7	20.5	10.3	13.8	16.7	3.1
1970	18.8	18.1	16.6	13.1	15.3	17.0	11.6	16.3	20.0	15.5	18.8	10.1	13.8	15.8	2.8
1969	19.5	17.8	16.9	12.9	15.1	17.8	11.1	16.4	19.5	13.6	17.8	10.3	13.7	15.6	2.9
1968	19.4	18.2	15.6	13.3	14.4	18.3	11.1	16.0	18.8	12.9	17.1	9.4	*13.4*	15.2	3.0
1967	*18.8*	17.3	14.3	12.7		18.5	11.3	15.2	18.3	12.0	15.8	9.4	12.6	(14.7)	
1966	18.1	16.5	13.2	11.6	15.9	17.2	10.6	16.8	16.9	11.0	14.6	8.8	12.5	14.1	2.9
1965	17.8	16.1	12.2	10.6	15.8	16.6	10.3	14.8	15.7	10.9	13.6	8.5	*11.7*	13.4	2.8
1964	*17.6*	14.5	12.8	10.0	15.4	16.1	10.2	12.9	*14.5*	10.7	13.1	8.4	11.9	12.9	2.6
1963	16.2	15.3	12.4	9.8	15.1	15.9	9.9	12.7	13.6	10.6	12.3	7.8	11.2	12.5	2.5
1962	15.8	15.2	12.2	9.7	14.5	*15.6*	9.9	11.9	11.8	10.1	11.3	7.8	11.2	12.1	2.4
1961	14.7	15.3	10.9	*9.1*	14.0	15.0	9.7	11.4	*11.4*	9.4	10.9	7.7	10.9	11.6	2.4
1960	13.8	15.3	11.1	8.7	13.4	16.3	9.6	11.7	11.1	9.4	11.0	7.5	11.0	11.4	2.3
1959	14.5	15.6	11.7	*9.3*	13.4	16.9	10.1	11.9	11.0	9.5	*11.0*	7.6	*10.9*	11.7	2.5
1958	14.4	14.7	11.7	9.0	*13.5*	15.9	10.3	11.5	*11.2*	8.9	11.0	7.7	9.87	11.6	2.5
1957	13.1	13.3	10.5	9.0	13.7	14.4	10.1	10.6	10.1	8.0	10.5	7.5	9.6	10.9	2.3
1956	12.9	13.1	10.4	7.9	13.7	*14.2*	9.5	10.5	8.3	7.5	10.1	7.1	9.7	10.4	2.3
1955	12.8	*13.2*	9.8	*7.6*	13.4	13.6	9.3	10.0	8.4	7.5	9.9	6.8	9.5	10.2	2.4
1954	13.7	13.7	9.8	7.5	13.2	13.9	9.0	10.5	7.6	7.3	9.4	6.7	9.7	10.1	2.5
1953	14.5	13.6	9.8	8.1	12.9	14.1	8.9	9.8	7.6	7.1	8.9	6.4	10.2	10.1	2.6
1952	14.2	12.5	9.5	7.4	12.6	13.7		9.2	7.9	6.2	8.4	6.4	9.4	(9.7)	
1951	12.9	11.7	8.2	6.3		14.8		8.5	7.1	5.7	7.7	6.0	9.9	(9.1)	
1950	12.4	12.5	8.4	6.7				8.5	7.1	5.7	8.3		10.0	(9.3)	
1949	11.6	11.9	8.1	6.7				8.2	7.1	5.5	8.2			(9.2)	

Breaks in statistical concepts which impair calculation of annual changes are indicated by the use of italics.

20% in the Netherlands — was twice as high as the minimum level reached in Switzerland (10%).

Notwithstanding the marked growth of the 1960s social spending continued to increase its share in GDP by another 6.6 percentage points in the 1970s. As Table 2 shows the pace of growth of the social expenditure ratio has in fact been increasing consistently throughout all five quinquennial periods since 1950. Departing from the modest increase of 0.9 percentage points in the first half of the 1950s it accelerated to an impressive peak of 5.4 percentage points in the first half of the 1970s.[2]

Table 2 Quinquennial increases of the average Western European social expenditure ratio

1950—55	0.9	1950—60	2.1
1955—60	1.2		
1960—65	2.0	1960—70	4.4
1965—70	2.4		
1970—75	5.4	1970—77	6.6
1975—77	(1.2)		

By 1977 the average Western European social expenditure ratio had reached 22.4% of GDP. Sweden was the biggest social spender with an expenditure ratio of 30.5%. Switzerland spent least with a ratio of 16.1%. Only three other nations — Finland (19.3%), Ireland (18.3%), and the United Kingdom (17.3%) remained below the level of 20% (cf. Table 1).

Throughout the post-war period phase-specific variations in the pace of annual increases of the expenditure ratio are very similarly distributed over the 13 countries (see Table 3). On average the GDP share of social spending increased by half a percentage point every year. Five phases stand out as periods of accelerated growth in several countries: the years 1952-53 (average increases of 0.68 and 0.42 percentage points); 1957-58 with consecutive increments of 0.52 and 0.68 percentage points; 1966-68 with increases of 0.77, 0.73 and 0.58, respectively; 1971-72 with a growth of 0.99 and 0.67 percentage points, and the period 1974-76 in which the expenditure ratio jerked up by 0.97, 1.82 and 0.77 points.

The generality of these phases of accelerated growth is striking. In 1952-53 9 of the 13 countries witnessed above average increases of 0.7 percentage points or more, In 1957-58 only France, Switzerland, and the United Kingdom deviated from the general pattern of accelerated growth. In the second half of the 1960s the expenditure ratio rose overproportionately in all countries without exception. In 1971-72 only Austria, Switzerland, and the United Kingdom abstained from heavy increases, whereas the upsurge of the

Table 3 Annual changes of the GDP share of social security expenditure in Western Europe*

Year	AU	BE	DE	FI	FR	GE	IR	IT	NE	NO	SW	SZ	UK	Av.
1977	0.1	1.1	-0.2	1.3	1.3	0	-0.8	0	0.6	0.7	3.1	0.2	-0.3	0.55
1976	0.8	0.8	1.8	1.9	1.9	-0.1	-0.6	-0.3	0.2	0.4	1.2	0.8	1.2	0.77
1975	2.0	2.7	1.4	0.7	0.7	3.2	3.9	1.7	2.0	0.7	1.8	1.2	1.6	1.82
1974	0.3	0.9	0.1	0.2	0.2	1.6	2.1	1.7	1.4	0.6	2.9	0.7	-0.1	0.97
1973	-0.2	0.6	0.4	-0.1	-0.1	0.4	-0.1	-1.1	0.5	0.5	0.8	2.1	0.5	0.32
1972	-0.8	0.9	1.8	0.8	0.8	1.1	0.3	1.6	0.8	0.8	0.2	0.1	0.3	0.67
1971	0.2	0.4	2.1	1.2	1.2	0.4	1.0	2.2	1.1	1.2	1.7	0.2	0	0.99
1970	-0.7	0.3	-0.3	0.2	0.2	-0.8	0.5	-0.1	0.5	1.9	1.0	-0.2	0.1	0.20
1969	0.1	-0.4	1.3	-0.4	-0.4	-0.5	0	0.4	0.7	0.7	0.7	0.9	0.3	0.26
1968	0.6	0.9	1.3	0.6	0.6	-0.5	-0.2	0.8	0.5	0.9	1.3	0	0.8	0.58
1967	0.9	0.8	1.1	1.1	0.9	1.3	0.7	-1.6	1.4	1.0	1.2	0.6	0.1	0.73
1966	0.3	0.4	1.0	1.0	1.0	0.6	0.3	2.0	1.2	0.1	1.0	0.3	0.8	0.77
1965	0.2	1.6	-0.6	0.6	0.6	0.5	0.1	1.9	1.2	0.2	0.5	0.1	-0.4	0.50
1964	0	-0.8	0.4	0.2	0.3	0.2	0.3	0.2	0.2	0.1	0.8	0.6	0.7	0.25
1963	0.4	0.1	0.2	0.1	0.6	0.3	0	0.8	1.8	0.5	1.0	0	0	0.45
1962	0.9	-0.1	1.3	0.6	0.5	0	0.2	0.5	0.4	0.7	0.4	0.1	0.3	0.45
1961	0.9	0	-0.2	0.3	0.6	0.2	0.1	-0.3	0.2	0	-0.1	0.2	-0.1	0.14
1960	-0.7	-0.3	-0.6	-0.3	0	-1.3	-0.5	-0.2	0.1	-0.1	0	-0.1	0.1	-0.30
1959	0.1	0.9	0	-0.3	-0.1	-0.6	-0.2	0.4	-0.2	0.6	0	-0.1	0.9	0.12
1958	1.3	1.4	1.2	0.3	-0.2	1.0	0.2	0.9	0.9	0.9	0.5	0.2	0.2	0.68
1957	0.2	0.2	0.1	1.1	0	-1.5	0.6	0.1	1.8	0.5	0.4	0.4	-0.1	0.52
1956	0.1	-0.1	0.6	0.3	0.3	0.2	0.2	0.5	-0.1	0	0.2	0.3	0.2	0.21
1955	-0.9	-0.2	0	0	0.2	-0.4	0.3	-0.5	0.1	0.2	0.5	0.1	-0.2	-0.06
1954	-0.8	0.1	0	-0.6	0.3	-0.3	0.1	0.7	0	0.2	0.5	0.3	-0.5	0.0
1953	0.3	1.1	0.3	0.7	0.3	-0.2		0.6	-0.3	0.9	0.5	0	0.8	(0.42)
1952	1.3	0.8	1.3	1.1		0.4		0.7	0.8	0.5	0.7	0.4	-0.5	(0.68)
1951	0.5	-0.8	-0.2	-0.4		-0.9		0	0	0	-0.6		-0.1	(-0.25)
1950	0.8	0.6	0.3	0				0.3	0	0.2	0.1			(0.29)

*Annual changes do not correspond to the differences of the ratios reported in Table 1, if there were changes of statistical concepts. All changes reported here rely on identical concepts. The years in which breaks of the statistical concepts occurred are marked in Table 1.

expenditure ratio around 1975 was again a general phenomenon shared by all countries.

After 1975 the pace of growth began to slow down again. Several nations saw either stagnation (Austria, Switzerland) or even decreases of the GDP share of social outlays in 1976/77 (Denmark, Germany, Ireland, Italy, United Kingdom). Whether this denotes a turn of the secular trend towards welfare state expansion remains to be seen. In the past, similar phases of stagnation (1954–55, 1959–60, 1969–70) were only temporary and did not halt the long-term trend towards expansion.

The post-war period was thus characterized by a general pattern of social expenditure growth throughout the Western European democracies. Not only did social spending consistently increase its share in GDP, but the pace of this increase also accelerated over time. These common tendencies are, however, accompanied by some important national variations. In fact the Western European welfare states have not become more similar during the phase of general expansion. If we take the standard deviation of the social expenditure ratio as indicator, there is no trend towards convergence but towards increasing heterogeneity instead (see Table 1).

The increasing heterogeneity of social expenditure levels was accompanied by distinct national patterns of welfare state development which significantly changed the rank order of high and low spending countries over time (see Table 4). Only the 1950s were a period of outspoken stability in which all countries practically maintained their relative positions. Throughout the decade neither the four leading social spenders with expenditure ratios above 10% from the outset (Germany, Belgium, Austria, and France) nor the three laggards (Finland, Switzerland, and Norway) were replaced by other nations. The rank order correlation between the positions held in 1950 and 1960 is correspondingly high (0.90).

The 1960s saw much greater dynamics of change. With heavy increases of their social expenditure ratios the Netherlands and Sweden moved into top positions, whereas Norway climbed up by three ranks. Germany, France and the United Kingdom, on the other hand, increased their ratios only modestly and consequently moved down in the rank order of Western Europe nations. In 1970, Germany, the long standing pioneer of social policies in Europe, found itself in the fith position, whereas the United Kingdom had dropped from the fifth place occupied in 1950 to the tenth position. In the 1970s Sweden and France dynamically expanded the welfare state whereas Austria, the other European pioneer of social policies beside Germany, was much more restrictive and fell behind most other nations. In 1977 the rank occupied by each country bore little resemblance to its relative position in 1950 ($r_s = 0.35$).

Over the entire post-war period Sweden, the Netherlands, Denmark, Italy, and Norway (in this order) registered the highest increases of the social expenditure ratio. Sweden as the most dynamic country augmented its GDP share of social spending by more than 22 percentage points. The Netherlands were following

Table 4   Rank-order of social expenditure ratios in 1950, 1960, 1970 and 1977

	AU	BE	DE	FI	FR	GE	IR	IT	NE	NO	SW	SZ	UK
1950	3	2	7	11	4	1	9	6	10	13	8	12	5
1960	3	1	6.5	12	4	2	10	5	6.5	11	8.5	13	8.5
1970	3	4	6	11	9	5	12	7	1	8	2	13	10
1977	8	4	5	10	3	6	12	77	2	9	1	13	11

close behind with an increase of 20.5 percentage points. The other three dynamic countries just mentioned each had increases above 14 percentage points. In contrast, Austria, Ireland, Germany, and the United Kingdom only increased their ratios by less than 10 percentage points. This differential pattern of growth is partly a function of the initial levels reached in 1950. With the exception of Ireland, all nations with sluggish growth had already reached above average expenditure levels in 1950. On the other hand, all of the more dynamic countries had ranked among the half of welfare state laggards at that time (Italy and Denmark were in the middle positions 6 and 7). Despite this pattern the post-war process of welfare state expansion is not adequately described as a catch-up phenomenon in which previous laggards closed up on the pioneers. Rather, it is a process of interchange, whereby former laggards have moved into top positions (Sweden, Netherlands) while traditional leaders have fallen behind (Austria, Germany).

Following the phase of heavy growth in the 1970s the Western European welfare states may be classified into three groups with markedly different profiles of social expenditure: At one extreme we have nations with high levels of social expenditure and extended growth in the 1970s (Sweden, Netherlands, France, Belgium, Denmark); in an intermediate position we find countries with medium levels of social spending and only moderate recent growth (Austria, Germany, Italy); at the other extreme, finally, there are nations with low levels of social outlays and low or modest growth in the recent period of greatest welfare state expansion (United Kingdom, Norway, Finland, Ireland, Switzerland).

Besides the different paths of social expenditure development, there are some other important dimensions of variation among the Western European welfare states. Thus the functional distribution of expenditures may vary, the systems of financing show considerable heterogeneity, and there are important differences with respect to the institutional models of social policies pursued in each country.

In respect of the latter, we may distinguish three basic models of social policies. Universal social security schemes seek to provide for a minimum level of economic security for all citizens independent of their status in the labour market. In these systems all residents are entitled to benefits, and the social transfers have a strong egalitarian component in which flat rate benefits play a prominent role even though they may be complemented with earnings-related supplements. Status preserving systems, on the other hand, define welfare entitlements in strict relation to the beneficiaries' status in the labour market. In these systems the social programmes are frequently fragmented into a variety of special schemes for various occupational categories. Coverage is often tied to income-limits, and the earnings-related benefits transmit the relative position which the recipients have acquired in the labour market into the system of social transfers. Thus they tend to preserve rather than modify the structure of social inequality. Finally, there is the selective model of social policy which seeks to reserve public benefits to indigent groups which have no or scarce potential of effective self-help. In this model the definition of entitlements is highly restrictive, but the benefits have a strong redistributive effect.

Although this model figures prominently in recent political debates on the welfare state, it so far is of little practical relevance in Western Europe. None of the major welfare schemes is strictly selective in any of the countries studied here. Empirically only the social assistance programmes bear some resemblance to the model. The universal and the status preserving types of social policies are, however, pursued in actual practice. In Denmark, Finland, Norway, Sweden, and the United Kingdom the social programmes are shaped according to universalistic criteria. The coverage of their schemes frequently embrace all residents, the programmes are administratively unified, and benefits combine flat rate and earnings-related components. Austria, Belgium, France, Germany, and Italy, on the other hand, follow the status preservation approach. In these countries the social security systems are institutionally split up into a variety of special programmes for different occupational categories, coverage is often limited according to earnings, and the income-related benefits strongly reflect the position obtained in the labour market.

The Western European welfare states thus display many common features together with important national variations. All countries have established public schemes of social security which were considerably expanded in the post-war period. Today the welfare state is a common structural element of all Western European democracies. In 1977 even the country with the lowest GDP share of social expenditure (Switzerland) had reached a level of social outlays which no other European nation had attained before the mid-1960s. On the other hand, the dynamics of social expenditure growth differed markedly from country to country and the functional distribution of expenditures shows common elements together with distinct national patterns. The national systems of financing are widely discrepant and the institutional profiles of social policies show marked variation. Despite the common trend towards expansion the Western European welfare states do not seem to converge.

Both phenomena, common trends and national variations call for scholarly explanation.

Determinants of the growth of social expenditures

Although the social science literature on the welfare state has been blossoming in recent years, general theories of welfare state development are still in short supply. Maybe we can distinguish three broad streams in theorizing, i.e. the Marxist tradition, the Durkheimian tradition, and the perspective of political sociology. In the Marxist perspective the growth of the welfare state is rooted in the logic of capitalist development. From a Durkheimian view the expansion of social policies reflects the weakening of social integration and the anomic tendencies in modern societies. In the perspective of political sociology the growth of the welfare state is the by-product of the changing power relations in Western countries where labour unions and left parties have increasingly gained influence on governmental policies. *Capitalism, anomie* and *social democratic reformism* are thus respectively identified as the major sources of welfare state expansion.

If the Marxist theory which relates welfare state development to the logic of the capitalist mode of production were correct we would expect to find significant difference in the development of social security expenditure in Western European and Eastern European countries. Figure 1 compares this development to the post-war experience of Western European countries by showing the average values in Western and Eastern nations together with the respective maximum and minimum social expenditure ratios.[3]

1   The post-war development of the social expenditure ratio in Western and Eastern Europe

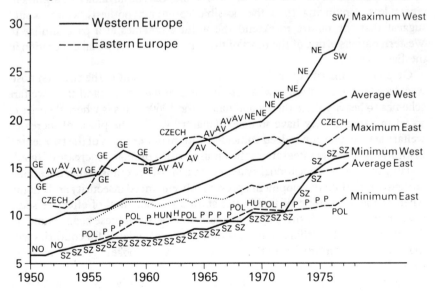

Up to the mid-1960s social security expenditures in Eastern and Western Europe show very similar patterns of development. The average expenditure ratios of communist countries is only slightly below that of the capitalist democracies, while the ratio of the Eastern country with maximum social outlays (Czechoslovakia) closely corresponds to that of the leading Western nations (Germany, Belgium, Austria). The laggards of social security spending in the East (Poland, Hungary) even slightly surpassed the spending efforts of Switzerland as the Western laggard. This basic similarity only begins to fade in the second half of the 1960s. The Eastern average ratio now increasingly falls below the average of the West. Czechoslovakia as the big spender among communist countries no longer holds the pace of spending in the leading Western countries (Austria, Netherlands, Sweden). Only the laggards of social spending in both contexts remain similar. In the 1970s, then, even the average expenditure ratio in the West surpasses the maximum value of the East, while the Eastern average falls below the values reached by Switzerland as the Western laggard.

In their present formulation theories of the Marxist orthodoxy do not seem capable to explain these patterns. Obviously the welfare state schemes are no peculiarity of capitalist countries. In capitalist democracies as in communist people's democracies social security spending has been rising in the post-war period. Even the pace of growth was similar up to the second half of the 1960s, diverging only afterwards. Marxist authors may argue that the growing gap reflects the increased necessity of capitalist countries to secure mass loyalty after the end of the post-war reconstruction period, but in the light of the internal tensions in nations such as Poland and Czechoslovakia this argument seems less convincing than the possible counter-hypothesis which would suggest that the failure to extend the welfare schemes at a pace similar to Western nations is one of the roots of the repeated crises of social integration in the East.

Given the similarity of social expenditure development in the two first post-war decades the question is what made Western nations expand their welfare schemes so heavily since the second half of the 1960s. This is where theories of social integration may have some explanatory value. The phase of increased welfare state expansion indeed coincided with major changes of the two central institutions of social integration: the family, with a dramatic increase of family instability, and the educational system with a massive expansion of educational participation. Both developments presumably enhanced insecurity and anomie whereas the weakening of family ties shifted the potential of effective social support to the state. If there is a systematic link between these changes and the development of the welfare state we should expect a tendency for countries with high family instability to experience the most outspoken growth of social expenditure.

Up to the mid-1960s crude divorce rates remained fairly constant in Western Europe. In a comparative perspective they were on a relatively high level in

Austria, Denmark, and Sweden, on a relatively low level in Belgium, France, the Netherlands, Norway, and Britain, with the remaining countries close to the European average (Flora, 1981). In 1965 there was no relationship between the level of family instability and the level of social expenditures ($r = 0.05$). In 1975 there was still no correspondence between the two developments ($r = 0.09$), but as the following cross-tabulation shows, countries with heavy increases in divorce rates between 1965 and 1975 also tended to show the heaviest increases in social expenditure ratios in that period. The average growth of the expenditure ratio consistently increases from 6.2 percentage points in countries with little change in family instability to 7.3 in the middle group and 8.8 percentage points in the group with highest increases in divorce rates.

Table 5 Family instability and social security expenditure development 1965–1975*

Increase of family instability 1965–75	Level of family instability 1975			Average increase of exp. ratio
	Low <1.4	Medium 1.40–1.73	High 1.98 +	
Low 0.27–0.55	BE 23.6/7.5 FR 24.1/8.3 SZ 15.1/6.6	AU 20.2/2.4		6.2
Medium 0.68–0.73	NO 18.5/7.6	GE 23.5/6.9		7.3
High 0.97 +1		NE 26.8/11.1	FI 16.1/5.5 UK 16.2/4.5 DE 22.4/10.2 SW 26.2/12.6	8.8
Average level of exp. ratio 1975	20.3	23.5	20.2	

*First figure: expenditure ratio 1975/second figure: increase of expenditure ratio between 1965 and 1975.

A closer examination of the relationship shows that similar changes in family instability did not preclude discrepant patterns of welfare state development. However, the correlation of both changes is clearly positive ($r = 0.45$). Excluding the deviant case of the United Kingdom the correlation coefficient would even go up to 0.79.[4] The weakening of social integration with the rapid increase of family instability since the mid-1960s in fact appears as one of the roots of accelerated welfare state expansion.

Anomie theories of welfare state growth cannot explain, however, why individual countries increased social outlays in greater independence from the weakening of social integration than others. The perspective of political sociology would suggest that this may at least partly be related to the varying power relations in different national settings. If it is true that the degree of welfare state expansion is a function of the power resources of the underprivileged classes, and if socialist participation in government strengthens their power position we would expect diverse growth patterns of social expenditure to reflect the partisan composition of governments.

The conventional strategy to test this hypothesis consists of static cross-sectional comparisons of the social expenditure ratios in countries with different lengths of socialist representation in cabinets. Based on our time-series data we can here analyze more specifically if different party governments had an impact on the annual changes of social outlays (relative to GDP) in the Western European nations. Table 6 shows how social expenditure grew under different governments in each country. Cabinets classified as centre-right consist of conservative, christian democratic or liberal parties excluding parties of the left. Centre-left coalitions refer to cabinets in which workers' parties participated in a minority position. Left-centre governments are either coalition cabinets with socialist dominance or cabinets exclusively controlled by left parties.

Table 6 shows that the welfare state grew under all types of governments, but that left cabinets tended to increase the social expenditure ratio markedly stronger than cabinets which excluded socialist parties or centre-left coalitions (0.57, 0.42, and 0.36 percentage points per year, respectively). The difference between single party cabinets of the left and of the right is particularly striking (0.53 vs 0.20). Participation of liberal or conservative parties in cabinets dominated by socialists did apparently not contain welfare state development. In fact the social expenditure ratio grew even stronger under left coalition governments than when socialist parties ruled alone (0.61 bs 0.53). Centre-right coalitions also promoted social expenditure growth in a more pronounced way than cabinets formed by a single 'bourgeois' party (0.55 vs 0.20). The growth of social spending under centre-right coalitions even came close to the dynamic under governments dominated by left parties. Among the coalition cabinets only centre-left governments did not record enhanced social expenditure growth. Under centre-left rule the social expenditure ratio increased in fact even less than under centre-right governments (0.36 vs 0.42).

The general tendency for a stronger growth of social expenditure ratios under governments of the left is confirmed for seven individual countries. Austria, Belgium, Denmark and Norway experienced higher increases of the GDP share of social outlays when parties of the right were in power. The two Scandinavian countries demonstrate most clearly how misleading conclusions based on cross-sectional analyses can be. Although both countries were mostly governed by the left, a sizeable part of social expenditure growth occurred

Table 6 Nation-specific increases of the social expenditure ratio under different governments*

Country	CENTRE-RIGHT			CENTRE-LEFT		LEFT-CENTRE			Average
	Total	Single party	Coalitions	Total	Coalitions	Total	Coalitions	Single party	
AU	0.48(4)	0.48(4)	–	0.29(16)	0.29(16)	0.21(8)	–	0.21(8)	0.29
BE	0.76(13)	0.43(4)	0.91(9)	0.26(10)	0.26(10)	0.28(5)	0.28(5)	–	0.50
DE	0.74(8)	0.10(1)	0.83(7)	–	–	0.50(20)	0.30(8)	0.63(12)	0.57
FI	0.30(11)	–0.10(3)	0.45(8)	0.51(8)	0.51(8)	0.53(9)	0.53(9)	–	0.44
FR	0.53(22)	–	0.53(22)	0.03(3)	0.03(3)	–	–	–	0.47
GE	0.08(16)	–	0.08(16)	0.10(3)	0.10(3)	0.73(8)	0.73(8)	–	0.27
IR	0.21(17)	0.21(17)	–	0.71(7)	0.71(7)	–	–	–	0.35
IT§	0.33(11)	0.11(7)	0.70(4)	0.35(8)	0.35(8)	0.83(9)	0.83(9)	–	0.50
NE	0.63(12)	–	0.63(12)	0.32(9)	0.32(9)	1.06(7)	1.06(7)	–	0.64
NO	0.85(6)	–	0.85(6)	–	–	0.45(22)	0.60(4)	0.41(18)	0.53
SW	3.10(1)	–	3.10(1)	–	–	0.71(27)	0.47(6)	0.78(21)	0.80
SZ	0.20(6)	–	0.20(6)	0.41(20)	0.41(20)	–	–	–	0.36
UK	0.16(16)	0.16(16)	–	–	–	0.36(11)	–	0.36(11)	0.24
Average	0.42(143)	0.20(52)	0.55(91)	0.36(84)	0.36(84)	0.57(126)	0.61(56)	0.53(70)	0.46

*Average yearly increases (in brackets: number of years with respective government).
§Special classification; centre-left: including social democrats, excluding socialists; left-centre: 'centro-sinistra' coalitions including socialists.

under liberal/conservative rule. In France and Sweden social outlays also grew more markedly when parties of the 'right' were in power, but due to the overproportionate dominance of only one type of party government both countries offer little basis for systematic comparisons of welfare state developments under different cabinets.

Changes of the social expenditure ratio reflect to a large extent changes in economic output. If economic growth is low, increases of social spending find much more easily expression in rising expenditure ratios than in times of prosperity. It cannot be excluded, therefore, that left governments appear as promoters of welfare state development simply because they were in power when economic growth was slackening. It is possible to control for the impact of different economic contexts by examining the increases of the social expenditure ratios under various governments on a yearly basis (neglecting the different national contexts).

This analysis confirms the enhanced growth of social expenditure under governments which were dominated by socialist parties. In 12 of the 28 years since the war expenditure ratios increased most strongly under left-centre coalitions. Nine years saw the strongest growth when centre-left cabinets were in power. Centre-right governments without socialist participation reported the highest increases of social spending effort only in 7 of the 28 years. While they had the lowest increases in 10 of the years under study, socialist dominated cabinets reported the lowest dynamic of social expenditure growth only in 5 years (with one tie). The following cross-tabulation shows the rank-order of annual increases in more detail (Table 7).

Table 7   Rank-order of annual social expenditure ratio increases under different governments (no. of years on each rank)

Rank	Centre-right	Centre-left	Left-centre	Years
1	7	9	12	28
2	11	6.5	10.5	28
3	10	12.5	5.5	28
Years	28	28	28	

The impact of the party composition of government apparently diminished over time. In the 1970s there was in fact only one year in which the social expenditure ratio grew strongest under left-centre cabinets (1971). In the 1960s and 1950s, on the other hand, six and five (one tie) of the ten years witnessed strongest increases of social spending when governments of the left were in power. Accordingly, centre-right governments reported the most heavy increases only in one year (with one tie) in the 1950s and 1960s, but in three of the eight years in the 1970s. As the following comparison of the average annual increases under each type of government shows, the social expenditure ratio grew most heavily under left-centre governments in the 1950s and 1960s, but not in the 1970s when centre-right governments took the lead. Centre-left governments consistently experienced the lowest annual increases. The differences between the more dynamic and the most stagnant group consistently decreased from one decade to the other.

Table 8   Average annual increases of the social
expenditure ratio under various
governments in the 1950s, 1960s and 1970s

Decade	Centre-right	Centre-left	Left-centre
1950s	0.24	0.19	0.37
1960s	0.36	0.30	0.47
1970s	0.85	0.71	0.78

Contrary to an hypothesis advanced by Heclo (1981) according to which partisan conflicts shape social policies most noticeably in times of austerity, the impact of parties thus diminished with the decrease in economic growth rates in the 1970s.

Notes

1. All data presented here were compiled from various editions of the I.L.O. series 'The cost of social security'. Percentages rest on absolute figures which are presented together with explanatory footnotes in the forthcoming data-handbook of the HIWED-project (Flora *et al.*, 1982). As the HIWED-collection ends in 1974, social expenditure ratios for the years 1974–77 are directly taken from the tenth edition of the I.L.O. series.
2. Since the ratio is a function of both, social spending in the calculator and GDP in the denominator, this does not preclude that the growth rate of social outlays in absolute terms (at constant prices) has been declining over the post-war years.
3. The expenditure ratios in Eastern European countries express social security spending as a percentage of the net material product. Since it excludes the service sector, this concept is not fully comparable to the Western gross domestic product, but this should not seriously hamper comparisons of developments over time.
4. The divorce rates for Britain refer to England and Wales only. Including Scotland and Northern Ireland, the growth in divorce rates may be lower.

References

Flora, P. (1981) Solution or source of crisis? The welfare state in historical perspective, in W.J. Mommsen (ed.), *The Emergence of the Welfare State in Britain and Germany,* Croom Helm, London.

Heclo, H. (1981) Towards a new welfare state? in P. Flora and J. Heidenheimer (eds.), *The Development of Welfare States in Europe and America,* Transaction, New Brunswick.

Issues of Redistribution in State Welfare Spending

Michael O'Higgins

A major element of the post-war consensus in British economic and social policy was the belief that economic growth would allow increased social expenditure which in turn would produce greater equality. Even though economic growth was often lower than expected, the first part of this belief proved sufficiently accurate for the Welfare State to be labelled the 'residual beneficiary of the Growth State' (Klein, 1980, p.29). The arrival of the No-Growth State in the mid-1970's might have been expected to lead to a discussion of how to achieve more social expenditure, and thus more equality, in a static economy; in fact, it has generated a critical debate about the second part of the belief — does increased social expenditure actually lead to greater equality?

The debate has not been favourable to social expenditure. Le Grand (1982) documents evidence indicating that spending on free or subsidized public services (health, housing, education and transport) benefits the rich more than the poor, and sometimes fails even to reduce inequality. The extent to which this has become the received wisdom of social policy is indicated by Taylor-Gooby:

> . . . a growing body of academic work shows increasing disillusion with the achievements of state welfare and pessimism about its potential for achieving redistribution to those in need (1982, p.345).

Parallel with this egalitarian disillusionment, social expenditure has been subject to an ideological attack from the political right wherein it has been variously accused of being inefficient, of undermining incentives and of diverting too many resources from 'productive' areas of the economy.

These critiques of state social expenditure and redistribution appear to be mirrored in recent survey evidence of popular perceptions on redistribution. When asked who got the 'best value for money from the system of taxes and benefits taken as a whole', non-manual workers, high income earners and

Conservative supporters were more likely to respond 'low income groups'; manual workers, lower income groups and Labour supporters plumped for high income groups. As Taylor-Gooby reports:

> ... there was ... a strong relationship between household income and a tendency to think that the state welfare system as a whole benefits other income groups (1982, pp. 337–338).

State welfare spending, therefore, seems to present not one, but two paradoxes: it is ideologically vulnerable from left and right, and it cannot rely on the perceived self-interest of either rich or poor for its defence. As Oscar Wilde might have said, to suffer from one paradox is unfortunate; to suffer from two is downright careless.

This chapter examines recent evidence on the distributive impact of state welfare spending and of the tax benefit system as a whole. It indicates that whilst the aggregate impact of government taxing and spending is by no means as redistributive as official statistics suggest, lower income groups receive a markedly higher share of state welfare spending than they do of market-generated income. In Westergaard's terms, therefore, the welfare state by no means achieves 'substantive equality of condition', but it brings about a significant measure of 'diffuse redistribution' (Westergaard, 1978, pp. 84–93).

Social Expenditure and Income Distribution

Public expenditure in the United Kingdom has in recent years accounted for between 40 and 45% of national income. Expenditure on those areas traditionally defined as social welfare — health, personal social services, social security, education and housing—amounts to around half of total government spending, or a little over one-fifth of national income. Although each of these proportions is much as it was in the mid-1970's, the balance between the various social welfare programmes has shifted. By far the largest is social security which is now almost 30% of government spending, compared to just over 20% in 1976/77; at the other extreme is housing, now down to less than $2\frac{1}{2}$% as compared to 7% in 1976/77. Education and the health and social services programmes absorb respectively just under and just over 12% of government spending, with education declining recently but health and social services growing slowly (O'Higgins, 1983, Table 2; HMG, 1983, Vol. 1).

Neither these individual expenditure programmes, nor changes in their sizes, are motivated by explicit policies to alter the distribution of income; they have a more specific purpose, such as providing social care for the elderly, primary education for schoolchildren or replacing some of the income lost due to unemployment or invalidity. Yet each expenditure has distributive consequences: some groups or individuals may either benefit more than others from particular expenditures or, even if benefitting less, may be better off than they would otherwise have been. Similarly, taxes may be required primarily to finance these expenditures, but they also have distributive effects: some people will be harder hit by an increase in VAT than in income tax, for example. Therefore, even though public policies may usually be changed for other reasons, information on the pattern of income redistribution allows one to assess the distributive impact of shifts within social welfare spending, between social welfare and other public expenditure, from one tax to another, or of a package of cuts in both expenditure and taxes.

The CSO Studies of Income Redistribution

The major source of information on the distributive effects of taxes and benefits is a series of studies produced annually since the early 1960's by the Central Statistical Office (CSO). These studies do not attempt to calculate the effect of every tax and government expenditure, but deal only with those taxes and benefits where there is a clear, measurable gain or loss to particular individuals. They, therefore, exclude expenditures, such as defence, which are 'not generally seen as conferring benefits on individual households', and spending such as roads and public parks where there is deemed to be insufficient information to calculate who benefits (Boreham & Semple, 1976, p.281).

The effect of these exclusions is that less than half of public expenditure is included in the CSO exercises; this allocated portion consists entirely of social welfare expenditure and over 90% of current expenditure on social welfare is allocated. Effectively, therefore, the CSO measure the redistributive impact of social welfare spending, which may be expected to be more progressive than public expenditure as a whole.

About 60% of government revenue is included in the CSO studies, the main exclusions being corporation and capital taxes, expenditure taxes which are assumed to fall on investment or government expenditure rather than consumers, and non-tax revenue. Therefore, the CSO studies allocate more taxes than expenditures so that the average household is shown as having a net loss from the redistribution process.

The CSO procedures are explained in Stephenson (1980) and the most recent details are in CSO (1982). O'Higgins (1980) provides a critical discussion of the methodological issues and the limitations of the CSO analysis. In this chapter, discussion of methodological issues will be restricted to those occasions when they may significantly affect the measurement of the redistributive impact of taxes and benefits.

The data on income redistribution may be examined in three stages:

(1) The impact of the various social welfare expenditures allocated by the CSO;

Table 1 The distribution of welfare spending, taxes and income by quintile 1971, 1976 and 1981

Percentage shares of:	1971 QUINTILES OF ORIGINAL INCOME						1976 QUINTILES OF ORIGINAL INCOME						1981 QUINTILES OF ORIGINAL INCOME					
	Bottom 20%	21-40%	41-60%	61-80%	Top 20%	As % of average original income	Bottom 20%	21-40%	41-60%	61-80%	Top 20%	As % of average original income	Bottom 20%	21-40%	41-60%	61-80%	Top 20%	As % of average original income
Original income	1.6	10.9	18.6	25.5	43.4		1.2	9.7	18.7	26.5	44.0		0.6	8.1	18.0	26.9	46.4	
Cash benefits	47.6	22.9	11.5	9.7	8.0	10.5	46.0	28.4	11.4	7.7	6.8	12.4	40.6	28.7	13.0	9.7	8.0	16.3
Health	19.4	19.4	20.1	20.3	20.7	5.4	19.0	20.0	20.4	19.9	21.0	6.7	23.3	21.3	19.1	17.9	18.4	8.0
Education	9.3	16.3	21.3	26.4	26.6	6.6	9.5	14.4	23.4	26.0	26.7	7.1	8.9	15.4	24.0	26.1	25.5	7.1
Housing subsidies	23.5	22.5	19.5	18.5	13.5	1.1	29.4	19.9	20.2	15.9	14.2	3.0	29.5	22.8	21.3	14.3	11.7	1.6
Total welfare spending	29.1	20.3	16.6	17.3	16.4	24.0	29.0	22.1	17.3	15.9	15.8	29.8	29.0	23.8	17.5	15.4	15.1	33.5
Original income and total welfare spending	6.9	12.8	18.2	23.9	38.2	124.0	7.5	12.5	18.4	24.1	37.5	129.8	7.7	12.0	17.9	24.0	38.6	133.5

						Av. Nos.						Av. Nos.						Av. Nos.
Direct taxes	0.4	8.0	17.0	24.6	49.8	17.8	0.2	6.5	17.0	26.8	49.5	22.1	0.2	6.3	16.5	26.9	50.1	22.1
Indirect taxes	7.4	14.2	19.7	23.7	34.8	20.5	7.5	13.6	19.8	24.5	34.5	18.9	7.9	13.9	19.2	23.7	35.3	23.1
Total taxes	4.2	11.3	18.5	24.1	41.8	38.3	3.6	9.8	18.3	25.7	42.6	41.1	4.1	10.2	17.9	25.3	42.5	45.2
Gross income	5.9	12.1	18.0	24.0	40.1	110.5	6.1	11.7	17.9	24.4	39.9	112.4	6.2	11.0	17.3	24.5	41.0	116.3
Disposable income	7.0	12.9	18.1	23.8	38.2	92.7	7.6	13.0	18.1	23.8	37.6	90.3	7.6	12.1	17.5	23.9	38.9	94.3
Final income	8.1	13.4	18.1	23.7	36.6	85.7	9.4	13.8	18.4	23.3	35.2	88.7	9.5	13.0	17.8	23.4	36.3	88.3
Composition of Quintiles						*Av. Nos.*						*Av. Nos.*						*Av. Nos.*
% of people	11.7	18.1	22.1	23.7	24.5	2.8	11.9	16.7	22.3	23.6	25.5	2.7	12.7	17.4	22.1	23.2	24.6	2.7
% of adults	14.2	17.8	20.1	22.5	25.4	2.1	14.5	17.5	20.3	22.0	25.6	1.9	14.1	17.5	19.9	22.3	26.2	2.0
% of children	5.0	18.8	27.4	26.9	22.0	0.8	5.3	14.5	27.1	27.7	25.4	0.8	8.6	17.1	28.6	25.7	20.0	0.7
% of workers	2.9	15.6	21.8	27.0	32.6	1.4	2.3	13.4	22.3	27.6	34.4	1.3	3.0	12.6	22.2	28.1	34.1	1.4
% of retired households within each quintile	72	12	2	1	1	18%	77	25	2	1	1	21%	76	32	3	2	1	23%

Derived from CSO (1978) and CSO (1982); the 'composition of quintiles' data for 1971 and 1976 are derived directly from FES microdata tapes for 1971 and 1976 and are thus more accurate than the 1981 figures which are derived from published data.

1. Original income is income before taxes and benefits; gross income is original income plus cash benefits; disposable income is gross income less direct taxes; and final income is disposable income minus indirect taxes plus non-cash benefits.
2. Total welfare spending includes welfare foods as well as the benefits specifically listed.
3. The 1981 final income data presented here are adjusted to exclude certain benefits (rail travel subsidy, option mortgage expenditure and life assurance premium relief) which the CSO allocated in 1981 but not in 1971 or 1976.
4. The housing subsidy data for 1976 also include food subsidies which it was not possible to identify separately. The food subsidies, which did not exist in 1971 or 1981 amount to around 20% of the total subsidy expenditure in 1976.

(2) The effect of taking account of those taxes allocated by the CSO;

(3) The difference, if any, to the pattern of redistribution if all taxes and government expenditures are included in the analysis.

The Distribution of Social Welfare Spending

Table 1 presents data on the distribution of social welfare spending, of taxes and of various measures of income for each of the three years 1971, 1976 and 1981. In each of the three years a similar pattern emerges for the various components of social welfare expenditure: social security spending is most redistributive towards those in the lower income quintiles followed by housing subsidies and then health care. Education is the only one of the four spending categories which is consistently most beneficial to those in the top two quintiles.

In 1971 almost half of social security expenditure went to the bottom 20%, and although this had declined to two-fifths by 1981, most of the gain went to the second quintile whose share increased from 23 to 29%. The shares of each of the top two quintiles did not reach 10 per cent in any of the years examined.

The inclusion of food subsidies expenditure in the housing data for 1976 means that it is better to confine comparisons to the 1971 and 1981 data. These show an increase in the redistributive impact of this expenditure; by 1981 almost 30% of the benefit was going to the lowest quintile compared to less than a quarter in 1971, whilst the shares of each of the top two quintiles dropped. A similar, though smaller effect occurred with health expenditure: while quintile shares were more or less equal in 1971 and 1976, the bottom two quintiles were benefitting by slightly more than average in 1981. The distribution of education expenditure only marginally changed over the decade with a slight increase in the share of the middle quintile at the expense of each of the others.

The distribution of total welfare spending is obviously dependent not only on the pattern of distribution of each programme but also on their relative sizes, that is the relative levels of expenditure on each programme. It would, for example, be possible for each programme to become more redistributive over time and yet for their combined impact to be less redistributive—if there had also been an expenditure shift from the more redistributive to the less redistributive programmes. In these data the average importance of each programme, relative to original income, grew between 1971 and 1981, but the most rapid growth was in social security and health. By 1981, cash benefits alone averaged one-sixth of original income, compared to one-tenth in 1971. Therefore, the reduced share of cash benefits going to the lowest quintile was largely offset by the greater importance of this most redistributive programme, so that 29% of total welfare expenditure went to the lowest quintile in each of these three years. The other changes combined to produce a slight increase in redistributive impact, with the overall shares of the second and third quintiles increasing at the expense of the top 40% of the distribution. Despite these shifts, however, each of the top two quintiles still received over 15% of total welfare spending in 1981, so that more than 30% of welfare spending went to the top 40% of the distribution.

The Distribution of Taxes

Table 1 also presents data on the distribution of those direct and indirect taxes which the CSO studies allocate. In order to assess the progressivity or regressivity of these taxes, the distribution of direct taxes should be compared to that of gross income, since this is the income measure which most closely resembles the base for direct taxation. Similarly, indirect taxes are compared to disposable income, which measures spending power.

Direct taxes fall heavily on the top two quintiles with around a half being paid by the top quintile and a quarter by the next quintile in each of the three years examined. Less than 10% of direct taxes come from the bottom two quintiles. Comparison with the distribution of gross income gives a more qualified but still clear picture of the progressivity of direct taxes. The tax shares paid by the lowest two quintiles are significantly less than their gross income shares; the next two quintiles play slightly less and slightly more tax than their income shares respectively, whilst the top quintile pay half of direct taxes while having two-fifths of gross income.

Indirect taxes are slightly regressive compared to disposable income: the bottom two quintiles generally pay a slightly greater share of indirect taxes than they receive of disposable income, whilst the reverse is true of the top quintile. While only slightly regressive in themselves, however, indirect taxes bear much more heavily on lower income quintiles than do direct taxes. In 1976 and 1981, the bottom two quintiles paid more than three times as great a share of indirect as of direct taxes, while the top quintile's share of indirect was only two-thirds as large as its share of direct taxes. Therefore, a shift from direct to indirect taxes makes the tax system less progressive and, as the data demonstrate, this occurred between 1976 and 1981. While direct taxes averaged 22.1% of original income in each of those years, indirect taxes rose from 18.9 to 23.1%, and the share of total taxes paid by the bottom two quintiles increased by almost one percentage point.

The combined effect of direct and indirect taxes leaves the tax system marginally progressive compared to gross income: lower income groups pay only slightly less and higher groups slightly more than they would do under a proportional tax system.

The Combined Effects of Taxes and Benefits

The tax and benefit systems cannot, however, be examined in isolation from each other: a regressive tax funding a benefit for the poor may produce an overall redistribution to lower income groups, even if the redistribution is less than would have been the case if the tax had been progressive. When the tax and welfare spending sides of the CSO studies are examined together, it becomes apparent that the system may be characterized as almost proportional taxation funding progressive benefits. The tax share of lower income groups is considerably lower than their benefits share, whilst the reverse is true for the higher quintiles.

This has the effect of reducing income inequality over the successive definitions of income used in Table 1. Gross income is significantly more equal than original income, and further though smaller increases in equality can be seen in disposable and final income.

Measuring increases in equality by comparing income measures to original income can be misleading, however, if original income is interpreted as 'what income distribution would have been if the state had not intervened'. In the absence of state redistribution through, for example, social insurance, people would make other arrangments to provide for contingencies such as retirement, sickness and unemployment. It can be argued that those arrangements would be less favourable to the poor than state benefits, but it is clear that the income share of the bottom 20% would be greater than the 0.6 per cent of original income which they had in 1981. Original income also includes all salary and occupational pension payments made by the state: if civil servants, doctors and teachers were all 'privatized', the distribution of original income would doubtlessly be different.

Original income is not, therefore, a fully satisfactory counterfactual against which to measure the redistributive impact of the state, but it is nonetheless clear that the share of welfare spending and of the net benefit from the tax and welfare spending system going to the lower income groups is greater than they would receive from market sources of income.

Extending the CSO Studies

It was noted earlier that the CSO studies of income redistribution, from which the Table 1 data are drawn, allocate less than half of public spending and about 60% of public revenue. Whilst there are methodological problems in making a more complete allocation, a partial allocation may distort the redistributive impact of the state, particularly if government policy switches taxing or spending from allocated to non-allocated items, or vice versa.

O'Higgins and Ruggles (1981) attempted to measure the redistributive impact of all taxes and public expenditure for the United Kingdom using 1971 data. To sidestep some of the methodological problems, they used a variety of assumptions to allocate some of the expenditure items about which there was most methodological disagreement. Their results suggest that whilst the distribution of taxes is only a little less progressive than the CSO data indicate, being basically proportional, the distribution of expenditures is notably less so. Whereas the Table 1 data indicated that the lowest quintile receives about twice as great a share of public expenditure as the highest, the O'Higgins and Ruggles data show that each quintile receives about an equal share of total public spending. It should be emphasized that even on these data the distribution of net gains (or losses) from the total tax and expenditure system still clearly redistributes towards lower income groups, but the gain is much less than the partial data suggest.

The income redistribution data therefore show that cash benefits and housing subsidies are of greater benefit to lower income groups, that the benefits of health expenditure are fairly equal across income groups whilst education benefits higher income groups most. Total welfare expenditure is therefore more favourable to the lower income quintiles, but total public expenditure appears to be equally beneficial to the different parts of the income distribution. Although the overall tax system is effectively proportional, the combined effects of taxes and public expenditure reduce income inequality.

Understanding Income Redistribution

In order to explain or understand the data on the distribution of taxes and public expenditure by income group, four factors need to be considered:

(1) The composition of the various parts of the income distribution;
(2) The socio-economic environment within which distribution and redistribution take place;
(3) The method of allocating taxes and benefits to different groups;
(4) Government policies concerning taxes, welfare and redistribution.

As the issues raised by these factors are linked it is easiest to discuss them together in relation to each category of expenditure.

A notable feature of Table 1 is the rise in the inequality of original income from 1971 to 1981 and the growth and changed distribution of cash benefits. Both are due, at least in part, to the same phenomena — rising unemployment and the growing proportion of elderly people in the population. These phenomena both increase the inequality of the original distribution and the amount of 'redistribution' which then takes place through state benefits. For example, the second quintile's share of original income drops from 10.9% in 1971 to 8.1% in 1981, whilst its share of cash benefits increases from 22.9 to 28.7%, and of health care from 19.4 to 21.3%. The 'composition of quintile' data at the foot of Table 1 show that over the same period the proportion of households within this quintile which were retired rose from 12 to 32%. Elderly people generally have low original incomes, draw state pensions and are assumed to make greater use of the NHS than other groups — hence the changes in the shares of the second quintile.

Whilst it is easy to measure the amount of cash benefit or housing susbidy which an individual receives, the benefit they get from a free health or education service is not so clearly quantifiable. Whilst some argue that the benefit should be measured by what the individual thinks it is worth, the CSO studies follow the principle of cost allocation, that is they seek to apportion among individuals the actual cost of the NHS and of state education. (A defence of the practice of cost-apportionment can be found in O'Higgins & Ruggles, 1981, p. 300–301).

The cost of the NHS is allocated to individuals differentiated by sex and age (there being eight age groups). Within each age-sex group individuals are allocated the cost of the average use of services made by people in that group. The distribution of health expenditure in Table 1, therefore, reflects the different age and sex compositions of each quintile as well as the different numbers of individuals in each. The cost allocations have been criticized for failing to take account of the extent to which middle-class people receive a better quality of service (even if they 'use' the NHS to the same extent), (Le Grand, 1982, Ch. 3). They are also not a guide to policy since they record use rather than use relative to need; the evidence suggests that people in different classes use the NHS equally, but since working class people suffer from worse health the middle class get greater benefit relative to need (Le Grand, 1982, Ch. 3). The Table 1 data, therefore, provide a useful indication of the way resources are being distributed by income class, but are not adequate as a guide to the effectiveness of policy.

Cost-allocation of state education spending means that households are attributed a benefit equal to the cost per pupil of particular types of school for each member of the household attending that type of school. The apparently inegalitarian distribution of education in Table 1 therefore largely reflects the composition of the quintiles (in particular the dominance of retired people at the bottom and the fact that most children are in households in the middle and upper half of the distribution). Again, different types of measure are required to assess policy effectiveness. Le Grand has gathered other evidence to indicate that the state education service provides relatively equal benefits to children from different classes up to the compulsory school-leaving age, but secondary education after the age of 16 and tertiary education provides notably more benefit to children from middle and upper income backgrounds (1982, Ch. 4).

The composition of the quintiles obviously does not account for all the inequality in Table 1: if the distribution of any of the concepts of income is compared to the distribution of people significant inequality remains. To increase the extent to which state services reduce this inequality may, however, conflict with other social policy objectives, such as universality. For example, the more equalizing distribution of housing subsidies in 1981 compared to 1971 reflects the shift from general subsidies (through low local authority housing

rents) to specific subsidies (means-tested rebates and supp
payments) which took place during that period. 'Privat
education, with residual state services for the poor, wo
redistributive impact of state spending — since only the po
from the residual state activity — but would probably inc
within the distribution of total health care or educa
Redistribution is one policy criterion, but it cannot proper
outside the context of the wider distribution of resources, whether through the
state or through the market.

Conclusions

The evidence suggests that state welfare plays a valuable, if limited, role in
increasing the share of resources going to lower income groups. What then
explains the egalitarian disillusionment noted at the beginning of this chapter?
Three explanations may be offered.

First, in examining distribution and redistribution insufficient attention is
paid to the composition of different parts of the distribution. The degree of
redistribution brought about by state welfare spending appears greater
when measured against the distribution of the population across the
quintiles.

Second, the different forms of equality which might be policy objectives are
inadequately distinguished. We might usefully take account of Rae's
distinction between marginal and global egalitarianism where marginal implies
distributing a particular good or service equally, whilst global implies
distributing it unequally in order to achieve a more equal overall distribution of
resources (1981, Ch. 3). Some of the major elements of state welfare — in
particular the NHS, child benefit and parts of state education — are designed to
promote marginal egalitarianism and will not, therefore, seem particularly
effective if judged by criteria of global egalitarianism. To expect the NHS to
increase equality, other than in access to health care, is to expect something for
which it is neither designed nor capable.

This leads to the third explanation which is that disillusionment may indicate
the illusory nature of previous expectations about the scope for increasing
equality through welfare spending. Welfare spending is notably more
egalitarian than income distributed through the market, but the market is still
the major contributor to average income. A substantial reduction in inequality
requires either a further reduction of the role of the market or a reduction of
inequalities within it. Welfare expenditure alone cannot eliminate
inequality.

References

Boreham, J. and Semple, M. (1976) Future development of work in the government tatistical service on the distribution and redistribution of household income, in A.B. Atkinson (ed.) *The Personal Distribution of Incomes*, George Allen and Unwin, London.

CSO (1978) The effects of taxes and benefits on household income, 1976, in *Economic Trends*, No. 292, February 1978.

CSO (1982) The effects of taxes and benefits on household income, 1981, in *Economic Trends*, No. 350, December 1982.

HMG (1983) *The Government's Expenditure Plans 1983-84 to 1985-86*, HMSO, Cmnd 8789, London.

Klein, R. (1980) The welfare state: a self-inflicted crisis, in *Political Quarterly*, (January), Vol. 51, No. 1.

Le Grand, J. (1982) *The Strategy of Equality: Redistribution and the Social Services*, George Allen and Unwin, London.

O'Higgins, M. (1980) The distributive effects of public expenditure and taxation: an agnostic view of the CSO analyses, in C.T. Sandford *et al.* (eds.), *Taxation and Social Policy*, Heinemann, London.

O'Higgins, M. (1983) Rolling back the welfare state? The rhetoric and reality of public expenditure and social policy under a Conservative government, in C. Jones and J. Stevenson (eds.), *Yearbook of Social Policy in Britain 1981/2*, Routledge and Kegan Paul, London.

O'Higgins, M. and Ruggles, P. (1981) The distribution of public expenditures and taxes among households in the United Kingdom, in *Review of Income and Wealth*, (September), Series 27, No. 3.

Rae, D. (1981) *Equalities*, Harvard University Press, Cambridge, Mass.

Stephenson, G. (1980) Taxes, benefits and the redistribution of income, in C.T. Sandford *et al.* (eds.), *Taxation and Social Policy*, Heinemann, London.

Taylor-Gooby, P. (1982) Two cheers for the welfare state: public opinion and private welfare, in *Journal of Public Policy*, (October), Vol. 2, No. 4.

Westergaard, J. (1978) Social policy and class inequality: some notes on welfare state limits, in R. Miliband and J. Saville (eds.), *The Socialist Register, 1978*, The Merlin Press, London.

Poverty Under Thatcher

Nicholas Bosanquet

The Whig interpretation of history lives on among students of social policy, deny it though they may. History is implicitly presented as a forward movement in which one generation of welfare reforms builds on the last. Even more important, people on the whole, get more compassionate and more willing to tolerate redistribution.

There has always been another view well put in the recent past by J.K. Galbraith in *The Affluent Society*. In 1958 he predicted a 'profoundly interesting although little recognized change in what may be termed the political economy of poverty. With the transition of the very poor from a majority to a comparative minority position, they ceased to be automatically an object of interest to the politician. Political identification with those of the lowest estate has anciently brought the reproaches of the well-to-do, but it has had the compensating advantage of alignment with a large majority. Now any politician who speaks for the very poor is speaking for a small and also inarticulate minority (Galbraith 1963, p.264). There would be the odd moment of altruism but little reason to expect any sustained shift of income and opportunities towards the less well off. Even with levels of unemployment current in Britain in the early 1980s the poor remained a minority and an unrepresented one.

Such sustained redistribution did come about between 1939 and 1950. This was a time when perhaps 70% felt themselves potentially threatened by economic insecurity. There was nothing new about that. More especially it was one where full employment and declining inhibitions in public finance made it possible to do something about the insecurity. The war added both to urgency and to solidarity. Both labour market and political forces were making for greater equality. Rowntree's survey in 1936 had shown that unemployment had been the most important cause of poverty: now the labour market had dramatically changed. The balance of voting strength was on the side of the poor and the war had brought a new interest in fairer shares.

The period 1950–79 is sometimes presented as one of steady erosion of the Beveridge ideals: but the record was in fact more mixed than that. The weaknesses of the Beveridge plan were first apparent in terms of growing poverty among pensioners. They were one group which could command a good deal of public support and who could also deploy voting power. The future of pension schemes dominated the politics of social security, and their interests were well to the fore. It was only in the 1960s that attention began to turn to child poverty. As early as the 1959 election, the then Conservative Government thought it worthwhile to steal Labour's clothes by introducing a new pension scheme shortly before an election. There was certainly downward pressure from the labour market on the incomes of the less well-off. By itself the course of labour market change would have made the poor poorer. In fact there was a rather marked reduction in the share of labour market income accruing to the poorest 40% of households. In 1961 they had 15.6% of labour market income: by 1976 this share had fallen to 10.2% (R.C.D.I.W. 1979, p.75). Poorer households found their share of income reduced by a third. But especially for those in retirement improvements in social security benefits offset these reductions in income from the labour market. Fiegehen, Lansley and Smith concluded that . . . 'comparative incomes of the poor seem to have been more or less constant between the early 1950s and the 1970s at about 48 to 49% of the median level' (Fiegehen *et al.* 1977, pp. 113–114). The Royal Commission on the Distribution of Wealth concluded in its Report on lower incomes that the real value of lower incomes from 1961 to 1974 showed an increase of 'about 40% in line with the growth of GNP' (R.C.D.I.W. 1978, pp. 142–3). Studies published in the early 1960s such as *'The Poor and the Poorest'* stressed that the numbers of people at below or just above the Supplementary Benefit level were rising (Abel-Smith & Townsend, 1965): later work has confirmed this but has also brought in new evidence that such people did share even if modestly in the returns to economic growth.

From the late 1970s onwards the number of households in poverty by the conventional line of the Supplementary Benefit scale rate began to increase. This increase probably began before the Conservative Government took office in 1979 but accelerated under it. The number of people in households dependent on Supplementary Benefit or with incomes below the SB level was 6m in 1979. By 1982 the number had risen to 8m at a minimum. Of the 8m, 6 million were in households directly dependent on SB and 2 million were in households which were not claiming but which had incomes at or below that level. Eight million must be taken as a minimum estimate in that it assumes cautiously in the absence of recent data that the numbers of working poor and other non-claimants had remained constant at 2m since the last official estimate in 1979. In fact given the trends in pay and unemployment to be described later, this number had probably risen by 1981 to at least 2.5m. Almost all the total increase was among people of working age. There was also greater pressure on people with incomes just above the SB level. The number of families claiming Family Income Supplement (FIS), the means tested form of income support for families with a head in full-time work, rose from 80,000 in 1979 to 143,000 in 1982.

Our aims in this chapter are first to examine how this change in the extent of poverty came about and then to relate the change and the policy response to history. We shall argue that social policy towards poverty and social security tends to show, other things being equal, slow change over long periods of time. We are dealing here with policies which relate to the life cycle of individuals over decades and to underlying changes in the labour market in levels of real income and in social and political attitudes which take time to develop. However this natural tendency to gradual evolution can be interrupted by two types of crises which can be triggered off by changes in public opinion or in economic circumstance. These are the crises of commitment in which political pressures point to new systems and higher levels of income support: and the crises of retrenchment when changes in economic circumstance put pressure on past attitudes and commitments. We shall look at the early Thatcher years as an example of the second type of retrenchment crisis.

The increase in poverty resulted both from general changes in the economy and from particular actions in social policy. The costs of the recession fell mainly on the poorest third of the population: and government social policy imposed further costs. The costs of the recession were those arising both from deliberate economic policy and from economic changes which were less open to government control. These were probably the more important of the two kinds of cost. The imposed costs were mainly those arising from policy on taxation, social security and housing. The combined effect of all these changes taken together from 1979 to 1982 was to produce the sharpest increase both in poverty and in inequality seen for many years.

These events of 1979–1982 have to be seen against a background of longer term change in the labour market (Bosanquet 1983, p.127). For the past twenty years the demand for labour has been shifting away from semi-skilled and unskilled male manual workers. It has shifted towards non-manual workers and towards women workers. In 1951 one out of ten of male employees were in the upper non-manual occupations: by 1978 one in three with most of the change coming about from 1961 onwards. The figures in Table 1 show the full extent of the change.

Within a falling total demand for male employees, the pattern of demand shifted much more suddenly than in any previous period, of comparable length. Yet the available work-force — labour supply — remained set on an older pattern. The new jobs were filled with new entrants, many of them newly qualified in the expansion of higher education after the Robbins Report in 1963. Older manual workers were faced with a situation where the total number of unskilled and semi-skilled jobs available to them shrank from 4.8m to 2.8m in a matter of seventeen years. The change reflected both shifts in the composition of employment within industries and shifts between sectors away from manufacturing and towards private and public services. All industries were employing a higher proportion of the more qualified and there was also a shift towards sectors which employed especially high proportions of them.

Nicholas Bosanquet

Table 1 Distribution of Employees by Occupational Class:
Men Great Britain

	1961		1978	
	Number 000	%	Number 000	%
Upper Non-Manual (including higher professional, lower professional and managers and administrators)	2516	17.8	3969	31.9
White-collar and Supervisors	1775	12.5	1613	13.1
Skilled Manual	5095	35.9	3985	32.2
Semi-skilled Manual	3501	24.7	2182	17.7
Unskilled Manual	1284	9.1	636	5.1
Total	14,171	100.0	12,385	100.0

Source: R.C.D.I.W. Report No.8, Table 2.7

Already by 1979 this underlying change was having some clear effects. One was in high rates of unemployment among manual workers. The general unemployment rate averages the experience of various groups. By 1979 a general unemployment rate of 6% already meant a rate for manual workers of about 12%. Falling demand had particular effects at the beginning and end of the working life. Rates of youth unemployment 2% or less in the early 1960s were now running at above 10%. There was a particular rise in long-term unemployment affecting workers in all Regions including the South-East. Some people were dropping out of the work-force completely. The activity rate for workers over 55 and especially over 60 began to fall. In some of the older industrial areas by 1979 up to 20% of men aged 55–59 and up to 30% of men aged 60–64 were effectively out of the work-force. Unemployment rates for adult workers under 55 remained rather low at this stage at 5% or less. Changed patterns in the labour market were reducing incomes and opportunities for some and raising those of others, in a rather decisive way. The change in the labour market also favoured the South East and the suburbs as against the North and the Inner Cities.

From 1975 onwards unemployment rose and then remained on a plateau around 1.5m. The main impact of any recession is on those jobs which are on the margin of viability which are likely to be those affected by long-term shifts in demand. Both economic and social forces protect the more qualified during recessions. The employer wants to protect his investment in training especially where there is hope that demand will recover in the future. More qualified workers also tend to have more bargaining power and to work within more structured internal labour markets where decisions take time and negotiation.

The main effect of the first recession after 1974 was to increase the shift against less skilled manual workers and to bring about a reduction in the share of labour market income going to the poorest two fifths of households — a prelude to much greater changes after 1979.

The new recession beginning in 1980 was unusually severe not just in the increase in unemployment which it brought about but also in a loss of projects and a growth of insecurity which affected people at all income levels. Yet the main thrust of the recession was still towards greater inequality. It added a further shift in the demand for labour to the long-term change which had already been taking place. The number of workers in manufacturing fell by a fifth between 1979 and 1982; this is still the area of the economy which employs the greatest proportion of male manual workers. This special change was not only due to the world recession: the appreciation in the sterling exchange rate which had begun in 1977 as the availability of North-Sea Oil reduced oil imports and improved the balance of payments, and also contributed to it. This appreciation had particularly serious effects on competitiveness in manufacturing. Like a boom town, turning to a ghost town, Britain found that its oil wealth has unexpected and harmful side effects on the normal pattern of economic activity. The downturn in public sector investment also had particular effects on the construction industry which used to employ less skilled manual workers.

The recession sharply reduced the share of original labour market—income — going to the poorest 40% of households. Their share was 10.2% in 1976; by 1978 it had fallen to 9.8% and by 1980 to 9.0%. Their shares of final income — after all taxes and benefits—also fell from 20.4% in 1976 to 19.1% in 1981. The tax and social security system was no longer operating as it had done in the past to offset losses in labour market income for poorer households. Economic Trends data on household incomes is only available with a two year delay so the full effects of the recession were not known at the time.

The recession increased local disparities in unemployment. The most obvious were between communities in the South East and the rest of the country. But within each region there was a great difference between unemployment in the core of the old inner cities of Liverpool, Birmingham and Newcastle and unemployment in the more suburban areas. The rise in unemployment did not affect just the traditionally depressed regions and the few communities such as Consett and Corby where dramatic closures of steel works were well-publicized. It affected many communities outside the South East which had been little affected before. In Table 2 we can see some of these local disparities, for communities which had been well outside the news. Manual workers in these communities faced specific unemployment rates which were well above these average rates.

Some effects of the recession simply accentuated longer term and well established trends. The rate of withdrawal from the work-force by older men increases further. By 1982 unemployment would have been rising much faster

Nicholas Bosanquet

Table 2 Unemployment by Local Area
         Oct. 1982 (%)

Crawley	6.8	
Basingstoke	7.8	
Hertford	6.4	
Ashton-under-Lyne	15.3	(1979: 4.4)
Bradford	15.6	(1979: 6.5)
Dudley/Sandwell	16.6	(1979: 4.6)

Source: D.E. Gazettes

if it had not been for this withdrawal. The inflow onto the Register was as large as it had been at the beginning of the recession but it was being offset by an unusually heavy out-flow not into work but into retirement or limbo (National Institute Economic Review, November 1982, pp. 18–19). The recession doubled the rate of youth unemployment from 10 to over 20%. More particular to the new recession after 1980 was the rise in unemployment among the core labour force of adult experienced workers. By late 1982, the unemployment rate for men aged 25–34 was 14.5% and that for men aged 35–55 about 11%. There were similar increases among the core work-force of experienced women workers with an even higher rate of withdrawal from the work-force associated with the higher measured unemployment rate. This change in pattern, towards unemployment among adult workers in mid-career, of course had serious implications for family poverty. By October 1982 there were 611,000 people in the 25–54 age group who had been unemployed for a year or more. The recession added to unemployment: this was part of an old pattern. More surprising and in fact unprecedented were the effects on relative pay. Lower paid manual workers not only stood a higher chance of becoming unemployed. Even if they did manage to stay in work their pay rose less than that of non-manual workers. The early 1970s had seen a narrowing of the differentials between manual and non-manual workers. Now they widened again, as can be seen in Table 3. The lower paid felt one part of a wider change affecting the manual work-force as a whole.

Thus the gross earnings of the lowest paid manual workers rose by 42% while those of the highest paid non-manual workers rose by 63%. Both market and bargaining power forces seemed to be working for the higher paid. Such changes in differentials over a short period of time had no precedent either in direction or in size: they more than reversed the changes that had taken place in the early 1970s.

Most of the direct costs of the recession in terms of higher unemployment, and reduced household income fell on the less well-off third of the population. But in addition there were costs which were the result of deliberate government

Table 3 Percentage Changes in Gross Pay 1979-82

Lowest Decile	*Lowest Quartile*	*Median*	*Upper Quartile*	*Highest Decile*
Male Manual Workers				
42	42	42	43	46
Non-Manual Workers				
50	53	57	59	63

Source: New Earnings Survey, 1982

decisions in the field of tax, social security and housing. From 1976 to 1979 the tax threshold, the level of income at which liability for tax is incurred, rose both for low income families and for others. This reversed a trend towards lower thresholds, which had set in over twenty years. But from 1979 onwards the tax threshold fell again, mainly as a result of the abolition of the reduced rate band which had helped tax payers with low incomes. Tax paying liabilities increased for most but the increase was greater for poorer households. From 1978/9 to 1981/2 the real increase in taxation for a married couple with two children earning three quarters of the national average was 17%. A family of the same type on average earnings was paying $14\frac{1}{2}$% more tax. In contrast a family with an income of twice the average was paying only $9\frac{1}{2}$% more and a very prosperous family on five times the national average has benefitted from a $6\frac{1}{2}$% reduction in its tax liability. Assuming that the tax-payer was continuously in employment and that he had a pay increase at the average rate, his real income would have improved. Pay settlements over the period were greater than the rate of inflation. However the average covers non-manual as well as manual workers and the evidence on pay suggests that many low paid manual workers will have got increases below the average, in pay. As a result of the changes in tax, taken together with these specific changes in pay, many poorer households experienced a fall in their real incomes.

Changes in tax rates were adding to the average tax liability of poorer households: at the same time changes in social security were reducing their income if they were unemployed and adding to insecurity if they were sick. One immediate change made in 1980 was that unemployment benefits rose by 5% less than the rate of inflation. For the longer term the government abolished earnings-related unemployment benefit and made all short-term benefits subject to tax. There was certainly a case for looking again at the earnings related benefit. It had had contribution conditions attached to it which meant that it was never in fact claimed by more than a quarter of the unemployed. It could be claimed only in the first six months of unemployment. There might have been a case for redistributing support for the unemployed through some improvement in benefits for the long-term unemployed: but the case for the net reduction in support just at the beginning of a major recession seemed hard to make. Significantly the decision was not defended in terms of increasing labour market incentives but simply as a means of reducing public spending.

The effect of these changes was to make unemployed people more dependent on Supplementary Benefit. By 1982 only one-third of the unemployed were getting any national insurance benefit. The Beveridge ideal of a minimum income in unemployment through a contributory benefit which could be claimed without test of means had receded into the far distance. Unemployed people were now generally dependent on a non-contributory and means tested benefit. By December 1981 2m people were living in households where the head was unemployed and which were entirely dependent on Supplementary Benefit.

The changes in sickness benefit might have seemed on the face of it more neutral in their effects on poorer households. By these changes the employer became responsible for making sickness payments for the first eight weeks of sickness and would pay lower national insurance contributions in return. Employers had to make a minimum level of payment corresponding to the current national insurance minimum. The new scheme has to be seen against the background of a labour market which is divided between primary employers offering security and good levels of pay and fringe benefits and secondary employment where the workers' position is much more insecure. Secondary employers would have considerable incentives to evade the payment of sickness benefit and their employees might feel rather hesitant about pressing their claims. These effects were a matter of speculation: it could be predicted with much more confidence that the new scheme would be a disincentive to employers to take on employees with a poor sickness record. The new scheme would encourage employers to hire people with good records.

The Beveridge Report and the legislation based on it had established a commitment to a minimum income for all in sickness, unemployment and old age. The government's changes taken together amounted to a further significant retreat from the Beveridge principle already eroded by the introduction of lower short-term rates of Supplementary Benefit for some groups in 1973 (Metcalf, 1980). The government did not attempt further changes in other kinds of income support. Child benefit proved popular not just with the Child Poverty Action Group but with the Conservative Women's National Advisory Council although the government was able to make some savings by stealth through its failure to index child benefit fully. It was committed both to the existing and to the new earnings related pension scheme. The Conservative Government even brought about some improvement in the benefits available to single parents. But housing conditions for the less well-off third of the population were worsening significantly continuing a change which had begun earlier. The House Conditions surveys showed for 1981 that at least a quarter of dwellings in the housing stock were either unfit, lacking in basic amenities or in need of major repairs. Many of these were lived in by the poor. The decline in parts of the owner occupied sector had particular effects on elderly owner occupiers: it was in the area of housing rather than income that the relative conditions of the elderly deteriorated during this period. Poor households below retirement age were more affected by declining standards of maintenance on local authority estates and by the rapid increase in rents which was a feature of the period 1979–82. Council house rents rose much faster than prices generally: by 109% as compared to the 44% increase in prices, over the period. The worst position of all was that of tenants on some new large estates: they had to pay rents higher than the average while often facing major problems both of maintenance and of unpleasant environment.

The effects of the changes in tax, social security and in council rents on poorer households need to be looked at together. One effect was to strengthen the poverty trap — or to use a phrase that was gaining currency at the time — to widen the poverty plateau. The poverty plateau described the range of income over which increases in gross income led to little increase in net income because of erosion by higher tax payments and by the loss of means tested social benefits (Bradshaw, 1980). Poorer families were now facing higher marginal tax rates: they were also finding that rent rebates were more available to them. As they increased their gross income so they found that the additional rent to be paid was greater than in the past. These changes reduced the incentive for those in work but with low incomes to earn more. At the same time, changes in unemployment benefit were reducing the real incomes of poorer households without a full time earner. The effect of all these changes was highly perverse. The government and the recession had reduced the real income both of those with low incomes in work and of poorer households out of work: the net effect for many people was a reduction in work incentives.

Although Supplementary Benefit scale rates were low, they provided a better net standard of living than many poorer families with children were able to earn for themselves. The children's allowances remained free of tax even after the adult scale rate became taxable in July 1982. The payments made for child support were inadequate though they were more generous than child benefit. Housing costs were paid in full, and a range of means tested benefits such as free school meals and free prescriptions were automatically available. Hermione Parker calculated in a pamphlet that received much attention at the time that gross earnings of at least the national average for manual workers of £125 a week would have been needed to produce a return to work for families with two children dependent on Supplementary Benefit (Parker 1982, pp. 47–49). Even on official estimates for 1979, 800,000 adults of working age were in a poverty trap: affected by implied marginal tax rates of at least 40%. Parker's fairly speculative estimate was that in 1982 perhaps 5½m (i.e. about 20%) of the workforce were at risk from either the poverty or the unemployment traps. There could well be argument about whether this did have the strong immediate effects on behaviour that Parker and others implied. It may well be that some people were not well informed: there may also have been delays in benefit loss or tax payment which meant that in practice the marginal tax rates were not as high as they were on paper. Social pressures, personal pride and fear of boredom may have impelled people to work even when they had little to gain from it.

Chance or circumstance might reduce or qualify the impact of these changes on particular households. But it would be hard to deny their significance in the longer term. The combination of high levels of unemployment, low earnings for those in work, reliance on means tested benefit and low levels of universal child benefit had produced a special economy for a very large number of people. It was an economy in which rewards were meagre but in which a special pattern of incentives operated. It was an economy unknown to the luckier half of the population with higher incomes. They looked to the occupational and fiscal systems of welfare rather than to a social security system which was becoming selective and dependent on means tests. The dream of income support which would be open to all and meet the needs of all had faded. Instead was a separate world both of economic prospects and of social institutions. As the economic prospects worsened so the full logic of the social security system in this new form came into play.

Our discussion has been of changes in poverty using the narrow conventional definition of the Supplementary Benefit scale rate. Poverty can be defined more broadly either in absolute or in relative terms. In absolute terms poverty is about hardship which threatens the physical basis of life itself. It is about destitution rather than just desperation. In relative terms poverty is about exclusion from opportunities and shared pursuits in an advanced society. Ideally we would like to be able to infer from a range of data about households what poverty by the conventional definition actually meant in terms of these other definitions. We lack the full evidence required to do this. On absolute poverty the evidence from 1979–82 was ambiguous, about the measure most commonly used in the past, that of mortality rates. There was some evidence that unemployment might have raised mortality rates among adults affected by it, although this view associated with the work of Harvey Brenner (Brenner, 1979) was seriously challenged (Stern, 1981). On balance it seemed likely that the experience must have effects both on physical and mental well-being, so serious that they might lead to some changes in adult mortality. However infant mortality fell during the early Thatcher years. There were many reasons for this but the absence of a strong upward movement in infant mortality did suggest that the connections between changes in poverty as conventionally defined and changes in 'absolute' poverty were no longer very close.

Families around the Supplementary Benefit level of income had a number of ways in which they could try to protect their living standards. One was to have more than one member in paid work and as compared to the 1930s many more households had some chance of continuing income from work. Another was to do some declared work and to take advantage of earnings disregards by which they could earn small amounts without losing benefit. There were also chances in the black economy. For council tenants there was the possibility of buying time through rent arrears. The amounts of rent arrears rose steeply after 1979. In this case bureaucratic delays worked in favour of the poor household. Non-payment of electricity bills carried a greater immediate risk but could also be a buffer in the short-term. Many families had some assets or savings over from times of greater prosperity.

The threat of actual destitution was probably greater for single people than for families. Benefit levels were lower and they did not have the guarantee of shelter given to families by the 1977 Housing and Homeless Persons Act. Official figures tended not to cover single people without permanent addresses and this led to an under-estimation of the effects of the recession on them. For families there were some ways in which they could try to stop poverty turning into severe privation.

The recession had clearer effects on poverty in the relative sense. It involved a wholesale loss of prospects and greater insecurity for many people. This had effects throughout the social structure but the effects were more serious for those who had least to start with, But such changes did little to generate any spirit of revolt or protest. They seemed to produce apathy and a stable state of depression in the communities most affected. The recession proved once again that communities and individuals — given some minimum of income support — can adjust to long-term unemployment. People in Northern Ireland had known about the blighting and depressive effects of long-term unemployment: now many more families and communities elsewhere in the British Isles came to experience them.

The system of income support worked fairly smoothly: there were surprisingly few incidents of the sort which draw protest. Although there were financial strains at the national level in meeting the costs of supporting 3m unemployed, these strains were much less than if unemployment relief had been financed through a separate fund as it was in the 1930s. Income support through supplementary benefits were paid for out of general taxation and there was not the special crisis involving possible 'bankruptcy' of a fund such as had occurred in 1929–31. The recession also coincided with changes in the Supplementary Benefit system which made it easier to meet extra custom locally. There had been a growing emphasis in the 1970s on discretionary allowances given only after review by staff. The new pattern after 1980 involved some improvement in the basic scale rates and disengagement from discretionary allowances. New 'cases' could be dealt with using less staff time and the system accommodated 2m extra people with surprisingly little friction. This contrasted with experience during the recession in the United States where support for the unemployed was low, often uncertain and inconsistent between States.

The increase in poverty came about through two sets of changes in the economy and in particular policies for social security. In general the macro-economic effects were the most important. Higher unemployment and other labour market pressure on low incomes were the main reasons why more people became poor. This was particularly the case for families. The particular changes in social security may well have had their greatest effect on single people, who have less to hope for both from the social security and the housing world. For families the main social security effect was on incentives rather than directly on income levels. The separate world of the poverty trap and of the Supplementary Benefit trap further developed and came to involve more people.

Social policy for poverty has usually been about raising incomes over a long period of time. The emphasis in the Beveridge Report on dealing with interruptions of earnings of a short-term or at least a reversible kind, has been unusual as well as far too optimistic. Income support involves commitments which may last two decades or more in the case of a family with children or three decades for a pensioner moving from retirement to extreme old age. Policy for poverty involves commitments and financial arrangements which take many years to mature. Its natural pace is rather slow. This stable state with its routines of benefits claimed and contributions paid can be disturbed by two kinds of crisis. One is a crisis of 'commitment'. This requires a major change in public opinion about the distribution of income. Thus the growing evidence on poverty from Booth, Rowntree and others created in the early years of this century a new mood and a feeling among many people. But the crisis of commitment must also involve a changed attitude to public finance. There must be a greater willingness to tolerate new taxes or at the very least a public readiness to sign post-dated cheques. The commitment crisis around the Lloyd George Budget of 1910 and the National Insurance acts involved such a change. The stamp was a new method of taxation which met some protests but more general acceptance. At the same time there were plans to widen the tax base by increasing payments from the wealthy.

The other type of crisis is that of 'retrenchment'. This occurs where change in the macro-economy such as a severe recession puts pressure on public spending. There are moves to reduce levels of income support in order to balance budgets. Given the political difficulties of doing this such plans normally only proceed in times of severe recession. Decisions made in the earlier crisis of commitment may in fact contribute to the later crisis of retrenchment. The tendency is to spread commitments forward so that they mature in the future: making the initial change more acceptable but increasing difficulties for successors. It requires a major crisis in the public finances to set off such a crisis of retrenchment. The existence of an unfavourable 'image' of welfare and of unsympathetic attitudes to the poor are not enough in themselves without such a crisis.

Since 1905 in Britain we can trace two major crises of commitment. The first was over the introduction of national insurance in 1910–12. The second was around the Beveridge proposals from 1942–46. In the second crisis as in the first, there were changed attitudes to the idea of a national minimum and changed possibilities in public finance. There have also been two major crises of retrenchment and the early Thatcher years can be seen as the second of these alongside the crisis of 1929–31. However this second retrenchment crisis was much less central to the politics of the time. The question of income support for the unemployed wrecked a government in 1931 and was at the heart of politics. The second crisis of retrenchment was played out on the sidelines with little interest either from voters or from the main economic pressure groups. However its general implication for policy in the longer term was perhaps even more important than the particular measures taken. Social Security had in the past acted as a counter-vailing force making up for income lost to poorer households in the labour market. Now it was no longer playing this role. The longer term social implications also seemed clear. The poorest third of the population seemed to be moving further into a separate world in terms of incomes, prospects and incentives. The rise in poverty was only one sign of a new and deepening division in society.

These changes for the worse in the position of the poor no doubt reflected apathy and a sense of fatalism in part, as well as the tilt in political balance foreseen by J.K. Galbraith. But they were greatly assisted by certain changes in ideology which seemed to have much longer term effects. The post-war consensus was not just about macroeconomics: it had also included a complementary approach to social policy, first set out in the Beveridge Report to which Keynes himself made a notable contribution. From the mid 1970s on the consensus began to wear thin and a new conventional wisdom began to develop. There were several aspects to this shift to the 'Right'. In macroeconomics, it involved the rejection of Keynesianism. It included a preference for market solutions in many detailed areas of policy: finally, it involved a hardening of attitude towards poverty, extending at times almost to a glorification of inequality.

The new ideology was supported by a rather crude kind of social cost benefit analysis. Greater inequality was essential to higher growth: growth would produce benefits which would trickle down to the poor. A dynamic society needed great inequality. The new ideology was supported by a new method of dividing the poor. The distinction was increasingly made between a minority of genuinely afflicted and those who had failed to better themselves. The opposition to the New Right had failed to develop any ideology which could be an effective counter to this. The old consensus had made the case for redistribution in terms of a shared sense of society reinforced by a certain sense of paternalism. In practice rapid growth had made it easy to spend more on social services. But what was to be the case for redistribution now that the growth process had stopped, tax levels were much higher and the sense of society much weaker? The focus from day to day for these issues was on the role of social spending: but behind that debate lay a wider debate about ethics and about how society was to adjust to much more difficult economic conditions than had been known in the three decades after the War.

References

Abel-Smith, B. and Townsend, P. (1965) *The Poor and the Poorest*, G. Bell and Son, London.

Bosanquet, N. (1983) *After the New Right*, Heinemann, London.

Bradshaw, J. (1980) An end to differentials, in *New Society*, 9 October, 1980, pp. 64–5.

Brenner, H. (1979) Mortality and the national economy: a review and the experience of England and Wales, in *The Lancet*, September 1979, pp. 568–73.

Department of Employment (1982) *New Earnings Survey 1982*, HMSO, October.

Fiegehen, G.C., Lansley, P.S. and Smith, A.D. (1977) *Poverty and Progress in Britain 1953–73*, Cambridge University Press, London.

Galbraith, J.K. (1963) *The Affluent Society*, Penguin Books, Harmondsworth.

Metcalf, D. (1980) Goodbye to national insurance, in *New Society*, 26 June 1980, pp. 349–50.

Parker, H. (1982) *The Moral Hazard of Social Benefits*, IEA, London.

Royal Commission on the Distribution of Income and Wealth (RCDIW) (1978), Report No. 6, *Lower Incomes*, HMSO, Cmnd 7175, London.

Royal Commission on the Distribution of Income and Wealth (RCDIW) (1979) *Fourth Report on the Standing Reference*, HMSO, Cmnd 7595, London.

Stern, J. (1981) *Unemployment and Its Impact on Mortality and Morbidity*, L.S.E. Centre for Labour Economics Discussion Paper No. 93, London.

The Inefficiency and Inequalities of the Health Care Systems of Western Europe

Alan Maynard

The objective of this paper is to argue that substantial inequalities exist in health and in health care in Western Europe and that the impact of the State in the last 30 years in mitigating these inequalities has been limited. Most health care systems in Western Europe purport to strive after greater equality but in fact do not perform in ways consistent with these objectives. Evidence to support these arguments will be drawn from the countries of the European Community and, in particular, from the British health care system.

The paper is divided into three sections. The first brief section is concerned with the distinction between health care and health status and this is emphasised by the enunciation of three maxims for health care researchers. The second section is concerned with inequalities for health care (inputs) and health status (outcomes). The final section examines the future of health and health care policy in Western Europe and presents an analysis of some general problems which are likely to beset all health care systems, and some specific policies which may increase equality, if societies wish to achieve such an objective (which is doubtful).

Health Care and Health

One of the most popular errors amongst health service researchers, commentators, and citizens is to assume that an increase in the provision of health care leads to an improvement in the health of the individual or the nation. It is important to distinguish between:

(i) health care inputs (e.g. hospital beds, health care expenditure, doctors, nurses etc.)

(ii) health care services: a measure of throughput (e.g. number of cases, patient days).

(iii) health status outcomes: a measure of the output of health care services.

It is foolish to believe that increases in health care inputs and throughputs lead to increases in health status outcomes, i.e. increased inputs do not always and everywhere lead to increased outputs. For increased inputs to increase the outputs of the health care system, the effects of such inputs on the health status of individuals should be positive and beneficial. The fact of the matter is that most health care has not been evaluated in a scientific fashion, and that which has been evaluated has not always been demonstrated to be effective.

A major problem facing anyone concerned with measuring the effectiveness and efficiency of health care systems is that there is no measure of the output for this large industry, currently spending £8,000 m a year in the United Kingdom. We can examine doctor-patient ratios, bed-population ratios and expenditure statistics but these are all measures of input. How does one measure the output of your general practitioner? How do you measure the output of a hospital? (The number of patients who come out boxed-up or dressed-up?) Mortality and morbidity statistics are inaccurate because of data collection problems and because they are the outcome of many influences other than health care inputs.

At this point the faint hearted might give up but such behaviour is irresponsible and immoral. Every day doctors make decisions about who to treat. A decision to treat Thatcher will consume resources and deprive Callaghan of health care. A decision to provide one heart transplant uses resources sufficient to provide four kidney machines. In deciding to allocate his resources to Thatcher or Callaghan, or to heart or kidney patients, the doctor makes judgement about the potential benefits of treatment. The problem is articulating these evaluations and creating robust measures of output. As yet this process has barely begun, largely because decision makers have been willing to evaluate effectiveness in relation to inputs rather than outputs.

However it is possible to approximate output with proxy measures. Let us examine some examples. In the 1960's the N.H.S. spent millions of pounds establishing expensive coronary care units (C.C.U.'s) in hospitals. In the late 1960s, Cochrane, Mather and others proposed to evaluate hospital care (including C.C.U.'s) and compare their efficacy with home care for patients with acute myocardial infarction (heart attacks). There was considerable professional opposition to this trial for ethical reasons but eventually a trial went ahead and the results were quite startling. Outcome was measured in terms of survival after one year and the trial, which was double blinded and random, demonstrated that the alternative patterns of care (hospital and home care) provided identical outcomes. However, hospital care is more expensive (Mather *et al.*, 1976).

This trial has been replicated (Hill, Hampton & Mitchell, 1978) and has been much debated. It now seems that the results are due to the fact that most deaths from acute myocardial infarction take place in the first four hours after the onset of the attack, and, in many cases, patients are not in the health care system by this time, i.e. health care (in hospital or at home) may be irrelevant unless it can be provided early.

Using similar methods, randomised control trials (R.C.T.s) which randomly assign patients to the alternative treatment regimes, Russell, Devlin *et al.* (1977) have demonstrated that day case surgery for hernias and 24 hour stays for haemorrhoids are as effective clinically, cheaper economically, and socially more accpetable to patients. Hirsch *et al.* (1979) has shown that short stay care for mental illness patients is equally as effective clinically, as long stay care.

These studies are unusual in that they are scientifically rigorous: a lot of clinical evaluation results are garbage because of the failure to design experiments carefully and to guard against biased results. The majority of medical therapies in use today have never been scientifically evaluated (Cochrane, 1972). When therapies are evaluated, the results often demonstrate inefficient resource usage (Bunker, Barnes & Mosteller, 1976).

So it may be the case that an expansion in health care expenditure may be 'money down the drain' if it used to provide therapies whose efficacy is limited or negative (i.e. harmful). Throughout any discussion of health care the following maxims should be adhered to:

Maxim 1. Do not confuse inputs (expenditure, doctors, beds etc.) with outputs (improvements in the health status of the community).

Maxim 2. Do not assume that increased inputs lead to increased outputs. This has to be demonstrated scientifically.

Maxim 3. Do not assume that increased inputs of health care are the only, or indeed, the best way of improving health status.

The expansion of health care systems in Western Europe, and indeed all over the world, has been carried out with scant regard to maxims 1–3. It has been assumed that increased inputs lead to increased outputs. It has been assumed that increased expenditure on health care was an efficient way of improving health status, and relatively more efficient than alternatives such as income,

Diagram 1. The Production of Health

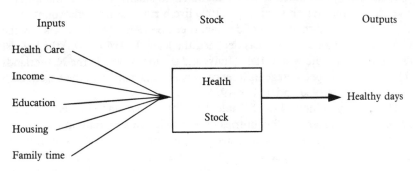

education, family time and housing. Hundreds of millions of pounds have been spent on the basis of hope and value judgements, rather than on the basis of scientific evidence. Politicians have pandered to the wishes of powerful interest groups and doctors have behaved in ways inconsistent with the efficient use of scarce health care resources. It is hardly surprising that amidst this rush to allocate resources inefficiently, the outcomes of health care systems in terms of distribution equality have been rarely analysed and little affected by public policy.

Inequalities in Health Care and Health

The discussion in this section is about inequality. It will discuss inequality in inputs and outputs and it will examine inequality from geographical and social class perspectives. The analysis is terse because of space constraints and seeks not to say whether these inequalities are 'good' or 'bad', but to determine, if policy makers (as agents of society) are seeking greater equality, whether they have been successful. The analysis in the subsequent section addresses the policy problems involved in achieving greater equality if this is a policy objective. If greater equality is not the concern of society then these sections may be of little policy interest.

The analysis of inequality below is divided into two sub-sections. In the first sub-section output measures such as mortality are presented and national and international trends in inequality are analysed. The second subsection is concerned with the analysis of inputs, i.e. differences in consumption and provision patterns for health care. Both sections present incomplete data. However, this seems to be the best that is available and indicates clearly the need for better data collection if we are to appraise distributional outcomes more clearly.

Inequality in outputs

In Table 1 mortality data for the 8 largest countries of the E.E.C. is presented (Luxembourg is excluded as its population is so small). Table 1, columns 1–3 gives the infant mortality rates (per 1000 live births) for the eight countries in 1960 and 1974 and their rates of decline. It can be seen from these data that the U.K.'s infant mortality rate has declined the least. In 1960 (1974) the highest infant mortality rate was in Italy (Italy) and the lowest was in the Netherlands (Denmark). The percentage difference between the worst and the best in each year was 145 in 1960 and 114 in 1974.

The data in column 4–5 of Table 1 indicates that standardized mortality ratios (S.M.R.) rose in all countries except Belgium and Italy in the 1960 to 1974 period. The S.M.R. is calculated by comparing the expected total number of deaths based on age/sex specific death rates in the E.E.C. as a whole, whilst allowing for concurrent changes that take place in the sex and age distribution

Table 1 Infant mortality and standardized mortality ratios in the E.E.C. 1960 and 1974

| Country | Infant mortality rate (per 1000 births) | | Percentage decline | Standardized mortality ratios | | Maternal mortality rate (per 100,000 births) | | Percentage change |
| | 1960 | 1974 | | 1960 | 1974 | 1960 | 1974 | |
	1	2	3	4	5	6	7	8
Belgium	31.2	17.4	44	105	104	40.7	13.7	66
Denmark	21.5	10.7	50	89	90	30.2	5.6	81
France	27.4	14.7	46	95	95	51.6	23.8	54
Germany	33.8	21.1	38	107	107	105.7	30.3	71
Ireland	29.3	17.8	39	108	114	57.6	23.2	60
Italy	43.9	22.9	48	101	96	115.0	41.2	64
Netherlands	16.5	11.3	32	81	85	39.3	13.4	66
United Kingdom	22.5	16.8	25	100	104	39.1	14.4	63

Notes: 1. In column 4 the datum for Ireland is for 1961
2. In column 5 the datum for Denmark is for 1973
3. In column 7 the datum for Italy is for 1972

Sources:
United Nations, *Demographic Yearbook*, 1961, 1962, 1963, 1975, 1976, 1977.
Ministere de la Santé et de la Famille, *Santé et Securité Sociale Tableaux* 1975–76.
INSEE, *Annuaire Statistiques de la France*, 1976
Statistisches Bundesamt, *Statistisches Jahrbuch*, 1976
Central Statistical Office, *Annual Abstract of Statistics*, 1980

of the population. N.B. Figures for 1974 are not standardized on the population of 1960. If the S.M.R. rate is used as an indicator of output, the health care systems seem to have been very unproductive. Health care budgets during this period for these countries grew rapidly, e.g. between 1960 and 1974 the N.H.S. budget increased annually by 6.5% in real terms. (Office of Health Economics, 1979, p.4).

The final three columns of Table 1 show maternal mortality rates in 1960 and 1974, and the percentage change between the two dates. The high maternal mortality rates in West Germany and Italy are particularly striking, as is the very low statistic for Denmark in 1974.

Clearly the 'outcomes' in Table 1 may be the result of a variety of inputs, only one of which is health care. The point to emphasize is that the experiences of the E.E.C. diverge quite considerably in some respects, particularly with regard to infant mortality rates and their rate of decline.

National statistics such as those in Table 1 hide differences *within* countries. This point is well illustrated by the data in Tables 2 and 3. The data in Table 2 indicates that the male standardized mortality rate for social class V in England and Wales worsened between 1949–53 and 1970–72. This combined with the improvement of the life-chances of social class 1 males, means that over the first 25 years of the N.H.S. the divergence between the life chances of the "rich" (social class 1) and the "poor" (social class 5), as measured by this particular statistic, actually worsened. It seems that if 'free' health care, via the N.H.S., has any effect, it is to improve the life chances of the rich (i.e. social class 1 and 2 as opposed to social classes 3, 4 and 5)!

Table 2　Male standardized mortality ratios: by social class England and Wales

Social Class	*(1)* 1949-52 (age 20-64)	*(2)* 1959-63 (age 15-64)	*(3)* 1970-72 (age 16-64)
I	86	76	77
II	92	81	81
III	101	100	104
IV	104	103	113
V	118	143	137

Source: Brotherston (1976), page 73, table 1

Table 3 shows the neonatal (death within 4 weeks of birth) and post-neonatal (death in weeks 5–52 of life) per 1000 live births in Scotland. It can be seen from this table that the neonatal class difference (social class 1 compared to social class 5) increased in period 1950 to 1977; the class V statistic as a percentage of the class 1 statistic rose from 142 to 216. The post-neonatal mortality difference between the classes rose until 1970 and declined only after this date (425 in 1950 to 433 in 1970 to 280 in 1977).

Table 3 Neonatal (post-neonatal death) rates by social class Scotland 1950-1977

Social Class	1950	1960	1970	1977
I	20.0 (5.9)	13.0 (2.7)	9.2 (3.0)	6.7 (2.5)
II	16.5 (7.7)	17.2 (4.3)	8.8 (3.1)	8.9 (3.7)
III	22.7 (14.3)	17.1 (7.2)	12.3 (6.3)	10.2 (4.0)
IV	24.9 (18.9)	20.7 (10.2)	14.3 (7.9)	10.8 (4.5)
V	28.5 (25.1)	21.0 (12.8)	18.8 (13.0)	14.5 (7.0)
V as percentage of I	142 (425)	161 (474)	204 (433)	216 (280)

Source: Registrar General Scotland Annual Report (1977) Pt. 1. Mortality Statistics, H.M.S.O. 1978 Table F1.4 page 371

Similar data are available for other countries. Walters (1980) presents infant mortality data for England and Wales with characteristics similar to those in Table 3. These data are presented in Table 4 with French infant mortality data. As with the Scottish data (see Table 3) the differences in post-neonatal mortality are greater than that in the first four weeks of life (neonatal mortality). The social class differences are of a similar magnitude to those in Scotland.

Table 4(A) Neonatal (and post-neonatal) and infant mortality in France

	1956-60 mortality rates Neonatal (Post-neonatal) Infant	1966-70 mortality rates Neonatal (Post-neonatal) Infant	Percentage decline Neonatal (Post-neonatal) infant mortality
1. Liberal professions (Class 1)	12.7 (4.1) 16.8	8.8 (3.0) 11.7	31 (27) 30
2. Unskilled manual (Class 5)	23.1 (21.7) 44.8	18.4 (12.0) 30.4	20 (45) 32
3. 2 as percentage of 1	182 (529) 267	209 (400) 260	64 (167) 107

Table 4(B) Neonatal (and post-neonatal) and infant mortality in England and Wales

	1949-50 mortality rates Neonatal (Post-neonatal) Infant	1970-72 mortality rates Neonatal (Post-neonatal) Infant	Percentage decline Neonatal (Post-neonatal) infant mortality
1. Liberal professions (Class 1)	13.5 (4.9) 18.4	8.7 (2.9) 11.6	35 (41) 37
2. Unskilled manual (Class 5)	21.9 (17.9) 39.8	17.6 (5.8) 23.4	20 (68) 41
3. 2 as percentage of 1	162 (365) 216	202 (200) 202	57 (166) 111

Notes:
Neo-natal mortality is death within four weeks of birth
Post-neonatal mortality is death in weeks 5-52 of life
Infant mortality is death within the first year (52) weeks of life
All data are rates per 1000 live births

Source: 4A: INSEE (1976) Taldeaux démographiques et socióux 1976
      4B: Walters (1980)
          Office of Population Censuses and Survey, (1978)
          Occupational Mortality Registrar General's Decennial Supplement for England and Wales 1970-72, HMSO, London

Both the English and the French data show that the neonatal class gap shows little sign of declining, although the post-neonatal class gap is shrinking. Overall the infant mortality experience of the different classes seem to be showing some signs of converging in recent years but the gaps are still very considerable.

From the poor data that is available in the United Kingdom and elsewhere it seems clear that whilst some but not all, (e.g. see Table 1) mortality measures of output have shown improvements over the last 30 years, in some cases the relative differences in the life chances of different social classes have widened. These changes have taken place in a period of massive increases in health care expenditure and the outcomes are depressing, as was argued in the U.K. context in a recent report (Department of Health and Social Security; 1980).

Inequality in inputs

In Table 5 a variety of health care input data are presented. The first two columns indicate how the percentage of GDP spent on health care has risen, i.e. health care acquired an increased slice of an increased GDP 'cake' over the period 1960–1974. In the final column, the number of doctors per 100,000 population is set out and it can be seen that the U.K. had the least doctors and the Italians the most: by 1985 if the forecasters are right, Italy may have three times as many doctors as the U.K. As Cochrane *et al.* (1978) have argued statistically there is a relationship between higher doctor stocks and higher mortality rates!

Table 5 Health Care Inputs in the E.E.C.

Country	Health care expenditure as a percentage of G.D.P.		Doctors per 10,000 population
	1960	*1974*	*1975*
Belgium	4.4	5.1	17.6
Denmark	3.2	5.8	–
France	4.0	6.1	14.6
Germany	4.5	7.6	19.9 (1)
Ireland	2.6	5.0	12.0 (2)
Italy	4.0	6.0	20.5
Netherlands	5.6	7.9	15.9 (3)
U.K.	4.0	5.0	11.8

Notes: (1) Data for 1976   (2) Data for 1977

Sources:
United Nations, *Yearbook of National Account Statistics*, 1966, 1968, 1978
United Nations, *Statistical Yearbook*, 1963, 1976.
Eurostats, *National Accounts*, 1977.
O.E.C.D. (1977), *Public Expenditure on Health*.
C.R.E.D.O.C. (1979), *Comptes Nationaux de la Sante*, 1950.1977.
Ministry of Health and Environmental Protection (1977), *Health Care in the Netherlands, Financial Analysis, 1972-1981*.

Another aspect of spatial disparity in expenditure and resources is budget allocation between the regions. The British in an attempt to reduce regional disparity in the allocation of N.H.S. monies have introduced separate budget allocation formulae in England, Wales, Scotland and Ulster. These formulae

distinguish the intra-U.K. disparity in the allocation of resources. For instance
if the English budget formulae (R.A.W.P.) is applied to the U.K. health budget
the Scots and the Irish would lose 14.9% and 13.6% of their monies, and the
budgets of England and Wales would rise by 2.3% and 7.6% respectively
(Maynard & Ludbrook, 1980a; 1980b).

Table 6   The Allocation of Hospital Resources: the application of a
RAWP-type formula to England, France and the Netherlands

	Distance from target as a percentage of actual hospital allocation	
	Best endowed region	*Worst endowed region*
England (1979-80)	+ 12.98	− 8.76
France (1976)	+ 31.23	− 57.33
Netherlands	+ 13.56	− 22.70

Source: Maynard and Ludbrook (1980c).

Not only are services and budgets distributed unequally, there is evidence
that there are significant differences in the health care consumption patterns of
the different social classes. Le Grand (1978) has shown that on average N.H.S.
patients in social class 1 consume 40 per cent more health care per illness
episode than patients in social class 5. Unfortunately this 'one off' study has not
been replicated in the United Kingdom or elsewhere in the E.E.C. Clearly it is
an area requiring careful further study.

Overview

The differences *between* and *within* the countries of the E.E.C. with regard to
mortality experiences and the distribution of health care (geographically and
between different social classes) are very considerable. These differences show
little sign of declining despite the massive increases in health care expenditure
during the last 30 years. Although E.E.C. governments, to varying extents,
have espoused the cause of greater equality in their health care systems, they
have signally failed to set detailed objectives and to adopt efficient policies to
achieve these objectives. Most public policy making in this area is characterised
by vague intent and very limited action. Presumably many politicians favour
the status quo?

Future Policies with Regard to Health and Health Care

If greater equality (in inputs and outputs) in health care is a policy objective of the health care systems of the E.E.C., its pursuit will require health care researchers to invest much more time and effort into two areas. Firstly they will have to identify much more clearly which therapies are cost effective, and ensure that those procedures which are not cost effective are discarded. Secondly, they will have to evolve more effective policies to ensure that the distribution of health and health care is more equal. In this section these two problems will be discussed briefly.

Greater efficiency

At present the health care systems of the E.E.C. are all facing the consequences of a much lower rate of expansion in health care budgets. This is a novel experience after the recent period of affluence and rapid budget expansion. This tightness in the budget is to be welcomed because it is forcing the principal health care resource allocators, doctors, to face up to the reality of economic life. Resources are scarce and not all health care demands can be met. It is inevitable that the demand for care will exceed its supply and rationing will take place. Doctors are the rationing agents. Their decisions determine who will live and who will die; and who will live in what degree of pain.

It is unfortunate that although the doctors' training is long (it takes at least ten years to train a specialist) and expensive (the medical school training alone costs around £60,000), they receive little or no training in economics and management. The ethos of evaluation is dormant in many medical schools and many doctors are not trained to think of the costs and benefits of their resource allocations (Maynard, 1979; Maynard & Walker, 1977).

It is essential that doctor resource allocations are made aware of the costs and benefits of their behaviour. The gap between clinical decision making and the economic responsibility for the efficient use of society's scarce health resources must be removed. Mechanisms such as peer review and medical audit may be helpful: they will oblige doctors to monitor each others performance and reduce deviance from group practice norms. However, it is probable that more radical measures may be necessary. One obvious policy is to give hospital ward teams a budget and an output objective, charge them for the inputs they use, and let them manage their own resources. In general practice doctors should be given drug budgets, charged the economic cost of all drugs they prescribe to their patients, and given a share (a bonus or a salary deduction) in any surplus or deficit on their drug accounts.

Policies of evaluating the costs and benefits of health care, and of requiring doctors to take this information into account when they treat people would ensure, if effectively enforced, that scarce resources are used efficiently within the health care sector. However, it is possible that the productivity of resources spent on health care may be less than those spent on other inputs which improve health status (e.g. education, income and the other factors set out in diagram 1).

There is very little evidence concerning the cost-effectiveness of preventive health care. However it is possible to show that the major causes of premature death are motor vehicle accidents, heart disease, cancers and cirrhosis of the liver. The causes of some of these diseases are unknown but others are amenable to change if government is prepared to construct policies to change people's behaviour.

In Table 7 some European causes of premature death are presented. It can be seen that deaths from cancer increase through the life cycle. An important component of this is lung cancer: in England in 1976, 2695 out of 5914 men aged 55–64 years who died of cancer, died of lung cancer (13.7% of all deaths in this group). It is important to realise that the risk of death from lung cancer is greater for social classes 4 and 5 than classes 1 and 2 because they (the poor) smoke more: the 1978 General Household Survey showed that whilst 60% of social class 5 males smoked, only 25% of social class 1 males smoked.

The incidence of heart disease, particularly in the higher age groups, is particularly striking in the U.K., the Netherlands, Ireland, and Denmark. Again, behavioural changes may reduce this cause of death. More exercise, more sensible diets, less smoking and other sensible behaviour patterns may reduce the chances of death from this cause. Clearly from U.S. evidence and from U.K. evidence about the reversal of the social class profile of death from heart disease (Marmot *et al.* (1978): in the 1950s heart disease killed more of the bourgeoisie than the proletariat, but now the opposite is the case!) it is possible to alter heart disease death rates substantially over quite short periods of time (Marmot *et al.*, 1978). The lower incidence of heart disease in France and Italy is remarkable but its causation is not clear: Cochrane *et al.* (1979) have suggested that it may be associated with high wine consumption.

Even if this is association exists it may mean that the French and the Italians substitute death from liver cirrhosis for death from heart disease, although the degree of the substitution is not complete.

The propensity of the youth of Europe to kill itself in motor vehicle accidents is very marked. Thirty-four percent of all male deaths in France in the age range 15–24 years were due to motor accidents, whilst in Germany and the Netherlands the proportion is over fifty per cent.

One conclusion which can be drawn from the data in Table 7 is that premature death could be avoided in many cases by preventive measures such as more rigorous road safety legislation, better education about diet and the virtues of exercise, greater taxation of alcohol and tobacco and education about its dangers, and related measures, (although such measures would ensure that people live on to burden the N.H.S. in old age!).

Thus if health care resources are to be used more efficiently the maxims in section 1 must be remembered. In particular:

(i) doctors must evaluate the costs and benefits of their resource allocations.
(ii) doctors must be trained at medical school to evaluate their behaviour.
(iii) the cost effectiveness of health care and preventive medicine must be investigated more extensively.

Table 7 The European Way of Dying, 1972

	Belgium		Denmark		France		Germany		Ireland		Italy		Netherlands		U.K.	
	M	F	M	F	M	F	M	F	M	F	M	F	M	F	M	F
(i) cancers																
age 15-24	7	14	10	13	7	10	6	10	10	16	9	17	7	14	9	16
age 25-44	16	33	18	40	15	25	13	31	18	34	20	35	18	41	19	37
age 45-64	28	36	29	45	28	35	25	38	24	33	30	37	31	44	28	40
(ii) heart disease																
age 15-24	0.91	0.26	0.26	0.67	0.15	0.38	0.38	0.43	0.35	–	0.78	0.72	0.33	0.85	0.4	0.3
age 25-44	12	4.6	11	4.5	4.6	1.2	8.4	2.7	17	5.1	8.3	2.7	18	5.8	21	5.6
age 45-64	24	12	32	14	10	5.5	23	10	35	20	16	8.4	33	14	37	18
(iii) motor vehicle accidents																
age 15-24	50	35	46	37	34	28	53	37	39	22	46	24	53	37	39	25
age 25-44	21	9.7	15	7.1	13	7.9	18	8.1	16	6.4	19	7.2	19	7.0	11	4.5
age 45-64	3.2	2.1	2.4	2.1	4.2	2.3	3.0	1.7	2.6	1.4	4.6	2.0	2.9	2.5	1.3	1.1
(iv) cirrhosis																
age 15-24	0.20	–	–	–	0.08	0.25	0.31	0.71	–	0.78	0.48	1.1	0.16	0.42	0.17	0.48
age 25-44	1.6	1.5	1.9	1.1	6.13	9.8	5.7	3.2	0.8	1.0	7.6	4.5	0.85	1.0	0.98	0.77
age 45-64	2.0	2.1	2.4	1.8	8.3	7.2	5.2	3.2	0.8	0.91	8.4	4.8	0.98	0.87	0.69	0.85

Notes: All data are percentages of death from all causes by age and sex (M = male, F = female). French data are for 1970, Belgium data are for 1971, U.K. data are for 1973. Heart disease is international classification R26.

There is good evidence that what the individual does (or does not) do for himself affects his health status more than additional health resources (Newhouse & Friedlander, 1980).

Greater equality

Greater equality in the consumption and provision of health care (inputs) must be seen only as the means to greater equality in outcomes: life chances and life expectancy. It is pointless to seek greater equality in health care (inputs) if these are ineffective. Consequently policy with regard to the pursuit of greater equality must take account of the findings from evaluative research, and ensure such findings are implemented.

The achievement of greater equality in the consumption of (effective) health care will require positive discrimination in favour of the poor. The creation of the N.H.S. removed the price barrier to consumption but it did not remove other (e.g. time) costs associated with demanding care. Perhaps the simplest way to increase health care consumption by the poor is to pay them to consume it.

Health inequalities could also be reduced perhaps by positive discrimination in favour of the poor in income distribution and education policies. Larger child benefits, more extensive provision of free school meals and school milk and similar policies might improve the nutrition of the poor and lead to improvements in their health status. However, as the Government reaction to the Health Inequalities document showed (Department of Health and Social Security, 1980), such policies are expensive and unlikely to be adopted by an administration determined to increase inequality in the hope that incentives will fuel British economic growth.

Greater geographical equality in the provision of health care could be achieved by mechanisms such as R.A.W.P. (Department of Health and Social Security, 1976; Maynard & Ludbrook, 1980a; 1980b). Mechanisms like this will, if implemented vigorously, shift resources from the Tory south and east to the Labour north and west. The application of the R.A.W.P. formula to the whole of the U.K. would shift resources out of Scotland and Ulster. Both policies have severe political difficulties which should not be ignored in a world of vote maximising selfish politicians.

The pursuit of greater equality in health status requires the preceding policies, together with substantial reforms associated with preventive medicine, education, and greater equality in income distribution. Clearly current economic policies, if successful will be the opposite of this and these policies, together with unemployment, will probably worsen the health status of the lower socio-economic classes. Also it is clear that powerful interest groups will oppose preventive measures which reduce alcohol and tobacco consumption and shift resources away from the N.H.S. to other social services.

It is unlikely that either political party in the U.K. will adopt these policies vigorously until they can be demonstrated to be cost effective and it can be shown that it will be in the interests of the politicians to pursue such policies. Clearly a lot of work needs to be done on both these aspects of implementation.

At present health care policies in the E.E.C. pay lip service to the ideas of efficiency and great equality. The health care industries of the Nine are characterised by inefficiency and inequality, and a great reluctance to monitor and evaluate their performance. Perhaps the 1980's will see the beginning of the great task of bringing scientific rigour to the management of the health care systems of Europe.

References

Brotherston, J. (1976) Inequality: is it inevitable? in C. O. Carter and J. Peel (eds.) *Equalities and Inequalities in Health*, Academic Press, London and New York.

Bunker, J.P., Barnes, B.A. and Mosteller, F. (1977) *The Costs, Benefits and Risks of Surgery*, Oxford University Press, New York.

Cochrane, A.L. (1972) *Efficiency and Effectiveness: random reflections on health services*, Nuffield Provincial Hospitals Trust.

Cochrane, A.L. *et al*. (1978) Health service 'input' and mortality 'output' in developed countries, *Journal of Epidemiology and Community Health*, 32.

Cochrane, A.L. *et al*. (1979) Factors associated with cardiac mortality in developed countries with particular reference to the consumption of wine, in *Lancet*, 1, 12 May.

Cooper, M.H. and Culyer, A.J. (1970) An economic assessment of some aspects of the operation of the National Health Service, Appendix A of *Health Services Financing*, British Medical Association, London.

Cooper, M.H. and Culyer, A.J. (1971) An economic survey of the nature and intent of the British National Health Service, in *Social Science and Medicine*, 5.

Cooper, M.H. and Culyer, A.J. (1972) Equality in the National Health Service: intentions, performance and problems in evaluation, in M.H. Hauser (ed.), *The Economics of Medical Care*, Allen and Unwin, London.

Department of Health and Social Security (1976) *Sharing Resources for Health in England*, HMSO, London.

Department of Health and Social Security (1980) *Inequalities in Health*, London.

Hill, J.D. *et al*. (1978) A randomised trial of home versus hospital management for patients with suspected myocardial infarction, in *Lancet*, 1, 22 April.

Le Grand, J. (1978) The distribution of public expenditure: health, in *Economica*, 45.

Marmot, M.G. *et al*. (1978) Changing social class distribution of heart disease, in *British Medical Journal*, 2.

Mather, H.G. *et al*. (1976) Myocardial infarction: a comparison between home and hospital care for patients, in *British Medical Journal*, 1.

Maynard, A. (1979) Pricing, insurance and the National Health Service, in *Journal of Social Policy*, 8, 2, pp. 157–172.

Maynard, A. and Ludbrook, A. (1980a) Applying resource allocation formulae to the constituent parts of the U.K., in *Lancet*, 1.

Maynard, A. and Ludbrook, A. (1980b) Budget allocation in the National Health Service, in *Journal of Social Policy*, 9, 3.

Maynard, A. and Ludbrook, A. (1980c) Thirty years of fruitless endeavour? An analysis of government intervention in the health care market, paper presented to World

Congress of Health Economics Leiden, September.

Maynard, A. and Walker, A. (1977) Too Many Doctors?, in *Lloyds Bank Review*, July.

Newhouse, J.P. and Friedlander, L.J. (1980) The relationship between medical resources and measures of health: some additional evidence, in *Journal of Human Resources*, 15, 2.

Office of Health Economics (1979) *Compendium of Health Statistics*, London.

Royal Commission on the National Health Service (1979) *Report* (Chairman: Sir A. Merrison), Cmnd. 7615, HMSO, London.

Russell, I.T., Devlin, H.B. *et al.* (1977) Day case surgery for hernias and haemorrhoids, in *Lancet*, 1.

Walters, V. (1980) *Class Inequality and Health Care*, Croom Helm, London.

Acknowledgement

This paper was presented at the 1980 meeting of the British Association for the Advancement of Science, University of Salford. The author would like to acknowledge the Social Science Research Council for a programme research grant in Public Sector Studies at the Department of Economics and the Institute of Social and Economic Research at the University of York, and to thank Anne Ludbrook for her assistance in the preparation of this paper.

The Personal Social Services: Incrementalism, Expediency or Systematic Social Planning?*

Adrian Webb and Gerald Wistow

Introduction

For the purposes of this chapter we shall deem the personal social services (PSS) to consist of the 116 local authority social services departments established in England and Wales in 1970/1. To these must be added the wide range of related social care and support provided by voluntary organisations and mutual aid groups, as well as neighbours, friends and kin of people in social need. Alongside these statutory, voluntary and informal care systems there is also a significant body of 'private enterprise welfare', ranging from residential homes and hostels in which the 'welfare' component can be readily recognised, to clubs and entertainment establishments in which commercial goals and relationships are paramount but around which patterns of friendship and mutual aid may flourish. The personal social services, therefore, cannot be viewed as other than a 'mixed economy of welfare' (Webb & Wistow, 1982).

Does the existence of a 'mixed economy' limit the significance of public expenditure; how feasible are the alternatives to state provision? Despite the growth of professional social work, it is still much easier to accept that there is an alternative to professional, state, personal social services than is the case in health care. Not only are professional field workers a relatively small part of the paid labour force of the personal social services (Wolfenden, 1977, p.36), but much of the need met by the services permits a considerable degree of substitution: of voluntary, informal or private provision for state services and of unpaid and 'untrained' labour for paid and professional labour.

Unpaid women — relatives, friends and volunteers — always have been, and remain, the core source of help for people in need of 'tending' (Parker, 1980). Their work prevents an immeasurable volume of care for old, young, handicapped, sick and socially isolated and downcast people falling upon the state. The fact of this high degree of substitutability accounts in large measure

*From Walker, A. (ed.) (1982) *Public expenditure and social policy*, Heinemann, London, pp. 137–64 (updated and abridged 1983).

for the very late emergence of the personal social services as the 'Fifth Social Service': a sharp dichotomy, between state institutional care (rooted in the Poor Law) and informal and voluntary care, characterized provision long after a comprehensive range of state services had been developed in other fields.

Once the commitment to a larger state role was accepted in practice, public expenditure was bound to rise; but public expenditure is also the bedrock on which much voluntary, and private, care is founded. These formal services are in turn an important means of underpinning much informal care, they enable hard-pressed relatives to obtain advice, temporary relief and support. The apparent failure of much formal service provision to measure up to the actual needs of informal carers (Bayley, 1973; Robinson, 1978) does not negate the essential point that public expenditure 'ripples' through the 'mixed' economy' and directly buys or indirectly calls forth a much larger body of care than is provided by the state services themselves. There is therefore no feasible alternative to significant levels of public *expenditure* even though there are alternatives to state service *provision*.

Substantive Policy in the PSS

No complex field of public administration rests upon a single statement of policy and the PSS are no exception. Policies abound. Nevertheless, the analysis of public expenditure on, and the planning of, the PSS can reasonably be based on a gross simplification. Let us assume that the policy which underpinned the development of these services consisted of two main components: a commitment to respond to unmet and changing levels and types of need in the personal social services and a commitment to 'community care'. The former seems straightforward enough; the latter requires closer examination.

Community care: a guiding concept?

What kind of policy is 'community care' and what does it imply for the planning and financing of the personal social services? The answer cannot be simple. Community care can be understood as a policy with its centre of gravity in the personal social services themselves, in the health services, in the health and personal social services conceived as an interlocking system of services, or in the entire field of social policies conceived of in system terms. It may also be seen as a policy which places any one of the following to the fore: client need and well-being; the reduction of state expenditure *per se*; or the balancing of needs and scarcity and the attainment of the optimal use of resources. (These latter perspectives correspond to our three types of planning noted later.) By permutating the 'centres of gravity' and the key perspectives, the apparently simple commitment to community care is fractionalised into a variety of significantly different policies, each with distinctive planning implications.

Taking the *personal social services as the centre of gravity,* community care has taken two main forms. The first, which held sway throughout the 1960s and early 1970s, emphasised the need to develop domiciliary care, day care, sheltered housing and support services in order to avoid the unnecessary institutionalization of people in residential homes and also to enrich the lives of needy people living in the community. The implication was that a sufficient level of service development could both reduce unmet need and lead to a more optimal use of resources, but the minimum necessary level of residential care and the structure of services to be sought could only be established by monitoring the well-being of clients in different forms of care. The second notion of community care gained strength through the second half of the 1970s and emphasized 'care *by* the community', that provided by family, friends, neighbours and volunteers, It recognized the importance of perceiving the personal social services as an interlocking set of statutory and non-statutory, formal and informal, paid and unpaid sources of care. Whether this recognition was, or is, inspired primarily by considerations of client well-being or of public expenditure containment remains uncertain. The cost-effectiveness of any particular structure of caring also remains uncertain, but the alternatives to statutory and professional care are widely assumed to be a cost-effective investment for the state.

If one locates the *centre of gravity in the health services,* a community care policy could begin to look rather different. As a policy rooted in medical and nursing interpretations of client need and of good professional practice, for example, it could imply the production of those community-based services essential to a curative medical model. The 'blockage' of acute hospital beds by the elderly is a prime instance of the importance of community services to an optimal throughput of patients in acute wards. However, 'blockage' is not confined to the acute sector: a slow throughput of patients also inhibits the practice of the curative model of medicine in what have traditionally been the chronic, or long-stay, specialisms (for example, geriatrics and mental health). The double pressure for 'throughput' would require heavy investment in non-hospital services and a significant part of it would be for socially dependent clients with a temporary or long-term need for residential-type services. This provision could be the responsibility of the health services themselves (for example health service hostels), the local authority social services departments, other local authority departments (for example sheltered housing), or the voluntary and private sectors. The precise implications for the local authority social services departments would depend upon the balance struck in this mixed economy, but it is clear that *capital* expenditure would be crucial.

The curative medical approach could be and has been seen to make economic as well as professional good sense. However, an even broader and more cost-conscious strategy might emphasize the expansion of *preventive* policies and the careful evaluation and containment of the curative model. Such an approach could suggest a further expansion of care services.

The ambiguity inherent in community care as a policy conceals a sharp dilemma; pursued within the personal social services it involves reducing dependence on residential-type provision by expanding domiciliary and day care; pursued within the health and personal services conjointly it involves a *further* expansion of domiciliary and day care *and also the maintenance, or expansion, of residential-type provision.* Increasing need adds a further pressure and in the case of very elderly people this includes heavy demand for residential care or high intensity care substitutes (for example, very sheltered housing).

Both the level of expansion of provision and the service structure to be aimed at are therefore problematic features of the community care policy. The only clear fact is that high levels of growth are implied in both capital and current expenditures. The Poor Law inheritance (especially residential homes for old people) and the post-war neglect of the PSS also added a need for replacement and improvements in quality, including the quality of staff training. From the point of view of the planning and management of the PSS, therefore, the task has been one of repairing an old pattern of service and creating a new one simultaneously in order to cater for the changing needs of growing client populations referred directly 'from the community' and also rehabilitated 'to the community', while the very meaning of community-based care has been expanding from that of local authority provision to include the 'informal care system'. No better case could be found for the development of social planning which moves beyond incremental growth and change.

Let us specify, therefore, an 'ideal' policy environment in which local authorities could reasonably be expected to respond creatively to the diverse pressures on the personal social services. It would include the following features: first, service 'packages' would need to be designed specifically to meet increased demand from the community at large *and* to effect those transfers of patients from the NHS which would prove to be appropriate and cost-effective; second, these desiderata take two forms which can be summarised as the 'expenditure' and 'policy' components. We have outlined a stringent, but straightforward, set of expenditure desiderata: adequate and *steady* growth on both capital and revenue accounts. This would include political acceptance of the fact that a disproportionately high rate of growth in the PSS is not a 'luxury' but an essential component of a policy which is believed to be cost effective, as well as in the best interests of clients.

The policy component of our desiderata would entail a precise elaboration of how community care was to be achieved and how, in service development terms, it was to be related to changes in the level and nature of client demand. This precise specification would provide the planning base for costing objectives and translating them into expenditure projections. In practice, however, detailed national estimates of need for each type of service have not been published as a basis for planning; planning in the PSS has never been that firmly centralized. For this very reason, it is impossible conclusively to argue that any particular expenditure growth rate has, or has not, been adequate.

This state of affairs can be defended. There has been no universal agreement on how best to cater for the frail elderly or the unemployed, mentally ill ex-offender with family responsibilities, for example. Experimentation in service provision, rather than central prescription, has been a key need in most client groups and the DHSS approach has been far from *dirigiste;* it has not stifled local variation. Nevertheless, the possibilities of centrally led discussion and analysis of service possibilities has been demonstrated by the National Development Group in the care of the mentally handicapped and the lack of a similar focal point in other fields has been marked.

A second crucial element of the policy component can be best characterised as the specification of priorities. In the event that the flow of resources proved to be below the level needed to achieve all policy objectives, priorities would be needed to guide a more limited form of progress. Given a central government policy linking health and personal social services development, the setting of priorities is necessarily a central government task to a large extent. The need for firm guidance on priorities, however, can best be judged by considering the history of expenditure on the PSS. We have outlined an ideal expenditure environment. Has this been approximated in reality?

Trends in Public Expenditure on the PSS

On the major criticisms levelled at the Seebohm Report was that, unlike other major social policy reports of the time, it did not provide a systematic analysis of need from which to argue for increases in public expenditure (Townsend, 1971). In this sense the Seebohm Committee could be said to have produced the first report of the era of welfare state austerity and defensiveness rather than the last of the era of welfare state growth and self-confidence. Yet the Committee met during, and helped to accentuate, a period of rapid growth in the personal social services. The paradox is explained by the political caution of the Committee which contrasted to the general growth in social public expenditure during the 1960s and early 1970s and with the upsurge of political sympathy and power which the personal social services enjoyed in many local authorities.

The general expenditure picture in the PSS is one of more rapid growth than that in any other social service, but *from a very low base line.* In 1955, the equivalent of what are now the PSS accounted for 0.2% of GNP; by 1976 the PSS accounted for 1.0% (Gould & Roweth, 1980). This fivefold increase in their share of national income was mirrored by a similar, though smaller, expansion of their share of all public expenditure, from 0.6% in 1955 to 1.9% in 1976 (Gould & Roweth, 1980). The social services have been favoured within the general field of public expenditure, but expenditure on the PSS has nevertheless grown twice as fast as all social expenditure. The same pattern of differential growth has also been repeated within the health and personal social services programme; the PSS accounted for 11.6% of the health and PSS programme in 1970/1 and 15.2% in 1979/80 (Treasury, 1975; Treasury, 1980). . . .

While the period of growth did much to establish the PSS on a relatively firm footing, the increase in the share of public expenditure enjoyed by the PSS seems to have come to an end by the mid-1970s and to have approximately stabilized. The share of all public expenditure reached a peak in 1977/8 at 2.0% and the share of the health and personal social services programme peaked in 1976/7 at 15.0%, regaining that level only in 1979/80 (Treasury 1975; Treasury 1980). This suggests that the harsh economic and public expenditure climate of the late 1970s put an end to further differential growth and brought the community care strategy into question. It is therefore a period which will be considered in more detail below. . . .

Expenditure on local authority services in influenced by three primary factors: centrally planned levels of future expenditure, the levels of expenditure actually allowed for the current year by central government, and the decisions made by local authorities about levels of rate-borne expenditure and the distribution of expenditure between services. In looking more closely at expenditure in the 1970s, therefore, it is useful to bear in mind both the expenditure environment created by central government and the nature of the local authority response.

In the 1971 public expenditure white paper, the first following the creation of the social services departments, the commitment to community care was reaffirmed and budgeted for in the following terms: a major objective for local authority personal social services is to shift the balance of care from hospitals to the community where this is more appropriate. The new group of local personal social services is planned to show a growth rate at constant prices of 9.2% in 1972/3 and thereafter an average annual compound rate of 6.8%, compared with a growth rate for hospital services of 3 and 3.5% respectively (Treasury, 1971, p.53). The following year this growth rate was raised to 8.5% for the years to 1976/7 (Treasury 1972a, p.73). That central government did not envisage unlimited growth as the price to be paid for community care became clear in December 1973, however. Local authorities had in fact promoted, or not prevented, expenditures which 'substantially exceeded [those] forecast' (Treasury 1973: 101). The out-turn figures showed rates of growth over previous years of 17.2% in 1972/3 and 18.7% in 1973/4.

World oil prices were dramatically raised in 1973, of course, and local authority 'overspending' was therefore not the only cause for concern, but the future was still seen to be one of steady and significant growth. A growth rate of 7% was projected for 1972/3 to 1977/8 (Treasury, 1973) with enough room for the pursuit of several objectives simultaneously. In the event, the local authorities continued to pursue more than the planned level of expenditure and the growth rate for 1973/4 to 1974/5 proved to be 13.8% on current account (Treasury, 1975). Capital expenditure had taken a severe tumble, however, from a rate of growth of 38.3% in the previous year to a *reduction* of 25.2%. The first sign of retrenchment notwithstanding, current expenditure had grown by two-thirds and capital expenditure by nearly one-half (at constant prices) in the first five years of the 1970s compared with an increase of one-fifth in total public expenditure (see Table 1). Central government had maintained a policy of differential development in favour of the PSS and the local authorities had responded more than fully.

Table 1 The growth in net outturn expenditure in the 1970s.

| | 1970/1 to 1974/5 (at 1974 survey prices) | | 1975/6 to 1979/80 (at 1979 survey prices) | |
	£m	%	£m	%
Current expenditure	209.9	66.2	114	12.4
Capital expenditure	27.4	47.8	–45	–36.8
Total PSS expenditure	237.3	63.4	99	7.7
Total public expenditure	6756	21.2	2354	3.2

Sources: Treasury (1975) Table 2.11 and Treasury (1980) Table 2.11.

It is from this point that the 1970s becomes a litany of cuts with capital expenditure having to be savagely pruned in order to make possible a sharp reduction in the rate of growth of current expenditure. From the 1975 public expenditure white paper onwards, the projected growth rate in current expenditure fell to, and below, the 2% level deemed necessary to meet increasing demand and it was not until the 1978 white paper (Treasury, 1978) that future growth was seen to be able to rise to 3% (in 1981/2). On the capital side a consistent trend downwards was planned, with cuts in the order of 30 to 45% in the early years. Positive rates of projected growth in capital (scheduled for 1980/1) did not reappear until the 1978 white paper. In addition, the system of cash limits introduced in 1976 precipitated uncertainty in the budgeting of expenditure during the course of each financial year. Consequently, far from exceeding planned expenditure, in the years 1976/7 to 1978/9 local authorities underspent by 2, $1\frac{1}{2}$ and $\frac{1}{2}$% respectively (Treasury, 1978; 1979b). The effect of the environment created by central government and the local authority response was reflected in the overall growth figures for the second half of the 1970s: current expenditure grew by only one-eighth while capital expenditure fell by more than one-third (see Table 1).

The PSS suffered in the mid-1970s; the adjustment was a difficult one. But did the confluence of central and local government restraint break the previous pattern of differential treatment? Had other services fared less well? The central government intention was certainly to maintain this pattern to a very limited extent by offering some protection to the PSS. Many local authorities, though by no means all, also continued to give particular support to these services. The figures in Table 1 suggest that a real degree of protection was achieved, but the PSS share of total public expenditure and of the health and personal social services programme did level off in the late 1970s.

Nevertheless, it must be remembered that a low rate (2%) of real growth remained the government target for the PSS in the second half of the 1970s, with cuts concentrated on capital. Moreover, by the time Labour left office in 1979, a slightly faster rate of growth had been built into forward planning, and the need for increased capital expenditure had also been recognized. To this must be added the introduction of joint financing, money earmarked within the health budget to be spent primarily on local authority services relevant to the health services (DHSS, 1976b). This new mechanism for transferring resources within the health and PSS programme provided the DHSS with a tangible means of protecting the PSS by emphasising the link with the health services.

Despite this slightly more optimistic note, however, we cannot avoid the conclusion that the expenditure desiderata of the community care strategy had been shattered in several ways in the mid-1970s. Capital expenditure had been savagely cut and although some growth had been preserved on current account it was insufficient for the pursuit of multiple objectives and the revenue consequences of the earlier capital programme. Perhaps most important, however, was the uncertainty which had been injected into the resource and political environments. This uncertainty favoured a radical shift in local authority thinking about 'community care'. Because central government financial support for local government is not hypothecated, or 'earmarked', a particular service cannot easily be exempted from a general worsening of the environment in which local government operates. The mid-1970s heralded the beginning of a period in which local authorities have been particularly subject to calls for economies and to charges of pushing public expenditure out of control. The pressure contains *a fortiori*, but the scene was set by the Environment Secretary's blunt announcement in May 1975: 'The party is over' (Crosland, 1975).

By the mid-1970s, therefore, the second element of the policy component of the community care strategy had become crucial: guidance was needed on priorities. To consider this further we need to examine government approaches to planning the PSS.

Social Planning and the PSS

A rudimentary typology of approaches to planning

If we think of planning as a systematic attempt to develop and implement policies for specified periods into the future, we can see that different types of planning could be expected to result from different resources and intellectual climates. Let us identify three 'ideal-types': *demand (or need) planning, supply planning,* and *demand-scarcity planning.*

In the first the intellectual and political climate, and/or the relative abundance of resources, enables demand considerations to dominate. The task is to determine what needs should be met and how. An appropriate flow of resources through time is then planned such that need objectives will be achievable. Problems on the supply side may intervene in the form of temporary scarcities which necessitate the rephasing of programmes. Nevertheless, supply side considerations are a minor and technical issue in this form of planning. We could argue that this position was approximated at times during the 1960s and the early 1970s (until approximately 1975/6) and that the welfare state ethos supported such an approach to planning.

Supply planning, by way of contrast, could be characterised as planning dominated by a preoccupation with retrenchment, the pursuit of 'market compression' at all costs. The scarcity of resources is the *leitmotif* of this approach to planning and need considerations are subordinate to them, as are those routes to cost-effective expenditure which produce slow results or which require short-term increases in expenditure if they are to be achieved. The domination of supply considerations may arise from politically exogenous forces which give rise to extreme pressure on resources or to extreme unpredictability of resources (for example long-term economic decline, or international determinants of energy supplies). A commitment to supply planning may equally reflect political ideology and a desire to restrict public expenditure. It is a strong candidate for the post-1979 years, and possibly for occasions during the years after 1975/6.

Demand-scarcity planning, on the other hand, refers to an approach which attempts to reconcile demand (need) with scarcity, the latter provoking a search for 'market *limitation*' (rather than 'market *compression*') and for cost-effectiveness. The conjoint recognition of need and scarcity would therefore *not* lead to a search for market compression *at all costs*. Demand-scarcity planning has been advocated with increasing rigour by public sector economists and in so far as public expenditure has always been subject to limits it was never far from the surface even in the heyday of growth. Nevertheless, it could be expected to have characterized particularly the period from 1975/6 to 1979.

The general philosophy of governance espoused by governments may have seemed less relevant to the analysis of planning had not the Conservative party come to power in 1979. However its commitment to 'roll back the frontiers of the state' has found expression in the PSS in a firm criticism of the *dirigiste* approach to planning which previous governments are said to have adopted (Jenkin, 1979). It is a criticism which needs more careful consideration than we can give, but its very existence has challenged what had remained axiomatic since Enoch Powell (as Minister of Health in 1962) inaugurated ten-year planning exercises: namely, the exercise of central government influence (especially through long-term planning) in an attempt to achieve a coordinated strategy towards community care across the health–social services boundary. It emphasises the importance of 'styles' of planning, the centralist–decentralist dimension within planning, and also the extent to which planning is primarily seen as either a means of gaining direct control over, or as a means of providing incentives to, actors at the periphery.

The point of identifying these ideal types of planning is not to 'periodize' recent history. Rather it is to draw attention to the way in which planning rests on an intellectual climate, dominant values sets and ideologies, particular resource environments, and on differing analytical skills and academic disciplines. If planning closely approximates ones of the ideal types, it will presumably be because the underpinning factors are substantially in accord. Let us trace the principal changes in planning during the periods of growth and retrenchment.

1960–75/6: a period of demand planning?

Can the years of rapid growth reasonably be described as a brief flowering of demand (need) planning: was it *demand-led?* Was it *planned* growth? The absence of comprehensive need data in the Seebohm Report was not critical in one sense. The period was increasingly characterised by a consciousness of unmet need, many need estimates had already been produced by the time the Seebohm Committee was established, and the creation of research units within the new social departments resulted in a powerful increase in social need research after 1970 (most obviously in response to the Chronically Sick and Disabled Persons Act, 1970). The concept of demand-based planning was also built into the community care policy. The recognized need for community services was actively to be translated into demand by central government; hospital provision was to be restricted for the long-stay patients who had hitherto depended on the health services for social care. Moreover, need was also translated into direct client demand by the creation of the social services departments; whether because of improved accessibility, increasing need, or a 'higher profile', the services became more 'popular' with potential clients.

However, the major part of this period of growth actually took place within a very loose planning framework; they were years of demand planning, but with the emphasis of demand rather than planning. The ten-year plans of the mid-1960s were intended to coordinate health and social services provision. Yet, while a degree of direct central government control was available within the health services, the local authorities were merely exhorted to take account of health service intentions when developing their own plans (Ministry of Health, 1962; 1963). Central government influence was exercised directly through capital expenditure approvals, but the influence on current expenditure was limited primarily to the impact of community care as a generalized statement of policy intent. Moreover, the services which were to be brought together as a result of the Seebohm Report (1968) were still scattered across several local authority departments until 1971 and the technical skills needed for planning were equally scattered, in so far as they existed at all. The great advantage which the prospect of long-term growth brought, however, was flexibility. Rapid increases in capital expenditure could be achieved, when economic policy permitted, precisely because there was real hope of the revenue expenditure implications being met from future growth.

The abiding irony of the history of the personal social services is that a more systematic attempt at forward planning was launched just before the growth bubble burst. The 1972 ten-year planning cycle represented the first step towards a 'central guidance' planning approach embracing capital and revenue and based on an assumed annual growth rate of 10% on current account (DHSS, 1972). . . . In reality the guidelines were essentially arbitrary. But they clearly specified the necessity of developing a continuum of care to meet a variety of contingencies. This was an essential goal for a service struggling towards the universal and comprehensive social service model upheld in other areas of social policy. . . .

The plans foundered on public expenditure restraint almost before the ink was dry. Growth continued at a relatively rapid pace for several years after 1972/3, but the expectation of a long-term average of 10% growth per annum was lost in the upsurge of economic uncertainty.

1975/6–79: a case of rational, 'need-scarcity', planning?

The onset of severe expenditure restraint promoted potentially valuable planning developments as well as introducing dislocation and distortion. The reaction to restraint was not negativism. The central government, and many local authorities, attempted to respond creatively. In addition to the fact that the personal social services were somewhat protected from the full impact o of expenditure cuts, an attempt was made to develop priorities and to implement them. A radical approach to resource reallocation was also initiated in the health service and the requirement placed on health and local authorities to engage in joint planning was emphasized by the introduction of joint financing (DHSS, 1976b). It is for this reason that the period merits consideration as one of 'needs-scarcity' planning, rather than a blind market compression.

On what criteria could priorities be established in the mid-1970s? The first was that of *need:* priority could be given to services and client groups in which need was growing most rapidly, or to those groups that had been accorded low priority in the past and in which there was considerable unmet need. The most obvious priority in terms of increasing need was the elderly, especially the very elderly frail and infirm. The groups which had a claim on the basis of past neglect, however, were the mentally ill, mentally handicapped and the younger physically handicapped. The second possibility was professionally and politically mediated *demand.* From the point of view of the local authority member, and of field social workers, services for children and families were the 'natural' priority because they gave rise to 'mainstream' social work tasks and because of the media attention given to non-accidental injury. From a personal social services perspective, therefore, there were entirely good reasons for trying to give attention to all client groups, which is hardly surprising in view of the concentration of highly vulnerable people in these services.

The third criterion, *cost-effectiveness*, raises different considerations, however. . . . From the NHS-PSS perspective, personal social services provision for children and families is least critical, the dependence of the NHS on a continuum of community care services is more immediate in the other client groups. But we have also noted that cost effective community care could *mean different things* from these different perspectives. Given the widespread belief that the cost-effective use of resources within the social services department requires a reduction in residential provision, one would expect local authorities to behave accordingly given the opportunity. The opportunity to minimise residential provision depends on two factors: the proportion of the client population capable of living 'in the community' given support services; and the extent to which local authorities can control the flow of clients through their services.

The combined effect of these two forces gave local authorities more opportunity for change in the child-care services. The Children and Young Persons Act 1969 had reduced the control over the disposal of children exercised through juvenile courts and thus allowed local authorities to experiment with different patterns of service. The onset of public expenditure restraint therefore created a 'natural experiment' in need-scarcity planning. different criteria existed on which to base priorities and different degrees of 'systems-interaction' were implied in the concepts of community care and cost-effectiveness in the various client groups. How broadly or narrowly was the planning task perceived in practice? What priorities were established? By whom? And how far did planning change the pattern of service provision?

The central government response to expenditure restraint gradually evolved into a significantly altered approach to planning. The effective collapse of the 1972 attempt at ten-year planning heralded an interregnum in which a variety of somewhat contradictory advice was given to local authorities. The clearest message was that services to clients should be preserved at the expense of administrative and other 'unproductive' functions. It is a message which has endured. One of the targets for cuts that was specifically singled out was research and development (DOE. 1975a), despite the fact that this resource was quite rapidly being redeployed from social need research to work on cost-effectiveness, resource allocation, and management information systems. Another suggestion — one that has gained ground steadily over time — was that local authorities should utilise voluntary organizations more fully and generally become more engaged with the non-statutory sector (DOE, 1974). A third was that long-term preventive work would have to be sacrificed (DOE,

1975b). This particular piece of advice merely reflected the deep and continuing uncertainty about the real meaning of community care.

By 1976/7 this initial period of unsystematic advice had given way to a far more specific and well orchestrated central government response. It took two main forms: the publication of consultative priorities documents in 1976 and 1977 (DHSS 1976a, 1977b) and the reinstatement of a planning cycle on a three-year, rather than a ten-year, time scale (DHSS, 1977a). The planning guidelines approach adopted in 1972 was retained, but the priorities documents provided a broad framework within which they could be set. Both these developments emphasised the DHSS intention of seeking a coordinated use of resources across the NHS–PSS boundary and not merely within each service separately. The internal organisation of the DHSS and the programme budgeting approach both had been developed to facilitate a unified view of client groups across the health and personal social services. The priorities documents were a public reflection of this concern and were widely hailed as a valuable contribution to strategic planning in hard times.

From the PSS point of view, however, the criticisms of the docucments were inevitable. All the major PSS client groups were identified as of high priority in recognition of demand and need pressures and community care objectives, with the highest rate of growth allocated to services for the mentally handicapped and the mentally ill (DHSS, 1976b; Annex 2). Nevertheless, the PSS were only allowed a marginally higher growth rate (2%) than that permitted in the health services (1.8%) for the years from 1975/6 to 1979/80. As we have seen, this revenue growth was itself bought at the price of a decimated capital expenditure programme.

The very achievement of a unified approach to priorities had also re-emphasised the fundamental weakness of social planning in this field. The health services and the medical perspective command far more attention and public and political support than do the PSS. Moreover, the DHSS *manage* a national health service organised on the basis of field decentralization, but central government's relationship with social services departments is essentially advisory. The DHSS were able to develop an integrated set of expenditure projections, but the Department could not control the resource allocation mechanisms which determined actual expenditure, nor could it greatly influence the national and local political climates in which the social services departments operated.

The Pattern of Services Produced by Local Authorities

. . . What have been the outputs of local expenditure processes, in aggregate terms, in relation to changes in need and to the policy objectives discussed above?

We may begin by specifying three hypotheses about the ways in which local

Table 2 Provision of selected services for the elderly 1974/5–1980/1 (England and Wales)

	1974/5	1975/6	1976/7	1977/8	1978/9	1979/80	1980/1	Per cent change 1980/1 on 1974/5
Residential care								
Total in Care	188,397	120,256	125,479	127,034	126,083	125,152	122,174	+3.2
Per thousand population 65+	17.9	17.7	17.9	18.1	17.7	17.5	16.7	−6.7
Per thousand population 75+	49.7	49.2	49.7	50.2	48.1	47.0	44.2	−11.1
Home help								
Total number (WTE)	36,598	43,623	40,563	42,373	43,231	42,221	43,711	+19.4
Per thousand population 65+	5.5	6.4	5.8	6.1	6.1	5.9	6.0	+9.1
Per thousand population 75+	15.4	17.8	16.1	16.8	16.5	15.8	15.8	+2.6
Total cases	542,342	583,299	600,051	629,006	637,216	665,074	624,611	+15.2
Per thousand population 65+	81.9	85.6	85.7	89.8	89.3	92.7	85.3	+4.2
Per thousand population 75+	227.7	238.5	237.4	248.8	243.1	249.5	225.9	−0.8
Total hours service	71,599,571	70,141,417	70,042,328	72,083,228	71,327,619	72,415,063	72,902,116	+1.8
Per thousand population 65+	10,816	10,298	10,008	10,295	9,995	10,097	9,952	−8.0
Per thousand population 75+	30,069	28,674	27,715	28,510	27,207	27,170	26,364	−12.3
Meals								
Total number	38,329,536	41,275,988	42,381,635	41,035,792	40,262,859	42,650,718	41,251,827	+7.6
Per thousand population 65+	5,790	6,060	6,056	5,861	5,642	5,947	5,631	−2.7
Per thousand population 75+	16,097	16,873	16,770	16,230	15,358	16,003	14,918	−7.3
Elderly persons								
Total aged 65+	6,619,722	6,811,158	6,998,515	7,001,496	7,136,732	7,171,976	7,325,480	+10.7
Percent of total population	13.9	14.2	14.4	14.4	14.7	14.8	15.1	+8.6
Total aged 75+	2,381,195	2,446,260	2,527,241	2,528,318	2,621,657	2,665,261	2,765,247	+16.1
Percent of total population	5.0	5.1	5.2	5.2	5.4	5.5	5.7	+14.0

Source: CIPFA, 1974/5–1980/1. Table updated since original publication.
Notes: 1. Number of authorities covered (maximum 116): 1974/5 = 110; 1975/6 = 111; 1976/7 = 112; 1977/8 = 113; 1978/9 = 113; 1979/80 = 112; 1980/1 = 114.
2. Home help figures assume the elderly consume 87% of total home help provision which is consistent with the percentage reported in 'Health and Personal Social

authorities might have allocated resources during the period under review. First expenditure growth and reductions were determined and distributed *incrementally*. Second, resource allocations were made through *'rational' planning processes* with the object of (i) responding to changes in the nature and extent of need; (ii) implementing community care in one or more of its various guises; (iii) shifting priorities between client groups; and (iv) protecting direct services to clients in the search for savings. Third, reductions in expenditure were dictated by *expediency*, that is they were determined by political acceptability and the 'ease' with which they could be made.

Regrettably, the nationally available evidence on which we must rely in reviewing locally determined levels and patterns of service is not always complete or conclusive. . . .

Within these limiations, however, the material presented in Tables 2–6 does enable trends to be identified in patterns of spending and service production during the greater part of the 1970s. If the relationship of such trends to need is not fully apparent, this is partly because of the absence of authoritative national need estimates. . . . In the absence of locally relevant need estimates, therefore, DHSS norms and guidelines have to be relied on as proxies for need. . . . Whatever the weaknesses of planning guidelines as need proxies, the extent of underprovision compared with official targets is clear.

In the case of the elderly, shortfall is now growing rather than diminishing. Between 1962 and 1976 the proportion of elderly persons receiving domiciliary services doubled (Bebbington, 1980). This advance was partially offset, Bebbington argues, by the fact that, age for age, levels of disability among the elderly were greater in 1976 than 1962. Nonetheless, the gains were real in contrast with the position since then. As Table 2 shows, the growth of residential care, meals, and home help hours have all failed to keep pace with the growing numbers of elderly persons in recent years. The disparity is even more pronounced for the over 75s than the newly retired, among whom need levels tend to be lower. . . .

Table 3 and the LAPS data (DHSS, 1979a) indicate that the proportion of expenditure devoted to the elderly is declining marginally, quite in contrast to national guidance. There has been insufficient growth in the second half of the 1970s to meet multiple objectives. An apparently endless stream of *causes célèbres* have made deficiences in services for children highly visible. Provision for the mentally handicapped, although inadequate in comparison with planning guidelines, has also absorbed an increasing proportion of PSS expenditure. It is the elderly who have suffered most noticeably from these pressures: services for the elderly provide some of the most ready opportunities for making savings. Table 4 shows that domiciliary services used mainly by the elderly were the first to suffer the effects of the reduced rates of expenditure growth. Holidays and support for sheltered housing were also cut, while the rate of growth for aids and adaptations was also very substantially reduced. Residential services (except for children) and day care services continued to

Table 3 Allocation by client group of personal social security expenditure 1972/3 and 1977/8 (England).

Client group[1]	1972/3 %	1977/8 %
Children and families	22.6	23.1
Elderly	35.5	33.2
Younger physically handicapped	3.5	2.4
Mentally handicapped	6.7	7.2
Mentally ill	0.8	0.6
Fieldwork	11.5	11.5
Administration (including research and development)	15.2	15.8
Other[2]	4.2	6.2

Notes: 1. Expenditure on home help has been allocated to individual client groups in proportion to their use of the service as shown in 'Health and Personal Social Services Statistics'.
2. Other expenditure includes expenditure on multi-purpose day centres and clubs, aids, adaptations, telephones, holidays, support to sheltered housing schemes and unallocated home help expenditure.

Source: Derived from 'Local Government Financial Statistics', 1972/3, Table 4.2, and 1977/8, Table 9B.

expand significantly. We may speculate that these developments did not reflect an explicit reversal in the degree of priority accorded to the elderly or to the expansion of domiciliary services in comparison with residential and day care. It seems at least as likely that this pattern was an expression of the need to accommodate the revenue effects of the earlier capital programme out of much constrained revenue budgets. One of the ironies of the late 1970s, therefore, was that expenditure restraint, at least initially, produced a shift to patterns of service development which were expensive in PSS terms.

Incrementalism, rationality or expediency?

With this apparent suggestion that expediency has dictated the shape of service production, we return to the three hypotheses with which we began this section. What light do our data shed on them? Was incrementalism, rationality or expediency the hallmark of expenditure decisions during the 1970s? Did the pattern vary with changes in the expenditure climate and in relation to different client groups?

The data showing the distribution of expenditure between the major types of service and client groups (Tables 2 and 5) appear to support the incrementalist

Table 4 Trends in Service Provision During the Period of Resource Restraint (England and Wales)

	1975/6	1976/7	1977/8	1978/9	1979/80	1980/1	Per cent change 1980/1 on 1975/6
	000s	000s	000s	000s	000s	000s	%
Residential care (occupied places)							
Elderly	120.3	125.5	127.0	126.1	125.2	122.2	+1.6
Children	37.3	37.3	36.3	34.2	33.3	30.8	-17.4
Mentally Ill	3.6	4.2	4.6	4.6	5.0	4.6	+27.8
Mentally Handicapped Adults	9.1	10.2	11.3	11.7	12.9	13.0	+42.9
Mentally Handicapped Children	1.8	1.9	2.1	2.1	2.2	2.4	+33.3
Physically Handicapped	6.0	6.6	6.9	7.3	7.5	7.0	+16.7
'Community care'							
Home Helps							
Number (WTE)	50.1	46.6	48.7	49.7	48.5	50.2	+0.2
Cases	670.5	689.7	723.0	732.4	764.5	717.9	+7.1
Hours Service	80,622.3	80,508.4	82,854.3	81,985.8	83,235.7	83,795.5	+3.9
Meals	41,276.0	42,381.6	41,035.8	40,262.9	42,650.7	41,251.8	-0.1
Telephones							
No. of installations assisted	15.1	11.5	14.7	17.9	14.2	9.4	-37.7
No. of rentals assisted	70.0	73.6	82.6	85.8	98.8	87.5	+25.0
Aids	240.5	241.5	274.6	289.8	275.1	287.7	+19.6
Adaptations	50.3	54.5	57.7	68.0	53.7	53.3	+6.0
Holidays	101.2	87.2	86.3	89.7	90.3	71.1	-29.7
No. of sheltered housing units assisted	90.4	93.3	91.3	75.3	78.0	69.4	-23.2
Children boarded out	31.8	34.0	35.1	35.5	37.2	36.6	+15.1
Fieldwork staff	21.0	22.2	23.0	24.0	25.3	24.6	+17.1
Administrative staff	17.2	18.8	19.7	18.8	18.4	18.4	+7.0

Source: CIPFA, 1975/6–1980/1. Table updated since original publication.
Notes: Number of authorities covered (maximum 116): 1975/6 = 111; 1976/7 = 112; 1977/8 = 113; 1978/9 = 113; 1979/80 = 112; 1980/1 = 114.

hypothesis. Neither the injection of 'double digit' growth nor its withdrawal appears to have had other than a very marginal effect on the share of the budget taken by different kinds of spending.

The evidence in Tables 4 and 6 that disproportionately high growth rates were experienced by day care services (up to 1978/9) and domiciliary services (up to 1975/6) merely reflects the low bases from which growth began and the relatively low cost of producing additional units of service in comparison with that of additional residential places. . . . In the longer term, the combined effects of minimal growth (barely sufficient to do more than cover social service department's joint finance pick up), together with a continuing expansion of joint financing, might begin to crack the incrementalist mould. Nevertheless, for the 1970s as a whole, the national aggregate data imply that incrementalism was the dominant force determining patterns of expenditure.

In support of a 'rational planning' hypothesis, however, we might cite the relatively large growth of domiciliary and day care provision for the elderly into the mid-1970s (Table 6) and the shift in the systems-wide balance of care in favour of the mentally ill and handicapped. . . . Further support for this hypothesis is to be found in the clear trend towards non-institutional patterns of child-care. Between 1974/5 and 1978/9 the proportion of children in care fostered rose from 32.8 to 36.2% while that for children in residential care fell from 38.2 to 34.8% (CIPFA 1976, 1980). Some of the other evidence is ambiguous. The recent reduction of administrative costs (Tables 4 and 5) could be seen as a rational attempt systematically to protect services to clients; DHSS advice has certainly promulgated this line of thought. In the longer term, however, it could undermine the capacity for rational planning through the reduction of research and management 'thinking' time. Similarly, cuts in population-specific levels of domiciliary provision could be seen either as undermining the pursuit of community care within the PSS or as a rational pursuit of community care across the health-personal social service boundary. Whether we have been witnessing 'supply planning' or 'scarcity-need planning' depends to a large extent on how individual local authorities have actually been using their services.

The influence of expediency in dictating the allocations of resources might be detected in a number of areas. The decimation of the capital programme threatened the system-wide concepts of community care. but it was also a 'rational' means of commissioning capital schemes already underway. The cuts experienced by most of the domiciliary services might also be evidence of expediency (Tables 4 and 6): home help hours, meals, aids and adaptations are all expenditure 'taps' which may be turned on or off with relative ease and certainly with little effect on the employment of professional staff. Again, however, the argument is by no means clear-cut because such action might be justified as a short-term planned measure to permit the consequences of the earlier large-scale capital spending to be taken into the main budget. Lastly, the trend to internalise spending within social services department budgets and thereby transfer the consequences of reduced growth to other agencies might also be suggested as evidence of a form of expediency. For example, there is evidence of reductions in the take-up of places in voluntary homes (DHSS 1979b: Table 1) and in assistance to sheltered housing, the very form of accommodation which could have a considerable effect upon demand for residential care (Table 4).

Table 5 Allocation of PSS expenditure by type of service, 1972/3–1977/8 (England)

	Gross expenditure			Net expenditure		
	1972/3	1975/6	1977/8	1972/3	1975/6	1977/8
	%	%	%	%	%	%
Fieldwork	9.5	9.9	9.8	11.5	11.6	11.5
Residential care	49.7	48.7	48.3	42.8	43.1	42.4
Day care	10.3	10.4	11.5	10.6	10.7	11.8
Community care	17.6	17.4	16.9	20.0	19.1	18.5
Administration (including Research and Development)	12.9	13.6	13.5	15.1	15.5	15.8

Note: 'Community care' includes home helps, meals, the boarding out of children, aids, adaptations, telephones, holidays, material and financial assistance to families under section 1 of the 1963 Children and Young Persons Act and support to sheltered housing schemes.

Source: Derived from 'Local Government Financial Statistics' 1972/3; 1975/6; 1977/8.

Little of the evidence is clear-cut and quite different interpretations are possible in a number of cases. Judgement is further complicated by three other factors. First, our data are of a national aggregate nature. The resource experience of individual local authorities has varied considerably as has their response to growth, constraint and government guidance. Second, our data provide almost no indication of changes in the way that services are deployed and used. It is known, for example, that admission criteria for, and the population of, homes for the elderly reflect increasing levels of disability.... In addition, we have not considered the extent to which homes are being used to provide short-term care and thus to support 'community based' care. . . .

Third, and perhaps most importantly, we are unable to identify how far apparently rational or incremental patterns of *expenditure allocations* and *service outputs* flow from correspondingly rational or incremental *planning processes*. . . . Relatively small changes in the share of spending on residential

Table 6 Personal social services: the growth of service provision 1971–8 (Great Britain)

	1971 (thousands)	1975 (thousands)	Per cent change 1975 on 1971	1976 (thousands)	1978 provisional (thousands)	Per cent change 1978 on 1976	Per cent change 1978 on 1971
Residential accommodation places							
Elderly	120.0	132.0	+10.0	137.0	141.0	+2.9	+17.5
Younger disabled	12.3	12.4	+0.8	11.0	11.2	+1.8	−8.9
Mentally ill	3.3	5.0	+51.5	4.7	6.3	+34.0	+90.9
Mentally handicapped	7.2	11.8	+63.9	12.4	16.4	+32.3	+27.8
Children	43.0*	45.9	+6.7	46.4	46.0	−0.9	+7.0
Day care places							
Multi-purpose	†	10.9	—	13.0	12.0	−7.7	+81.8
Elderly	†	13.9	—	19.7	23.3	+18.3	+77.9
Younger disabled	†	11.9	—	10.2	12.1	+18.6	+9.0
Mentally ill	†	3.8	—	3.4	4.7	+38.2	+23.7
Mentally handicapped	30.1*	37.7	+25.2	38.5	47.9	+24.4	+59.1
Day nurseries	25.3	30.8	+21.7	32.3	34.1	+5.6	+34.8
Domiciliary services							
Home helps — cases	504	708	+40.5	740.0	785.0	+6.1	+55.8
Main meals served	24 791.0	43 862.0	+76.9	44 772.0	45 197.0	+9.5	+82.3

Notes: * 1971 data not available: 1972 figure used.
† Data not available.

Source: Expenditure white papers. Cmnd 6721-11, p.79; Cmnd 7439, p.141: and Cmnd 7844, p.104.

care, for example, might be quite consistent with the simultaneous development of non-institutional forms of treatment for children and of non-hospital care for the mentally handicapped. . . .

This discussion serves to underline two points. First, the multiple objectives of community care make interpretation of the data exceedingly difficult. . . . Second, the rationality or otherwise of budgetary *processes* cannot be determined solely from the study of budgetary *outputs*. . . . How far the patterns we have observed were in fact intended and how far social services departments themselves were able to impose a rational pattern upon the flow of resources and clients, upon the inheritance of neglect and partial development, and upon the confusions and conflicts surrounding community care, is an issue which must remain unresolved at present. To that extent the cases for incrementalism, rationality or expediency remain largely untested and untestable at the national level.

The Conservative government: an exercise in supply planning?

The 1970s ended with the election of a Conservative government committed to the reduction of public expenditure, critical of much social work practice and anxious to secure a growing role for non-statutory forms of care within the PSS (see Webb & Wistow, 1982).

The new government's first expenditure white paper (Treasury, 1979b) marked a radical break with the past: the protected status of PSS spending was overturned. A period of rigorous supply planning, in which systems-wide concepts of community care would be sacrificed perforce, appeared to be under way. In practice, however, local authorities have continued the tradition of protection, as indeed they were urged to do by the Social Services Secretary. But it seemed likely that a two percent annual increase in expenditure would be enough to avoid real cuts in the levels of provision (especially population-specific levels). As (the subsequently revised) Tables 2 and 4 demonstrate, such fears were fully borne out by later events. An analysis of this failure to maintain service levels despite the real growth of personal social service expenditure was presented to the Social Services Committe of the House of Commons and published in Webb and Wistow (1983).

On the policy front the major thrust, as revealed in ministerial speeches, has been an advocacy of expansion in non-statutory welfare and especially in informal patterns of caring. This has been seen both as an attempt to reconcile growing demand with resource constraint and also as an expression of the kind of individual initiative and responsibility which the government wishes to promote in all sectors of economic and social life. By late 1980 few concrete initiatives had been taken. Indeed, it is unclear how far the government feels able to go beyond general exhortation: it appears to fear that intervention might undermine the spontaneity, creativity and independence of non-statutory welfare, the very features which it is most anxious to see preserved and extended. Previous administrations have shown interest in extending voluntary and informal care but without placing it at the centre of their approach to the PSS in quite the same way.

The role of the statutory sector is under review in relation to the wider issues of the balance of responsibilities within the mixed economy of social care. The central issue is the balance to be struck in social work and social services departments between direct service provision and the stimulation of local networks of informal care. The latter has been presented as a reassertion of Seebolm's suggestion that such care should be interwoven with, rather than replaced by, professional services. Ministers appear to be hoping that the Barclay Committee of Inquiry into the role of social work will give some priority to this issue (Barclay, 1982).

For the foreseeable future, the reinstatement of the growth rates experienced in the early 1970s seems improbable under governments of any political colour. While the PSS can legitimately claim an element of preferential treatment, it seems unlikely that sufficient resources will be available to meet the growth of need (including that arising from increased unemployment) and the transfer of social care responsibilities from the NHS. Two developments seem necessary, therefore. First, it will be increasingly necessary to create 'growth' out of existing budgets. This implies the pursuit of cost-effectiveness within the PSS and the transfer to them of resources from the NHS, where the expansion of PSS provision brings financial savings to the former. The latter approach is being actively considered within the DHSS, especially in relation to mental handicap, and some kind of initiative is probable in 1981. Difficulties to be overcome include the resistance of nursing unions; the requirement for short-term *additional* funds to permit the buildup of social services departments facilities before NHS provision can be wound down; and the Treasury's need to ensure that such transfers are effectively tied to real reductions in NHS provision. An initiative of this type is currently essential if the PSS are to play a growing part in the realisation of systems-wide concepts of community care.

The second element of a strategy for responding to severely limited growth involves a reassessment of the role of social services departments in community development. However, there is a real need to examine critically the potential and the limitations of informal care and of the organised voluntary sector. Again there is the difficulty that the expansion of non-statutory care implies at least a short-term injection of additional public funds to generate higher levels of activity. We simply do not know its longer-term implications for levels of expenditure, or care. Nonetheless, it seems highly possible that social services departments, caught between the twin pressures of growing demand and scarce resources, will increasingly seek a contribution from non-statutory sources.

References

Barclay, P.M. (1982) *Social workers, their role and tasks*, Bedford Square Press, London.

Bayley, M. (1973) *Mental handicap and community care*, Routledge and Kegan Paul, London.

Bebbington, A.C. (1980) Changes in the provision of social services to the elderly in the community over fourteen years, in *Social Policy and Administration*, Vol. 13, No.2, pp. 111-23.

Chartered Institute of Public Finance and Accountancy (CIPFA) (1976) *Personal social services statistics 1974/5 actuals* CIPFA, London.

Chartered Institute of Public Finance and Accountancy (CIPFA) (1980) *Personal social services statistics 1978/9 actuals*, CIPFA, London.

Crosland, A. (1975) The finance of housing, in *Housing Review*, Vol. 24, No. 5, pp. 128-30.

DHSS (1972) *Local authority social services ten year plans 1973-1983*, circular 35/72, DHSS, London.

DHSS (1976a) *Priorities for health and personal social services in England*, HMSO, London.

DHSS (1976b) *Joint care planning: health and local authorities*, circular HC(76)18, DHSS, London.

DHSS (1977a) *Forward planning of local authority social services*, LASSL(77)13, DHSS, London.

DHSS (1977b) *The way forward*, HMSO, London.

DHSS (1979a) *Local authority personal social services — summary of planning returns 1977/78 to 1980/1*, DHSS, London.

DHSS (1979b) *Health and personal social services statistics 1978*, HMSO, London.

DOE (1974) *Rate fund expenditure and rate calls in 1975/76*, circular 171/74, DOE, London.

DOE (1975a) *Local authority expenditure in 1976/7 — forward planning*, circular 68/75, DOE, London.

DOE (1975b) *Rate support grant settlement 1976/7*, circular 129/75, DOE, London.

Gould, F. and Roweth, B. (1980) Public spending and social policy: the United Kingdom 1950-77 in *Journal of Social Policy*, Vol. 9, No. 3, pp. 337-57.

Jenkin, P. (1979) *Speech to social services conference*, Bournemouth, 21 November 1979.

Ministry of Health (1962) *A hospital plan for England and Wales*, cmnd. 1604 HMSO, London.

Ministry of Health (1963) *The development of community care*, cmnd. 1973, HMSO, London.

Parker, R. (1980) *The future of the personal social services*, Seminar paper, Policy Studies Institute, London.

Robinson, A. (1978) *Parliament and public spending*, Heinemann Educational Books, London.

Seebohm Report (1968) *Report of the Committee on local authority and allied personal social services*, cmnd. 3703, HMSO, London.

Treasury (1971) *Public expenditure to 1975/6*, cmnd. 4829, HMSO, London.

Treasury (1972) *Handbook on methodology* HMSO, London.

Treasury (1973) *Public expenditure to 1977/8*, cmnd 5519, HMSO, London.

Treasury (1975) *Public expenditure to 1978/9*, cmnd 5879, HMSO, London.

Treasury (1978) *Public expenditure to 1981/2*, cmnd 7049, HMSO, London.

Treasury (1979) *The government's expenditure plans 1980/1*, cmnd 7746, HMSO, London.

Treasury (1980) *The government's expenditure plans 1980/1 to 1983/4,* cmnd 7841, HMSO, London.

Webb, A. and Wistow, G. (1982) *Whither State Welfare? Policy and Implementation in the Personal Social Services, 1979–80,* Royal Institute of Public Administration, London.

Webb, A. and Wistow, G. (1983) Public expenditure and policy implementation: the case of community care, in *Public Administration,* Vol. 1, No. 1, Spring.

Wolfenden Committee (1977) *The Future of Voluntary Organizations,* Croom Helm, London.

PART IV

Contemporary Issues in Social Policy

Introduction

In this last section we examine some of the developing issues in social policy which in many ways seems likely to characterise the debates of the 1980s — mass unemployment, scroungerphobia, calls for greater self reliance and a pervasive aura of crisis.

Michael Hill details the development of government policies to combat unemployment. The strong focus on the supply side of the labour market which has characterized more recent programmes, particularly those promising a new future to the young unemployed, has not produced any corresponding pull from the demand side of the labour market. Indeed, in spite of the promise of the MSC's Director, Geoffrey Holland, that less than 10% of Youth Opportunity Programme graduates would find themselves, in his word, 'reunemployed' (*Observer*, 2 April 1978), the level of youth unemployment rose faster than the capacity of MSC programmes. As more young people became unemployed and entered MSC schemes so any advantage previously gained from a place on an MSC programme disappeared. In pursuing wider economic policies which failed to increase the demand for labour and, in fact, helped to reduce it, the Callaghan and Thatcher government's commitment to developing special programmes lacked any overall coherence.

The development of large scale programmes to provide training or work experience for the unemployed was an innovation in British policy but the failures of the programme could have been anticipated. Marris and Rein, in a seminal work on the American War on Poverty, noted the failure of American programmes designed to assist the disadvantaged unemployed into work, particularly when no such work was available:

> However resourceful the project's employment programmes, they could do little to influence the economy which determined how many usable skills were in demand.

In fact what many trainees found was not work but disillusionment: 'As each door they opened led to nowhere, they were continually adding anterooms in which an appearance of hopeful activity disguised the ultimate frustration' (Marris and Rein, 1974, pp.125–126). It was an experience soon to become familiar to hundreds of thousands of British young people.

Those who could not find work encountered a social security system which was simultaneously under increasing pressure from growing numbers of claimants and cost cutting measures from government. They also experienced a press reaction to unemployment which in its pursuit of the spectacular trickster seemed concerned to devote more attention to the genuinely undeserving handful than to the growing army of the authentic impoverished. The effect of such media coverage, coupled as it was with growing government surveillance of claimants (which in true moral panic form could trigger further media outbreaks of scroungerphobia) is difficult to measure. That some of the unemployed were deterred from claiming must be obvious, that others failed to gain their entitlement, in a situation where it became increasingly difficult to secure even an interview at a local office, must be assumed. Alan Clarke examines the politics of scrounger bashing and argues that it reflects an important aspect of a wider political strategy.

The rhetoric of community care has not been the preserve of any one government. Successive politicians have urged us to do more for ourselves and bemoaned the loss of community, frequently accelerated by insensitive redevelopment schemes backed by their colleagues. In fact most care is already provided in the community, for example, only 5% of the elderly are in residential institutions, and less than 3% receive meals on wheels. Those caring for elderly relatives or handicapped children would find little resonance in appeals for community self-reliance which neglected to note the absence of adequate support from either statutory or voluntary services.

Nick Derricourt, in looking beyond the rhetoric of community, argues that we need to be alert to different meanings which might be given to community care policies. The central question must be whether such policies are premised on a commitment to meet need, which is uncovered by more effective links between service providers and the localities they work in, or whether they are premised on a commitment to redefining government responsibilities in the social welfare field in order to cut spending.

The situation in Northern Ireland offers a special case for students of social policy, one which may offer some disturbing pointers to developments on the mainland. The high levels of poverty and unemployment which the province has historically experienced have not been marked by any commensurate political response. Poverty is widely under recognized even by those who might be thought to suffer from it. The wider sectarian conflict has precipitated the incorporation into mainstream social policies of repressive measures so far unknown on the mainland — most notably in the area of debt collection.

Ditch's critical evaluation of the notion of crisis suggests that it may well obscure a perceptive understanding of the issues. Certainly the experience of Northern Ireland suggests that for the poor and unemployed on the mainland the situation could deteriorate much further without any ameliorative political response. This is a lesson that history has driven home to the American poor, whose inner city ghettoes, once viewed with disdain from this side of the Atlantic, now have an increasingly familiar appearance.

References

Marris, P. and Rein, M. (1974) *Dilemmas of Social Reform*, Penguin, Harmondsworth.

Government Responses to Unemployment

Michael Hill

Introduction

Government responses to unemployment may be separated into what may be described as 'macro' and 'micro'. The former are the battery of measures which may be used to influence the working of the economy as a whole. These are, in the author's view, quite the most important of the potential responses. Their analysis involves, however, considering a very wide range of issues, alongside the alleviation or prevention of unemployment, about the relationship between the government and economy as a whole. In particular, in this context, the trade off between unemployment and inflation, and the impact of measures upon the balance of trade, must be given consideration. This chapter is however concerned with the other category of responses, the 'micro' ones, designed to have a direct impact upon the demand for or supply of specific segments of, or group within, the labour force. However, it will be argued that it is inappropriate to consider such measures without relating them to the macro-economic context in which they occur. Specific government manpower policies, and responses to the needs of the unemployed, need to be portrayed, explained and evaluated in their wider economic context.

This chapter will therefore start with a brief survey of the recent history of government policy in this area, designed to relate specific policies to the various prevailing theories about the role of government as the manager of the economy. Following that particular contemporary responses to unemployment will be discussed, but always in their wider context.

The Development of Responses to Unemployment in the Twentieth Century

It is an over-simplification to suggest that unemployment is a 20th century concept. But it is nevertheless appropriate to argue that the analysis of this subject, outside the relatively limited numbers of economists and politicians

241

already influenced by the work of Karl Marx, tended before the 20th century to approach unemployment as a facet of the behaviour of the labour force rather than as a defect in the working of the economy. The idleness and sloth of the working class, and the need for punitive social policies and carefully controlled charitable interventions were stressed rather than a concern for the victims of a malfunctioning labour market. Indeed, the dominant economic theory of the time did not recognise the notion of a malfunctioning market, so long as governments refrained from interfering with the free interplay of economic forces. Hence, worklessness was explained in terms of the failure of workers to accept wages at their true market level. The only appropriate government response to unemployment was that provided under the 1834 Poor Law, designed to force reluctant workers to lower the price of their labour to the market level under threat of incarceration in the workhouse.

But then, as now, political responses to unemployment were not solely determined by the accepted economic orthodoxy. Politicians had always been fearful of the urban 'mob', who were increasingly evident as the Western European countries industrialized and urbanized. Towards the end of the 19th century two phenomena enhanced the political threat of the 'mob'. One was the tendency for geographical imbalance to develop between the supply of labour and the demand for labour. The other was the fluctuation of the strength of the demand for labour over time, the 'trade cycle'.

The orthodox view had relatively little difficulty in taking the former of these phenomena into consideration. In societies which had experienced vast population movements consequent upon industrialization it was relatively easy to come to terms with the view that continued progress required further adjustments. Naturally the emphasis was upon the need for labour mobility not industrial mobility. At the end of the 19th century in Britain a variety of voluntary 'colonization' schemes existed. These were designed to move unemployed workers not only overseas to the colonies but to new industrial settlements within Britain. The government sought to encourage these developments (see Harris, 1972).

It was a similar concern about matching the supply of labour to the demand for it which stimulated the establishment, by local authorities and voluntary bodies, of 'labour exchanges'. Subsequently central government itself seized upon the idea and set about, with legislation in 1909, to establish its own network of exchanges (Harris, 1977; Fullbrook, 1978).

The fluctuations of the trade cycle raised much greater problems for classical economic theory. It was not until the 1930s that an explanation of this phenomenon acceptable to economic policy makers really began to be established. (For a discussion of relevant economic theory see B. Showler in Sinfield and Showler, 1981). Keynes was the seminal theorist here, providing legitimation for a much more radical governmental approach to the management of the economy. But governments began, in *ad hoc* ways to try to mitigate the effects of the depressed part of the trade cycle long before that. In

Britain the ban on 'outdoor' cash relief for the unemployed implicit in the 1834 Poor Law had never been complete. Local crises required responses of a more radical kind. The 1905 Unemployed Workmen Act recognized the need for such special responses, and tried, largely unsuccessfully, to ensure that efforts to relieve the unemployed were channelled into work creation projects (Harris, 1972). But the most significant government response to unemployment at this time was the development of an insurance scheme, designed to enable groups of workers affected by the trade cycle to receive cash help when temporarily out of work. This idea, developed in Germany, Belgium and Switzerland, reached Britain with the Unemployment Insurance Act of 1911 (Harris, 1977). Contributions to the British scheme were provided by employees, employers and the government. Benefits were for a limited period of time, and the scheme was initially confined to occupations where employment opportunities were only periodically interrupted by downturns in trade.

In Britain the inter-war period saw the extensive elaboration of the unemployment insurance scheme and a vast extension of relief for the unemployed by means of cash payments. This was the key response to the problem of depression during this period. Initially, after the First World War, the government were panicked by fears of unrest into extending the insurance scheme, particularly to protect returning soldiers. This rapidly undermined the insurance principle and 'bankrupted' the scheme (see Gilbert, 1970; Deacon, 1976). A complicated series of *ad hoc* responses followed leading eventually to legislation in 1934 which provided a means tested benefit system to replace poor relief and to underpin a limited insurance scheme unsuited to a prolonged depression. This dual system remains relatively unaltered as the social security response to the needs of the unemployed to this day. We will therefore return to it in a later section.

The work creation option, which the British government briefly flirted with at the beginning of the century, remained suspect in this country because of the recognition that its extension on any effective scale would entail a substantial interference with the working of the free market. But, of course, the growth of non-commercial public enterprise during the 20th century suggested new approaches to this option which might not be damaging to the capitalist system. The Fascist dictatorships in Europe tended to discredit this option by becoming its leading exponents, but after 1932 the United States increasingly espoused it. In Britain by the late 1930s it had begun to be accepted that a combination of public enterprise, and public aid to private enterprise might be used to aid the most depressed regions (see Booth, 1978). The advocacy of a more radical response came largely from the Liberal group led by Lloyd George. Keynes, in his *The General Theory of Employment, Interest and Money,* transformed thinking about this option by showing that far from threatening capitalism it could save it by counteracting the downturn of the trade cycle. But Keynes' impact upon government thinking on this issue was not significant until the 1940s.

At the end of the Second World War the British government seemed to have accepted the case for macro-economic intervention along Keynesian lines to counter the effects of the trade cycle. Such intervention might involve fiscal measures, or the stimulation of public expenditure or even conceivably public economic initiatives. In practice the post-war economy proved to be much more buoyant than anyone expected. The Keynesian measures of fiscal intervention and public expenditure adjustment became a form of 'fine tuning' in which the limitation of inflation was a much more significant concern than the stimulation of employment. Britain enjoyed levels of unemployment until the 1960s much better than those outlined as the minimum tolerable in policy statements in the 1940s (Deacon 1981, in Sinfield and Showler).

However, during this period of near 'full employment', — between about 1945 and 1970 — three issues about unemployment continued to secure attention. First, the regional imbalance so very evident in the 1930s, still remained. Hence, from the war period onwards efforts were made to tackle the continuing presence of depressed areas within a bouyant economy. Second, although now in a muted form, the trade cycle fluctuations still occurred and government interventions of a fiscal, macro-economic kind, were, particularly in the later part of the period, perceived to be often too late and too imprecise (Brittan, 1971). Hence it began to be felt that Keynesian economic management would work much better if accompanied by manpower policy measures. Perhaps the main argument for these was that inflation stimulated by over-full employment could be counteracted by measures to assist employment placing, training and labour mobility (Mukherjee, 1972). Third, though this was very much the issue which received least attention, some concern was recognized for those who seemed to make the weakest claims for employment and tended to be the victims of each mini-depression. While a general protective measure for the disabled had been enacted in Britain during the War, it was poorly implemented and this issue was otherwise largely neglected until the 1960s.

In the 1960s the markedly successful economies of Germany and Sweden were given attention by people concerned about the weaknesses of British manpower policy. The very comprehensive 'active' labour market policies adopted in Sweden particularly seemed to provide a model worthy of further study (Mukherjee, 1972). These seemed to deal with all three of the unresolved issues. The geographical ill-distribution of work in Sweden was tackled both by regional policies and by assistance with employee mobility. The trade cycle problem was explicity addressed through the expansion of training during the down-turn, and through a system of investment reserves to be taken out at the top of the cycle and released at the bottom. These interventions were underpinned by a range of special measures to assist the least privileged competitors in the labour market, through training, subsidies and sheltered employment. The key institution for the implementation of these policies was, and is, a National Labour Market Board on which both sides of industry are represented.

In Britain some of the lessons from Sweden began to have an impact in the 1970s, by which time they were largely too late. The overall level of unemployment shifted markedly upwards and the trough of the trade cycle became much deeper. In 1973 responsibility for manpower policy was given to the Manpower Services Commission, on which both employers and trade unions are represented. This body set about vigorously transforming the employment services. A new system of Job Centres was created, aiming to provide a dynamic placement service. It was claimed that the old employment exchanges had acquired a 'dole queue image', associated with chronic unemployment, which deterred both employers and potential employees from using them effectively. Similarly the training activities of the services were recognized in an attempt to make them more relevant to contemporary needs (Department of Employment, 1971).

It is debatable whether the reorganized British employment service dealt more effectively with the third of the issues outlined above. Indeed, the author suggested at the time that there were many signs that losing the dole queue image implied ignoring the needs of the system's most disadvantaged clients (Hill, 1974). Nevertheless, it is now fair to say that while the rise in unemployment effectively prevented the Manpower Services Commission from developing a clear Swedish style active manpower policy the new service which was created seems to have been adept at developing quickly a whole battery of new policies for the unemployed. Clearly, while it is an untestable proposition that it has been better at this than the old system would have been, the MSC has become a source of sophisticated analyses of the contemporary problem of unemployment and of the measures required to cope with it.

The rest of this chapter will carry forward the themes discussed in this brief account of the 20th century development of British manpower policy. It will look at the way the issues explored so far have taken new forms as unemployment has returned to levels which were thought to have been left behind in the 1930s. To them must be added, however, a new concern, non-existent in the inter-war period, to directly attack the problem of unemployment through measures to provide temporary work or training, or to persuade individuals to withdraw from labour market participation. What however is significant about these new measures is that they have to be seen against the background of the abandonment of the Keynesian economic theory which became so popular in the 1940s and 1950s. To attack the problem of unemployment directly through reflation is now seen, by a broad spectrum of opinion (going well beyond the ranks of the hard-line monetarists who want the government to return to a 19th century *laissez-faire* stance on unemployment) to entail dangerous consequences for Britain's inflation rate and therefore for its international competitiveness. Instead, therefore, measures have been espoused, and are still being sought, which combine a maximum impact upon unemployment with a minimum demand upon public expenditure.

The Employment Service at a Time of High Unemployment

Before moving on to discuss the special measures developed to deal with high unemployment it is necessary to take a brief look at the way the ordinary employment service and benefit system operate in this context. This will be done in this and the next section.

The modernization of the employment exchange system has continued so that most communities are now served by high street 'job centres'. At the end of the 1970s MSC produced evidence that new centres were 'capturing' a greater share of the vacancies arising (MSC, 1978). However, the marked fall in the number of vacancies in the 1980s has created increased problems for all employment agencies, both public and private. In 1980–81 the team led by Sir Derek Rayner commissioned to look at efficiency in the civil service examined the employment service. They recommended that the continuation of the requirement that all unemployment people should register with the service served little purpose, proposing that registration should only have to be with the offices administering the benefit system. This proposal was implemented in 1982, severing, it may be suggested, the last link with the 'dole queue' image. It might have been fully consistent with the ideology of the government which commissioned his study if Rayner had recommended the elimination of public employment agencies altogether. Certainly there are grounds for doubt about either the economic or the social policy ends fulfilled by a service handling a small proportion of the limited number of employment vacancies at a time of high unemployment.

During the 1970s the work of the training services branch of the public employment service expanded rapidly. The MSC had some success in making their new courses, known as TOPS courses (Training Opportunities Scheme), more relevant to the needs of industry. Numbers of trainees grew rapidly, their growth perhaps hastened by a decline in training within industry. In the 1980s reduced employment opportunities naturally undermined this growth, since the MSC are committed to ensuring that TOPS courses lead to employment opportunities. At the time of writing the whole future of publicly financed or sponsored industrial training is in the melting pot. The government has begun to wind down the Industrial Training Board system which has required employers to provide, or contribute to, training; the traditional apprenticeship system has declined markedly; and, as suggested above, TOPS courses face a crisis. At the same time a new initiative for the young unemployed stresses training. We will return to discuss that further below, and to examine some of the underlying problems about developing relevant training in the face of very high unemployment.

The other ingredient in the battery of manpower policies developed between the 1940s and the 1970s is not, in general, the responsibility of the MSC. That is regional policy. This chapter cannot go into this complex subject in any depth.

In the late 1970s various special measures, to be discussed below, were particularly targetted to the regions and areas with the heaviest unemployment. The political problem for the 1980s has been the vast increase in areas calling for special treatment. While regional differences in experience of unemployment remain, the pattern has changed markedly. Some hitherto prosperous regions, such as the West Midlands, have joined the depressed group, and even the most fortunate regions have their own special 'black spots'. In all regions the decline of inner-city areas has attracted political concern, especially since the urban riots of 1981. Hence there has been something of a shift from regional interventions to more localized ones. The government has seen the stimulation of inner city economic development as a special priority, attempting various experiments in local subsidy and loosening of planning controls. Local authorities have also begun to see employment creation as amongst their tasks. These new initiatives cannot be said to have been satisfactorily evaluated as yet, but there is an increasingly voiced suspicion that in the face of high overall unemployment any local initiative will have a marked 'beggar my neighbour' aspect. Certainly this is a conclusion that many experts draw about the earlier regional policy initiatives.

The Benefit System

As pointed out above, the system of financial support for the unemployed, although much changed in detail, remains that established in 1934. The contributory unemployment benefit scheme provides flat rate benefits, plus additions for dependents, subject to previous contributions, for up to a year of unemployment. The problems about this are

a) that the rates of benefit (particularly since earning related supplements were abolished in 1982) are too low for the subsistence needs (as determined by the supplementary benefit scales) of many of the unemployed;

(b) that it exhausts after a year when in practice nowadays many are out of work for longer than that; and

(c) that the contribution conditions exclude both new entrants to the labour market and those who have had recent lengthy spells of unemployment.

Hence, a substantial proportion of the unemployed have to secure means-tested supplementary benefits to meet their income needs.

Throughout the history of income support for the unemployed politicians, journalists and others have, from time to time, alleged that the benefit system sustains some workless people in voluntary idleness. In the 1970s the issue of the extent to which benefit levels, particularly for the fathers of large families, were above wage levels for low skill work received considerable attention. The Supplementary Benefits Commission initiated an investigation of this issue and concluded that this could be true only for a very small proportion of the unemployed (SBC, 1977). Since that time benefit levels for the unemployed have risen more slowly than wage rates or the cost of living. However, the issue remains a live one for those who believe the route to eliminating unemployment lies in reducing wage levels until the 'market clears', regardless of how those levels relate to the minimum subsistence levels determined for the benefit system.

The whole issue is further complicated by the availability of benefits for low income workers — notably family income supplement, housing benefits, remission of health charges and free school meals — which are assessed by various agencies using varied and sometimes obscure means-testing rules. Hence, unemployed people may conclude incorrectly that they will be worse off in work simply because they do not know about, or understand, the benefits to which they will be entitled.

However, the presence among the unemployed of a minority who prefer, for whatever reason, to remain out of work hardly seems, to this writer, to be a cause for attention when unemployment is so high and so many are eager for work. Nevertheless the concern about voluntary unemployment continues to be voiced, and it has been alleged that MSC's abandonment of the traditional responsibility for the administration of the 'dole queue' has reduced the pressure upon the reluctant, or discouraged, elements amongst the workless (Layard 1979). To counter this the government has continued to use some civil servants in DHSS to interview, and perhaps coerce, the long term unemployed. The fact that such officials do seem to have some success in accelerating some people's return to work, and inevitably uncovering some fraudulent claims, is regarded as justifying the maintenance of these 'unemployment review officers'. What, however, DHSS's studies of the 'successes' of these officials cannot prove is that these are not merely achieved at the expense of other (perhaps more willing!) job seekers.

Special Measures: Youth Unemployment

A particular feature of the rise of unemployment in the late seventies and early 1980s has been the dramatic rise in youth unemployment. The special measures developed by the government have particularly concentrated upon this group, generally defined as those between 16 and 18. The specific measures tried have been varied combinations of job creation and training, with 'work experience' featuring as a (not always happy) compromise between these two. The general tendency has been for the training emphasis to receive increasing attention. Hence, at the time of writing, in late 1982, the government is just beginning the third radical revision of the special youth employment programme, introducing the Youth Training Scheme. This aims, by September 1983, to guarantee all youngsters without jobs, who left school at the minimum age, a year's 'foundation training'. Sponsors, principally from private enterprise, are being sought to provide this publicly funded training. What the scheme implies is still a mixture of course based training and work experience. It remains to be seen to what extent the new scheme will be able to provide relevant training, and to what extent it will still fall into one or other of the two traps which critics of the older schemes have alleged exist. These have been either that the training provided (particularly by colleges) has been irrevelant, or that the work experience has been merely employment at the taxpayers' expense. The early record of work experience seemed to suggest that a high proportion of trainees were subsequently offered work by their 'employers'. This was regarded by MSC as proof of the success of the scheme but could alternatively be taken to be evidence that employers who could have offered normal jobs secured a trial period for new young employees at public expense. However, as unemployment worsened a rapidly diminishing proportion of youngsters moved from work experience to work.

All job creation efforts by the government need to be evaluated in terms of three considerations. Firstly, whether, in the light of the government's rejection of the straightforward Keynesian alternative of direct stimulation of the economy through fiscal measures or public investment, jobs can be created at minimum cost. Hence calculations are now widely attempted to relate job creation costs to benefit costs saved and additional taxes recovered. (See, for a review of these, Metcalf, 1982). Second and third whether the drawbacks which economists call 'deadweight' and or 'displacement' occur. These two problems are described as follows by Metcalf:

> Subsidies have two big problems. First, there will always be some *deadweight* — in some instances firms will be paid for hiring workers whom they would have hired anyway. This represents a windfall to the firm and raises the Exchequer cost per extra job . . . Second, subsidised workers may *displace* non-subsidized workers, either inside a given firm or as the output of the subsidised firm displaces output of non-subsidized firms (Metcalf, 1982).

Clearly as the youth programme has shifted away from job creation towards training the latter two problems have been minimized. As far as the costs issue is concerned clearly the training is, at least in the short run, unproductive. A great deal of the cost therefore depends upon the issues of the resources to be used for training and the allowances to be paid to the trainees. The latter has been cut back to a level little different from that paid to the young unemployed on supplementary benefit. However, there is an emergent problem about the payment of trainees. This is that if a 16 year old stays in full-time education he or she normally gets no income at all (the exception here is the small minority of very poor students who get educational maintenance allowances). If he or she leaves school and goes on benefits then an income is acquired but parents lose child benefit. If admitted to a training scheme then a different benefit comes into payment. The issues are whether there should not now be some kind of benefit for 16 to 18 years old regardless of whether they are at school or not and what should the relativities be between the money available in different situations including their relationships to likely earnings in full-time work.

In the evolution of new training ideas for young people a great deal has been made of the inadequacy of the conventional educational provision for entrants, especially unqualified entrants, to the labour market. The theory behind the new initiatives is that better preparation for the world of work can be provided. To some extent it is true to say that a 'battle' has occurred between the educational system and the Manpower Services Commission for control over the 'training' of un-academic 16–18 year olds and the latter has 'won'. But there is not much evidence that a satisfactory public debate has developed as part of this 'battle'. The education system has largely lost the confidence of a high proportion of children by the time they reach 16, and has few new good ideas. Moreover the MSC have been able to point to the impact of technological change on unemployment, diminishing opportunities for the low skilled and demanding new skills. However, the impact of new technology is far from clear, and much disputed. Its most obvious effect is to reduce job opportunities in general, not to produce a clear imbalance between a lack of demand for low skilled workers and an excess demand for high skilled ones.

To suggest that 16 year old school leavers need training to equip them for the labour market seems implausible when a few years ago employers were only too happy to take them on, and the actual training packages on offer do little to stretch the abilities of the trainees. Certainly the new training programmes do not seem to be particularly concerned with training for high technology jobs. There is no evidence of a supply of jobs, so such training would be regarded as raising unrealistic expectations (a regular careers officers' refrain about this group!). Therefore the author is led to conclude that there are clear signs here of what has been called the 'blame the victim' phenomenon (Ryan, 1971). The arguments about the case for training suggest that high youth unemployment is somehow to do with the inadequacies of the unemployed. That is what much of the contemporary talk, about the need for training, experience of the work situation, help with self presentation at interviews etc. seems to imply. Of course all these efforts may enhance the job prospects of some young people, but surely at the expense of others. Training may be the best way to spend the two years from 16 to 18, but the education system could perhaps fight back more effectively upon behalf of forms of education which might be justified in their own right quite apart from any labour market opportunities they convey.

Special Measures: Job Creation and Preservation

While job creation was, in the 1970s, one aspect of the youth programmes, the recent tendency has been to see this kind of measure as more appropriate for older groups, with some tendency for a concentration of help upon those just beyond the 16–18 group. It is in relation to job creation that the problems of 'deadweight' and 'displacement' most significantly occur.

In the late 1970s a direct attempt was made at job preservation through the 'temporary employment subsidy' available to employers who would otherwise make people redundant. It was accepted that the displacement effects of this would be high, but hoped that to some extent they would operate outside our own economy by making some British firms more competitive at the expense of foreign ones. Metcalf argues that there is some evidence that the scheme did do precisely this and 'this is why the EEC put a stop' to it (Metcalf, 1982). It was replaced by a subsidy scheme for part-time work, which remains a significant element in the government's anti-unemployment measures. At its peak, in 1981, it kept nearly 200,000 individuals out of the unemployment register (see Metcalf, 1982, p.57). It is not open to the same objection as the Temporary Employment Subsidy because 'it simply shares out the available work by reducing the working week' and therefore subsidises leisure rather than work (Metcalf, 1982, p.56).

It has been much more difficult for governments to engage in actual job creation without falling foul of one of the pitfalls for this activity. Job creation in the private sector inevitably encounters the problems of 'deadweight' and 'displacement'. It may be attempted on a limited scale so long as it is recognized that it is a government subsidy to industry which may be used to

(a) increase the extent to which it is labour-intensive rather than capital-intensive, and
(b) to enhance the job prospects of groups who might otherwise be very weak competitors in the open market.

But develop this measure on any large scale and it becomes simply a different general stimulus to industry. In this case it may be barely distinguishable from the kind of general reflationary measure which recent governments have sought to avoid.

In the public sector job creation may be more rapidly controlled to avoid substitution effects. However, the objection again arises that if it is to be developed on any scale it involves a Keynesian type stimulation to public expenditure. However, contrasts have been made between, for example, individual job creation and major new public investments (like the Channel Tunnel or the Severn Barrage) which suggests that the former creates work at much lower overall costs than the latter (see Select Committee of the House of Lords, 1982). What however annoys public authorities is that they may be asked to engage in job creation projects of low priority when the government is preventing them proceeding on capital projects or normal staff expansion schemes of much higher priority.

The government's desire to use job creation to have the maximum effect upon unemployment at minimum cost led them to develop, in 1982, a new version of their adults job creation scheme, the Community Enterprise Programme, in which a substantial majority of the jobs provided were to be part-time. It was claimed that this meant the 'wages' available to many participants with family commitments compared unfavourably with benefit levels (Unemployment Unit, 1982, p.5). In relation to both this scheme and the new training scheme for young people the government was shifting towards mechanisms to take people off the unemployed register into activities rewarded at no better than supplementary benefit levels. Fears have been expressed, reinforced by a previous proposal attempt to do this in relation to the youth scheme, that the next step will be some measure to compel participation.

Special Measures: Withdrawal from the Labour Market

One of the characteristics of the crisis of unemployment is that the number of people who wish to be within the labour market has grown substantially and will continue to grow through the 1980s. This has two special features: the growth in labour market participation by women, and the contrast between the high number of young people entering the labour force and the low numbers of older people (the relatively small First World War birth cohorts) leaving it. Consequently one approach to the reduction of unemployment involves the reduction of labour market participation. Clearly the measures for young people outlined above operate, at least temporarily, in this way. The stimulation of further and higher education both for youngsters and for others could have a similar effect, but is presumably taboo because of its public expenditure effects. So Britain remains a country which offers post-school education to a remarkably small proportion of its population, by comparison with other European countries.

Efforts to stimulate withdrawal from the labour market have been concentrated upon elderly people. A Job Release Scheme, paying subsidies to men of 62 and over (or 60 and over if disabled) and women of 59, has been operating for some time. In January 1982 about 50,000 people were covered by this scheme. The government has preferred here a selective scheme, subsidizing early retirement where employees are going to be replaced, to a more indiscriminate measure lowering the retirement age. That would be much more costly because of its general effects upon pension rights and contributions.

Experiments are proceeding at the time of writing with the development of job-splitting schemes, with government subsidies for the resulting part-time work. The House of Lords Select Committee on Unemployment particularly commended this as a measure for elderly people in the preretirement period. (House of Lords, 1982, para. 10.63). The widespread extension of job-sharing seems unlikely unless much more effective policies develop to protect part-time workers.

Amongst the trade unions other apporaches to work-sharing are popular, notably the reduction of working hours and the lengthening of holidays. However it does not seem to be the case that the advocates of these measures envisage lower incomes for less hours of work. Hence, Metcalf's pithy summary of the implications of these ideas expresses what would probably characterize a government reaction:

> Lower basic working hours, reduced overtime or longer holidays will generate a permanent increase in employment only under circumstances most people in employment would not like. Work-sharing is about income-sharing (Metcalf, 1982, p.56; see also the similar conclusions of the House of Lords Select Committee, 1982, para. 10.59).

Conclusions

In the 1920s and 1930s governments believed that they could do very little about unemployment. They sought to mitigate its worst effects, and to reduce the unrest so caused, by the development of a comprehensive, but often means tested, benefit system. In the 1940s, 1950s and 1960s it was believed that Keynesian economy management had banished unemployment as a substantial problem. It was also believed that any government that tolerated a substantive rise in unemployment would drastically lose electoral support (Deacon, 1981, in Sinfield and Showler). In the 1970s British governments gradually came to treat inflation as a greater evil than unemployment in the face of evidence that the simple Keynesian trade off between unemployment and inflation no longer operated. At the end of that decade unemployment and inflation rose markedly *at the same time*. In the early 1980s we have a government which remains surprisingly popular despite very high unemployment rates. However, unlike its predecessors in the 1930s it has remained committed to programmes, developed under Labour in the late 1970s, which aim to reduce the numbers on the unemployment register. They have succeeded therefore in marginally stemming the growth in worklessness. What, however, is significant about these programmes is that they are not Keynesian contra-cyclical measures. The government has taken a great deal of trouble to try to ensure that the special measures operate with a minimum of public expenditure costs (many indeed cost little more than the social security benefits that would have been paid out) and a minimum of inflationary impact.

However, it would be wrong to leave these last observations as if they were simply criticisms of the Thatcher government. It has become the new orthodoxy that, while the Conservative' commitment to the reduction of inflation through an attack on public expenditure and some degree of espousal of monetarist measures has probably worsened the impact of a world recession upon Britain, the underlying factors of overall changes in the pattern of world trade, the development of new technology and the growing potential labour force imply that there will be no easy way of returning to full employment. Certainly there is no longer any simple confidence in the Keynesian remedies for a depression. Hence we are likely to see, in the absence of dramatic new economic remedies (whose possibility the present author is not qualified to evaluate) a continuation into the indefinite future of measures like those described here. The short and medium run manpower policy questions seem, therefore, to entail choices about the balance between the various (temporary or permanent) withdrawal from the labour market options, most of which are already being tried in some ways. The predominant political concern on the agenda is, it may be suggested, a more cynical desire to reduce the numbers actually registered as unemployed in as inexpensive a way as possible.

References

Booth, A.E. (1978) An administrative experiment in unemployment policy in the thirties, in *Public Administration* 56.

Brittan, S. (1971) *Steering the Economy*, Penguin Books, Harmondsworth.

Deacon, A. (1976) *In Search of the Scrounger*, Bell, London.

Department of Employment (1971) *People and Jobs*.

Fullbrook, J. (1978) *Administrative Justice and the Unemployed*, Mansell, London.

Gilbert, B.B. (1970) *British Social Policy, 1914-39*, Batsford, London.

Harris J. (1972) *Unemployment and Politics: A Study in English Social Policy 1886-1914*, Oxford University Press, Oxford.

Harris, J. (1977) *William Beveridge*, Oxford University Press, Oxford.

Hill, M.J. (1974) *Policies for the Unemployed: Help or Coercion*, CPAG pamphlet, London.

Layard, R. (1979) Have job-centres increased long term unemployment?, Centre for Labour Economics Discussion Paper 62, London School of Economics, London.

Manpower Services Commission (1978) *Job Centres: An Evaluation*, London.

Metcalf, D. (1982) *Alternatives to Unemployment*, Policy Studies Institute, London.

Mukherjee, S. (1972) *Making Labour Markets Work*, Political and Economic Planning Broadsheet 532, London.

H.M.S.O. (1982) *Report from the Select Committee of the House of Lords on Unemployment*, London.

Ryan, W. (1971) *Blaming the Victim*, Orback and Chambers, New York.

Sinfield, A. and Showler, B. (1981) *The Workless State*, Martin Robertson, Oxford.

Supplementary Benefits Commission (1977) *Low Incomes*, London.

Unemployment Unit (1982) *The Unacceptable Face of the Special Measures*, Briefing No. 4, August, London.

Prejudice, Ignorance and Panic! Popular Politics in a Land Fit for Scroungers

Alan Clarke

Amongst the promises in the Conservative Party's Manifesto for the 1979 General Election there was a section called 'Making sense of social security'. We were told that when the Conservatives formed the next Government:

> The rules about the unemployed accepting the available jobs will be reinforced and we shall act more vigorously against fraud and abuse. (Conservative Central Office; 1979; p.27).

This article is concerned with the way that the Conservative Government put social security fraud on the political agenda after their victory at the polls. But the moral panic around 'scroungers' is only the latest chapter in a long-running saga about the undeserving. We shall see that although the particular form taken by the different outbreaks alters over time, the central concern with the importance of the work ethic links them all. By sketching in some of these historical connections, it is possible to evaluate the campaign against the scrounger as part of a specific political strategy. In particular the article attempts to show that the argument is based on emotional rather than factual appeals to a particular construction of what made Britain great. Hence I shall begin by outlining the moves of the 1979 Conservative Government which will then be contrasted to the historical construction of the problem of the undeserving.

Any doubts that this aspect of the manifesto was taken seriously were quickly dispelled by the Chancellor and the Department of Health and Social Security (DHSS). Sir Geoffrey Howe gave the ideas a clear direction when in his first budget speech he announced 'urgent measures to tighten up on abuse and fraud' in the social security system. By the end of November, only six months after the election, 600 more staff had been recruited to investigate suspected frauds. In a gesture which caught in the imagination of the press, many of these investigators were supplied with high-powered binoculars.

As one official said:

> When you know a man is on the fiddle and is picking potatoes in the middle of a muddy 20 acre field, binoculars are the best way to catch him out and get the evidence.

Although this is clearly one use for binoculars, more suspicious people thought they might also be trained on bedroom windows to acquire the evidence of cohabitation necessary to stop benefits. Not content with these measures, the Government announced a further 1,060 investigators would be employed in the two years 1980–81 and were expected to save over £50m 'of the taxpayers' money'. Reg Prentice, the Minister responsible, commented at a press conference:

> Any kind of fraud in our society is something evil and something we should attack . . . . It is intolerable that some people should be cheating the system at a time when both national and local government are being forced to make economies in soical services which affect vulnerable people (*The Times, 14 February 1980*).

At the time of these political initiatives, much was being made of the failures of the courts in disciplining the abusers. Following this process of exposing the 'soft' and lenient sentences, the courts were awarding prison sentences to those guilty of fraud and abuse. As Lord Justice Lawton said, prison was 'the only possible way of dealing with this class of offence . . (which is) rife from one end of the country to the other.' (Quoted in *The Times*, 27 February 1980.) Deterrence was not only the aim of the courts, for a change of policy within the DHSS in 1980 meant that the investigation teams were encouraged to see themselves as a deterrent to the undeserving claimant.[1]

An internal document explained:

> In the past, as many cases as possible were pursued to prosecution but, in future, while the deterrent effect of successful prosecutions will continue to be borne in mind, the cessation of a claim might be regarded in appropriate cases as the most cost-effective way of dealing with the matter (quoted by Moore, 1981; p.138).

The cost effectiveness of the 'non-prosecution interview' cannot be doubted as evidence mounts that people are withdrawing their claims after a visit from one of the new specialist investigators. Some of the cases reported on the *File on 4* programme 'Social Insecurity'[2] appear to suggest that some of the teams are being over-zealous in their interpretation of their powers, despite an explicit warning in the *Fraud Investigator's Guide* about the danger of such an approach:

> Take care to avoid any approach which could lay (you) open to an accusation of pressurizing the claimant into withdrawing his claim. For example, you should not suggest a bargain — 'Admit you are not entitled and we won't prosecute.' The only justification for terminating a person's benefit as opposed to withdrawing his

claim is that facts have definitely been established which show that he is not entitled. You should never recommend withdrawing benefit on inadequate evidence in the hope that the claimant will not protest (*ibid.*, p.138).

However as early as 1969 one of the DHSS investigators had detailed the measures taken by him when confronting potential cases of abuse — suggesting that the claimant would be better off not coming to the benefits office the following week, and threatening prosecution even though there was no evidence to support the trial. These revelations, in *The Spectator*, led to Page being dismissed for a breach of internal security after which he published his grievances and reminiscences in a book (Page, 1971). This stands as an eloquent testimony to the shortcuts taken within the system to prevent the payment of money where there is any element of doubt about the claimant.

The Poor Are Always With Us

The criteria used in identifying such claimants are derived from the values of the work ethic which are a dominant part of the national morality. Thatcherism has once more drawn up the work ethic as an integral part of its political rhetoric, urging the individual to take responsibility for their own lives. This responsibility is to be taken on in the return to the free market and is cast within the imagery of the work ethic. A just reward, we are told, is a fair day's pay for a fair day's work. So those who expect something from the Welfare State for nothing — which is often how their claims are viewed — are claiming on the rest of us. What makes this worse is that some people take benefits for granted, accepting them with no thought of seeking proper employment, and although this may not be illegal it is considered by some to be immoral.

Many of the themes raised in the brief historical account which follows frame the way in which welfare claimants are viewed now. The rules of the game were officially recognized when legislation distinguished three groups of the poor in 1553. The three categories were the impotent (the aged, orphans, chronic sick); casualty (war-wounded); and thriftless (the idle, vagabonds and rioters). Long histories of this process have been written identifying the categorisation of the people described by one reformer as 'the workless, the thriftless and the worthless.' (Peek, 1888, p.62). Golding and Middleton conclude a review of this early period, by saying:

> By the time Beveridge arrived, stalking his Five Giants of Want, Disease, Ignorance, Squalor and Idleness like so many characters in a morality play, the imagery of poverty and welfare with which the new utopia was to be constructed were deeply engraved into popular expectations. Three key ideas formed the tripod on which public understanding of poverty and welfare rested. These were efficiency, morality, and pathology: efficiency of the labour market and the economy; morality of the work ethic and self-sufficiency; and the pathology of individual inadequacy as the cause of poverty (Golding & Middleton, 1982, p.48).

Work is still seen as positively beneficial in that it allows people to live their own lives, free of state support which should exist only in the literal sense of a 'safety net' for that minority of people unable to work. Equally important is the pejorative case which asserts that the people who claim assistance from the state are in fact claiming against the earnings of those people who are working. Each new claimant is seen as an added burden on the tax payer. According to this view of welfare payments it is psychologically damaging for the honest, hard-working citizen to see the scrounger enjoying benefits in 'idle luxury'. At the turn of the century, there was growing concern at the excessive sheltering of the able-bodied in workhouses. The 'luxuries' of the workhouse came under constant attack especially in the new popular press. The *Daily Mail*, for instance, ran a report of 'The Workhouse de Luxe', a veritable 'poverty palace' in Camberwell. Working on a well-worn image the report claimed that the building was a 'haven of rest from worldly turmoil' and 'a paradise', an 'oasis in poverty's desert.' (Daily Mail, 12 April, 1905). Well worn because as early as 1866 the *Daily Telegraph* was warning its readers of the dangers of any improvement in the standards of the workhouses, stressing that: 'it was necessary to make the workhouse an undesirable habitation, because a system of more spacious benevolence would have been a direct discouragement to industry.' (Daily Telegraph, 20 April, 1866). Another interesting example of this line of thinking can be found in Deacon's analysis of a much later panic in 1947.[3] The target then were 'spivs' and 'drones' who existed without any recognisable form of employment — the spivs by living off the Black Market and other people's shortages; the drones existing on private incomes. With a desperate labour shortage, the Government was seeking to introduce legislation to 'direct' labour to jobs of importance to the national well-being. *The Times* observed that the registration of the spivs and drones was 'psychologically necessary' if the other controls were to be observed. 'Direction cannot be applied to the majority of workers, who are in no sense idle or useless, if no attempt is made to control the behaviour of the minority whom public opinion suspects of economic malingering or sharp practice' (Quoted in Deacon, 1980; p.447). What is unusual in this case is the attack on the 'drones', demonstrating that the public anger can be directed at the rich as well as the poor.

In more recent times the public outrage has been directed to those receiving benefits and especially to those who appear to be obtaining more than they need. Figures are often quoted of the level of benefits paid to claimants with large families, both to comment on the largesse of the state and to criticize the recipients' sexual morality. This letter from the *Daily Mail* (11 January, 1983) sums up these reactions:

On the State
YOUR story Love on Dole Fiddlers leaves one with the impression that Harold Frances is a voice crying in the wilderness, i.e. Liverpool.

In our part of the soft south-east we echo his beliefs that there are women about who set out deliberately to milk the State system. For instance, an unmarried mother of three children automatically gains more housing points than a married couple with one legitimate child. And the Homeless Persons Act gives a battered woman with children higher priority than a 'normal' family.

The upshot is that if you live an upright life, you get no advantages thereby. But if you are freckless, spend thrift or dissolute, somebody, usually the Social Services Department, will come along and put you on your feet.

The advantages do not look all that great compared to, say, the average wage. But guaranteed free housing, help with other bills and statutory and discretionary grants all add up to a tidy tax free sum.

C.R. Cheeseman (Secretary)
Merton Women's Aid Ltd, London

However some of these reactions are mild by comparison to *The Times* comment on the provision for family support in the 1834 Poor Law Bill:

> ... which allows the worthless self-gratifying sluggard to people every parish *ad libitum* and which imposes the consequences of the scoundrel's self-indulgence on the industrious and honest rate-payer, which in fact gives a letter of licence without check control or punishment to every brutal libertine to scatter his profligate image round the land — can such a bill be considered a cure for the evils consequent on reckless debauchery? Is it not rather a premium on vice? (*The Times*, 23 June, 1834).

Nor is the problem confined to sexual morality, as the critique of welfare adduces a general moral decline from the receipt of state benefits. As Golding and Middleton observe, Peek was a passionate opponent of indiscriminate charity 'by means of which the vicious thrive ... And these unwise schemes for the relief of destitution ... are in reality sources of demoralization and a direct encouragement to vagrancy and mendicancy' (Quoted *op cit*. 1982, p.3). One of the direct consequences of this demoralization is that some people would be tempted to forego work and allow the state to support them.

The threat of national pauperism, the product of the erosion of the national spirit, is one of the motivations of Thatcherite politics as it seeks to re-establish a sense of national identity. As we shall see returning responsibility to the individual in a free market is also thought to restore the moral integrity of the nation. This strategy began when the Conservative Party were in opposition with the revelations of one Conservative M.P., Iain Sproat, about the extent of 'scrounging'. As Patrick Jenkin, the Opposition's spokesman on Social Services, observed — when the British Association of Social Workers asked him to comment:

> I am sure you realize that there is a great deal of indignation among the ordinary taxpayers of this country that so much of their hard earned cash is squandered on the scroungers. (*Social Work Today* 5 August, 1976; p.291).

How to be a failure . . . and get paid for it

The common sense acceptance of this position increased with the constant usage of the term. The lexicon may have changed from the 'indolent' and 'the loafer' to the more contemporary condemnation of the 'scrounger' and the 'fiddler' but the threat was still clear. For as *The Times* observed in 1977:

> There is a widespread belief in this country that many people receiving social security payments are scrounging off the state. (*The Times*, 8 December, 1977)

In a moment of rare clarity the editorial continues to distinguish between two separable forms of abuse:

> One is the accusation of deliberate fraud, by which payments are obtained through false statements, which is a criminal offence. The other is a more subtle abuse of the system that stops short of fraud but leads to money being obtained from the state because the person concerned has made no serious effort to provide for himself. This is not a criminal offence but it is still a most damaging practice because, like fraud, it leads to the waste of public money, it undermines respect both for the social security system and for the vast majority of beneficiaries who are getting payments honestly, and it provokes justifiable resentment that some people should be helped who are not truly in need (*The Times*, 8 December, 1977)

Although this editorial makes the distinction between fraud and abuse which is rare in the reporting of social security, the argument provides a concise summary of the case against the scrounger.

This view of 'abuse' is well illustrated by one case which generated massive newspaper coverage. The event that 'launched a thousand clippings' was the trial of an unemployed, 42 year old Liverpudlian, Derek Peter Deevy, at Liverpool Crown Court in July 1976. The trial consisted of three specimen charges of obtaining supplementary benefits by deception. A grand total of £57 was the amount discussed in the court room, though the *Sun* carried the front page headline '**£36,000 SCROUNGER**' following an unsubstantiated claim made by Deevy himself that this was the amount he had received from his 41 aliases. *The Daily Telegraph* emphasized the '**£10,000 a year life-style for Dole Fiddler**', whilst the *Daily Express* talked of the '**£200-a-week tycoon on social security**'. As if the sums were not enough, every story included some reference to Deevy's cigars and his suits. The *Daily Mirror* began its story by stressing that 'Nothing was too good for Derek Deevy. His weekly cigar bill came to £25 and he regularly bought expensive suits. The fact that he was out of work didn't spoil his life at the top.' A clearer example of the waste of public money is hard to imagine! Deevy's case was also made the hook on which to hang calls for a thorough inquiry into the social security system — the *Daily Telegraph* even went so far as saying that 'the full inquiry into the Social Security system obviously carried out by **DEEVY**, the Fiddler of Genius, was a timely, if expensive, public service.' (*The Daily Telegraph*, 15 July, 1976). With less irony, the *Express* suggested 'there is a strong case for the view that the whole system needs to be looked at again. Even the perfectly legal largesse looks excessive.'[4]

The Deevy case also raises the other two points in *The Times*' indictment. Abuse does provoke 'justifiable resentment', particularly in the *Express*. In the same editorial quoted above the moral of the case was explained: 'It is no use inviting people to work harder for the country if they feel, with justice, that the product of their effort, in part, is going to cigars and drinks and a good tax-free life for bums.' It is little wonder that abuse undermines the respect for the vast majorities of honest beneficiaries when the 'scroungers' are condemned in such language. Indeed many of the stories create the impression that this assumed honest majority is not so vast as an innocent public might like to believe, with headlines like the *Daily Mail's* **'Biggest Scrounger of the Lot'** and the *Mirror's* **'King of the Dole Queue Scroungers'** implying that Deevy was one of many. In the words of the Conservative MP, Iain Sproat, Deevy was 'only the tip of the iceberg' (Sproat, 1976). If there was an iceberg, the welfare state was like a latter day *'Titanic'* and the ship was heading for trouble. Sproat invited the general public to write to him with details of other scroungers in their neighbourhood and he duly presented the DHSS with 765 allegations of fraud. This was somewhat lower than he might have expected having claimed that only half of those receiving unemployment benefit were really looking for work. And Field reports worse was yet to come:

> Some could not be checked, as the allegations were so vague. Of those letters which identified a family, 13% of investigations showed that no trace could be found of the person having been a claimant, let alone abusing benefit. In 67% of investigations, there was no suspicion of fraud. 22 cases — i.e. 3% — of previously undetected fraud were cited (Field, 1979, p.756).

At the time Stan Orme, the minister responsible, remarked that had the staff time been spent on manning the normal control procedures, ten times as many cases of possible abuse would have been found.

The numbers game can always be relied upon to provide an interesting diversion for any debate and the discussion of the scrounger is no exception, with two sets of figures open to question. Firstly there is the question of the amount of abuse, and here the statistics must only include criminal actions. Offical figures in this area are hard to come by and even more difficult to interpret. From the 1973 Fisher Committee on Abuse of Social Security Benefits (Cmnd 5228), we find an incidence of abuse in less than 1% of all claims. [5] Field reports the answer to his parliamentary question on the subject in the table on the following page.

These figures do not tell us much on their own and leave a great deal to the imagination. For instance to talk of nearly £4m of fraud would sound serious, but to present the per centage figure makes the fraud appear marginal. Again if

How many scroungers?		
1978/9: Type of benefit	No. of claims	Fraud as % of claims
Family Allowance or child benefit	661,296	0.042
Retirement pension	583,764	0.127
Unemployment benefit	4,383,000	0.563
other contributory benefit	13,330,958	0.061
supplementary benefit	5,547,396	0.596
TOTAL	24,506,414	0.273

Type of benefit	Detected fraud £	Fraud as % of benefits paid out
Family benefits	36,753	0.639
Unemployment benefit	437,972	0.664
Sickness and invalidity benefit	420,406	0.051
Maternity benefits	6,840 ⎫	
Widows' benefits	120,422 ⎬	0.025
Retirement pension	60,495	0.001
Industrial injury benefits	24,732	0.012
Supplementary benefits	2,802,052	0.138
TOTAL	3,909,672	0.027

Source: Field, 1979, p. 75.

the cost is compared to the overheads of detecting the fraud, the investigations seems quite sensible. The same figures when compared to the monies involved in tax evasion pale into insignificance.[6] However important these considerations are, the numbers game becomes much more pernicious when it is addressed to the level of individual benefits. For instance in November, 1976 the *Daily Mail* (16 November, 1976) presented a table which illustrated how 'the £75 a week man is better off on the dole.' David Howell, the Conservative spokesman on economic affairs, described as 'fiscal insanity' the fact that an average worker needed gross earnings of £77-a-week to keep up with 'the stay-at-home-Jones's'. Earlier in the week the *Daily Telegraph* (14 November, 1976) led with **'OUTCRY AT £5,000 A YEAR DOLES'** (14.11.76). This at a time when the Supplementary Benefit Commission's evidence to the Diamond Commission on Wealth was saying that there were few cases in which benefit exceeded potential earnings, although it did admit the gap was sometimes very close and that this narrowness could demoralize people returning to work. What is at issue here is the way that the figures quoted are not directly comparable. By taking the highest benefits available for people with many commitments — high rents, large families, etc. — and placing them alongside the average earnings of workers, the supposed attack on the work ethic is maximized. When these estimated excesses are presented as the norm, it fuels the image of a 'life of luxury on the dole' with 'the stay-at-home-Jones's'.

Although these statistics are important they are not the central terrain on which the arguments about the 'scrounger' appear, as they derive less from 'facts' than from a potent mixture of exaggerations and extreme cases from politicians and pundits in the newspapers. It is unlikely that many people bothered to probe the complexities of the Social Security system in July 1976 when the conversation concerned the size of Deevy's cigars. Whilst Deevy's case is illustrative of the general themes in the scroungers story line, there are two other types of scrounging stories which also feature prominently in the press and which are worth mentioning here. The first category concerns that staple diet of the 'gutter' press — sex. For despite the passionate exploitation of the titillating, papers such as the *Sun* and the *News of the World* demand a puritan moral code from the world they report. This contradiction is amply demonstrated by the *Sun* which can run guides on how to get your man ('Hook a Hunk') at parties, at the same time as it is condemning claimants for breaking the cohabitation rule. Related to this are the condemnations of claimants with large, or more accurately *'excessively'* large numbers of children. John Knight from Cornwall achieved notoriety on BBC 1's *Nationwide* programme because of his £130-a-week claims on Social Security to support his legal wife, his common-law wife and the 21 children they had borne. When the *Daily Mirror* picked up the story they headlined it **'Superdad or Superscrounger'** balancing the romantic elements of the large family with the temptation to condemn the lack of restraint within the family. Large families and their implied 'loose morals' are often linked to the second type of story, those dealing with the alien claimants. Most often this story line conjures up confirmation of the stereotypes of the idle West Indian and the cunning Asian but occasionally white foreigners make an appearance. The most spectacular cases have tended to involve airport arrivals housed at public expense, with the Malawi Asians placed in a Heathrow Hotel in 1976 being the most notorious (Troyna, 1980). In May 1979 an Australian mother became one of the few white immigrants to be subjected to this sort of press treatment. **'Scrounger Cynthia jets into new home'** declared the *Sun* (9 May, 1979) and the *Express* (10 May 1979) followed up with: **'Now, Free Furniture! That's the latest demand from superscroungers'**. The implications of these reports is that the country was becoming 'a land fit for scroungers' *(Daily Telegraph,* 29 July, 1976).

Scroungers and the Thatcherite Ideal

The echoes of these stories are still with us with new parallels of the scrounger with other forms of the undeserving, what is important now is to notice what is specific to the imagery of the 1970s. As Fitzgerald's article in this reader has suggested Thatcherism's central expression of neo-liberal doctrines has approached welfare in two ways which have affected the 'scrounger'. The immediate impact came with the advocacy of the 'monetarist' policies of reducing public expenditure which established parameters on the role of the social services. Even though the budget allocation for benefits has risen this has more to do with the hidden consequences of economic policies designed to halt inflation creating an ever-increasing number of claimants rather than the benefit levels having kept pace with wage increases or inflation. However more important than the cash limits on the social services has been the success of Thatcherism in transforming the political agenda for discussions of the welfare state. That agenda now begins from the question: should the state provide welfare support at all? David Donnison summed up the change in the Conservative Party and the country by saying:

> The older paternalistic brand of Toryism seemed to have died. After May 1979, as social security minister, Reg Prentice made the new philosophy brutally clear: 'If you believe economic salvation can only be achieved by rewarding success and the national income is not increasing, then you have no alternative but to make the unsuccessful poorer (Donnison, 1981, p.153).

It was a new question on the political agenda in the 1970s but one with a long history and a safe home in the Institute of Economic Affairs, who, in the shape of Alan Peacock, reminded us as early as 1961 that the 'true object of the Welfare State . . . is to teach people to do without it' (Peacock, 1961).

Thatcherism's appeal to the common sense understanding of the people has created a space in which the conservatives could develop a philosophy of the Right. This philosophy is rooted in a profound sense of moral integrity dependent upon the values of the work ethic, of individual responsibility. Boyson's earlier work on the poor became essential reading, as it contained many of the elements of the Thatcherite approach to social problems. He had warned:

> The moral fibre of our people has been weakened. A state which does for its citizens what they can do for themselves is an evil state; and a state which removes all choice and responsibility from its people and makes them like broiler hens will create the irresponsible society no-one cares, no-one bothers — why should they when the state spends all its energies taking money from the energetic, successful and thrifty to give to the idle, the failures and the feckless? (Boyson, 1971, p.5).

The political effectivity of the Thatcherite strategy stems from the position it has constructed as the representative of the British way of life, and the

Champion of the individual. The success has been in aligning this vision of the British way of life with the values of possessive individualism and the free market and with an attack on the ever expanding state. Thatcher gave voice to her vision at her first conference as the Party Leader, in Blackpool 1975:

> Let me give you my vision. A man's right to work as he will, to spend what he earns, to own property, to have the state as servant not as master — these are the British inheritance. They are the essence of a free country and on that freedom all our other freedoms depend (Thatcher, 1977, p.33).

Thatcherism secures the vision of the British inheritance by calling on the voice of history to align 'the people' with the 'traditional wisdom of the nation'. By referring to the British 'way of life' and the 'beliefs of the ordinary British people', the political strategies which the Conservative Party have constructed are made to appear not as something new but as the rediscovery of some half-forgotten 'true beliefs'. The scrounger fits into this model, raising issues from the past in the common sense conversation of the general public but locating these within a new framework. This new context gives the scrounger a double target, for 'scroungerphobia' draws attention not only to the individual abuse but also to the general critique of the welfare state. In this moral panic, the scrounger becomes a populist folk devil as a popular base for this critique is established in every day terms. The media have dredged popular myth to come up with the man who wants something for nothing, at the expense of everyone else. Indeed the beauty of the scrounger for popular politics is that even those on Supplementary Benefit can join in the condemnation. The figure is never 'us', but we can all recount the stories we have heard of people on the fiddle and share the outrage. By drawing on this media construction, already partially informed by actions of the politicians, Thatcherite policies have been presented — and present themselves — as grounded on popular support. However with public opinion fed almost exclusively with these negative images of the welfare state, it is not surprising that, when it is 'consulted', it has tendency to coincide 'spontaneously' with regressive opinion. As Hall declares, the assaults on the welfare state can be said to be:

> . . . what the people want! Thus 'the people' also come to be represented, as consenting to the erosion of their own hard-won and barely secured 'rights', in a society where massive inequalities of power, property and wealth continue to be secured. This is how a consensus *against* social rights is ideologically constructed (Hall, 1980, p.7).

Thatcherism has explicitly addressed the common sense thoughts of the electorate, gauging the general mood and forging it into a unit with their policies. However the role of the media in creating the terrain of this common sense has to be stressed, particularly where the lack of factual clarity heightens the impact of emotional outbursts. This final example comes from Lynda Lee-Potter of the *Daily Mail* and was headed **'scroungers by the Sea'**:

Our bronzed, healthy, young hedonistic army of self-unemployed are holidaying by the sea at our expense this year and yes, I do resent it. I resent working to support the idle loafers who have a laugh at our expansively generous system which allows them to get away with legalized plunder. The seaside Social Security Offices are thick with subsidized cigarette smoke, the smell of alcohol paid for by the state, and the smugly tanned faces of the leeches feeding off the hard-working, ordinary, silent majority.' *(Daily Mail,* 13 July, 1977).

This is the language of prejudice, ignorance and panic. It is devoid of any factual content but overflows with richly suggestive imagery. Never mind the facts, feel the indignation. However the facts are not the most important element in these stories as we have already seen and the emotive tone of the article appeals directly to that field of regressive opinion. It is a mistaken view to think that rigorous, factually supported, arguments are the only ones that are persuasive. Indeed in an area such as this 'facts' only have significance in the context of the terms of the argument that gives them meaning. When attempts are made to dispel the ignorance surrounding a particular issue, they are often thwarted by the stubborn disbelief of popular prejudice. But where the prejudice can be used to support a political direction, it can be a powerful motivating force. Thus it is said that the images of 'bronzed, healthy, young hedonistic army of self-employed' gain potency as they touch the untheorized prejudices of the respectable people against the 'undeserving'. The threat of the 'smugly tanned faces', along with the subsidized cigarettes and alcohol, is directed to our upholding of the work ethic and it is precisely the hard-working who feel this threat most directly. It is a moral panic of the silent majority, fuelled by the media stories and given direction by the politicians, that makes the scrounger such a significant figure in this society.

Notes

1. 'Operation Major' launched by the DHSS in 1982 became a classic example of these deterrent tactics. The scheme involved setting up a bogus DHSS office in a disused school building in Oxford. When the operation was closed, in what some newspapers described in terms of the film *'The Sting'*, 286 claimants were charged with filing false claims. Subsequently nearly all of these charges were dropped, but follow up research at Citizen's Advice Bureaux in the area revealed an increase in reluctance in claiming supplementary benefits (see Franey, 1983).
2. Roger Finnegan's Programme 'Social Insecurity' was broadcast in December 1982 and included interviews with claimants who had complained about the conduct of special claims control officers. One, Sue Love, said she had been treated like dirt and would never claim benefit again even if this meant having to live in a tent. The programme raises the question of whether such withdrawals should actually be counted as a success by the

teams of investigators. It opened with a statement that is worth repeating here to give some flavour of the feelings aroused by the deterrent tactics:

> I think that people should have the right whether they are social security claimants or millionaires to walk down the street without being followed. I think that people should have the right not to have their friends and neighbours questioned about them. I think they should also have the right not to be locked up without having charges pressed against them. And all of these kinds of things have happened and are still happening to social security claimants — by very virtue of their claiming, they are now considered suspicious.

3. The idea of panics comes from Cohen (1973) where he studied the role of folk-devils in generating moral panic. Moral panic describes a period where the moral order of society is seen to be threatened by a particular figure, characterized as the folk-devil. In Cohen's study of Mods and Rockers, he showed how these groups came to embody the 'threat' of the affivent young to the order of respectable society. The moral panic concentrates around the issues contained in the figure of the folk-devil, a modern demonology. Applications of the model have been used to account for the presentation of many social problems where there has been a central group to personify the issue.

4. It has been remarked that 'An unsuspecting reader of the British press could think that not only do the rich largely foot the welfare bill, but that much of what benefit is provided goes to 'scroungers', or as they are sometimes more positively called those without 'genuine need' (Field *et al.*, 1977, p.169). In a similar vein at the start of the Deevy case the editorial in *Social Work Today* asked: 'When did the *Daily Express* — whose headlines **'Tax payers insist that benefits do not go to these swindlers ... GET THE SCROUNGERS'** was the most remarkable of the whole affair—last publish a headline that said **'GET THE TAX FIDDLER'?** It never has'. (Vol. 7, (9), 5 August, 1976).

5. The Rayner Scrutiny of 1981 of the Department of Health and Social Security and the Department of Employment suggested that people were working whilst claiming benefits in 8% of cases. This figure is based not on prosecutions but on suspicion and cannot therefore be compared directly with Field's or Fisher's figures. The 8% figure is a reflection of the level of cessation of claims following 'non-prosecution interviews' by Special Claims Control teams.

6. The figures for tax avoidance (legal, but anti-social) and tax evasion (illegal) are necessarily impossible to calculate. However in the years 1963–72 almost £94m was recovered from tax evaders by the Inland Revenue. This compared with a figure of £304,000 in overpayment of benefit in 1972, the first year that figures were available. Another interesting comparison is with the number of benefits which go unclaimed. An article by Ruth Lister in *Poverty* (August, 1976) suggested that:

(a) 550,000 pensioners appeared to be eligible for supplementary benefits but did not claim;

(b) 360,000 appeared to be in the same position;

(c) 65–70% of tenants in unfurnished accommodation fail to claim rent allowances;

(d) 90% of tenants in furnished accommodation also do not claim the rent allowances to which they are entitled.

7. This collapse of moral fibre was made explicit in the *Daily Mail's* article **'The Welfare Junkies'** which began:

> One in ten of Britain's once proud people now depend on a last-ditch semi-charitable hand out from the state . . . there is a dangerously addictive influence at work in the welfare system. As in the world of drugs, it seems that young people are particularly susceptible (*Daily Mail*, 26 September, 1977).

References

Boyson, Dr. Rhodes (ed) (1971) *Down with the Poor,* Churchill Press.

Cohen, S. (1973) *Folk-devils and Moral Panics,* Paladin.

Conservative Central Office (1979) *The Conservative Manifesto 1979,* Conservative Central Office.

Deacon, Alan (1977) 'Scrounger Bashing,' in *New Society*, 17 November, 1977.

Deacon, Alan (1978) 'The scrounging controversy: public attitudes towards the unemployed in contemporary Britain', in *Social and Economic Administration*, 12(2).

Deacon, Alan (1980) 'Spivs, drones and other scroungers,' in *New Society*, 28 February, 1980.

Donnison, David (1981) 'The emergence of an issue,' in *New Society*, 22 January, 1981.

Field, F. Meacher, M. and Pond, C. (1977) *To Him Who Hath,* Penguin.

Field, Frank (1979) 'Scroungers: crushing the invisible', in *New Statesman*, 16 November, 1979.

Franey, R. (1983) *Poor Law: The Mass Arrest of Homeless Claimants in Oxford,* CHAR.

Golding, P. and Middleton, S. (1982) *Images of Welfare,* Basil Blackwell & Martin Robertson.

Hall, S. (1980) *Drifting into Law and Order Society,* The Cobden Trust Human Rights Day Lecture, 1979.

Lister, R. (1976) *Poverty,* Child Poverty Action Group.

Moore, P. (1981) 'Scroungermania again at the DHSS,' in *New Society*, 22 January, 1981.

Page, R. (1971) *The Budget Racket,* Tom Stacey.

Peacock, A. (1961) *The Welfare Society,* Institute of Economic Affairs.

Peek, F. (1888) *The Workless, the Thriftless and the Worthless,* Wm. Isbister Ltd.

POOR LAW REPORT 1834 Edition, edited by Checkland S.G. and E.O.A., Penguin, 1974.

Sproat, I. (1976) 'The Social Security Fiddle: I believe we have seen only the tip of the iceburg', in *Daily Express,* 14 July, 1976.

Thatcher, M. (1977) *Let Our Children Grow Tall: Selected Speeches 1975-1977,* Centre for Policy Studies.

Strategies of Community Care

N.J. Derricourt

Introduction: What kind of care? What community?

It is customary to begin a piece on community care by saying that it is a matter beset by confusion, and 'confusion' as Titmuss once observed, 'has often been the mother of complacency' (Titmuss, 1968, p.104). Philip Abrams illustrated this confusion with a wide variety of meanings that he had found in the pages of Community Care magazine: 'Three distinct types of care are regularly considered in that journal: services provided in residential but relatively client-centred and open settings — the deliberately constructed 'caring community'; services provided through the placing of professional and specialist personnel 'in the community'; and services provided in their own locality by residents on a voluntary and quasi-organized basis. In my definition, the first of these would be a form of institutional care, the second a form of community treatment, and only the third would be unequivocally community care.' (Abrams, 1977, p.78).

If community care, then, is regarded as an activity carried out by lay/non-specialists in open settings, it differs from work done by lay/non-professionals in closed settings and from work done by professionals/specialists in institutional and open settings. In this vein, Abrams (1977) suggested that community care be defined 'as a matter of the provision of help, support, and protection to others by lay members of societies acting in everyday domestic and occupational settings'. Nevertheless, we still have to acknowledge the role that professionals may play in stimulating and supporting community care, if they can find ways of doing it constructively and can avoid spoiling or overstraining existing support networks.

For this reason, this chapter will give examples of three different kinds of community care:

(i) activity initiated by professionals who expect to fulfil a more or less permanent supportive or monitoring role, using volunteers and low-paid helpers;

(ii) activity initiated by professionals who plan to be supportive for only a brief period, so that the activity can be continued without them;

(iii) activity undertaken by lay-people with relatively little help from professionals.

The range of activities which can be accommodated by Abrams' definition is enormous. The variety can be glimpsed in Windass' (1982) directory of local initiatives which describes a wide range of local projects for youth, the elderly and disabled, mental health, single homeless, the terminally ill, single parents, alcoholics, health projects, and general neighbourhood services. But in this variety of services and groups providing community care, what should one exclude? Certainly not the single parent groups supported by Sheffield Family and Community Services Department whose guiding principle is mutual help and support by members (see SCOOP, 1978). Should one then exclude women's hostels from the general definition of community care? The search for conceptual purity is likely to be time wasted.

A particular source of confusion about community care is the prefix 'community'. The term has attracted a great deal of criticism, and yet the word is still used to sugar all kinds of top-down interventions. From community service orders through the renaming of approved schools as community homes with education to the recently established Community Programme, what Robert Pinker (in Barclay, 1982, p.202) has called 'the fig-leaf of community' seems as popular a device as ever with which to conceal all kinds of confusions and contradictions. The ideal evoked for this purpose is that of the traditional community where social relationships were as woven together as a 'pig's entrails' (Rees, 1961, p.75), and kin, work and interests were coterminous. Long ago, Tönnies (in Bell & Newby, 1974, pp. 7-12) described these conditions as *Gemeinschaft*, which denotes sharing, familiarity, tradition, being-among-one's-own, neighbourhood, togetherness, and the organic. He opposed *Gemeinschaft* to *Gesellschaft* which was characterized by formality, commerce, achieving, calculated politeness, and the mechanical. Many community studies have attested the wearing away of these traditional patterns by the interaction between the demands for mobility of 20th century capitalism and citizens' mobile response, so that they can hardly be said to exist anywhere anymore. This is not to say that nothing has taken their place; most people now through their work, interest and kinship commitments relate to an over-lapping set of locality-related and non-locality-related interest groups. For some people this set is small, non-existent or defunct. In some traditional working class urban and rural areas a *form* of the traditional pattern may be lingering on or have gone through a sea-change, but that does not mean that we can say that most people exist within a pattern of informal care that gives them all the support they need. We just do not know how many people suffer from loneliness or go without the kinds of help and support which most of us regard as essential for an adequate existence. To talk about community or to introduce schemes prefixed by the word community might make us feel better or just make us feel out of joint because we cannot experience reality in the way that the work suggests we should.

Titmuss, in 1961, when discussing the failure of government and statutory services to turn the theory of community care into practice, said:

In the public mind, the aspirations of reformers are transmuted, by the touch of a phrase, into hard-won reality. What some hope will one day exist is suddenly thought by many to exist already. All kinds of wild and unlovely weeds are changed, by statutory magic and comforting appellation, into the most attractive flowers that bloom not just in the spring but all the year round (Titmuss, 1968, p.104).

Norman Dennis (1968) agreed with this general contention in his chapter 'The Popularity of the Neighbourhood Community Idea', and explains why ascribing the terms neighbourhood and community to a locality have long been found by urban managers to be one cheaper way of deflecting demands than affording citizens their civil rights in housing, education and transport services. The vision of a 'community' of working class residents who make up for their relative deprivation by giving each other support has been a popular one with government for at least several decades. The residents themselves may, of course, if they are not too depressed, have alternative visions of community which sustain them through the distressing conditions of poverty. So the term 'community' comes to be vested with all kinds of hopes, deceits, nostalgia and hopes for progress, so much so that it seems helpful to expunge it from discussions like this, and substitute a more cold-blooded word like locality or area.

A further confusion about the term 'community' should be noted; it is viewed differently from different political perspectives, and this has implications for the meaning of community care. For example, if Raymond Plant is right in arguing that the 'conservative' view of community leads to racist dogma, then 'looking after one's own' takes on a particularly sinister meaning. His argument goes like this:

> . . . the 'conservative' view sees the main emphasis of the descriptive meaning of community to be in terms of locality and cultural and kinship ties, and will be unable to make sense of a multi-racial form of community when 'multi-racial' implies that not *all* values are shared and not *all* ends are recognized, and this is why, with perfect if manic consistency, the new conservatives formulated the *Volkgemeinschaft* idea (Plant, 1974, p.46).

A liberal view of community, on the other hand, which is based upon the sharing of functional interests related to one's job, or housing, or pastime, is probably comparable with a degree of cultural mixing. Such a liberal (or pluralist) view of community care would acknowledge the eclipse of traditional community and regard it as necessary to stimulate functional groupings if the weak and casualities are to be cared for by lay people, whether by family, or friends. So statutory agencies must be organized to reactivate functional caring networks, and these are often called 'community' networks. The socialist view would regard any form of locality community, that has hitherto been thought to exist, as an illusion, although where caring by family and friends does exist, it may be taken as proof of the humane solidarity of the working class. While urban managers may try to exploit this humane behaviour for the benefit of capital, progressive functional groups based on issues related to locality should be kept alive as much as workplace combinations both to make gains and to testify to the idea of the fellowship of persons. In the genuine community of socialism, caring will not have to be induced. Many socialists would argue, with Westergaard (1965, pp. 107-8), that 'the solidarities of class and the solidarities of community are antithetical rather than complementary'.

It might be as well at this stage to say what community care ought at the least to be, and mention some of the problems which one would expect to meet in trying to make it happen. Firstly, it must plan to cover those people who are 'in the community' and have no reliable support, or whose normally reliable support needs relief. Not only must community care itself be reliable but it should be sensitive to changing circumstances. Clearly, one difficulty lies in the problem of establishing that you have or will have accurate information about the current circumstances of everyone likely to be in need of support. Another lies in the problem of combining the care-work of public services with that of lay members of the public, whether relatives, friends, or volunteers.

Philip Abrams (1980, p.13) has argued that community care *qua* the efficient delivery of bureaucratically administered welfare services to neighbourhoods is likely 'to militate directly against the realization of' community care *qua* the cultivation of effective informal caring activities within neighbourhoods by local residents themselves. Michael Bayley (1981) has in turn argued that the two need not be antithetical, but that great care is needed to achieve the 'interweaving' of the formal and informal in a way which avoids incorporation of the latter by the former.

One should not only be anxious about individuals in need that are not known about. Philip Abrams (1980, p.16) was insistent that 'the problem of those who had nothing to offer' in the pattern of reciprocal helping in localities would prove difficult for community care projects to solve. Certainly, in the fraught social patterns of disintegrated urban localities, one would expect the problems of the stigmatized and the disliked to remain acute.

The Different Meanings of the Terms Community Care and Community Development

Although community care is widely regarded as a *social welfare* strategy, its recent history is also tied up with that of community development, or community work as it is now more often called. Peter Baldock has defined community work like this:

> Community work is a type of activity done by people who are either employed or who find opportunities to help others to identify problems and opportunities that they have and to come to realistic decisions to take collective action to meet those problems in ways that they determine for themselves. . . . The community worker

also supports the contact population in the process of putting any decisions that they make into effect in such ways as help them to develop their abilities and independence of the worker (Baldock, 1974, p.18).

From this it will be seen that the community development worker or community worker tries to make herself accountable to the representative groups as well as to her employer and to her personal agenda. How this balance is struck has always vexed community workers. Workers have been dismissed apparently for advocating their clients' interests too vigorously, and have disappointed community groups which they encouraged to enter into conflict with the local council. But at least most of them listened to what people said was wrong with their daily lives and tried to be open about what resources and constraints they had. As will be seen later, community care schemes *qua* the cultivation of social networks and voluntary services to care for and be concerned about the welfare of residents, particularly the elderly and handicapped, have resulted from community development workers' efforts to work with residents over problems expressed by them, and many Tenants' Associations supported by community development workers have taken on community care duties, even projects.

Many community workers would quickly point out that the activities of Tenants' Associations which choose to fight for prompt housing repairs are engaged in a form of community care, and certainly the work of Brown and Harris (1978) on the origins of depression in working class women would support that view. Others would argue that resources distribution issues which affect housing should take priority over community care schemes. Although the typical activities of both case-work-oriented Social Service departmental staff and specialist community workers do appear to be distinct, both may, with some small modification of their role, become involved in supporting forms of community care in localities (see Baldock, 1974, pp. 114–117).

Seebohm: Community Development for Community Care

This section shows how both community development and community care were embedded in the new form of social work practice proposed by the Seebohm Report of 1968.

The Seebohm Committee on Local Authority and Allied Personal Social Services called for 'a community-based and family oriented service' that would 'enable the greatest possible number of individuals to act reciprocally, giving and receiving service for the well-being of the whole community' (Seebohm, 1968). More specifically, it stressed both 'the importance of community involvement' and the need to encourage informal 'good neighbourliness' as essential features of the new patterns of social welfare that it envisaged. Since 1968, the theme of encouraging good neighbourliness, of drawing an ever-wider range of local residents into an ever-wider variety of caring and helping activities has acquired a dramatic new emphasis in almost all areas of social policy (Abrams *et al.*, 1981, p.9). The Seebohm Report played a crucial part in transposing the meaning of community care as care *in* the community (as described in the original Government White Paper—*Health and Welfare: the Development of Community Care*) (Ministry of Health, 1963) to care *by* the community, provided primarily by the dependent person's family.

The Seebohm Report (1968, pp. 156–7) urged statutory agencies to use community development methods to develop 'community identity and assist mutual aid, particularly in areas of rapid population turnover, with high rates of delinquency, child deprivation, and mental illness . . .'. Further, local authorities should 'enlist the services of large numbers of volunteers', and 'the area team will be particularly well-placed to engage in community development and in preventive work if it has appropriate services'. The Report was acclaimed as something that would put social workers more in touch with the communities they served. But these hopes were quite quickly overtaken by the reappearance of social work specialisms through the back door, and the remote and bureaucratic character of the newly created Social Services Departments, some of which nevertheless did make attempts to outpost parts of their services, for example, Family Advice Centres in Tower Hamlets and Birmingham. The themes of unification and control of the growth of social welfare expenditure (from 4.2% of GNP in 1910 to 17.6% in 1961) seemed to be more powerful than that of decentralization. But Cockburn has argued that one of the main purposes of the Committee — to strengthen and rationalize the management of social welfare — was linked to the 'community approach', which was designed to integrate the local population into the local state system, so that it might govern more efficiently, but on its own terms. As Cockburn (1977, p.101) says 'in making use of state services, one does not necessarily become part of the system — in sharing in their administration one may well do so'. Nevertheless, this is not a risk-proof strategy for the state, for the more incorporated the working class becomes, so do the possibilities for disruption 'inside the state' become greater.

After 1968, many Social Services Departments did appoint Community Development Officers and Volunteer Liaison Officers, and funded voluntary organisations to reactivate community identity in localities. The story of how many CDOs instead worked with community groups to press for resources with which they might set up forms of community care (e.g. land for a self-help adventure playground) is incomplete. Better documented is the Home Office Community Development Project, the largest CD programme that this country has yet seen, which began with four of its eventual twelve area projects being set up in 1969. The project was set up by the Labour government to engender self-help and generate resources within the areas; but most of the area projects very soon made it plain that they endorsed further-reaching objectives which involved shifting resources into needy areas and identifying the causes of maldistribution both in the local economy and the national economy, (see Loney, 1983; and Home Office *et al.*, 1975). These importunate criticisms, which became sharper as the world recession announced itself in the mid-1970s made many local government sponsors think again about CD as a resource-generating strategy, and coincided with a time when voluntary organizations were finding grants more difficult to come by.

Between the late 1960s and mid-1970s community development work provided many good examples of professionals attempting to initiate work of a community care sort which could be continued without them by residents. One example from Clydeside of a successful piece of community development which resulted in a form of community care is the story of Gibshill Tenants' Association's fight to be fully consulted about redevelopment plans for the estate from 1972–76 (Gibson, 1979, p.52). During this fight, local residents put in a considerable amount of work to help Gibshill's older teenagers, who had a reputation for vandalism and getting into trouble with the police, to find and run a club. With the support of a neighbourhood worker, a contractor's hut was obtained via the police, and later the TA persuaded the planners to build a detached purpose-built youth centre as part of redevelopment, and to allow it to be managed by the residents it served. By 1977, about 400 young people attended regularly, and both vandalism and reported crime had dropped sharply.

Barclay: Community Social Work for Community Care

If the Seebohm Committee had licensed community development, few of the new SSDs had by the end of the 1970s whole-heartedly accepted it as a principal method. The Barclay Committee, which was set up in 1980 by the incoming Conservative government and reported in 1982 , recommended 'a community approach', and in doing so, professed to be doing little more than repeating the recommendations made by the Seebohm Committee in 1968.

> By (community social work) we mean formal social work which, starting from problems affecting an individual or group and the responsibilities and resources of social services departments and voluntary organisations, seeks to tap into, support, enable and underpin the local networks of formal and informal relationships which constitute our basic definition of community, and also the strengths of a client's communities of interest (Barclay, 1982, p.xvii).

This approach is not only concerned with working with supportive networks to help existing clients, but also 'with reducing the number of such problems which arise in future' (p.205). The Report contended that 'ordinary' people do most of the caring and supporting of each other both in and out of troubled times, but that these arrangements are informal and often both unreliable and inadequate. So in addition to working with individuals and families, social workers should help to set up, maintain and advise these 'caring networks'. To do this properly would require new forms of organizational arrangements which placed social workers in localities, where they would be better attuned to local needs and practices and more directly accountable to the local community that they seek to serve. The main report envisaged a number of different kinds of possible arrangements, including basing social workers in patch teams, resource centres, working in hospitals, attached to general practice, to schools, in specialist teams at area level or multi-disciplinary teams serving a wider population (Barclay, 1982, pp. 207–8). One of the two dissenting notes to the Report, Appendix A, argued that there should be full commitment to a patch team model, since only in this way could the required amount of integration be achieved at a community and management level. Populations covered should be much smaller than Seebohm's 50,000–100,000; area teams covering 20,000–30,000 with a number of sub-teams within each, covering areas of up to about 10,000, were suggested (Barclay, 1982, p.227).

It is not necessary here to weigh all the proposals of the Barclay Report. That the community approach was seen as an *alternative* to the 'welfare state approach' did not endear it to those who saw the welfare state as badly in need of defending against the attacks upon it launched by the Conservative government. In spite of Barclay's warning that the community approach would not be cheap, and the calculations that SSD staff would have to be trebled to place two to three workers in population units of 5,000–10,000, supporters of the welfare state feared that a switch to a community approach could be used to justify cutting social services expenditure further.

Many defenders of social work as a professional public service were dismayed by the Barclay Committee's unpreparedness to criticise the government's cutting of social services resources, which was making the practice of social work with an increasing number of distressed clients ever more difficult, so that, as one commentator put it, 'social workers find themselves having to perform Grand Opera in the setting of a *Tom & Jerry* cartoon' (Phelan, 1982, p.12). There were also qualms about the separation of second-tier specialists from front line generalists, about the scaling down of social work organizational units at the same time as the National Health Service's primary care units are being gathered into large units to cope with the demands and requirements of special knowledge, about the emphasis on the social worker's role as a resource *rationer*, and about the difficulty of taking on a truly preventative role without any influence over the supply of housing resources.

There were, however, 'welfare statists' who accepted the argument that the social services should sometimes offer a more preventive 'proactive' (rather than just reactive) strategy of intervention, and that some forms of localized schemes might contribute to a better understanding of how social problems get created and defined as such within the interaction which occurs between the institutions and networks of a 'community'; this *might* lead to more sensitive and better timed interventions (Welch, 1982, p.8).

Much critical concern revolved around the real nature of neighbourhoods and the 'informal caring networks'. Did they exist to the extent that some members of the Committee hoped? If they did not, could they be reactivated, and if they could, what kinds of burden would this place upon relatives and friends of those that need support? How reliable, benign, or comprehensive would that support be? Would the most dependent and unsociable be left out? While enthusiastically proposing this approach, the Report was not able to draw on concrete evidence which would conclusively answer these questions.

Examples of Community Care Strategies

What evidence is there to suggest that localised arrangements for social services delivery may be able to raise the level of community care?

Research both into one localized patch system at Normanton (Hadley & McGrath, 1982) and into Dinnington Neighbourhood Services Project (Bayley & Parker, 1980) have begun to offer information with which some limited progress can be made towards answering some of the foregoing questions. These two examples of work will be described in turn.

The Normanton Area team was divided into three patches in 1976, each with a population of between 5,000–8,000. Each of the teams is led by a grade three social worker — the patch leader — and is staffed by two unqualified ancillary workers — 'patch workers'. Home helps and wardens are also allocated to patches to make contact with the public easier; they are managed by the area domiciliary care organiser. The objective is to interweave the work of professional staff with voluntary and informal networks so that problems can be reached early and crises prevented from arising without warning. The patch teams are expected to get to know their locality well, and become well-known by the residents; in fact, most of the Normanton patch workers come from their own patches. They provide a range of basic support to cases held by the patch, arranging transport, acting as escorts, liaising with home helps and wardens and working with volunteers and local groups. The area officer has called these workers 'paid relatives' or local gatekeepers. They 'undertake the kinds of tasks families would expect of a competent close friend or relative and they have become well-known in their patches as available, well-informed and helpful people (Cooper, 1980). A necessarily short account of the Normanton patch team's work can give little of the flavour of the work itself, but we are more concerned here with the claims that a community-oriented method of social work provides a more responsive service and mobilizes more resources in the locality than conventionally organised area teams do. Hadley and McGraths's evaluation of the Normanton patch team 'suggests that in most respects the Normanton team had more knowledge of its users and potential users, and of their environment, was more accessible, and had mobilized more resources than either of the two more conventionally organized teams' to which they compared it. Further, they believed that there were 'good grounds for believing that the Normanton team has helped to improve the capacity of the local community to help itself and has provided more equitable treatment for the elderly'. (Hadley & McGrath, 1982, Ch. 9, p.23).

In the case of the Dinnington project, the most recent research on this pit village with a population of 7,000 is soon to be published by the National Institute for Social Work. In this work Bayley has suggested that 'informal care does exist, that it exists in quantity, but that it is highly variable'. Only 16% of those interviewed in a service user study 'had inactive or non-existent kinship networks . . . only 9% of all 187 users were without support from family or friends'.

The objects of the Dinnington Project which began in 1980 are to interweave informal care with the whole range of the statutory services, particularly the health and welfare services. The project seeks to understand *'existing'* local patterns of care, what local people think the needs are and the way in which they think they should be met. The pilot survey undertaken in 1978 revealed that although social workers had very limited contact with the elderly, wardens and home helps were well acquainted with the help given to the elderly by family, friends and neighbours. So the project was staffed by two social workers and one housing assistant (employed by housing) whose special responsibility it was to develop the services' responsiveness to existing informal networks. The work of the social workers with 'natural helping networks' has two main foci:

> . . . the focus on individual cases and the focus on networks as a whole. In dealing with individual cases, the worker might assist a client's family, friendship or neighbourhood network, to mobilise on the client's behalf, or he might help to identify specific services which the network cannot supply, and then use agency resources to plug the gaps in collaboration with the informal helpers; or he might match specific clients to appropriate networks that he knows are willing to extend their support to other people. Focusing on the network as a whole, the worker is either concerned simply to strengthen it for the benefit of all, or uses it as a route to individual clients who might otherwise not use the statutory services at all (Bayley & Parker, 1981, p.71).

Strengthening and using the network involves identifying key figures in it, supporting them with specialised knowledge when necessary, and feeding information about services into the network.

The data which will be produced by the Dinnington project will be particularly interesting because of the project's concern to monitor the co-operation of the health and social services. Yet neither of these projects are located in the disintegrated, far-from-homogeneous locality referred to by the Seebohm Report as being appropriate for the community development approach. It clearly makes sense to pilot an experimental approach in favourable conditions, but there must still be some considerable doubt about the most useful form that the 'community-approach' should take in disintegrated and deprived inner city areas. At present the most ambitious localised scheme is that being implemented (since 1981) by East Sussex County Council Social Services Department in over forty areas with eleven area teams; this authority has provided a substantial training budget in order to prepare staff for these new arrangements.

In both the Dinnington and Normanton schemes, professional staff seek to stimulate and support the 'informal caring network', and interweave their own formal services into that network. There are other schemes which attempt to combine the efforts of professional staff and paid helpers to provide a service to individual clients.

The Kent Community Care Project has been running since 1977, when it was piloted for over three years in the Thanet area of Kent with ninety frail elderly people (Challis & Davies, 1980). The purpose of the project was to discover if frail elderly people could be either prevented or delayed from going into residential care (old people's home or hospital) by arranging for social workers to have a budget of up to two-thirds of the cost of a residential place out of which neighbours, friends (and exceptionally relations), could be paid to provide a supervised in-home service under the auspices of the project social workers. Serious attempts were made to interweave the service of the helpers with conventional provision rather than substitute it, so as not to discourage existing care from continuing.

An interim report has confirmed some earlier findings that 67.4% of an experimental group of frail elderly receiving support from the project managed to remain in their own homes, compared with 44.8% for a control group (Challis & Davies, 1981, p.24). There was also a lesser probability of institutionalization and a lower probability of death in the experimental group. In comparing the Community Care Project approach with the patch approach, the same report suggests that while both appear to be able to mobilize human resources, and neither can be said to have the 'edge' in that respect on current evidence, the Community Care model can claim to be able to help in focusing the need to combine 'the handling of specific and complex social and psychological difficulties' with 'the mobilisation of resources (Challis & Davies, 1981, pp. 82–83). The similar Community Care scheme set up in Gateshead on Kent lines in January 1981 has certainly given evidence of the advantages of flexibility claimed for the model (Luckett et al., 1982). Budgeting for the service to each individual is under the control of the social worker, which makes it easier for the team to match provision to need and to make continual adjustments to the help given as the elderly person's circumstances change. If an old person is wanted back into the family home, the service can be changed to give relief to the person's children by means of day groups in the helper's home or the occasional use of a residential bed. The Gateshead scheme is thus designed not to replace existing networks, but to step in where these do not exist or are in danger of breaking down. The objective is to give existing carers sufficient help to enable them to go on offering as much care as they reasonably can, by fitting the extra help around what is already available so as to consolidate and enhance rather than undermine it. This means that the social workers work carefully with the carers to provide realistic boundaries to their commitment and reduce the level of stress which they are experiencing, rather than displace their caring role.

In all the examples mentioned so far, professional staff have played a salient role. This is generally less true of Good Neighbour Schemes, many of which have been initiated and maintained entirely by lay members of the public. Few of the 1026 Good Neighbour Schemes reviewed by Abrams *et al.* (1981) would claim to give or to attempt to give the systematic community care to which the established patch or Kent-model schemes aspire. Nevertheless, for what they are, organised attempts to mobilize local resources to increase the amount or range of help and care given to a wide variety of client groups, they merit attention. The review found that the incidence of schemes did not reflect the level of need in a given environment, but rather the availability of helpers and organisers; there is no reason to suppose that needs and resources were any better matched *within* cities and towns. The work of Knight and Hayes (1981) in four inner London boroughs supports this view. Schemes most readily developed where there was a large supply of women who do not do full-time work, but who can also meet the costs of being a Good Neighbour. So schemes flourish not where the need for care is greatest, but where need and a certain level of prosperity exist side by side. The South-East, for example, has the lowest need, and the higher incidence of schemes. The reviewers formed the impression that where schemes flourished in the North, it was mainly due to local authority funding and stimulation, and they concluded that in time of recession, schemes need organized public support, that organized welfare holds the key to their survival. But the schemes would be most helped by that support being established in the shape of a dialogue rather than a bid to control. The review contains some interesting examples of schemes, among which is one which arose from a Tenants' Association on a local authority estate in Greenwich in 1976 (Abrams *et al.*, 1981, p.72). Initiated by an employee of Task Force, the Barnfield Neighbourhood Care Scheme gradually emerged from dealings with an established TA, and, making use of the networks of the association, produced some very useful informal community care. The reviewers concluded that 'the contribution of an existing neighbourhood organization and a determined semi-professional who knows his way around welfare is not a bad formula'.

In all the projects referred to above, the voluntary and ancillary roles were predominantly filled by women, and this situation mirrors the position of women as the principal providers of care of relatives.

Finch and Groves (1980; 1983) have argued that as social welfare policies shift towards 'care by the community', so women will be expected to shoulder the main burden. Moreover, to the extent that community care policies rely on women's unpaid domestic labour and may necessitate their withdrawal from the labour market, such policies could be counter-productive to the promotion of 'equal opportunities'. The challenge is to devise community care policies which do not disadvantage women and which give men 'equal opportunities' to take on caring roles usually assigned to women.

Present Problems in the Policy and Practice of Community Care

In the speech of 1961 quoted at the beginning of this chapter, Titmuss was talking of government and statutory services' failure to provide proper support services in the community for mentally ill people discharged from institutional care. Enoch Powell, then Minister of Health, had the same year announced that in the next fifteen years, mental hospitals would be diminished by some 75,000 beds. The National Association for Mental Health prudently asked: 'who is to look after them?', a question which has a profoundly topical ring. Titmuss argued that:

> . . . to scatter the mentally-ill in the community before we have made adequate provision for them is not a solution; in the long-run not even for H.M. Treasury. Considered only in financial terms, any savings from fewer hospital inpatients might well be offset several times by more expenditure on the police forces, on prisons and probation officers: more unemployment benefit masquerading as sickness benefit: more expenditure on drugs: more research to find out why crime is increasing (Titmuss, 1968, p.106).

Many patients would be left to be looked after by those who don't want to, or know how to, instead of those who do (and know how).

In the early 80s, it looks highly likely that the situation which Titmuss was warning against will actually come about. The consultation document 'Care in the Community' (DHSS 1981) made several suggestions for moving people who do not need nursing care out of long-stay hospitals. In mid-1982, it became clear that the government was unwilling to respond to the document by increasing operational funds for community care services. It has been calculated that 'at least 5,000 mentally ill and 15,000 mentally handicapped are incarcerated unnecessarily.' The recent government comment was that 'progress now depends on making better use of what is already available'. Admittedly, schemes to move people out of hospital can now attract 100% joint financing for ten years, with reduced funding for a further three years. But this still leaves local authorities to fend for themselves after that period. Moreover joint funding is now over-committed, and cannot be regarded in any way as a substitute for the proper funding of community care service (Crine, 1982, p.16). By contrast, the Welsh Office has strongly endorsed the Report's recommendation for larger spending on community care schemes, promising to increase social services funds by up to £8 m by the end of five years and by a further £15 m per year over the following five years. An example of what can be done with this kind of support is NIMROD, a community based professionally-staffed service for handicapped clients which aims 'to ensure that each handicapped person is helped to live and behave in as "normal" a way as possible' in a catchment area of about 60,000 total population (Welsh Office, 1978).

The lack of government response to its own policy initiative in "Care in the Community" is clearly part and parcel of a monetarist approach to social welfare in which the strategies of promoting voluntary community care, reduction of social services expenditure, restructuring social services departments and the privatization of potentially profitable sections of the Welfare State, are combined, and justified by the doctrine of the 'finite cake'. This doctrine seeks to present as uncontentious both the halving of the housing programme between 1980/81 and the end of 1982/83 and real increases in defence spending. Current local authority spending on personal social services fell by 8.2% between 1979/80 and 1981/82, and total PSS expenditure fell by 7.2% (Stein, 1982, p.47: calculated at 1980 prices). The severity of these reductions is brought home when demographic data are taken into account. It has been conservatively estimated that expenditure will need to be increased in real terms by 2% per annum until 2001 to keep pace with the number of elderly in the community; that estimate does not allow for any improvement in the quality of service.

As we have seen, the effects of cutbacks are far from equally distributed. It is not just in education that middle-class areas are better placed to compensate for cuts by raising funds for books and equipment; the opportunities for voluntary efforts in welfare are no more equally spread. Certainly the strategy of *voluntary* community care rather than 'state action' has been forcefully espoused by the leading members of the Conservative government as a means of fulfilling their commitment to reduce the level of social services spending. In a speech to the WRVS National Conference on 19 January 1981 Margaret Thatcher spoke approvingly of the number of professionals in the social services who are 'increasingly determined to shift the emphasis of statutory provision so that it becomes an enabling service — making it possible for volunteers to do their job more effectively' (quoted in Loney, 1983, p.94). According to the information leaked from the Think Tank report on the welfare state (1982) this proposed a much bigger role for private health insurance and approved of the principle of demand-led welfare (Bosanquet, 1983, p.220) and subsequent reports indicate the attraction of these ideas in conservative party policy making.

But the restructuring of social services departments and their attempts to promote voluntary community care by reaching out into their areas, will certainly find more and more areas of need which will become more and more difficult to prioritize. For this reason, restructuring must entail organisational arrangements which both suppress the information about deprivation which localized schemes uncover and exert greater control over the professional workforce. If this containment and control is not achieved, localized welfare strategies could rebound.

At all events, a reliable and comprehensive community care service is unlikely to be cheap and will certainly require a considerable input from statutory sources. The experiments and research now being conducted into community care may give us some evidence which will enable us to choose which arrangements are most suitable for any given set of circumstances. Then, if we are careful and lucky, we may find a way of organizing ourselves and the social services which best looks after society's casualties without damaging our own interests or building even further on the specifically capitalist ideology of self-help.

References

Abrams, P. (1977) Community care: some research problems and priorities, in *Policy and Politics*, Vol. 6.

Abrams, P. (1980) Social Change, social networks and neighbourhood care, in DHSS *Social Work Service*, No. 22, February.

Abrams, P. *et al.* (1981) *Action For Care*, London, The Volunteer Centre.

Baldock, P. (1974) *Community Work and Social Work*, Routledge and Kegan Paul, London.

Barclay Committee (1982) *Social Workers: Their Role and Tasks*, Appendix B, Bedford Square Press, London.

Bayley, M. and Parker, P. (1980) Dinnington: an experiment in health and welfare cooperation, in R. Hadley and M. McGrath (eds), *Going Local*, Bedford Square Press, London.

Bosanquet, N. (1983) Is spending out of control?, in *New Society*, 10 February.

Brown, G. and Harris, T. (1978) *Social Origins of Depression*, Tavistock Publications, London.

Challis, D. and Davies, B. (1980) Community care for the elderly, in *British Journal of Social Work*, Vol. 10, No. 1.

Challis, D. and Davies B. (1981) *The Thanet Community Care Project: Some Interim Results*, Personal Social Services Research Unit, University of Kent.

Cockburn, C. (1977) *The Local State*, Pluto Press, London.

Cooper, M. (1980) Normanton: interweaving social work and the community, in R. Hadley and M. McGrath (eds.).

Crine, A. (1982) A commitment to the community, in *Community Care*, 30 September.

Dennis, N. (1968) The popularity of the neighbourhood community idea, in R. Pahl (ed.), *Readings in urban sociology*, Pergamon, Oxford.

DHSS (1981) *Care in the community: a consultative document on moving resources for care in England*, HMSO, London, July.

Finch, J. and Groves, D. (1980) Community care and the family: a case for equal opportunities?, in *Journal of Social Policy*, Vol. 9, No. 4.

Finch, J. and Grove, D. (1983) *A Labour of Love*, Routledge and Kegan Paul, London.

Gibson, T. (1979) *People Power*, Penguin, Harmondsworth.

Hadley, R. and McGrath, M. (1982) *Community Based Social Services: An Evaluation of the Normanton Patch Team*, Department of Social Administration, Lancaster University (awaiting publication).

Home Office and City of Coventry Community Development Project (1975) *CDP Final Report, Part I: Coventry and Hillfields; property and the persistence of inequality*, London, March.

Knight, B. and Hayes, R. (1981) *Self-Help in the Inner City*, London Voluntary Services Council.

Loney, M. (1982) Policies for community care in the context of mass unemployment, in G. Craig, N. Derricourt and M. Loney, (eds.), *Community Work and the State*, Routledge and Kegan Paul, London.

Loney, M. (1983) *Community Against Government*, Heinemann, London.

Luckett, R. *et al.* (1982) The Gateshead community care scheme, a new life for the elderly at home (to be published in *Community Care* in 1983).

Ministry of Health (1963) *Health and Welfare: The Development of Community Care*, Cmnd. 1973, HMSO, London.

Phelan, P. (1982) In the beginning, in *Social Work Today*, 22 June.

Plant, R. (1974) *Community and Ideology*, Routledge and Kegan Paul, London.

Rees, A. (1961) *Life in a Welsh Countryside*, University of Wales Press, Cardiff.

SCOOP (Sheffield Committee of One Parent Families, (1978) *Report*, St Paul's Chambers, St. Paul's Parade, Pinstone Street, Sheffield 1.

Seebohm Committee on Local Authority and Allied Personal Social Services, (1968) *Report*, cmnd. 2703, HMSO, London.

Stein, M. (1982) Personal social services under the Conservatives, in *Critical Social Policy*, Vol. 1, No. 3, Spring.

Titmuss, R. (1968) Community care: fact or fiction? in *Commitment to Welfare*, Allen and Unwin, London.

Tonnies, F. (1974) Gemeinschaft and Gesellschaft in C. Bell and H. Newby, (eds.), *The Sociology of Community*, Cass, London.

Welch, B. (1982) Love thy neighbourhood, in *Social Work Today*, 10 August.

Welsh Office (1978) *Nimrod: report of a Joint Working Party on the Provision of a Community-Based Mental Handicap Service in S. Glamorgan*, Cardiff, July.

J. Westergaard (1965) The withering away of class: a contemporary myth, in P. Anderson and R. Blackburn, (eds.), *Towards Socialism*, Fontana, London.

Windass, S. (ed.) (1982) *Local Initiatives in Great Britain, Vol. II Health and Community Care*, New Foundations for Local Initiative Support, Banbury.

Social Policy in 'Crisis'? The Case of Northern Ireland

John Ditch

An assumption of much recently published social policy literature has been that the welfare state is 'in crisis': a supposed conjunction of problems, almost traumatic, around three related dimensions: ideological, organizational and fiscal. Some commentators have attempted to trace back its origins but most have simply described the characteristics of social policy over the past five or six years and applied the epithet 'crisis'. One theme of this chapter is to question how useful and appropriate it is to conceive of the present (profound) problems, deficiencies and dilemmas in the area of social policy as consitituting a 'crisis'.

The literal meaning of the term 'crisis' is 'a turning point; a moment of danger or suspense in politics, commerce, etc' (Concise Oxford Dictionary). This would imply a specific point in time: a month, six months, or at most up to a year. Yet, for the past half decade or more, the British welfare state has been said to have been 'in crisis'. This will not do, and two related sets of argument will be advanced. First, there is a tendency for students of British social policy to forget that over 30 years ago, the same term was being applied to British welfare services. For example, two articles in The Times entitled 'Crisis in the Welfare State' were published in February 1952 (Jones et al., 1978, p.48). The problems to which attention was drawn were not substantially different to those to which attention has been drawn in the 1970s and 1980s. It is inappropriate to apply the adjective 'crisis' to a period which has existed for over 30 years.

A second theme looks at the development of social policy in Northern Ireland, examines its assumptions, objectives and socio-economic context and suggests that many of the characteristics of the alleged British 'crisis' were inherent in the introduction of welfare legislation into Northern Ireland in the 1940s and that they have remained both salient and significant since then. But most importantly it will be suggested that not only has Northern Ireland experienced for over 30 years the dominant characteristics of the supposed British 'crisis' in a more extreme form but has actually suffered from two other debilitating sets of circumstances which would, in the British context, undoubtedly have led many of the 'crisis' observers to have demanded even greater respect for their thesis. These factors are, first, that Northern Ireland has long experienced levels of multiple deprivation greater than that to be found anywhere else in the United Kingdom. Indeed reports from the European Regional Development Fund have consistently ranked the province as one of the poorest in the Common Market. Secondly, over the past fourteen years there has been manifest political instability, unknown on an equivalent scale anywhere else in Western Europe, which has resulted in 2,500 violent deaths; massive destruction of property; the erosion of citizen rights; and consequential challenges and acute dilemmas for both statutory and voluntary welfare workers.

The point is, according to the postulates of the 'crisis' thesis the Northern Ireland welfare state should be its expression par excellence. It is not: far from Northern Ireland undergoing a catharsis and discovering its capacity for growth and stability, it merely continues on a path of decline and malaise. There would appear to be little more than a tacit agreement between the public and their representatives to stand back and watch the process of collapse.

However, it must be emphasized that this argument does not in any way suggest or accept that the difficulties experienced by claimants, clients, welfare workers and others are not profound or extremely disturbing. It simply holds that it is wrong to continue applying the term 'crisis', because to do so is to facilitate the ongoing malaise by legitimating a social ideology which accepts as given such conditions as social instability and the impossibility of consensus, and, more importantly, allows for ad hoc statutory responses which are, at best marginalist, managerial or irrelevant and, at worse, insidiously corruptive of a commitment to social justice and citizens' rights. Just as C. Wright Mills wrote of the tendency of the American Government in the 1950s to be consistently constructing foreign policy 'crises' to which they could respond executively without full and democratic consultation, so in the 1970s and 1980s, in the context of a social ideology which accepts 'crisis' as a given, so participatory structures and other democratic and egalitarian objectives of social policy are either dismissed or decried. In this context there is no little irony that the British left have, albeit by default rather than design, acted as grave diggers for the welfare state and thereby provided sustenance for its critics.

British welfare legislation in the immediate post-war period was nurtured in the context of the shared experiences of war which promoted a degree of consensus about the aims and objectives of social policy and demonstrated the capacity of the state to effectively intervene to achieve them. As Derek Fraser has written '. . . the term 'Welfare State' is a useful description of that synthesis of past pragmatism and future aspirations which was the achievement of social policy in 1948. The Welfare State represented the social consensus of the British people in the middle of the 20th century'. (Fraser, 1973, p.222) The reason for the introduction of equivalent welfare legislation into Northern

Ireland cannot be assumed to be the same. Northern Ireland had not experienced the Second World War in the same way or to the same degree as Britain. First, there had been no military or industrial conscription. Secondly, there had been only four bombing raids on Belfast (though one resulted in the highest number of fatalities caused by enemy action in any city (other than London) in the British Isles for the duration of the war). Thirdly, the Northern Ireland economy did not respond to the exigencies of the war as efficiently as in Britain. Furthermore, domestic political considerations, and in particular the electoral security and dominance of the Unionist Party was for a while threatened by a number of challenges from Independent Unionists and the Northern Ireland Labour Party. Certainly there was growing concern for the political implications of poverty. As Lyons noted:

> The shabbiness, the poverty, the lack of adequate schools, houses, hospitals or roads, the ill-health, the squalor of the slums — all these things, which had to be put up with at a time when there seemed no way to do anything about them, became all at once an intolerable affront, to be wiped out as quickly as possible in the new world that men began to look for with growing impatience as the war drew near its close (Lyons, 1973, p.736).

It is against this general background that a number of more specific considerations may be identified. First, that the Northern Ireland Government was concerned to maintain the support of the Protestant working class and social reforms were a necessary element in this strategy. Secondly, the Stormont administration wanted 'to dish' the Government in Southern Ireland and demonstrate that Unionism could be progressive. Thirdly, that reforms can be seen as an attempt to generate 'conditional loyalty' from Catholics: welfare in return for political allegiance. In addition there are those who have argued that Northern Ireland had no alternative but to simply follow the British example; others who favoured reform for genuinely benign and humanitarian reasons and finally those who regarded reform as a necessary precondition for the restructuring of the Ulster economy. It is the mix of these diverse factors which is important. It is already apparent that the tranche of post-war social legislation in the province had as much to do with the exigencies of sectarian politics and the constitutional status of the province as with the welfare, per se, of its population:

> . . . the advantages of the welfare state have remained ever since a good propaganda point to use against those who desire union with the Republic (Barritt & Carter, 1972, p.108).

Even at its inception the 'welfare state' in Northern Ireland was both cause and effect of political dissension. Within the Ulster Unionist party a body of opinion was mobilized to re-designate the province as a Dominion in an attempt to 'save Ulster from socialistic legislation'. Within a few years Protestants were accusing Catholics of abusing the new welfare services.

Some credence was given to this accusation by the comments of Eddie McAteer, a Nationalist member of Stormont, who urged Catholics 'to get as much out of the state as possible and then 'act stupid, demand explanations, object, anything at all that will clog the Departmental machinery' (Barritt & Carter, p.112). Numerous other examples illustrate the point being made: The (Catholic) Mater Hospital was not included in the National Health Service because the NHS legislation in Northern Ireland did not include the 'Stokes clause' which had enabled hospitals with religious links to maintain their traditions within the Health Service in Britain. In 1956 an attempt was made to adjust the basis on which Family Allowance was paid so that a lower rate would be paid in Northern Ireland for fourth and subsequent children: this was interpreted as being an attack on Catholic families, which tended to be larger. The attempt failed but was an indication of a clear trend of thinking.

If consensus was one strand of the post-war political order in Britain then full employment was the other. Again, in Northern Ireland the situation was different. The rate of unemployment was consistently three times greater in the province than the United Kingdom average. Furthermore the rate of female economic participation within the labour market is lower and the duration of unemployment for both males and females longer. Unemployment in Northern Ireland has therefore been of 'crisis' proportions for as long as anyone can remember. The remarkable thing is the resignation of the unemployed and the capacity of state welfare services to contain if not ameliorate its consequences. Political campaigns around the issue of unemployment have been small scale and unsuccessful (Ditch & Morrissey, 1981).

The argument so far can be summarized as follows: in an historical context social policy as reflected in post war legislation was not just an expression of universally agreed responses to social need but in part an element in a grander strategy to maintain social order, accommodating, on a differential basis, diverse sections of the population. The Welfare State, to that extent, was based neither on consensus, full employment nor the existence of a social democratic movement. Over the past fifteen years the situation has deteriorated rather than improved. Two broad themes, political instability and rising deprivation, must be discussed and illustrated as a necessary background to an examination of more specific issues.

Since 1968 street disturbances, assassinations and bombings have claimed the lives of almost 2,500 people in Northern Ireland. The Northern Ireland Government introduced a series of reforms in the late 1960s and early 1970s, but were unable to retain the confidence of the British Government and were prorogued and subsequently abolished. In 1973 a Power Sharing Executive was established which functioned between January and May 1974 when it collapsed due to the hostility of sections of the protestant population. Since then the British Government has unsuccessfully attempted a number of initiatives, culminating in the Assembly of 1982. Both the substance and vocabulary of Ulster politics during this period has been permeated by the rhetoric of politicians more concerned with security, the border and the fulfilment of aspirations related to conceptions of national identity than to the sympathetic and rigorous consideration of socio-economic questions. The civil disturbances have resulted in a massive relocation of population, regarded as the biggest in Europe since the Second World War. This has exacerbated an already severe housing problem, particularly in West Belfast. Overcrowding and related social problems have generated new demands for social workers, who have also had to carefully reflect upon their role vis-a-vis both state and client (a point which will be returned to). Additionally 'the troubles' have caused new and, in some cases, acute problems for hospitals, the medical profession and the prison service.

Malaise is the dominant characteristic of the social and political economy of Northern Ireland. Known to be one of the poorest regions in the EEC, Northern Ireland has the highest regional rate of unemployment in the United Kingdom, the lowest wage structures, the highest infant mortality rate and the highest rate of dependence on statutory income maintenance schemes.

The staple industries of agriculture, textiles and shipbuilding declined greatly in the post-war years and the replacement sources of employment, such as man-made fibres and petro-chemicals, in turn collapsed in the mid-1970s as Northern Ireland entered its second profound phase of de-industrialization. A large number of studies have described and analysed this process. (Trewsdale, 1980; Ditch & Morrissey, 1980). In the first Annual Report of the Social Security Advisory Committee (1982) Northern Ireland is dealt with in a separate chapter, where the indices of disadvantage are well noted. The Report also refers to the Family Expenditure Survey of 1979 which demonstrates that total weekly household income 'was appreciably lower on average in Northern Ireland than in the United Kingdom as a whole; viz £106.13 compared to £120.45. Moreover, although only 20% of households in the United Kingdom had incomes below £54 in 1979, 40% of households in Northern Ireland had such low incomes. In 1979, 19% of average household income in Northern Ireland was derived from social security benefits compared to 12% in the United Kingdom as a whole and supplementary benefit helped support 14% of

Comparative Statistics on Housing Conditions

	% of dwellings statutorily unfit	% of dwellings without a bathroom	% of dwellings without a wash-hand basin	% of dwellings without an internal WC	% of dwellings lacking 1 basic amenity
N. Ireland 1979	14.1	15.4	15.9	15.7	17.9
England 1976	4.6	4.7	5.8	6.3	8.7
Wales 1976	9.8	9.7	9.7	10.2	13.7

Source: SSAC, 1982, p.51.

the population compared to around 9% in Great Britain'. (SSAC, 1982, p.50). They go on to note the higher cost of living in Northern Ireland and in particular draw attention to fuel costs which 'present serious problems for low income groups in Northern Ireland. Family Expenditure Survey data for 1979 show that because of the continuation of higher fuel costs and the greater reliance on coal the average household spent some 66% (£3.46) more per week on energy than the average household in the United Kingdom as a whole (SSAC, 1982, p.5).

Various surveys conducted by the Northern Ireland Housing Executive have shown the poorer condition of housing in the province.

In a recent report on housing by the Northern Ireland Economic Council it was concluded that:

> The primary objective of housing policy is to provide a minimum standard of housing for the population as a whole. In Great Britain this goal has been largely achieved but in Northern Ireland there is an overall shortage of dwellings and many of the existing homes fall far short of the minimum standard (Northern Ireland Economic Council, 1981).

These data and numerous other reports demonstrate that Northern Ireland is characterised by a scale of deprivation which is far greater than that experienced elsewhere in the United Kingdom. Also, and this is the important point, the deprivation is not merely structural but endemic, being a perduring characteristic of Northern Ireland's history. The vocabulary of 'crisis' is inappropriate in this context.

But what is even more remarkable are the attitudes of the Northern Ireland population to the causes of poverty; the possibility of its alleviation and the appropriateness of state intervention. For the past five years commentators have anguished about the phenomena of 'scrounger mania' and the 'blaming the victim' syndrome. For example, Frank Field has written:

> The poor are ... caught in a pincer movement. On the one hand there is reluctance to accept the existence of 'real' poverty, while on the other hand, because of the rise in national income, those who accept that poverty does exist in Britain today are likely to view it in terms of personal and sometimes moral failure (1981, 21).

He draws evidence from the 1976 EEC-wide opinion survey into the perception of, and attitudes to, poverty (EEC Commission, *The Perception of Poverty* 1977). Responses are published for each of the (then) nine member states. Re-analysis of the data allows for the identification of Northern Ireland responses and these show that in the province people are even less inclined to perceive poverty than in Great Britain and equally inclined to attribute its cause to 'laziness and lack of will-power' (Ditch, 1982b).

That Northern Ireland respondents appear to perceive little poverty in their immediate environment is unexpected particularly against the background of known indices of multiple deprivation. This seeming contradiction may be

Do You Perceive Poverty?

	% Yes	% No	
Great Britain	37	49	
Northern Ireland	24	61	
European Average	47	35	[X^2 NI v GB = 18.03
			p = 0.005 2 df]

Why are People in Need?

Because of:		GB	NI	EC Average
(a)	Injustice	16	15	26
(b)	Laziness and lack of willpower	43	40	25
(c)	Unlucky	10	11	16
(d)	Inevitable	17	18	14
(e)	None of these	4	4	6
(f)	Don't Know	10	9	13

X^2 NI v GB NS

explained in terms of relative deprivation whereby the experience of pervasive 'objective deprivation' adjusts upwards the perceptual threshold of what constitutes poverty. Furthermore, 'it may be that socio-economic issues (such as poverty, unemployment, housing, low pay) are not part of the normal vocabulary of political literacy in Northern Ireland to the same extent as elsewhere in the European Community. The absence of a strong Social Democratic movement within the province, and the importance of such political issues as the national question, security and terrorism conspire to deflect attention away from poverty and related issues' (Ditch, 1982b).

Responses to subsequent questions indicate that people in Northern Ireland were as optimistic about the decline of poverty as anywhere else in the European community and some 54% of respondents thought the state to be doing either enough or too much on behalf of those in poverty.

These responses tend to indicate that there is no necessary or inevitable relationship between high levels of social deprivation on the one hand and social awareness or support for state intervention to alleviate or ameliorate the consequences of poverty on the other. The erosion of support for social democratic values and objectives, characterized by a shift to the right in British politics in the late 1970s and regarded by some commentators as a further, ideological, dimension in the 'crisis' of the welfare state is something which has long been a part of political life in Northern Ireland. The political wing of the Labour movement has never developed a long standing influence within Northern Ireland politics and every indication is that vox populi is complacent about and compliant with the *inevitable consequences*. For example, in the recent Assembly elections support for left-of-centre political policies, such as the Workers Party, was very low — no more than 6% of first preference votes. Not a single socialist was elected to the Northern Ireland Assembly and therefore opposition to the social and economic policies of the Northern Ireland office is ad hoc and often contaminated by attempts to gain sectarian advantage, and in consequence public debate around distributional and other social policy questions is muted. Social immiseration has not, and will not, lead to a forging of consciousness or a strengthening of commitment to social justice.

However, social policy in Northern Ireland is far from being in a kind of suspended animation. Over the past decade nearly all of the welfare delivery structures (health, housing, personal social services, income maintenance, community work) have been significantly reformed. The nature of this restructuring, the assumptions upon which it was based and the general implications for people, as both givers and receivers of social service, will be the subject of the remainder of this chapter. (This draws heavily on Ditch & Morrissey, 1980; and Morrissey and Ditch, 1982.)

The process of reform began in 1968 with the emergence of the civil rights campaign and the involvement of Westminster in the affairs of Northern Ireland. While it is true to say that some of the inspiration for reform came from within the province the major dynamic was from London and must be seen as culminating with the introduction of Direct Rule in 1972. The reorganization of local government into 26 district councils and the transfer of many of their traditional functions and responsibilities to newly constituted Area Boards removed a focus for Catholic grievance concerning discrimination. Responsibility for housing was transferred to the Northern Ireland Housing Executive in October 1971, an organization infused with the principles of corporatism and managerialism. Its lack of accountability to tenants and public representatives has been a source of considerable controversy ever since (Shelter, 1981).

The reform of delivery structures in the area of health and personal social services was a complex and radical matter. As with housing, managerialism was a dominant theme. As the official guide to the new service explained:

The three separate branches of the personal health service — hospital, general practitioner and local health authority — were brought together within a unified administration. And three branches of the personal social services — local welfare services, social work within the health service and social work for the mentally subnormal — were also brought together, in partnership within the health services and within the same administrative framework (DHSS, (NI) 1974, p.1).

Four administrative boards were established, covering the whole of Northern Ireland and they have responsibility for the planning and provision of services. Each Area is divided into a number of Districts and at both levels are 'teams' representing the diverse medical, para-medical, social work and administrative specialisms. The team reaches 'decisions by consensus, accepting commitment to decisions taken and only when agreement is unattainable referring problems to a higher level' (DHSS (NI) 1974, p.8). Board members are appointed by the Minister of State in the Northern Ireland Office and are representative of a range of opinions and interests. Many have criticized the Boards for being inert, cumbersome and insensitive (Brown, 1979, pp. 21-23).

Within three years a research study found a number of serious problems: a top heavy administrative structure; that Area Boards lacked real independence from the DHSS (NI) such that they have subsequently been called 'legitimating cyphers for government policy'; that tenuous relations between Area and District levels lead to delays in decision making. Since then observers have noted not only the persistence but the reinforcement of professional jealousies, thereby effectively wrecking the operational strategy of 'programmes of care'.

Area Boards were also established for the education service and criticisms are frequently made about their lack of accountability. In addition there has been the creation of a range of quangos to deal with a number of more specific policy issues: The Fair Employment Agency; the Equal Opportunities Commission (NI); the Health and Safety Agency; the Labour Relations Agency and so on.

Underlying each of these reforms was a declared commitment to an improved and more efficient delivery of service. But it is also possible to detect another, more implicit objective, and that was to crucially shift the balance of responsibility for the determination of policy away from public representatives and the recipients of service thereby expanding the domain of the professional and generating problems of accountability. This is consistent with what Habermas (1971) has called 'a technocracising of policies' — a means whereby day to day issues and problems (housing, health, benefits and social services) are regarded as technical rather than either moral or ideological. Politics and political discussion become spectacle rather than substantively significant because issues of principle are thought to be no longer important in ordinary social administration. The opportunities for influencing the policy making process and commenting on the delivery of service are reduced. Administrator-experts, who are usually imbued with the ethos of line-management techniques and who do not have case-loads, or see patients or meet the public, construct policy on the basis of what they regard as objective and rational criteria. The emphasis moves away from consultation, participation and accountabililty to a detached concern with efficiency and cost-effectiveness by means of a calculus which has little time for the intrinsic and subjective experience of professional-consumer/client relationships because the quality of the latter is so hard to quantify.

It has been argued by some commentators that it was a 'security' crisis in late 1971 and early 1972 (evidenced by an escalation of street violence and bombings) which led to the prorogation of Stormont in March of that year. The argument of this chapter, however, is that by referring to the deteriorating security situation as a 'crisis' a *pretext* rather than a sufficient condition for the further restructuring of public administration in Northern Ireland was articulated. The removal of Stormont may, in retrospect, be seen as part of a more broadly based strategy concerned with the re-organisation of all public services in the province.

The 'troubles' and social policy are not inter-related at that level only. The state has generated a number of responses to specific events and difficulties which have subsequently been incorporated in standard social policy practice. The most notorious example is the Payments for Debt (Emergency Provision) Act (NI) 1971. Introduced to deal with the non-payment of rents and rates as part of a compaign of civil disobedience following the use of internment, the legislation allowed for debts to be recouped from benefits and wages at source. As a response to a direct political challenge to the state, this legislation may have had a degree of legitimacy, despite the considerable hardship it caused. However, when the rent and rate strike ended the Act was retained and subsequently used to facilitate deductions from benefit to cover all tenants in debt, irrespective of political persuasion. In 1978 the Payment for Debt Act was amended to allow for use against gas and electricity debtors. An exceptional and emergency piece of legislation had been incorporated or normalized as part of conventional social policy practice. Since the reform of the Supplementary Benefit Scheme in 1980 this piece of legislation has been superceded by an equivalent, albeit more humane, mechanism known as Direct Deductions. In June 1981 over 9,500 individual claimants in Northern Ireland were subject to this provision, which now also applies in Great Britain.

Social workers in Northern Ireland have inevitably been affected by the social and political context within which they work (Darby & Williamson, 1978). There are of course important differences in the extent to which this occurs and it would be both inaccurate and irresponsible to infer that social workers are under constant threat to life and limb. The point is that for over a decade they have been working in exceptionally difficult circumstances which find their nearest equivalent in the districts of St. Paul's Toxteth and Brixton in Great Britain.

In the North and West Districts of Belfast social workers are very much at the sharp end of the delivery structure as it meets urban deprivation and communal violence. Case-work, the dominant tradition of social work practice, has come under considerable pressure and has at times been abandoned altogether in favour of emergency service provision. At best it has adapted to the environmental context which has contributed to an increase in the number of single parent families, a dramatic rise in the number of detected cases of child abuse and neglect; massive overcrowding; a range of problems stemming from pervasive financial deprivation; and the effects of communal violence on children (Harbison, 1980).

By and large social workers have been vigorous to maintain 'an image of neutrality' (Bamford, 1980) thereby enabling themselves to function in difficult circumstances. But at the same time as new and increasing demands are made upon their services, so their capacity to respond has relatively diminished. As the Black Report (HMSO, 1979) noted, in September 1979 Northern Ireland was 164 (34%) social workers short of the number required to meet DHSS staffing guidelines. In consequence crisis intervention has been a dominant strategy in social work practice. Secondly, fear is something which many social workers have experienced — especially if they work in troubled areas or are called out in the middle of the night to deal with emergency calls. Finally, social workers have had to deal with emergency situations (caused by bombings and the like) for which they were inappropriately trained and ill-equipped.

This context has posed acute problems and dilemmas for social workers and in particular, probation officers. Furthermore any public perception of a close relationship between the security forces and social welfare workers could be especially dangerous to the latter and would seriously compromise their ability to function effectively. At various times they have come under pressure from both paramilitary organizations and the security forces. For example, social services have been regarded by some military strategists as a potential source of information about suspected terrorists. Robin Everlegh a senior army officer who served in Northern Ireland wrote of the value of such data for the purposes of counter-insurgency (Everlegh, 1979, p.66).

Social workers were acutely aware of their exposed position when in 1978 they resisted an attempt to computerize all social work records. The Northern Ireland Public Service Alliance, the trade union which organizes social workers in the province, supported their opposition and the proposal was dropped. As I have argued elsewhere 'The conflict has focused attention upon the need to expose the political postulates of social and community work theory and practice in Northern Ireland. The emphasis in conventional social work training upon casework and related strategies of professional competence stands in contrast to the experience of many welfare workers in the province during the 1970s when, at times, "normal" social service functions were suspended in favour of crude "resource mobilization" and "band-aid" intervention' (Ditch, 1982a).

Probation officers and medical practitioners, especially those employed by the Police Authority, have also experienced the acute dilemmas caused by conflicts of loyalty. For example the conflict for a doctor in an emergency situation is between his/her commitment to the values incorporated in the Hippocratic Oath and the duty under criminal law to reveal knowledge of terrorist offences. Even more tendentious is the role of doctors in the monitoring of suspects during this process of interrogation. In March 1979 the Bennet Report on Police Interrogation Procedures noted the persuasive evidence submitted by police surgeons to the effect that suspects had been ill-treated under questioning. As a result of their statements (based on what they regarded as ethical and professional values) a number of doctors were subjected to public abuse and condemnation.

This chapter has attempted to outline the development and contemporary nature of social policy in Northern Ireland. Lacking for its entire history either full employment or political consensus, and characterized by exceptionally high levels of deprivation Northern Ireland has, in addition, endured for the past 14 years, civil strife on a scale unseen in the British Isles since the English Civil War. Northern Ireland may not be a simple harbinger of things to come in Britain but the development of social policy over the past 30 years demonstrates its capacity to both survive and accommodate precisely those difficulties which are evidenced in discussions of the welfare state in Great Britian in the 1980s.

References

Bamford, D. (1981) Lessons for learning when home fires burn, in *Social Work Today*, Vol. 12 (47).

Barritt, D.P. and Carter, C.F. (1972) *The Northern Ireland Problem, 2nd Edition*, OUP.

Brown, M. (1979) The dubious advantages of integration, in *Social Work Today*, Vol. 10 (27).

Darby, J. and Williamson, A. (1978) *Violence and the Social Services in Northern Ireland*, Heinemann.

DHSS (NI) (1974) *A Guide to the Structure for Health and Personal Social Services*, September.

Ditch, J.S. and Morrissey, M.J. (1980) Recent development in Northern Ireland's social policy, in M. Brown and S. Baldwin (eds.), *The Yearbook of Social Policy, 1979*, Routledge and Kegan Paul.

Ditch, J.S. and Morrissey, M.J. (1981) *Unemployment in Northern Ireland*, mimeo.

Ditch, J.S. (1982a) Social policy, social work and community work in Northern Ireland. Supplementary Material for DE206, Open University.

Ditch, J.S., (1982b) *The Perception of Poverty in Northern Ireland*, mimeo.

Everlegh, R. (1978) *Peacekeeping in a Democratic Society*, OUP.

Field, F. (1981) *Inequality in Britian*, Fontana.

Fraser, D. (1973) *The Evolution of the British Welfare State*, Macmillan.

Habermas, J. (1971) *Towards a Rational Society*, Heinemann.

Harbison, J. and J. (1980) *A Society Under Stress*, Open Books.

HMSO (1979) *Legislation and services for children and young persons in Northern Ireland*, Report of the Children and Young Persons Review Group chaired by Sir Harold Black (Black Report).

Jones, K., Brown, J. and Bradshaw, J. (1978) *Issues in Social Policy*, Routledge and Kegan Paul.

Lyons, F.S.L. (1973) *Ireland Since the Famine*, Fontana.

Morrissey, M. and Ditch, J.S. (1982) The social policy implications of emergency legislation, in *The Journal of Critical Social Policy* Vol. 2, No. 1.

Northern Ireland Economic Council (1981) *Public Expenditure Priorities: Housing*.

Shelter NI Report (1981) *This Year . . . Next Year . . . Sometime . . . Never*.

Social Security Advisory Committee (1982) *First Annual Report*, DHSS.

Trewsdale, J. (1980) *Unemployment in Northern Ireland*, Northern Ireland Economic Council.

Contributors

JENS ALBER was formerly at the Universities of Mannheim and Koln. He is presently at the European University Institute in Florence; author of *Vom Armenhaus zum Wohlfahrtsstaat*, (1982) and numerous articles on the development of the Western European welfare states; co-author of the data handbook, *State, Economy and Society in Western Europe, 1815–1975*.

NICK BOSANQUET is a Lecturer in Economics at The City University. He edited (with Peter Townsend) *Labour and Equality* (1980) and has written about the social thought of Friedman, Hayek and the IEA in *After the New Right* (1983). He has contributed articles on low pay and unemployment to the *Economic Journal* and the *British Journal of Industrial Relations*.

DAVID BOSWELL has been Senior Lecturer in Sociology at the Open University since 1970, from 1977 to 1980 he was Professor of Social Policy at the University of Malta. He is the author of articles in *Social Networks and Urban Situations* (1969), *The Health Services: Administration Research and Management* (1972) *Urban Ethnicity* (1974) and *Mediterranean Studies* (1980) and co-editor of *The Handicapped Person in the Community: A Reader and Sourcebook* (1974).

MURIEL BROWN taught at Bristol University and since 1974 has been at the London School of Economics. She is author of *Introduction to Social Administration in Britain* (5th edn., 1982) and was editor, with Sally Baldwin of the *Year Book of Social Policy in Britain* (1977, 1978 and 1979). With Nicola Madge she wrote the final report on the DHSS/SSRC Programme of Research into Transmitted Deprivation *Despite the Welfare State* (1982), and she has edited a volume of research from that programme on *The Structure of Disadvantage* (1983) as well as contributed to numerous journals.

ALAN CLARKE is a research officer with South Yorkshire County Council. He was formerly a research assistant in the department of Sociology at the Open University. He has published articles on general election television, television crime series and televised sport.

JOHN CLARKE is Lecturer in Social Policy at the Open University. He was formerly a postgraduate student at the Centre for Contemporary Cultural Studies, University of Birmingham and Lecturer in Sociology at North East London Polytechnic. He is a co-author of *Policing the Crisis* (1979) and co-editor of *Working Class Culture: Studies in History and Theory* (1980).

NICK DERRICOURT is Lecturer in Community Work and Group Work at Lancaster University and is chairman of the Editorial Advisory Board of the Community Development Journal. He is co-editor of *Community Work and the State* (1982).

JOHN DITCH is Senior Course Tutor in Social Policy at Ulster Polytechnic. He has written a number of articles on social policy in Northern Ireland. He is an active member of the Northern Ireland Poverty Lobby.

TONY FITZGERALD is a research student in the Faculty of Social Sciences at the Open University studying contemporary changes in British politics.

MICHAEL HILL is Senior Lecturer at the School for Advanced Studies at the University of Bristol. He is the author of a textbook on social policy, *Understanding Social Policy* (1980) and of several other books. He carried out a study of unemployment in the early 1970s and continues to monitor developments in policies for the unemployed.

PHIL LEE is a Senior Lecturer in Sociology and Applied Social Studies at Sheffield City Polytechnic. He is a member of the *Critical Social Policy* Collective, and is writing, with C. Raban, *Marxism, Fabianism and Welfare*. He has written a number of articles in the areas of social policy and social work and has co-edited with R. Bailey *Theory and Practice in Social Work* (1982).

MARTIN LONEY is Lecturer in Social Policy at the Open University. His previous publications include *Rhodesia: White Racism and Imperial Response* (1975) and *Community Against Government* (1983). He is an editor of *The Crisis of the Inner City* (1979), *Social and Community Work in a Multi-Racial Society* (1982) and *Community Work and the State* (1982).

ALAN MAYNARD is Reader in Health Economics and Director of the Graduate Programme in Health Economics at the University of York. He has taught in Italy, Sweden and New Zealand and is a member of the York District Health Authority and the North Yorkshire Family Practitioner Committee.

MICHAEL O'HIGGINS is Lecturer in Social Policy at the University of Bath and, since 1980, a specialist adviser to the Social Services Committee of the House of Commons.

COLIN RABAN is Senior Lecturer in Sociology at Sheffield City Polytechnic. He is currently writing with P. Lee, *Marxism, Fabianism and Welfare*.

JOHN SAVILLE is Emeritus Professor of Economic and Social History at the Univeristy of Hull. He is chairman of the Oral History Society and of the Council for Academic Freedom and Democracy. His publications include; *Ernest Jones: Chartist* (1952) *Rural Depopulation in England and Wales 1851–1951* (1957) and numerous articles in learned journals. He is the editor with Asa Briggs of three volumes *Essays in Labour History* (1960–1973); with Joyce M. Bellamy, *Dictionary of Labour Biography*, Vol. 1 (1972) Vol. 6 (1982). He is the editor with Ralph Miliband of the Socialist Register, which has been appearing annually since 1964.

PATRICIA THOMAS is Deputy Director of the Nuffield Foundation. Before she took up her present position she worked as Committee Secretary at the Social Sciences Research Council.

PETER TOWNSEND is Professor of Social Policy at the University of Bristol and was Professor of Sociology at the University of Essex from 1963–1982. He is Chairperson of The Child Poverty Action Group and the Disability Alliance. His recent books are *Sociology and Social Policy* (1975), *Poverty in the United Kingdom* (1979), *Disability in Britain* (with Alan Walker), (1981) and *Inequalities in Health* (with Nick Davidson) (1982).

ALAN WALKER is Lecturer in Social Policy at the University of Sheffield. He is author of *Unqualified and Underemployed* (1981) and editor of *Disability in Britain* (with P. Townsend) (1981), *Public Expenditure and Social Policy* (1982) and *Community Care* (1982).

ALBERT WEALE is Lecturer in Politics and Assistant Director of the Institute for Research in the Social Sciences at the University of York. He is the author of *Equality and Social Policy* (1983) and of a number of articles dealing with problems of value in social policy.

ADRIAN WEBB is Professor of Social Administration and Head of the Department of Social Sciences at Loughborough University. He is co-author of *Income Redistribution and the Welfare State*, (1971), *Change, Choice and Conflict in Social Policy* (1975), *Across the Generations* (1975), *Teamwork in the Personal Social Services and Health Care* (1980), *Whither State Welfare* (1982). He is the Chairman of the Volunteer Centre.

ELIZABETH WILSON was formerly a social worker and is now a Lecturer in Applied Social Studies at the Polytechnic of North London. She is the author of *Women and the Welfare State* (1977) *Only Halfway to Paradise; Women in Postwar Britain, 1945–1968* (1980) *Mirror Writing* (1982) and *What is to be Done About Violence Towards Women* (1983). She is a member of the Editorial Collective of *Feminist Review.*

GERALD WISTOW is Research Fellow in the Department of Social Sciences, Loughborough University. His major research focus is the implementation and evaluation of community care policies. He is the author of *Planning and Scarcity: The Personal Social Services Since Seebohm*, co-author of *Whither State Welfare* (1982), and author of a number of articles.

Index